SPECULATIVE FICTION 2014

Edited by
Renee Williams and Shaun Duke

Foreword by
Kate Elliott

Cover by
Kenda Montgomery

Afterword by
Foz Meadows and Mark Oshiro

First published 2015 by Book Smugglers Publishing

Brooklyn & Cambridge
www.booksmugglerspub.com

978-1-942302-08-7 (Ebook)
978-1-942302-07-0 (Paperback)
Foreword copyright © Kate Elliott 2015
Introduction copyright © Renee Williams & Shaun Duke 2015
Afterword copyright © Foz Meadows & Mark Oshiro 2015

Cover by Kenda Montgomery

Series Editors
Ana Grilo & Thea James

Series Creators
Justin Landon & Jared Shurin

Book Design and Ebook Conversion by Thea James

CONTENTS

FOREWORD

INTRODUCTION

FANDOM: ESSAYS & CRITICISM

REVIEWS

AFTERWORD

CONTRIBUTORS

FOREWORD

FOREWORD

Kate Elliott

"(T)o win favor one had to attract attention and have at one's disposal a network of personal contacts."

Ignorance is bliss. When my first novel was published in 1988 I was a stranger yet to the pain of endless disagreements, storms, rants, and divisive arguments that have (as far as I can tell) been part of the speculative fiction community since its inception. Growing up as I did in a sub-culture that did not value or encourage direct confrontation, I found the first SFWA Forums I received in the mail (print only!) enlightening, appalling, entertaining, and, in their way, impressive for the degree of viciousness with which some writers use their words to wound others.

Of course internecine conflict is nothing new in human interaction; literary and aesthetic feuds are a staple of history, for better or for worse. But at the same time, as I made my first steps into the field, the SFF community felt comfortable, not because of the quarreling but despite it, because the amount of support and welcoming was also remarkable.

If the universe were a great skyscraper filled with nothing but large meeting rooms where loud cocktail parties were taking place (my idea of social hell), SFF was the cocktail party where I felt at ease. Honestly, I really love this strange and somewhat peculiar place with all its strengths and weaknesses, and so many of those strengths and weaknesses can be exactly the same things like, say, "stubborn intransigence" or "uncritical enthusiasm."

When I entered the field in 1988 there were a limited number of review columns and venues where discussion about topics of the day and the works themselves could take place. Where roads are few, gates loom large, and it was easier to hierarchize what was considered worth talking about when fewer people had a determining voice. It took me a long time to figure out that fandom existed or even what it was (and I am pretty sure I still have only the haziest handle on a vast amorphous creature that is growing by the day in ways no one can control).

One of the first things I learned was that "to win favor one had to attract attention and have at one's disposal a network of personal contacts (p. 162)."

The quote comes from the monograph *Courts and Elites in the Hellenistic Empires* by Rolf Strootman, that period roughly defined (in the West) as the era from the death of Alexander the Great in 323 B.C.E. through to the death of Cleopatra VII in 30 B.C.E.

Courts in the Hellenistic Age were both political and personal, centered around the reigning king, his immediate family, and his circle of friends and companions. Strootman notes that "most definitions consider the court to be a social space" (p. 31) rather than a physical one, that is "networks of personal relations" (p. 32) as opposed to, for example, a palace.

In the Hellenistic era, during which the arts and science were in many ways innovative and pioneering, poets, scholars, and scientists were often courtiers. "In world history, court culture often serves as a means to link dispersed local elites, creating coherence in culturally and ethnically heterogeneous empires (p. 163)."

I do not here intend to directly compare the SFF community with a Hellenistic court or any form of elite (however much I am tempted to compare our wranglings, disputations, and jockeying for position to the internal spasms and feuds of the Seleucid, Ptolemaic, and Antigonid courts) but rather to suggest that the advent of online forums, email, and social media have created a larger sphere of attention within which a wider network of contacts can be made.

Developing connections is nothing new, as Strootman points out: "The court, as a centre of social and economic distribution, was a place where the lines separating the hierarchical layers of society could be crossed. (p. 162)"

How familiar does this sound? I entered the field knowing basically no one and had to make my way in slow stages. Some people come into the SFF community with sterling professional contacts already in place. Others make connections within the complex world of fandom. Always so intertwined that it can be difficult to separate the two, the interaction between "fan" and pro" has become increasingly complicated and nuanced. Academics now study storyworlds and transformative works, terms that encompass fanfiction and a broad range of media and art. Elderly volunteer docents in tailored silk suits at the The Rubin Museum of Art in New York City know what *Game of Thrones* is and think maybe they should watch it, when five years ago they would likely have said, politely, "Yes, my great-nephew reads that sort of thing."

Science fiction and fantasy are now mainstream where once they were peripheral. We can talk to each other from all around the world.

But many readers, viewers, gamers, writers, artists, and developers still have little or no contact with the core SFF community and its in-jokes and obsessions and arguments. In this way the core SFF community—which I define all-embracingly as those who are at minimum tangentially involved in and concerned about the inner workings of what is still a primarily USA/UK-centered field—is a kind of "court" culture because it reflects a relatively small and circumscribed circle when compared to all the people who don't know about it, aren't interested, or for one reason or another can't or won't participate.

Speculative Fiction 2014's essays, reviews, and articles give a glimpse into what some people have to say, in this ever-expanding web of connection, about works that include a speculative fiction element and about the "big tent" of the SFF community itself.

Who reads, watches, and plays the various media that these days fall under the umbrella of speculative fiction? What conversations grip those who are interested in the debates and the audience? How many essays on *Captain America: The Winter Soldier* should one read in order to fully understand the totality of feels? How much are we talking "to ourselves" and how much are we engaging new people and new voices?

Do hierarchies remain? Of course. Some of the SFF community's biggest arguments swirl around concepts of hierarchies and definitions. But the flip side of conflict becomes the creation of spaces where people, who perhaps have lived (however happily or unhappily) among family and friends who profess no interest in speculative fiction, can find each other to talk to.

"After all, you have always existed in isolation," writes Chinelo Onwualu in her wonderful essay "The Unbearable Solitude of Being an African Fan Girl." She speaks to her specific situation, and yet also to one in which any dispersed individuals and groups can reach out. "You know you are not alone. You ask them to come and pour their hearts and stories into this space you've helped to create. You assure them that they are not alone, that in the vast spaces on the worldwide web, there are others like them."

INTRODUCTION

INTRODUCTION

Renee Williams and Shaun Duke

An SF academic and a fanfiction writer walk into a bar...

Fandom, as previous iterations of the Speculative Fiction series has defined it, circled a very small area of online discussion and engagement centered largely around the publication and reading of adult speculative fiction. The controversies and debates have tended towards repetition, if only because each iteration is, in theory, adding something new to an existing conversation. In their introduction to *Speculative Fiction 2013*, Ana Grilo and Thea James argued that it is "easy to dismiss these conversations as routine drama, or downplay their importance by calling them *kerfluffles* or infantile *brouhahas*. The simple position is to claim that these are just cyclical discussions that amount to nothing, except anger, frustration, and general divisiveness." However, the four of us agree that these instances are part of a process of change and that only by discussing these issues—and sometimes failing at doing so—can we forge a path towards a better, more inclusive fandom.

The *Speculative Fiction* series is an attempt, however limited, to represent the growth and scope of the conversations within the SF world. That scope, of course, is mediated through the interests and perspectives of its editors. Past editors Justin Landon and Jared Shurin brought a quirky sense of humor and seriousness to the myriad number of fandoms and opinions within those fandoms. They were followed by Ana Grilo and Thea James of The Book Smugglers who brought their optimism for new voices and belief in the power of conversations to produce growth within a community to the *Speculative Fiction* mantle. Ana and Thea loved editing the anthology so much that they became publishers themselves—and then took over the whole project in the quest for world domination. Watch out, future *Speculative Fiction* editors; you may get an itch!

In other words, we come on the heels of editors whose perspectives we greatly respect and whose prior work has done so much to shape the way we approached editing *Speculative Fiction 2014*. These teams were working from similar backgrounds with aligning interests. When we started this journey, we realized the view from the end of our anthology was going to be nothing the Speculative Fiction series had seen before. Our perspective was different, and that had everything to do with mediating the tension between our divergent communal and literary interests. Our different paths we experience as "fandom" made us particularly interesting partners as we sought to find and judge what the most important, creative, and impactful 2014 speculative fiction reviews and commentary were.

Shaun, for example, is an SF academic, toiling away in the furnace of theory and dusty library basements to produce a monstrous beast called a dissertation. Renee, however, is a fanfic writer, dancing through seas of Tumblr gifs, fawning over Sebastian Stan, and making up her own stories in the worlds she loves. Renee has a grudge against academia; Shaun doesn't read fanfic. Renee calls Tumblr a fannish home and reblogs gifs of attractive celebrities, cats, and Spiders Georg jokes; Shaun writes critical essays on his blog and rubs elbows with huge swathes of SF publishers, editors, and authors as part of his work on Skiffy and Fanty, his successful speculative fiction podcast. This can also be described in media terms by using the most divisive science fiction film of 2015 so far. Renee loved *Jupiter Ascending* unironically and immediately looked for Jupiter/Caine wing fic. Shaun is looking forward to using "No Award" should it make the Hugo ballot for Best Dramatic Presentation: Long Form. We're vastly different types of fans. It could have been a disaster.

But it wasn't. Instead, we learned that our perspectives gave us a unique strength as a team. We challenged each other to think deeper about something we might have dismissed, to change the way we looked at one another's fandoms and find what made essays on fandom economics and Bucky Barnes just as valuable as essays about the Hugo Awards or bigotry within the SF community. Sometimes it was obvious; sometimes it wasn't; and sometimes we hashed out the hows and whys and found common ground during long late-night deliberations involving swordfights and games of "who knows more about Captain America" (okay, not really). This gave us the ability to consider a debate, critique, or article more thoroughly than we would have otherwise. Through our differences, we found that we could represent a much wider community of fandoms and fannish voices (but it's still a good thing we won't have to decide which *Jupiter Ascending* commentary to include—crisis averted!).

The 2014 edition of the anthology is grounded in a wider definition of fandom, including works from Tumblr accounts, SFF blogs, mainstream media, and other regions where the tendrils of SFF have stretched out or been met by other fandoms. After all, the *Speculative Fiction* series is dedicated to honoring and saving ephemeral fan discussions, and there are countless types of fans, so many it's possible we could have year-long debates about what the perfect definition of fan might be. We've reached as far as we could into other fan communities, and we've brought you both familiar and new voices, names both big and small. Each voice offers a perspective on the myriad forms that fandom can take, touching on a wide range of media formats and properties and creating a somewhat disparate collection of people who are connected by the things they love. Because it's a submission driven anthology, the same community will likely rotate through it for years to come and expansion will be slow, but it's still important to reach out as far as possible when given the opportunity. This year, we were given that opportunity, and we tried to run as far as we could with it.

The 2014 edition is about saving our thoughts about media, such as the reaction to *Captain America: The Winter Soldier*, which you'll see discussed in "I'm the Tyranny of Evil Men" by thingswithwings. It's about saving our thoughts about the love we have for our fannish pasts, as you'll see in Juliet Kahn's article "Nostalgia as a Weapon: The Sailor Moon Renaissance is a Feminist Mission Behind the Lines of Pop Culture", about the manga and anime series which was a huge part of the fantastical lives of young girls. It's about valuing our thoughts on fandom culture, such as Worldcon, as highlighted in Bertha Chin's article "Conventions, hierarchies and forced diversity". It's about remembering the important conversations about fannish identity happening outside our Western perspectives, as we see in Chinelo Onwualu's article, "The Unbearable Solitude Of Being An African Fan Girl". It's about remembering important parts of our history, such as in Daniel José Older's "One Hundred Years Of Weird Fear: On H.P. Lovecraft's literature of genealogical terror". It's about remembering there's true value in our inevitable opinions on opinions of fan culture, such as in Saathi Press's "The Economics of Fandom: Value, Investment, and Invisible Price Tags" and Amal El-Mohtar's "Of Awards Eligibility Lists and Unbearable Smugness", the latter of which caused widespread discussion and engagement. There are serious articles that sobered us, fun articles that made us laugh, critiques that were hard to read but necessary, and because Ana and Thea are starting a new tradition of putting editors in the hot seat, two essays by us, showing you our very personal perspectives on one tiny part of media and fandom from 2014 through our own writing.

We hope you learn something new, meet a new writer you love, or find a piece of media to read or watch. We hope that when you finish the anthology, you come and find the current year's submission form and tell the next editors all the reviews, criticism, commentary, and meta you're currently loving that's changing how you perceive fandom and engage in fandom and fan communities. Help us keep expanding this anthology series, which becomes a time capsule from a specific perspective and a specific time in the life of a handful of fandoms, so it's only one small part of the history you help us write.

This was our attempt to capture a quick, fleeting moment in the life of a wide array of disparate, complicated, and growing communities. We hope it becomes a moment you enjoy reading about as much as we enjoyed creating it.

FANDOM

Essays and Criticism

A GUIDE TO FANFICTION FOR PEOPLE WHO CAN'T STOP GETTING IT WRONG

Gavia Baker-Whitelaw and Aja Romano

What is fanfiction? That's the question magazine articles and TV segments have been attempting to answer for upwards of 40 years now, usually without doing much actual research into the topic.

Maybe this was a valid question back when folks were still sliding Kirk/Spock zines under the tables at *Star Trek* conventions, but in the era of *Fifty Shades of Grey* (look, we had to namecheck it at some point) and Amazon's licensed, for-profit fanfic publishing service, you'd think that fanfic explainer articles would be on the way out.[1]

Most millennials are at least vaguely aware of what fanfic is, and their parents can presumably just Google it like anyone else. Right?

Not so much, apparently. More than a decade after the *Harry Potter* craze kicked fanfic culture straight into the mainstream, we're still seeing regular appearances from that most embarrassing of journalistic genres: the poorly researched thinkpiece expressing shock, horror, bemusement, and condescension for fandom and the (mostly female) fans who write fanfiction.

And it's not just fringe publications who get the whole concept of fandom wrong. It wasn't long ago that BuzzFeed enraged fans with one of those "How geeky are you?" quizzes. Although BuzzFeed of all places should have known better, its definition of what made someone a geek managed to leave out 90 percent of popular fandom activities, along with the vast majority of the geek population, i.e. not-a-white-dude.[2]

So for anyone out there who has just been hired to explain the intricacies of fanfic culture to a confused and ill-informed audience, here are a few misconceptions we can get out of the way before you even start:

Myth: It's written as "Fan Fiction"

No, it's not. The word is "fanfiction." It's not Fan Fiction or FanFiction or fanfictions or fan-fiction. It's just fanfic, for short. Get it right. Having lately added the term to its lexicon, the Oxford English Dictionary hedges its bets and includes both "fan fiction" and "fanfic." Here in fandom, however, we usually say "fic", "fanfic", or "fanfiction." The adjective form of fan is "fannish." This is most often used in the context of things like, "I feel fannish about X" or to discuss "fannish practices", i.e. all the things that fans typically do as a

1 http://www.dailydot.com/business/kindle-words-amazon-fanfiction-problems/
2 https://fozmeadows.wordpress.com/2014/04/12/exclusion-as-default-female-geeks/

culture. If we're talking about slash fic, it's "slash fic", "slashfic", or most often just "slash."

When you write fanfic as "fan fiction" you're implying that a) you're not one of us, because if you were, you'd call it fic like normal people, and b) you're thinking that "fan" is an adjective that somehow separates our fiction from normal-people fiction. Fanfiction is a literary format with its own subgenres. You wouldn't call a play "stage fiction" or a movie "film fiction." They're things. Fanfiction is a thing.

If you need help with other terminology, here's a handy way to brush up on your fangirl lingo.[3]

Myth: "Fandom" is a morphing of "kingdom"

It's a common misassumption, but no, the word "fandom" isn't a shortening of "fan" and "kingdom," but rather, as used originally by the sports fans who created the word back in the late 19th century, a truncating of "fan" and "domain." The difference between the idea of a "fan kingdom" and a "fan domain" may not seem like much, but in practice, the former is a fantasy that smacks of an unfairly attributed sense of entitlement. "Fan domain" is a more practical way to talk about the purview that fans have over their own community, not to mention the creative works, discussions, and other kinds of fanworks that they produce.

Myth: Fanfic writers are mostly dudes

No. No, no, and no.

Look, just Google that shit, dude—or look it up on Fanlore. In addition to the ample amount of research that academics and acafans (an academic who's also a fan) have done on the vast communities of women writing fanfiction on the Internet, we dare you to go to the Internet's main multi-fandom fanfiction hubs—LiveJournal, Wattpad, Archive of Our Own, Fanfiction. net, AdultFanFiction.net, Tumblr, Movellas, Quotev, AsianFanfics—and interact with the fanfiction writers there. Unless you specify that you're male, you will nearly always be assumed to be female or genderqueer until proven otherwise.

Women are the writers of fanfiction. You're on female turf when you enter fanfiction communities. Don't let anyone tell you otherwise. (Seriously, go to Wattpad and try to find a dude. We'll wait.)

Sure, there are definitely a bunch of men who actively participate in the fanfic community. But the vast majority of fanfiction writers on the Internet are women or non-cisgendered, we'd estimate around 95 percent.

Which leads us to the second frequently encountered stereotype by people who manage to get past this first one:

Myth: Fanfic writers are all teenagers or modest young women who shouldn't be exposed to this kind of Internet filth

The fanfic audience may mostly be women, but they're certainly not all kids or teenagers. Also, the places where pre-teen readers mostly hang out

---

(fanfiction.net and Wattpad, which we'll get to in a minute) don't allow adult material. Your typical fanfic fangirl is likely to be around college age, but there are also plenty of older participants—even on Tumblr, which is famous for being full of impenetrable teen subcultures. Without sounding like we're going out of our way to make fandom sound super normal and harmless, most fanfic readers are... super normal and harmless. And not 12-year-olds who are being psychologically warped after being indoctrinated into a sinister cult of Voldemort porn.

This kind of puritanical panicking about teenagers finding explicit material on the Internet is kind of self-defeating. If you're worried about your kids accessing porn, educate yourself about how the Internet works and talk to them about boundaries. As for older teenagers and college students, you're probably going to have to resign yourself to the assumption that they already know about sex. Sorry.

Myth: Fanfic writers are sexless, fat, repressed middle-aged spinsters

In the words of Lieutenant Uhura: "Sorry, neither." There's no template for what a fan looks like, how successful they might be, what age they might be, or what career they might choose. And if you've ever been to Comic-Con or Dragon Con or any number of cons, you'll note that con attendees run the gamut of all ages, ethnicities, and shapes. Writing fanfiction doesn't shunt you into the "lonely olds" category. But it's interesting how the two polar opposite conceptions about fanfic—that it's written by clueless tween fangirls *or* by loveless older women—both manage to co-exist as blatantly misogynistic stereotypes, isn't it?

Myth: Bronies are special

As we said above, male fans can be found in all corners of fanfiction-based communities. They're fans like the rest of us. You don't get a special hat because you happen to be a man who's decided to like this one Saturday morning cartoon. In addition to, oh, *all of Japan*, fandoms for animated shows like *Adventure Time, Avatar: The Last Airbender*, animated DC and Marvel adaptations, and your average Saturday morning cartoon all have vast and mixed fanbases.

The only thing special about bronies is that bronies decided they were special, and then decided they needed their own subculture name, special Web apps, navel-gazing documentaries, and even commercials in order to function as a fandom. Bronies have produced an impressive array of fanart, music, and even social media platforms, but this doesn't really make them different from what female-dominated, online fanwork-based fandom has been doing for decades.

For some reason, though, the media continues to see bronies as far more newsworthy than the Organization for Transformative Works or the Vlogbrothers' Nerdfighter movement, even though these fandom communities are, like bronies, engaged in social activism and outreach. *Most* fandoms are, in fact. Dig a little deeper, and you'll find that bronies are no different than any other fandom community.

We suppose it kind of makes sense for parents to be worried that reading and writing fanfic is going to teach kids bad literary habits or something.[4] It isn't as if fanfic has editors, right?

Wrong. Not only do fanfiction writers often become acclaimed and best-selling writers of original fiction, but in the *Twilight* fandom, fans got together and even created multiple fandom publishing houses staffed by fans as editors and publishers, all working to take popular *Twilight* fanfic and "file off the serial numbers" to turn it into marketable original fiction.[5] (And yes, this is exactly how your mom came to own a copy of *Fifty Shades of Grey*.) Hell, some of these writers even continue to write fanfiction after they're rich and famous.[6]

Most fanfic writers have "beta readers" who read over their work before it gets posted, checking for things like grammar errors and clumsy storytelling. In other words, editors. Plus, there's a long-running culture of feedback from readers—just take a look at Wattpad, where stories get millions of hits and thousands of comments from eager readers on every chapter. Even if your kid is reading nothing but poorly written boyband fanfic, they're reading regularly and improving their literacy.[7] And sooner or later they'll probably become more discerning, and move onto the good stuff. Of which there is a lot.

Which brings us onto our next point: Where do you find good fanfic?

Myth: Most fanfic is on Fanfiction.net

No. Look, just because you Googled "fan fiction" and the first result was fanfiction.net does not mean that FF.net (nicknamed "the pit of voles" by the rest of us fic writers) is where all fanfiction lives, breeds, and dies.

FF.net is just one website among many, and it's not even the *worst* website in terms of overall fic quality. We have Wattpad (home of the aforementioned tween boyband fanfic), which is famous for stories with ridiculously huge reader counts but poor literary merit.[8] Then there's the Archive of our Own (AO3), which is home to a lot of the most well-written fanfic, both adult-rated and suitable for children.[9] And we can't leave out longtime staple AdultFanfic.net.[10] There's also a myriad of individual fandom-specific archives and LiveJournal communities, and each of them have their own individual mini-cultures. Basically, if you're judging fanfic by skimming FF.net, then you may as well be judging the full span of Western literature based on the first book you pick up by the entrance of Barnes & Noble.

4 http://www.nytimes.com/2008/07/27/books/27reading.html?pagewanted=all&_r=0
5 http://www.themarysue.com/50-shades-of-grey-and-the-twilight-pro-fic-phenomenon/ and http://online.wsj.com/news/articles/SB10001424052702303734204577464411825970488
6 http://www.dailydot.com/culture/10-famous-authors-fanfiction/
7 http://www.thoughtleader.co.za/stevevosloo/2008/01/22/fan-fiction-improving-youth-literacy/
8 http://www.dailydot.com/fandom/wattpad-raises-50-million-investment/
9 http://www.dailydot.com/fandom/ao3-million-fanfic/
10 http://www.dailydot.com/interviews/adult-fan-fiction-apollo-interview/

Myth: Slash fanfic is the equivalent of lesbian porn for straight women

We can kind of see where this one is coming from, but it's really not true.[11] First of all, male/male slashfic is definitely not read exclusively by straight women.[12] In fact, in numerous self-reporting polls of fandom done over the years, the majority of members participating in traditional fandom communities have identified themselves as queer or otherwise non-hetero-sexual. For example, you'd be amazed by the number of lesbians who read and write exclusively about relationships between men, i.e. a gender to which they are not even attracted in real life.

The popularity of slash fanfic invariably seems like a weird kink or a total mystery to outsiders, but there are actually a number of factors at play. Yes, many people like to read male/male erotica because they find it hot, but there's also the obvious fact that pop culture is completely obsessed with male/male relationships already. As in, Kirk/Spock, Holmes/Watson, every buddy cop drama ever, and the vast majority of popular sci-fi/fantasy fiction and superhero movies.

In a male-dominated field that regularly focuses on close relationships between men while sidelining the women, it's not a huge leap to turn that ho-moerotic closeness into romance—particularly if you want to see more LGBT representation in popular culture but are thwarted at every turn. Take the TV show *Supernatural*, for example. Its fans are often derided for being slash-ob-sessed, but the fact is that *Supernatural* itself is dedicated to two male/male relationships: Sam and Dean Winchester, and Dean and the angel Castiel.[13] Female characters are routinely introduced as damsels, love interests, or sexy villains, and are then killed off to make way for the intense, obsessive loyalty and love expressed between these three dudes. Slash fanfiction is simply an extension of what viewers are already seeing onscreen.

One of the most obvious yet overlooked reasons for writing slash is that people who enjoy romance enjoy the emotional catharsis of a love that can overcome obstacles. There are few bigger obstacles in life than the social obstacles that gay and lesbian men and women have to overcome to achieve self-acceptance, community acceptance, and real and meaningful relation-ships. This is the reason that many straight men and women enjoy reading queer romance, be it slash or original fiction.

While gay men will often claim that slash is a way of fetishizing and ob-jectifying them, that's not really what's going on here. Again, the majority of slash writers are women raised in societies that constantly reinforce the par-adox that if they say no to sex, they're frigid, but if they say yes, they're a slut. Add to that the way women's bodies are routinely objectified while they're told that sex is shameful, and it becomes very hard for many women to ex-plore their sexuality. For many women and girls, exploring sexuality through male characters provides a safe, shame-free distance, while enabling them to simultaneously soften male characters and imbue them with emotions

11 http://www.dailydot.com/culture/beginners-guide-fandom-fanworks/
12 http://melannen.dreamwidth.org/77558.html
13 http://www.dailydot.com/society/jensen-ackles-homophobia-supernatural-fandom/

and characteristics that many real men find it difficult to show because of masculine stereotypes.

Slash's Japanese cultural counterpart is yaoi, which shamelessly depicts its gay male characters as masculine/feminine archetypes (often regressive) so that young women can identify with the smaller, more overtly feminized uke character. Even though yaoi is about male romance, like slash it's written by women and is commonly acknowledged as an expression of feminine desire and sexuality. By the same token, slash allows many women to insert themselves into the emotional experience of a relationship.

On top of all this, many slashers claim that they prefer to ship male characters because the vast majority of female characters that exist in media lack agency. They're used as props for the main male cast, or are fridged, or otherwise debilitated to build up male characters in narratives.[14]

If you're a fan who wants to write your favorite characters going on adventures and falling in love, but you're faced with a vast sea of media populated by women who just don't get to have as much fun or be as complex as their male counterparts, then who would you rather ship Captain Kirk with—Yeoman Rand or Spock? Most slashers are going to ship the two most complex characters together. And for most media, that means the dudes.

Myth: All fanfic is super weird

Fanfic explainer articles love to give weird and creepy examples of fanfic concepts, probably because it makes for a better story than the reality of people writing harmless stories about Captain America and Iron Man falling in love (which, by the way, canonically happened in an alternate Marvel comics universe where Iron Man was actually a woman).[15] Tentacle porn! Dobby/Voldemort slashfic! Bizarre crossovers where the Super Mario Brothers have a threesome with one of the blue aliens from Avatar! LOL, it's all so weird!

Look, we get it. Fandom is home to some pretty eccentric ideas, and that's fine. There's something really heartwarming about the idea of a self-generated community where people can come together to write the Smaug/Bilbo Baggins dragon romance of their dreams. But whenever a mainstream media article exclusively describes fanfic in those terms, it's probably alienating awhole lot of people who would actually engage with more popular fanfic topics like Harry Potter sequel fics and homoerotic reinterpretations of the Sherlock Holmes books.

The fanfic community's overall output is extraordinarily diverse, but the vast majority of stories tend to be things that would make sense even to people who have never read a fanfic in their lives: romances where old friends are reunited and enemies recognize a mutual attraction, continuations of long-cancelled TV shows, and explorations of details that never got enough screentime in canon. Characterizing fanfic as a bizarre and threatening subculture full of poorly written Klingon erotica not only shames the people who actually like poorly written Klingon erotica (a perfectly harmless hobby), but it casually dismisses the merit of fanfic and the community that produces it.

14 http://en.wikipedia.org/wiki/Women_in_Refrigerators
15 http://marvel.wikia.com/Natasha_Stark_%28Earth-3490%29

Myth: Fanfic is just practice for "real" writing

"If these fanfic writers are so good, why don't they get published?"

This is one of the very first questions people ask when they're told that fandom is full of seriously talented authors and artists. Why not go pro? Well, first of all, some of them do. Several published authors admit to writing fanfic in the past, and countless numbers still operate under fanfic aliases while publishing books under their real names. However, becoming a "good enough" writer is not the goal of fanfiction. You may as well ask why someone spends their time knitting or playing football or practicing a musical instrument if they're not going to try and go pro.

For every fanfic writer who dreams of being the next J.K. Rowling, there's another who will only ever be interested in writing stuff based on, well, the *original* J.K. Rowling. The fanfic community forges friendships across the world and has developed a thriving gift economy where people write made-to-order stories as holiday gifts for total strangers. Even if you ignore the issue of literary merit, the way fanfiction is produced and consumed is nothing like the process of producing or consuming a novel, which is typically a very lonely venture on both ends of the reader/writer relationship.

Acafan Catherine Tosenberger has argued that fanfiction's greatest signifier is actually that it's un-publishable.[16] That is, really good fanfiction—and there's plenty of it—is actually so intrinsically tied to its canon that if you tried to just replace the names of characters and places you'd have something unrecognizable and unable to be severed from its original source. That's not to say that fandom isn't also churning out a million or so trope-laden, interchangeable coffeeshop AUs that could easily be turned into original fiction.[17] That can and does happen all the time. But at the core of every fandom are fanfiction writers who are drawn to explore those specific storylines. They don't want to write original fiction. They want to linger a little while longer in the world they love.

Myth: All fanfic is porn

We've already answered this, right? No, all fanfic is not porn. And all fanfic porn is not bad porn. You're actually way more likely to find well-written erotica from fanfiction writers on AO3 than from many writers of published erotica.[18] There's also the fact that when it comes to sexually explicit material, the fanfic community has a pretty unusual attitude compared to mainstream porn, erotica, and many other forms of popular entertainment.

Typically, the most popular and highly-recommended fanfics are long (about 20,000 words and up), well-written, and feature a mixture of plot, character study, and romance. In popular fandoms like *Sherlock, Teen Wolf,* and *Avengers*, the most popular longfics focus on a central relationship

---

16 http://muse.jhu.edu/login?auth=0&type=summary&url=/journals/childrens_literature_association_quarterly/v039/39.1.tosenberger.pdf
17 http://fanlore.org/wiki/List_of_Tropes_in_Fanworks and http://fanlore.org/wiki/Barista_AU
18 http://www.dailydot.com/culture/where-to-find-good-fanfic-porn/

like Sterek or Johnlock, but also have an action/adventure or mystery plot, and adult-rated sex scenes.

This type of cross-genre mixing is pretty rare within Hollywood narratives, particularly if you're looking for a sci-fi or action movie that also focuses on sophisticated adult relationships. This limitation is one of the reasons fanfic is so popular in the first place. Even in novels that include sex scenes, unless the book is categorized as New Adult, romance, or erotica, you're unlikely to get an equal balance of gripping plot and heady sex. Sure, you do see cross-genre mixing in mainstream fiction to a certain extent, particularly in Urban Fantasy novels and high-concept romance lit like Diana Gabaldon's *Outlander* series. But it never happens in the kind of popular entertainment most fanfic fandoms are inspired by: *Sherlock, Supernatural, Harry Potter*, and so on.

Outside of romance and speculative fiction, fanfiction has been the driving force that unites "mainstream" narratives with underground tropes like sex, kink, and other forms of erotica. There's a huge gap between adult-rated shows like *Game of Thrones*, and actual pornography. In the world of fanfiction, this division is almost nonexistent. Fanfic sites like AdultFanFiction.net and AO3 are among the only places where you can find this kind of fiction in bulk, and have it be written about characters that you already know you'll love.

In the real world, we're used to seeing a pretty clear division between what is and isn't porn—or at least we were used to it prior to the rise in New Adult literature. New Adult often combines multiple genres with erotica and romance. And how did New Adult begin, again? With the success of *Fifty Shades of Grey*—a novel that started out as fanfiction.

Myth: Fanfiction is plagiarism

No, it's not. Where to begin with this frequently leveled accusation? Let's start with the basic fact that recursive literature and remix culture stem from centuries of telling and retelling stories that are living, breathing parts of our heritage and culture.[19]

Then consider the way that stories live on and teem and ferment inside of our brains, whether we like it or not. After reading *Pride and Prejudice*, Jane Austen's own niece wrote a letter to her while roleplaying in-character as Elizabeth Bennet. Fanfiction isn't a late-20th-century invention, nor is it a deliberately deviant choice made by infringing delinquents.[20] Fanfiction is something that has been around for centuries but only recently gained a name and a culture.

More practically, there's an immense and increasing amount of support for the legitimacy of fanfiction. For one thing, franchise tie-in novels and speculative television scripts written for profit are essentially fanfiction in all but name—the only difference is that this fanfiction is corporate sanctioned. (This is also why we deign to call Kindle Worlds a service for fanfiction when it is more accurately a very low-paying franchise tie-in generator.) For another, many modern classics are fanfiction: Donna Tart's *The Goldfinch* (fanfiction

19 http://bookshop.livejournal.com/1044495.html
20 http://www.jasna.org/persuasions/printed/number27/fergus.pdf

about a real painting); Pulitzer-winning novels like *March* (*Little Women* fanfic) and *A Thousand Acres* (*King Lear* fanfic); Robert Altman's classic noir film *The Long Goodbye*, which took famed detective Philip Marlowe and plopped him into the '70s, because that's what fanfiction does. The list is virtually endless, and it grows daily.[21]

More and more, authors are coming to be aware of the commonalities they share with fanfic. After he wrote his acclaimed sci-fi novel *Redshirts*, John Scalzi got referenced as having written *Star Trek* fanfic so often that he finally decided that's exactly what it was.[22] It helps that many of the authors who started out writing fanfiction now work as creatives and writers themselves, from fanfic writer-turned-acclaimed novelist Rainbow Rowell's *Fangirl* to Steven Moffat writing *Doctor Who* headcanons years before being tapped to be a showrunner.[23] When the lines between fans and creators grow blurrier every day, it's hard to keep up the myth of an exclusionary literary establishment. Increasingly, the fans are the establishment. And it's harder to keep up the argument that fanfiction is plagiarism, no matter how much some writers feel that it's like selling their children into white slavery. (And yes, that's an exact quote.[24] Oy vey.)

But what about copyright?

Like every other potentially infringing thing we do on the Internet every day, from reblogging a photo on Tumblr to uploading a song cover to YouTube, in the U.S. fanfiction writers are protected by a magical thing called the Fair Use clause. The Fair Use clause states that if use of someone else's work is "fair", it's OK. Traditionally, "fair" has usually been granted to purposes of education or commentary, but this is also the clause that allows and protects parody. In a landmark parody lawsuit, *Campbell vs. Acuff-Rose*, fandom found its cornerstone: the word "transformative."[25] This ruling created the legal precedent that the more transformative a work is from the original, the fairer its use, even if that use is commercial. That means that under current legal precedent, if your work of fanfiction truly transforms the original, like taking angsty teenage vampires from *Twilight* and turning them into high-powered adult businessmen who play around with BDSM, you can sell that work. Which is how we ended up, again, with *Fifty Shades of Grey*.

There is one other ruling that explicitly sets a precedent for the protection of fanfiction under copyright law, though it's recently been challenged. That ruling awarded transformative status to a '90s bestseller called *The Wind Done Gone*.[26] This book is a non-humorous, non-satirical, critical reworking of *Gone with the Wind*, but it was deemed a parody while acknowledging its transformative status. As we currently have no copyright ruling in place for fanfiction as a genre or as a grouping of works, this ruling is as close as we've gotten to a legal precedent. If a compelling case can be made for the fanwork

21 http://bookshop.livejournal.com/1044495.html
22 http://www.dailydot.com/culture/10-famous-authors-fanfiction/
23 https://groups.google.com/forum/#!topic/rec.arts.drwho/fNc0-Zpirpg%5B1-25-false%5D
24 http://bookshop.tumblr.com/post/37053347832
25 http://www.law.cornell.edu/supct/html/92-1292.ZS.html
26 http://www.edwardsamuels.com/copyright/beyond/cases/gonewindappnew.htm

as transformative, then the U.S. copyright "fair use" clause is fully protective of the work, whether it is done for free or for profit.

Copyright law is very outdated and has yet to catch up to current common copyright practice, which relies heavily on remix culture and the idea of "Creative Commons." Advocacy groups like fandom's Organization for Transformative Works and the Electronic Frontiers Foundation frequently engage in legal advocacy for fanworks. As they do, fanfiction gains more and more legal acceptance and protection.

And ultimately, it doesn't really matter, because, again, the itch to write your own story about that story you just heard is much, much older than copyright. Fanfiction is here to stay.

Myth: Reporters should ask celebrities what they think about the awkward fanfic fans write about them

No. First of all, asking a celebrity to simply "react" to fanfiction being written about the fictional character they portray (and occasionally the actor themselves) is actually shorthand for "I'm a lazy reporter who would rather exploit fans than do the work of rounding up real questions for this interview."

Secondly, this celebrity who is having lots of slash written about them has already been asked about their thoughts on slash by the other 145 million unoriginal reporters who came along before you and went, "What can I do to be edgy? Oh, I know, I'll show them the fanfiction about them on the Internet!" They are sick of being asked this question.

Thirdly, depending on any number of personal/social/contextual factors that have nothing to do with the show, the fandom, or the content of the fanfic, being asked about fanfic could make them feel uncomfortable, which means you were just rude and invasive for stupid reasons.

Fourthly, if the actor is worth their salt, they'll know that reporters asking them to comment on fanfic, on specific ships, and/or slash are all among the worst-case scenarios of that actor's fanbase.[27] No matter how the actor answers, fans will be hurt. It's rare to find fandom-savvy actors like Misha Collins and Orlando Jones, who talk about fanfic freely and see it as something to celebrate rather than avoid. And even then, those actors know that fans themselves like to stay on their side of the fourth wall that preserves fandom's subculture from prying eyes. In the words of Misha Collins, "Don't talk about it? Right! Because there's a line! There's a line! And you're crossing it! Right now!"[28]

Myth: The fourth wall is made to be broken

The fourth wall is the fandom-created idea that there should, at all times, be a necessary distance and separation between fans and the creators/creative teams of the things they love. The fandom shorthand for "creator/creative team/producers/actors/writers/etc" is TPTB, short for The Powers That Be. TPTB always have the power in any given situation where they interact with fans, because TPTB controls the product fans are consum-

27 http://www.dailydot.com/news/sherlock-fanfic-caitlin-moran/ and http://www.dailydot.com/society/jensen-ackles-homophobia-supernatural-fandom/
28 http://strangepicturesofmishacollins.tumblr.com/post/17440121256/misha-on-slash

ing. But fans always take those products and do things with them that are outside of the creators' control, like, oh, turning male characters you might have meant to be bastions of heteronormativity into deeply repressed gay superheroes. This disparity can sometimes cause friction between the two groups.[29] So when fans interact with creators, TPTB have to be extra careful not to disturb the balance that exists between their vision and how fandom has re-imagined their stories and characters. The fourth wall represents the idea that these things co-exist but don't overlap.

Increasingly, the concept of "the fourth wall" has become known among some fans as the idea that fandom is a hidden space that should be preserved and kept out of the limelight. Obviously that's something that conflicts with the idea of the free press, but it's also something that responsible journalists should consider before pulling fandom communities into the public eye. Fans should never have their real names tied to their fandom identities and then made public without their permission.

Journalists should also consider whether the purpose of quoting and linking to a piece of fanfic is to enhance a discussion of fandom, or whether the context is simply to incite mockery and titillate readers. If it's the latter, consider that you're contributing to a media culture in which fannish practices are routinely mocked, which contributes toward ongoing sexism and dismissal of the predominantly women-based communities that participate in them. Is it really worth it? And, again, 268 million other journalists have made the "fanfic is so weird and funny" joke already. It's far more rare and far more valuable as a statement on fanfic to talk about fanworks the way you would any other literature or creative practice.

If you must...

So, if you still feel the need to write an explainer article on "Just what IS this weird fanfiction phenomenon", there's one final thing that you really need to take into account: Fanfic is totally mainstream. We're serious. Jon Stewart references it on *The Daily Show*. There is a bestselling novel called *Fangirl*, written by an award-winning author who used to write Harry/Draco fanfic.[30] A fusty midwestern newspaper uses the word "fandom" in their headlines.[31] Writers for *Sherlock*, *Teen Wolf*, and other popular stories go out of their way to tease their audience of slash shippers, occasionally to disastrous effect.[32] So unless your target audience is retirees who don't use the Internet, it's probably time to give it a rest on the shock and awe, OK?

This article first appeared on *The Daily Dot* on June 17, 2014.
www.dailydot.com/geek/complete-guide-to-fanfiction/

---

29 http://www.dailydot.com/geek/supernatural-season-9-predictions/
30 http://www.dailydot.com/fandom/10-people-changed-fandom-2013-list/
31 http://www.indystar.com/story/entertainment/movies/2014/03/13/doctor-who-north-america-tardis-capaldi-bbc-indianapolis-bradbury-dalek/6361539/ and http://www.duluthnewstribune.com/content/mitch-albom-column-dark-side-sports-fandom
32 http://www.dailydot.com/news/sherlock-fanfic-caitlin-moran/

THE ECONOMICS OF FANDOM: VALUE, INVESTMENT, AND INVISIBLE PRICE TAGS

Saathi Press

'␣ve been thinking a lot lately about fandom in terms of the value/devaluation spectrum, as it's been a useful framework for my current mode of fandom behavior analysis. For instance, when talking about the hate that some prominent fandoms have for characters of marginalized identities (female characters, characters of color, etc), it's been handy to frame the issue in terms of value: tagged hate is an active attempt to *de*value those characters, dedicated celebration events or communities are an active attempt to generate or increase value for frequently-devalued characters or ships, and so on.[1]

These terms were only intermittently useful until I read a blog post by Rose Lemberg regarding recent Science Fiction/Fantasy fandom issues—issues which, not incidentally I think, seem to parallel a lot of current transformative works fandom (TWF) issues.[2] In it, she says: "…we see a flow of social capital from fans, in form of sales, praise, and support, towards […] powerful fans…"

And I went "oh, shit, yes, *social capital*." That's what I was missing in the whole puzzle of fannish value spectrums. Because when I say "value", people probably think of two things: *money* and *quality*. But in a subculture like TWF, where money is not the primary tool used to represent goods and services and where, in fact, goods and services are ostensibly offered/exchanged "freely" among the community, it's easy to misread "fannish value" as representing quality. Which is, I think, profoundly misleading.

Transformative Works Fandom has an economy, and I think calling it a "gift economy' misses the mark.

In other economies, the primary currency is, obviously, *money*. At its most basic level, money represents **work** (effort expended to provide goods or services) and **influence**. Admittedly, capitalism is a convoluted and thorny topic, well beyond the scope of this discussion, so I won't render any value(quality)-based opinions here on the *justness* of a capitalistic money-based

---

1 In Tumblr fanspace, tagging posts is a contentious issue. Many fans of a character or a ship search using that tag for content that *values* the character/ship, and they may become upset or frustrated when they encounter a consistent or overwhelming amount of posts doing the opposite.
2 http://roselemberg.net/?p=762

41

system, or how well one functions in the real world. But I think that definition of money is a fair, if a super-basic one.

Just like money-based economies, TWF has goods and services, as examined by Tisha Turk in "Fan work: Labor, worth, and participation in fandom's gift economy."[3] So, if producing goods and services is "work" in money-based economies, then it's still "work" in TWF. This is perhaps a radical definition, for some—but simply because it's *voluntary* work in fanspace doesn't mean it's not the same thing.

It's very, very easy to mistake "work" for "the thing we do because we *have* to, not because we *want* to", but in the simplest terms, work is an expression of *time* and *emotional energy*. I could say "enthusiasm" instead of "emotional energy", but I don't think that's quite right, in part for reasons that I'll talk about later, but also because the close relationships forged in fanspaces—as elsewhere—aren't always about enthusiasm, but can also be about support in rough times, commiseration, advice, and other immensely valuable elements that go beyond enthusiasm. I could add "skill" as a component of "work", too, but then we veer again into *quality*-based definitions of value, which as I said before can be misleading and create inaccuracies in this kind of discussion. Just as other economies don't consistently—or primarily—reward skill, neither does fandom.[4] Not to mention, time and emotional energy are essential aspects of skill-building, because it's rare to see skill without some form of dedicated practice and some kind of learning process.

The other thing that money can represent is influence. Now, we in fandom often hate to admit that we *do* grant greater influence to some members of our community—some call them BNFs (Big Name Fans), but that's a term many eschew due to negative historical connotations. Whatever you call them, we do value some voices more than others, and are more willing to *invest* in their creative outputs (see below about "costs").

Such status can be a reflection of privilege, just as influence often is in larger economies. Which language(s) an individual knows and how fluent they are can dramatically affect their experience in fandom; so, too, can access to technology like the internet, or the amount of free time available to spend in fanspaces. Also a factor: the money a fan can invest in things like travel, attending conventions, buying related merchandise or ephemera, in creating tangible fanwork, and so on.[5]

It's also valuable to remember the impact of intellectual ability &/or higher education. Fandom still responds better to certain ways people express themselves and articulate their thoughts and feelings than to others. "Correct" spelling and punctuation, clear if not always *formal* rhetoric—these things may get shrugged off in situations where "ZOMG FEELS!!1!" is not an unusual expression, but are absolutely valued in fanfic—and also in, say, meta essays like this one.

3 http://journal.transformativeworks.org/index.php/twc/article/view/518/428
4 http://penknife.livejournal.com/178090.html
5 This can include canonical or semi-canonical ephemera including (but not limited to) tie-in comics or novels, soundtracks, or Blu-Rays with full supplemental features, as well as noncanonical or *fanonical* ephemera like doujinshi, fanzines, and so on. Cosplay, for instance, can be a very expensive hobby; creating other non-digital fanwork can often require purchasing materials, and even digital fanwork can require hardware, software, and the ability to make prints/copies for resale as desired.

So: without money, how do we *express* value in fanspace? Different platforms or venues offer different methods of expressing value. The kudos button on AO3, the like button on facebook, and the little <3 or ✫ symbols on Tumblr and Twitter are straightforward "reward values." Reblogs are another example; positive gifs and "THIS" and "+1" in reblogs/comments can imply additional value. Recs—one of those fannish "services"—are also a form of value. More in-depth, positive comments express greater value, as they take more time and emotional energy (again: *work*) to employ.

This is perhaps why someone creating derivative work of other fans' transformative works—podfic of a fanfic, or fanart for a fanmix, or graphics for awards, or etc.—is one of the most prized occurrences in TWF. It's a sign that a fan is so enthusiastic about someone else's work that they're willing to expend creative energy of their own in response.

Essentially, fandom exchanges *work* for *work*. The greater the perceived value, the greater the reward in terms of the work other fans are willing to do in exchange.

Now let's talk about *costs*. In fandom, everything is "free", right? Nope. I hate to get all TANSTAAFL on ya'll, but um, in this case it's true.[6] In order to *value* a work, one must first "consume"—read, watch, look at, listen to, possibly buy—it. If "work" is "time and emotional energy", then consuming fanwork is an *investment*. It takes work to consume fanwork.

When someone says, "That fanfic was so bad, I had to hit the back button a quarter of the way through," that means that they did not feel they received the value they expected, and they decided to *invest* the rest of their time and emotional energy *elsewhere*. "Unfollowing" has the same connotation—space in one's "feed" (as on tumblr, twitter, livejournal or dreamwidth, RSS feeds, etc) is investing a regular fraction of attention, if not more. Which is why reblogging and reccing and other forms of "sharing" work have slightly greater value than kudos or likes: because someone valued something enough that they thought that *others* should likewise invest in that work. *Investment* of time and emotional energy is the "invisible price tag" in online communities and in fanspaces.

Aside from the "back" button and unfollowing, other ways to devalue work in online communities are *negative* responses. There aren't any "dislike" or "hate" or ☹ buttons on some of the aforementioned platforms, though there are things like "downvoting" in some forums or comment threads. However, fans may use expressive gifs, flames, or other forms of negative feedback. In TWF, "flames" (negative comments on fanworks) are generally frowned upon, but that's a nicety that not everyone observes or endorses. It seems that many transformative works fans perceive such devaluative work as wasted effort ("just hit the back button if you don't like it, sheesh")—and since I'm defining effort/work as a *reward* in TWF, the reasoning works out.

On the other hand, if someone takes the time to thoughtfully refute or rebut a post, it may not merely be a devaluation of that post, but an assertion of value for an opposing viewpoint. This is where fandom economics gets tricky and kind of fascinating: there are always multiple competing *concep-*

6 "There Ain't No Such Thing As A Free Lunch," a phrase popularized by Robert Heinlein's book, The Moon is a Harsh Mistress. http://en.wikipedia.org/wiki/There_ain%27t_no_such_thing_as_a_free_lunch

tual values within the fannish "marketplace." In some cases, dissent can even show that someone considered the *topic* valuable enough to invest work in discussion instead of simply ignoring/dismissing it.

That's why posting character/ship hate in the tags is considered a devaluation: it takes time and emotional energy to create such a post and to tag it. For fans of a character or ship, "tagged hate" can feel like negativity that saps them of a fraction of time and energy. Such negativity can then pile up, prompting resentment from fans, who may mobilize into "defense squads" or create blogs to document and counter hate, like FandomsHateWomen or FandomsHatePoC.[7] Think of tagged hate as a *devaluative microaggression* within fanspace, whereas sending anon hate to another fan or posting an anonymous flame on fanwork would be a form of devaluative *aggression*.

Moreover, if creating transformative works is *work* then it makes sense that collective devaluation can discourage creators from investing in some things they might otherwise value highly. If a fan fears that their investment of time and emotional energy may not be valued at all, or that their work will be met by active devaluation, then their output and enthusiasm is likely to be hindered.

This is why I try to promote thoughtfulness and consideration for all kinds of fans, especially from those with greater influence within fandom (like BNFs), why I promote ship egalitarianism, and why I dislike ship wars and single-perspective declarations about interpreting canon. Because if a single OTP (One True Pairing) "wins" and drives away all other kinds of shipping, or all fanon (fannish interpretation of canon) save one is devalued into silence or nonexistence, then we have a smaller community, a smaller amount of *collective value* to share and (re)distribute.

In short: those situations mean there's a *monopoly on the social capital in that fandom*. Furthermore, if a TWF "monopoly" reflects harmful kyriarchal constructs, instead of being truly "transformative", then I think we've lost one of the greatest *values* our community has to offer. (But as always: ymmv.)

This article appeared on *The Fan Meta Reader* on August 28, 2014.
thefanmetareader.wordpress.com/2014/08/28/the-economics-of-fandom-value-investment-and-invisible-price-tags-saathi1013/

---

7 http://fandomshatewomen.tumblr.com and http://fandomshatepoc.tumblr.com, respectively.

SMUGGLER'S PONDERINGS: HISTORY, FANDOM AND MASTERS OF SCIENCE FICTION

Ana Grilo

T his post started (as many things these days do) as a Twitter rant, which was then followed by a very thoughtful conversation between many parties (storify here).[1]

Actually, let me backtrack a little bit. This all started when I read an article called The Problem of Engagement written by Baen Books publisher Toni Weisskopf and later posted on According to Hoyt.[2] As a bit of context, this article has surfaced following the controversy surrounding Jonathan Ross and his brief stint as official Hugo Award MC for this year's Loncon. If you don't know what I am talking about, here is a brief recap.[3]

There have been many troubling aspects surrounding the Hugo-Ross controversy. One of them is the way that the surrounding narrative has been reframed in a way that calls those who voiced their concerns about Jonathan Ross hosting the Hugos "bullies"/"the PC crowd running wild"/"oversensitive zealots who are always offended by things" without any thought to the context in which their concerns are voiced. Kameron Hurley has written an incredible post about this phenomenon: Rage Doesn't Exist in a Vacuum.[4]

The fact is, I've been following this conversation from the very beginning (being up early here in the UK), I watched it all go down. I also watched as Big Media relayed events in such a way that was completely out of context, so unwilling to listen to the actual facts of the conversation, that it soon became clear to me:

This is history being rewritten in front of our very eyes.

***

Reading Toni Weisskopf's article was a bit like wandering through fog (or wading through mud, if we take into consideration some of the more abhorrent comments left after the post). I was not exactly sure as to what was the point of the article. It appears to be an earnest call to unite the different

1 http://storify.com/sl_huang/the-book-smugglers-et-al-on-sf-classics

2 http://accordingtohoyt.com/2014/03/10/the-problem-of-engagement-a-guest-post-by-toni-weisskopf/

3 http://corabuhlert.com/2014/03/07/the-media-spin-machine-at-full-power-or-this-is-totally-not-what-happened/

4 http://www.kameronhurley.com/rage-doesnt-exist-in-a-vacuum-or-understanding-the-complex-continuum-of-internet-butt-hurt/

"sides" of fandom involved in Ross-Hugogate. Of course, this call for unifi-cation would have been much more effective had the article refrained from referring to one of the "sides" as "fuggheads" who are "politically correct, self-appointed guardians of [...] everything" and participate in "fooforaws."

The post also calls for calmer minds and sings the praises of classic authors like Heinlein: "Of course we all read Heinlein and have an opinion about his work. How can you be a fan and not?"

My favourite part of this argument is the way it reminisces an idyl-lic time when folks thought that fandom ought to have "nothing to do with greater world politics, but should concentrate on the thing we all loved, that being science fiction."

Here is the problem with Weisskopf's presentation: when you use words like "PC" or "fuggheads" to describe groups of people (e.g. women, people of colour, LGBTQIA folks)—people who have been trying to become fully ac-cepted members of what you call Science Fiction Fandom—you are not only delegitimizing their fight but also reframing the narrative of the fight itself.

This is history being rewritten in front of our very eyes.

In addition: when you decide to use those charged words to describe those people? That's a choice. It's a choice to engage in the conversation in a certain way that has everything to do with "greater world politics" and very little to do with "loving Science Fiction."

***

I've been thinking about all of these things, and about history. And I have many questions, but not many answers.

It seems to me that there's this idea that Science Fiction—as genre and as fandom—has a "history." And that (real) fans should know this particular history.

My main question when hearing this argument is: "history" as perceived by whom? As defined by whom?

Why is it that this early history of Science Fiction fandom is presented as "idyllic" when we know for a fact that large groups of people stood out-side looking in? Isn't that history being rewritten in front of our very eyes? Try this: when you Google "best Science Fiction of all time" or "essential Science Fiction novels," you almost invariably get lists featuring works by the same group of people. Very few contain writers who are not white and male. The narrative that chooses this subset of people as the only worthy "masters" of the genre? Isn't that, too, rewriting history in front of our very eyes?

It is obvious to me that this idyllic period of Science Fiction "history" is told largely from an American, white, male perspective. It might be an im-portant part of a historical narrative, but it is not the *whole* narrative. Surely, it can't be. If we choose to brand only those works "masterful" and "classic" and "essential", what are we saying?

What about a bit more of personal context: I am Brazilian. MY history is that I've had little to no access to those "masterworks" of science fiction.

Am I a lesser Science Fiction fan if I have not read Heinlein or many other "classic" authors?

But what about my other hats? Am I a lesser reviewer or editor? I am torn about this. As a reviewer, I completely appreciate the point that it might be useful to be well versed in at least some of the tenets of the field in which you are reviewing. Even if some of those classics are racist, misogynistic, dated, and terrible, like I said before, *context* is always important.

But then I go back to the point: What is this "context"? Does "classic" SF really represent the entire extent of the genre? If I, as a reviewer, read only what has been branded "classic" to become aware of our "history" am I not choosing to be limited to a certain demographics? Where do the paradigms and criteria used to define "masters", "history" and "fandom" come from anyway? Are those ideas so easy, so simple to grasp and define?

(It seems to me that this is easy only if you believe you are approaching science fiction from a mythical objective place that is apart from "greater world politics"—but we know that that is history being rewritten in front of our very eyes).

When someone says to a piece of criticism "but have you read X [work of classic SF]?" isn't that a way of silencing criticism? This reminds me of something that happened when I was at university, when a History of Art teacher had an argument with another student over criticism theory. The student made very good points, but teacher shut him down by saying, "You haven't read Foucault, do not talk to me until you have." I was horrified.

Can't we criticise "new" without knowing the "old"? Is our reading "narrow" if we don't allow for the weight of "history"? This is coming from someone who tries to play catch any chance she gets. But here is another question: can *anyone* have read *everything* there is to read? To me it seems that there will be always blind spots you don't see.

At the end of the day, I am worried about the idea that one must do or read X in order to be a "real" critic/fan/aficionado. I understand wanting to read the "classics" for any number of reasons: for research, for context, for fun, for whatever. I also equally understand NOT wanting to read them for any reason at all. Because you want to frame your reading in a different way, because the "classics" do not represent you or worse: *mis*represent you. I fully understand not wanting to spend time reading something that equals being punched in the face.[5] I myself dislike that immensely.

I don't want the latter to define a "worse" type of reader or fan or critic than the former.

Am I a lesser reviewer because of that? I am filled with angst at the thought that what I write here means nothing at all because I have not been a part of fandom for long and I have not read a lot of "classics." Does that make my opinions and thoughts on new books or my involvement in fandom any lesser? I am also Brazilian (am I outside fandom?). A woman (am I outside fandom?). English is not my mother tongue (am I outside fandom?). I am not very young either (am I outside fandom?). I am a blogger (am I outside fandom?). I read YA and Middle Grade and Fantasy (am I outside fandom?).

5 http://www.annleckie.com/2013/10/21/real-heart-real-artificial-heart/

I know very little and I have few answers. I do know one more thing: that what I am saying here is not new or original and that many, many others have been talking about this since forever. I know this and I say this because I am not rewriting history in front of your eyes.

This article first appeared on *The Book Smugglers* on March 12, 2014.
thebooksmugglers.com/2014/03/smugglers-ponderings-history-fandom-and-masters-of-science-fiction.html

OH DEAR: SFWA BULLETIN PETITION

Natalie Luhrs

David Truesdale has written and circulated a petition (this was received directly from David Truesdale)—and gotten a number of SFWA members to sign it.[1]

That, however, was not what was originally circulating. This is.[2] And this is what I'll be responding to below.

It's full of appeals to the sanctity of the First Amendment—which, as a private organization, SFWA doesn't need to abide by—and a whacking great heap of sexism and racism, too. I don't understand why some people are constantly conflating their desire to say anything they want, wherever they want, with private organizations' right to moderate spaces that they own.

Enjoy some excerpts:

> The essence of the situation is that a writers' organization, of all groups, should not be establishing a committee to determine what is "unacceptable" or "inappropriate" or "offensive" in some contribution to one of its publications. SFWA should be the front line of defense for First Amendment issues, and not make itself part of the problem.

If one takes that argument to its logical conclusion, then why have an editor at all? Let's just publish whatever gets sent in! Also, again: SFWA is a private organization and the First Amendment doesn't apply. Just like this space is a not-the-government and I get to make the rules about who gets to talk here and who doesn't.

> The cover of the 200th issue of the Bulletin was part and parcel of the furor that has led to its suspension. Cries of "sexism," portraying women as "sex objects," and other like phrases reached the ears of the President and will now become part of the "review process" overseen by the new editor, "volunteers and an advisory board" and the President himself. Covers like the one shown here are not new. They have graced the covers of countless magazine and book covers for many decades. So have magazine and book covers featuring handsome, ripped and rugged males in various stages of dress, depending on the story and what the publisher hopes will appeal to his readership in order to advance sales. Yet there are those who object strenuously to a sexy female (scantily

1 http://pretty-terrible.com/wp-content/uploads/2014/02/Bulletin-petition3.pdf
2 http://pretty-terrible.com/wp-content/uploads/2014/02/truesdale-petition.pdf

clad or otherwise) on the cover of anything, and always somewhere in the mix of reasons, primary among them is that women are being portrayed as sex objects and that such covers are blatantly sexist and therefore are to be avoided, or removed, or are otherwise to be castigated and held up to ridicule and scorn.

Let's refresh our memory about that cover, shall we?[3]

It would be one thing if this cover had any sort of relationship to the contents of the Bulletin, but it didn't. It's a badly done painting of a not that sexy, mostly naked warrior at severe risk of frostbite. And the Resnick/Malzberg column was about how hot some lady editors were in their bathing suits and nary a mention of their facility with a red pen. Objectifying and dehumanizing. No wonder people objected.

And if the next two issues hadn't been a doubling down on said objectification and dehumanization, people would have let it pass. It was the fact that there were *three issues in a row* that were full of sexist and racist nonsense that caused the uproar—and rightly so in my opinion.

Then Truesdale embarks upon a long digression on how ogling objects of desire is something that everyone does (well, not exactly everyone) and how it should be completely okay. You know what? Not in a professional context—which the SFWA Bulletin is. The SFWA Bulletin should be about publishing and writing speculative fiction in an increasingly volatile marketplace, not about the good old days when the female editors were smokin' hot in a swimsuit and didn't let themselves be offended by red-blooded American male approval. Or, at least, didn't let on that they were offended.

Ladies these days. Just don't know anything about quiet dignity.

Then—oh then. Truesdale hauls out the very best part: he has a black friend![4] A black lesbian friend! Who is never named but who nonetheless goes on to agree with and bless every single one of Truesdale's arguments. If this friend exists, I feel sorry for them, as they've been reduced down to their racial and sexual identities.

> I want to emphasize that I am not trying to shut people up who hold deep feelings about their views on sexism (or any other topic). What I object to and find odious is that certain folks, in their self-righteousness, want their views to override all others, silencing them, and now they have a President in their hip pocket who is willing and able to do their bidding. Their views should be open for discussion—and print in the Bulletin—just like the views others hold on any variety of important subjects, but not to the exclusion of any opposing (and just as deeply felt) view or mode of expression from anyone else. That approach is the inclusivity and diversity you're looking for.

---

3 The cover of the 200th issue of *The Bulletin of the Science Fiction & Fantasy Writers of America* displayed artwork featuring Red Sonja in a golden bikini, standing with a bloody sword over the body of giant in snowy mountains.

4 http://tvtropes.org/pmwiki/pmwiki.php/Main/SomeOfMyBestFriendsAreX

> SFWA members don't pay their $90 annual dues to be told what to think or how they should express themselves in the pages of the Bulletin, nor do they want their own thoughts (through their articles or columns) to be deemed "acceptable" or "right thinking," or adhering to some jumped-up (always subject to change at whim) PC style manual by some hootenanny "advisory board" of boot lickers.

Okay, then. Again: I wasn't aware that the Bulletin was supposed to be a free-for-all, where anyone can say anything. I thought it was a professionally edited magazine for professional writers that is supposed to have content that is of use to the specific audience. I don't think six pages of Mike Resnick and Barry Malzberg going on about the good old days is really very useful to the membership; I read some magazines that have personal essays in them and they're usually one or two pages, at most. Six pages is a lot of real estate for reminiscing about how awesome it was to be a writer 30 years ago.

> Far from an editor, this person will be nothing more than a slave, dragging his bundle of copy to the mansion from the field, where the "review process," and some proposed "volunteer and advisory board," and the President himself will be making the real "editing" decisions. You gather the cotton, we'll spin it into what we think looks good for us.

Yep. He went there.

Ultimately, though, Truesdale's argument is thoroughly dishonest. He's trying to get people riled up over someone editing the publication and he's doing so in an incredibly offensive and gross manner. He's claiming that this is a free speech issue when it isn't. SFWA is not the government. They can't stop you from saying whatever damn fool thing you want. All they can do is stop you from saying it in their publication.

Luckily for you all, Sunny Moraine has written a handy guide explaining what the First Amendment means.[5]

C.C. Finlay makes the point more eloquently than I can as well.[6]

So hey: Don't let the door hit you in the ass on the way out.

EDIT 4:30 PM: I was provided a copy of the first (unedited) version with additional signatures. You can find it here.[7] This version was being sent out via email by David Truesdale as late February 8.

This article first appeared on *Pretty Terrible* on February 10, 2014.
www.pretty-terrible.com/2014/02/10/oh-dear-sfwa-bulletin-petition/

---

5 http://sunnymoraine.com/2014/02/09/political-censorship-a-helpful-guide-to-whether-or-not-its-happening-to-you/

6 http://ccfinlay.com/blog/editing-is-not-censorship.html

7 http://pretty-terrible.com/wp-content/uploads/2014/02/Bulletin-Censorship2.pdf

POST-BINARY GENDER IN SF: INTRODUCTION

Alex Dally MacFarlane

I want an end to the default of binary gender in science fiction stories.

What do I mean by "post-binary gender"? It's a term that has already been used to mean multiple things, so I will set out my definition:

Post-binary gender in SF is the acknowledgement that gender is more complex than the Western cultural norm of two genders (female and male): that there are more genders than two, that gender can be fluid, that gender exists in many forms.

People who do not fit comfortably into the gender binary exist in our present, have existed in our past, and will exist in our futures. So too do people who are binary-gendered but are often ignored, such as trans* people who identify as binary-gendered. I am not interested in discussions about the existence of these gender identities: we might as well discuss the existence of women or men. Gender complexity exists. SF that presents a rigid, unquestioned gender binary is false and absurd.

I intend to use this column to examine post-binary SF texts, both positively and critically, as well as for discussions of points surrounding this subject.

And I intend to use this column to go beyond Ursula K Le Guin's *The Left Hand of Darkness*.

Kameron Hurley wrote several years ago about the frustration of *The Left Hand of Darkness* being the go-to book for mind-blowing gender in SF, despite being written in 1968.[1] Nothing written in the decades since has got the same traction in mainstream SF discourse—and texts *have* been written. For a bit of context, 1968 is almost twenty years before I was born, and I'm hardly a child.

One of the reasons Hurley considers for this situation (raised by someone on a mailing list she belonged to) is that:

> ...perhaps Le Guin's book was so popular because it wasn't actually as radical as we might think. It was very safe. The hetero male protagonist doesn't have sex with any of the planet's inhabitants, no matter their current gender. We go off on a boys' own adventure story, on a planet entirely populated by people referred to as 'he,' no matter their gender. Le Guin is a natural storyteller, and she concentrates on the *story*. It's not overly didactic. It's engaging and entertaining.

The Left Hand of Darkness certainly has been radical, as Hurley says, in its time, in the subsequent years and in the present. I have spoken to several

1 http://www.kameronhurley.com/leguin-boys-own-adventure-and-the-fire-art-of-genderfucking/

people who found *The Left Hand of Darkness* immensely important: it provided their first glimpse of the possibility of non-binary gender. The impact that it has had on people's realisations about their own gender is not something I want to diminish, nor anyone else's growth in understanding.

However, I do think it can be very palatable for people who haven't done a lot of thinking about gender. It is, as Hurley says earlier in her post, the kind of story that eases the reader in gently before dropping the gender bombs, and those bombs are not discomfiting for all readers. Of course they're not. How can one text be expected to radicalise every reader?

I don't want to cast *The Left Hand of Darkness* aside. It's an important part of this conversation. What I do want to do is demonstrate how big that conversation truly is. Other texts have been published besides *The Left Hand of Darkness*, many of them oft-overlooked—many of them out of print. Some of them are profoundly problematic, but still provide interesting questions. Some of them are incredible and deserve to be considered classics of the genre. Some of them are being published right now, in 2014.

Amal El-Mohtar wrote a piece about the process of finding—having to find—a pioneering woman writer, Naomi Mitchison, and followed it up with a post where she said:[2]

> It breaks my heart that we are always rediscovering great women, excavating them from the relentless soil of homogenizing histories, seeing them forever as exceptions to a rule of sediment and placing them in museums, remarkable more for their gender than for their work.

It seems to me that there's a similar process for post-binary texts: they exist, but each reader must discover them anew amid a narrative that says they are unusual, they are rare, they sit outside the standard set of stories. This, at least, has been my experience. I want to dismantle the sediment—to not only talk about post-binary texts and bring them to attention of more readers, but to do away with the default narrative.

That process of (re)discovery is probably inescapable. A bookshop, a library or a friend's/family member's bookshelves can't contain every book ever published, so new readers will always have to actively seek out stories beyond the first ones they encounter. What if, El-Mohtar wonders, the first books often included Naomi Mitchison? What if the first books often included multiple post-binary texts as well?

Conversations about gender in SF have been taking place for a long time. I want to join in. I want more readers to be aware of texts old and new, and seek them out, and talk about them. I want more writers to stop defaulting to binary gender in their SF—I want to never again read entire anthologies of SF stories or large-cast novels where every character is binary-gendered. I want this conversation to be louder.

To that end, I'll be running this column: posting every two weeks, with discussions of books and short stories, as well as interviews and roundtables with other writers and readers of post-binary SF, because I strongly be-

2 http://www.npr.org/2014/01/01/258384937/crossroads-and-coins-naomi-mitchisons-travel-light and http://amalelmohtar.com/2014/01/02/crossroads-and-coins-naomi-mitchison-and-travel-light/

lieve it's important to hear multiple voices. I'm particularly interested in science fiction at the moment, but I expect I'll cross genres as I run the column. I hope you'll join me in making the default increasingly unstable.

This article first appeared on *Tor.com* on January 21, 2014.
www.tor.com/blogs/2014/01/post-binary-gender-in-sf-introduction

THE TAXONOMY OF GENRE: SCIENCE FICTION AS SUPERGENRE

Shaun Duke

I recently stayed with Maureen Kincaid Speller and Paul Kincaid, two wonderful people whose book collections would make almost any SF fan drool. One of the brief discussions we had before I headed off for my final days in London concerned the often pointless debates about what science fiction "is." Paul suggested that thinking of SF as a "genre" in the narrative sense is not accurate to the use of "genre." Unlike romance or crime, there is nothing unique to the narrative practice of SF that can be separated from everything else. This might explain, for example, why there has been so much discussion about the nature of SF as a cross-pollinating genre—crossovers being so regular an occurrence that one would be hard pressed to find an SF text which does not cross over into other generic forms.

Paul's observation, it seems to me, is spot on. Even if I might define SF by such vague features as future time and extrapolation, these are merely functional terms to explain SF to someone who does not know what it is; outside of that narrow space, these definitions are practically useless, as the academic world has yet to define SF in any concrete, generally accepted sense—as opposed to other fields, such as biology, whose name defines itself (the study of life). Likewise, no two people can agree on what SF "is", with academics and non-academics alike debating the wide range of critical definitions, from Darko Suvin to Carl Freedman to Istvan Csicsery-Ronay, Jr.

During this conversation, I suggested that it might be more fruitful to think of SF as a supergenre rather than a straight genre, as doing so would allow us to apply the crossover potential of SF to a different set of parameters: namely, the interaction of subgenres or genres with the supergenres to which they belong. The supergenres would include realism, science fiction, and anti-realism, with the traditional genres of crime, romance, historicals, fantasy, and so on underneath. These supergenres would not necessarily define the genres beneath them, but they would suggest a relationship between genres that moves beyond narrative practice, but never quite leaves it behind. A fantasy novel might be as much historical as it is anti-realist; the former is a narrative practice, while the latter is a conceptual "game."

In this respect, SF would be defined by its most basic roots—its conceptual concerns, not its narrative ones. Futurity, extrapolation, and social or hard science, to give a rough sketch. Of course, SF can interact with the other supergenres, producing SF-nal works which are more realistic than not (or the other way around); this seems a supergeneric necessity, as to define "realism" as anything other than "literature which attempts to represent the world as it is" would not allow for the widest range of possibilities, which I submit a supergenre requires in order to be defined as such. A terminological shift from "as it is" to "as it could or might be" is fairly negligible in the long run. Thus, an SF text can adhere to the rigors of science in its imagining of a possible real future, and a realist text can do the same in reverse order; whichever conceptual mode is dominant would determine the supergenre to which that text most aptly belongs, but the divisions would never be hard so as to discount the cross-supergeneric influences. One might think of a typical Asimov or Bacigalupi novel as more SF-nal than realist and a Jane Rogers novel as more realist than SF-nal. Naturally, this could make things rather messy.[1] In a similar fashion, one might think of Tolkien's Lord of the Rings as both anti-realist and realist at once, which might suggest a contradiction if not for the fact that the rigor with which Tolkien wrote LOTR would seem to subvert the anti-realist tendencies of fantasy, if only minutely. I'd suggest that LOTR is dominated by its anti-realist practices simply by being more tied to myth and folklore than to the Realist tradition (in the literary sense, not the supergeneric sense). In that respect, one would place myth, fairy tales, and folklore firmly under the anti-realist banner.

Defining genre this way would also kill the endless discussions about how to classify texts which seem to borrow narrative traditions from all over the place. A romantic comedy featuring a detective could be shoved into three separate genres (or subgenres), neither marring the value of the other in relation to the text. Whether dominance should determine classification at this point is up to debate, though I suspect out of a need to keep conversations about texts relatively smooth and unencumbered one would need to focus on the dominant trait rather than apply a text's multiplicities. Outside of conversation, an acronymic practice might make things easier.[2]

These are all preliminary thoughts—ones which I'm expounding upon while on my train to London Victoria. I do think they are worthwhile ones, though. Expect more on this in the future.

And on that note: I leave the comments to you lot.

This article first appeared on *The World in a Satin Bag* on August 25, 2014.
wisb.blogspot.com/2014/08/the-taxonomy-of-genre-science-fiction.
html

---

1 Obviously, this concept is only useful outside of the marketing apparatus.
2 If one is clever, the acronyms could be turned into clever words. A romantic comedy set in 18th century France would become a HRC, or "horic."

SHATTERING IT TO BITS: WOMEN AND THE DESTRUCTION OF SCIENCE FICTION

Vandana Singh

"...Would we not shatter it to bits and then
Remould it closer to the heart's desire..."
(Omar Khayyam, as translated by Fitzgerald)

The June 2014 issue of Lightspeed is a special issue called "Women Destroy Science Fiction."[1] With an all female guest editorial team and an impressive roster of women writers, the issue is a great start toward a newer, richer science fiction. I have not finished reading all the stories, but the ones I've read achieve a fine balance of style and substance. There is of course no doubt in my mind that women can write science fiction, being one of those women myself. But in many ways I feel we are still at the start of the journey. The journey began with Mary Shelley, with Rokeya Sukhawat Hussain, later it got a fresh start with Joanna Russ, Ursula Le Guin, Eleanor Arnason, Octavia Butler among others, and even later with a new crop of women writers, increasingly international and diverse, among whom I feel privileged to count myself. Each start was from a different place, and each part of the journey carried all of us women writers, and indeed science fiction itself, into new and strange places. It is in this sense that I refer to the special issue as a "start."

So what does it mean to "destroy science fiction"? The guest editor, Christie Yant, says this:[2]

Why "Women Destroy Science Fiction"? Are we really trying to destroy it? As you read the stories in this issue, you may very well think so. Here you'll find galactic gastronomy and alternate astronomy, far-future courtship and a near-future food court—right alongside alien invasion and deep-space salvage missions. My hope is that one or more of these stories will reach a reader who never realized that kind of story is science fiction, too, and will seek out more like it. And I hope that one or more will convince those writers—the fantasists, the poets, the ones more comfortable in Middle Earth or the Midwest than on Mars—that they, too,

1 http://www.lightspeedmagazine.com/issues/june-2014-issue-49/
2 http://www.lightspeedmagazine.com/nonfiction/editorial-by-women-destroy-science-fiction-editorial-team/

can create science fiction stories and participate in the expansion of the field.

So to "destroy", in this sense, is to expand the boundaries of the field. And in fact writers like Ursula Le Guin have done this as well—in her case, bringing intelligent sociological/ anthropological speculation to science fiction, thereby allowing SF to emerge from its adolescent boys-with-toys stage.

Earlier in her editorial, Yant states:

> There was—is—something else going on, too, something apart from the attacks from the outside. It's a smaller, quieter attack from within, and it's just as pernicious. Too many accomplished writers are convinced that they aren't qualified to write science fiction because they "don't have the science." I've heard this worry from men, too, but more often I hear it from women. I don't know which is worse: the men who tell us we're doing it wrong, or the voice within ourselves that insists that we'll fail if we try.

This is a very important point—women thinking they "don't have the science." It is easy to conclude, from these two paragraphs, that Yant's solution to the problem of women's discomfort with science (and therefore with science fiction) is to expand the definition of science fiction, and thus avoid any real engagement with the hard sciences. I don't know if this is intentional on the part of the editor, although a couple of comments in the article seem to assume that. I'm going to keep an open mind about the editor's intention, but I will address the issue of women's diffidence about the sciences, particularly here in America, since this is a topic of deep interest to me, both in my professorial and writerly capacities.

I am going to attempt to ask the question I posed a few paragraphs ago in a slightly different form.

What does it mean to *me* to "destroy science fiction?"

Science fiction is dominated by certain assumptions, definitions of what is science fiction, and what is good science fiction or real science fiction. Science fiction is deeply influenced still by the Campbellian "golden age" paradigm. Here, scientific and technological achievement are the province of the white cis male. The worldview is materialistic, science is a source of power and glory, "progress" in the Western capitalist mode is naturally and unquestionably good. Space-faring heroes colonize and exploit other worlds, mimicking without engaging with or critically examining the problematic history of colonialism here on Earth. Space missions are invariably in the mode of a military chain of command, because what other options are there? Natives exist to provide exotic color, to be conquered and rescued, and to be uplifted through the magnanimity of the white heroes, to whom they can never be equal. Women and non-human animals play similar roles in these fictions.

In the above I've over-simplified somewhat, but I hope the idea is clear. Although the field has diversified and expanded through the decades, I find some form or other of these assumptions still extant in SF, sometimes including SF by women. So to me, to destroy science fiction means to examine these assumptions, to engage with them, to stretch our imaginations by coming up with alternative visions. Such science fiction should:

- Expand the field, as Christie Yant has stated.

- Diversify the field, so that we are presented with a kaleidoscope of voices and visions (I've written at length about diversity in SF in another post).[3]

- Question the enterprise of science and technology. Examine the notion that science, technology and progress are necessarily good no matter the circumstance. This entails examining the state of the sciences today. I say this as someone with a deep love of the sciences, as a scientist who, to echo Robert Frost, has a "lover's quarrel" with the way science is done.

- Science has origins in a "masculine" Western culture whereby rationality, logic and science are associated with men, and gushy emotionalism, or anti-science, is associated with women. This view of science is pathologically limited, essentialist, and misses a lot. I've written at length about it in a series of three columns for Strange Horizons: Science, Emotions and Culture.[4] For this series I interviewed scientists and people who study science cultures, and read books and papers on the subject. It is inevitable that a science culture still informed by such notions is going to give rise to a similar phenomenon in science fiction.

- The idea of science as a search for truth has been blemished by the use of science by vested interests. The co-optation of science by war and industry deserves better scrutiny in and out of science fiction.[5] Consider the tobacco industry's propaganda in the name of science. The pharmaceutical industry is rife with examples of products and concepts that may not stand scrutiny. How does the profit motive affect, promote, dilute and contaminate science? Much of the SF I've read from the American canon (mostly short stories because I often only have time to read these) seem to take for granted that the public interest and corporate interest always coincide.

- Perhaps related to item 3a) is the fact that much of science as practiced today is based on the reductionist paradigm—that if you understand the parts of some system, you can deduce from it the properties of the whole.[6] This is powerful indeed and has enabled us to get to where we are today in terms of technological advance. But a relatively neglected field of study—that of

3 https://vandanasingh.wordpress.com/2014/05/27/alternate-visions-some-musings-on-diversity-in-sf/
4 http://www.strangehorizons.com/2011/20111212/singh-c.shtml
5 http://www.inference.phy.cam.ac.uk/sanjoy/science-society/2004-winter/physics-war.pdf
6 http://en.wikipedia.org/wiki/Reductionism

real world complex systems—is telling us that reductionism can only go so far. If we are to think intelligently about issues like global climate disruption, we need to change the paradigm. I wonder: if there had been more diversity in the sciences, would we have developed the science of complexity earlier? For a great short essay on what I'm driving at here, read Willy Ostreng on holism versus reductionism.[7] One way that science fiction can be "destroyed" is to imagine a scientific world-view that is based on an appreciation of complexity rather than solely on re-ductionism. So for instance how to re-imagine future medicine based on this idea? And it turns out that scientific paradigms affect human society—modern urban cultures are based on a Newtonian world-view—the atomistic division of society into nuclear families and individuals, for example. The "clockwork universe" notion that arose as a response to Newton's discov-ery of some of Nature's laws led to the industrial revolution and all the modern "isms", from capitalism to communism. Yet we know the universe is not Newtonian. What would a society based on a different paradigm look like?

• Include more science, not just more tech. Since this is a person-al list, I am allowed to put this here. As science fiction writers we are good at thinking up futuristic gizmos, but what about scientific ideas, principles, concepts? There is quite a bit of technological fiction out there, but not enough that plays with science itself. So for example, we could have a story in a uni-verse where the big bang didn't happen, or one where physical laws change with time (something that physicist Lee Smolin suspects about our own universe). This is not just intellectually interesting but can be personally meaningful as well. Science fiction, after all, is the only literature that is regularly concerned with our interactions with the physical universe. When playing with big science ideas we get to engage with philosophy as well, with big questions that can only make our work richer, multi-layered and resonant.

All this requires, obviously, some knowledge of science—I'd generalize this to include philosophy of science and history of science—so I am going to examine what Christie Yant mentioned with regard to women who feel they "don't have the science."

This leads me to examine the realm of "hard science fiction", because that is where women are outnumbered most hugely by men.

There are many definitions of hard science fiction, but what makes most sense to me is this: *hard science fiction is fiction where the people in the story are engaged with science and technology to such an extent that the story would not hold up if the said science and technology were taken out or*

7 http://www.cas.uio.no/Publications/Seminar/Consilience_Ostreng.pdf

substituted with something else. The sci-tech has its own story that braids with the story of the humans.

To me the crucial thing is the *engagement* of the people with the science and technology, so that the sci-tech is not merely a backdrop. Nor is the story a *story* without a well-developed human element—subtract that, and it is a speculative essay or manual. (Which eliminates, for me, almost all classic hard SF that is written with wooden dialog, cardboard characters, stereotypes of gender, race and sexuality, and "as you know, Bob" infodumps). I add the bit about the sci-tech having its own story to mean that the sci/tech story, in the form of how it (device/ universe/ scientific idea) works, what is discovered, how it might affect the humans, how it is invented, calculated, tested, experimented with—that sci-tech story must be a primary part of the story as a whole. (An elegant story would accomplish this without indigestible infodumps).

I wonder to what extent stories written by women are simply overlooked as hard SF, because it is assumed that women can't write the stuff. It would be interesting to compile a list of hard SF by women through the ages that are consistent with the definition above. This would give historical context to some of the stories in Lightspeed's "Women destroy Science Fiction" special issue.

Looking at the table of contents of "The Hard SF Renaissance" (edited by Hartwell and Cramer), I see the names Nancy Kress, Joan Slonczewski and Sarah Zettel, three women among a list of 40-odd authors. In the "The Ascent of Wonder: The Evolution of Hard SF" I find stories by Ursula K. Le Guin, Kate Wilhelm, Anne McCaffrey, James Tiptree Jr., and Katherine MacLean. Of these most don't write hard SF on a regular basis. Off the top of my head I can add stories by Pat Cadigan and Octavia Butler. These are all, of course, writers from the West. Of the history of hard SF by women elsewhere I know almost nothing.

Of more recent-ish hard SF by women that come to mind: there is Rosemary Kirstein's Steerswoman series, elegantly written and well conceptualized (I'd like to offer a detailed critique sometime); there's this post praising three novels I have yet to read.[8] There are many other women who at least some of the time write hard SF, and I hope that somebody more widely read than me (and with more spare time) will compile a list of their names and works. I suspect that part of the problem is that hard SF stories written by women are simply not often recognized as such.

[I mention in passing that several of my own stories are hard SF in the sense described above, but I don't know that anyone familiar with my work thinks of me as a hard SF writer.[9] My hard SF work puts science first and technology second as far as ideas go, and people are as important as ideas. I write with attention to words. My work has speculative physics and biology in it as well as good, old fashioned Newtonian physics. In many stories I've tried, with varying degrees of success, to come up with alternative paradigms of science and doing science. My dream is to write hard SF that anyone will

---

8 http://www.tor.com/blogs/2013/05/sleeps-with-monsters-recentish-hard-sf-by-women
9 http://vandana-writes.com/short-stories/

want to read, even if they don't like science, and that they will finish the story with a different way of thinking about the world. (I can dream, can't I?!)]

To write this sort of fiction, one must be willing to engage with the science. In my personal experience the notion that *women are not good at science* is much more prevalent in the U.S. than in India, where I am from. (We have our gender issues, but that seems to not be one of them, or not one of the major ones). This is consistent with data on the percentage of women enrolled in physics degree programs around the world.[10]

Some of the diffidence women have about the sciences here in the U.S. likely comes from a) *social-cultural expectations* of what is appropriate for women and what they are capable of, and b) *the bad PR about science*, especially the physical sciences, so prevalent in a popular culture that is proudly anti-intellectual, which portrays science as boring, and scientists as exceptionally weird and smart, so they are clearly outside the norm and difficult to identify with, and c) *a culture of science that is still unwelcoming to women*. The first and third are discussed in a paper by Potvin and Hazari that I reference in Part II of my essay series, for those interested.[11] Here's my take on these three factors.

- Women are capable of any intellectual enterprise that men are also capable of. The nice thing about socio-cultural expectations is that when you examine them enough to know when they are untrue, you have the privilege of saying "the hell with that!" However socio-cultural expectations and assumptions are so powerful (as one can see in such phenomena as stereotype threat) that thumbing one's nose at them is only the first step.[12] What I imagine a woman needs other than the guts and honesty and perseverance to go against deeply ingrained stereotypes is a truly supportive community of other women. More on that anon.

So can we take it as given that women, when they have the chance, can bloody well do science, talk about and write about science, and write hard science fiction just as well as men? Which allows us to posit the possibility that women can bring new perspectives to these fields that might well revitalize these enterprises, but more on that anon.

- You go to a party, and at some point someone, let's say a woman, although it could well be a man, asks about you and what you do. You admit to teaching at a university, and inevitably they want to know what you teach. Looking hard at the salad, you admit to having a background in theoretical particle physics, at which the person then does one of these things: 1) drop their jaw and say OMG, you must be so smart, 2) tell you how boring and horrible their sole physics class in high school was, and how much they hate physics, and 3) get a glazed look in their eyes and change the subject, and move away as soon

10 http://www.aas.org/cswa/status/2002/JUNE2002/IUPAPMeeting.html
11 http://www.strangehorizons.com/2011/20111010/singh-c.shtml
12 http://www.reducingstereotypethreat.org/definition.html

as possible. Of these I much prefer 3), although I sometimes get a genuinely positive, interested response that makes me very happy. But there are so many misconceptions about the sciences in this single encounter that I barely know where to begin. One, the fact is that scientists are no more smart than anyone else—what it takes to do science is hard work, passion, curiosity and perseverance. And two, there is enough research out there to indicate that intelligence is not a fixed amount of smarts you are given at birth, but something you can grow.[13] I've seen that again and again in the transformation that some of my students undergo. Three, physics is anything but boring, although there are many people who teach it as though it were a solution to insomnia. Physics is not 'about facts,' nor is it about memorizing disconnected blobs of meaningless information. Physics is about the underlying patterns in nature that result in the awesome physical universe we inhabit. Rocks falling, planets turning, sunsets, rainbows, ballerinas spinning, matter changing state, blood coursing through our veins, blue skies—we are surrounded by the manifestations of physical laws. How can this be anything short of amazing and wonderful? Science in general and physics in particular have an aesthetic aspect that so many people miss because they have had a bad first exposure to the subject. For writers in particular, these disciplines are rife with gorgeous metaphors too.

- I have sufficient personal and anthropological evidence to support the assertion that the physical sciences still present a "masculine" (as constructed by the West) culture marked by confrontation, competitiveness and "son-of-bitch-ness" which can be unwelcoming to many women. (I am not being essentialist here; I am talking about enculturation, and women are rarely enculturated to be confrontational in that way, and not all confrontation has virtue in any case. Where would modern science be without teamwork and collaboration?) In a similar fashion I suspect the culture of *science fiction* in the U.S. is territorial about science and hard SF, dismissive of women's abilities to write the "hard" stuff, and generally unwelcoming to women. It would not surprise me that even women who get past barriers a) and b) are turned away by c). [For more on these, see my essays in Strange Horizons].[14]

These are of course musings based on my personal experience and informal investigations. I'd be delighted to hear from women who write or want to write "hard" SF about their experiences.

---

13 http://learningandtheadolescentmind.org/people_01.html
14 http://www.strangehorizons.com/2011/20111212/singh-c.shtml

How do we overcome these barriers? Women can learn about science in many ways, not just from books but also from news magazines (I recommend New Scientist), by taking free online courses taught by fabulous professors from top universities (check out coursera.org and edx.org), and taking college classes if and when possible. We can watch NOVA and other shows like Cosmos to ignite our sense of wonder and dispel the bad PR about science as a boring, dry-as-dust enterprise. We can read about the history of science to realize how very human is this enterprise. We can read critical works that examine how science has been co-opted by vested interests. But to do learning well, and especially if that learning is to be transformed by and into story, we need more. We need to work hard, to not give up, to familiarize ourselves with the research on intelligence (I HIGHLY recommend the work of Stanford University educational psychologist Carol Dweck) so that we can dispose of the myths about science smarts. In addition we need to be persistent. Perseverance and persistence move mountains. I once helped run a writers' workshop in which a woman writer wanted to know how much time would pass for a person on a spaceship relative to the people they had left on earth. She prefaced that by saying "I don't do math, just give me the answer." The mathematics of relativistic time dilation is not that hard. "It's just square roots" I said, offering to show her the formula and how it worked so that she'd never have to ask anyone the answer. She didn't want to deal with it. I respect her right to make her own choices. But there are too many women I've come across who are content with staying safely within their comfort zone. I sympathize (I was once math-phobic myself, until tenth grade, after which I did mathematics for stress relief). Being female, I am distressingly familiar with the temptation of the easy way, the safe, familiar, well-trodden way, in a world that bristles with barbed wire fences as far as we're concerned. But we do need to trascend the barriers that restrain us from realizing our full potential.

How do we do this? I imagine a community. Indulge my fantasy for a moment. I imagine—to start with—a two-week-long workshop of women SF writers who get together in some fabulous place with great views and wonderful food. We have daily presentations on the physical sciences as they relate to science fiction. So there's cosmology, Newtonian physics, Einsteinian relativity. Add planetary geology, some atmospheric chemistry and biochemistry. We also have classes or workshops on the history of science, both Western and non-Western, on science and gender, and science and colonialism, and discussions that intelligently critique scientific enterprise. We do lab experiments, befriend mathematics, and read science news articles. We discuss these to clarify our understanding, to critique, to speculate on the consequences of new discoveries and technologies, and to come up with story ideas. (I've sometimes used science news stories as story prompts for practice, and it is fun). We use the afternoons and evenings to write and to critique our writing. This experience then becomes the seed for a true community of women writers who support each other, give each other honest critiques and share both failures and triumphs.

This sounds positively science-fictional, but perhaps someday someone will take the initiative.

So, in summary: women can and do write science fiction, and science fiction is as broad a canvas as the universe, or the imagination. All the different kinds of SF have their own virtues and pleasures. Among these, hard SF is historically the most unfriendly to women. For women (or anyone) to write hard SF well, an engagement with the sciences is essential, and while it might be difficult, it is also rewarding. But to write hard SF intelligently, one must go beyond the "golden age" paradigm to something more daring, critical and visionary. Women, I believe, are particularly well-placed to do so.

I grew up loving the arts and humanities as well as the sciences. It was a terrible thing to have to make a choice, in eleventh grade, between science and humanities. Before that all subjects were mandatory, which exposed me to their variegated wonders. Now I feel very lucky, because between my job and my writing I have the best of both worlds. There are days during which I might spend time reveling in the poetry of Kalidasa, or reading with delight the wonderful novel of childhood by Guinean writer Camara Laye, after which I might turn to pondering the dipole moment of the ozone molecule, or travel in my imagination to the moon, and observe the electrostatic dust fountains on the barren lunar surface caused by the solar wind.[15] This privilege, of having access to the full spectrum of human accomplishment, is one for which I am deeply grateful. (It does not come without struggle). One doesn't have to have a background in the sciences to learn about and appreciate science, and also to interrogate and critique how science is done in our world. Women are particularly well-positioned to do this, because many of us know what it is to be marginalized. So we can go into this endeavor fueled by our outrage and our anger, as well as our curiosity. We can look around with unprejudiced, wondering, and critical eyes at what science is, and how it is done. We can notice, as many female scientists did, in archeology and developmental biology for instance, things that the men missed. We can ask why we study this thing or that thing without studying the relationship between them. Science in my not-so-humble opinion is a natural human response to the gorgeousness of the universe. So let's take it back. Let's take it back from the corporations and governments. Let's talk to scientists, especially women scientists, and do some learning, on our own and together. And let us write our bravest stories, undaunted by categories and restrictions. Let us continue to take back *science fiction*, including hard SF—destroy it and recreate it, redefine it and enrich it.

More power to us!

This article first appeared on *Antariksh Yatra* on August 9, 2014.
vandanasingh.wordpress.com/2014/08/09/shattering-it-to-bits-women-and-the-destruction-of-science-fiction/

---

15   http://en.wikipedia.org/wiki/K%C4%81lid%C4%81sa

DISABILITY METAPHORS IN SCIENCE FICTION AND FANTASY

Corinne Duyvis

I'm a co-founder of the website Disability in Kidlit as well as an author who regularly writes disabled characters; both my recently published fantasy novel *Otherbound* and my upcoming sci-fi novel *On the Edge of Gone* feature disabled protagonists.[1] On top of that, I'm disabled myself. It's pretty safe to say I'm a huge fan of disability representation. Specifically, I'm a fan of accurate, respectful, and *textual* disability representation.

However, when writing science fiction and fantasy, it doesn't just stop at featuring textually disabled characters. Many SFF stories contain disability metaphors. These span a wide range—from purposeful to unintentional, from obvious to subtle, and from well-done to inadvertently offensive.

Many authors tackle interesting questions through these parallels: questions about human dignity; about violation; about "natural" versus "unnatural;" about reliance on medication or assistive tools; about the likelihood of ever recovering; about whether people may not be better off dead. However, they don't always consider that these exact questions are regularly posed to and by disabled people in real life. Worse, authors commonly answer these questions in a way that's contrary to the way actual disabled people feel about their lives.

Many disabled people are fed up with these poorly handled disability metaphors, and with the common trope of the "magical disability." Even when disability parallels are handled wonderfully, it's frustrating when these metaphors or made-up, sci-fi disabilities are used in lieu of actual disability representation.

To give an idea of what I mean when I talk about disability metaphors and parallels, here are a handful of different approaches...

In Kit Whitfield's *Benighted*, the vast majority of society are werewolves; the main character is one of the few people who's human. She's seen as broken and lesser for it. A similar situation occurs in Janet Edwards's *Earth Girl*, in which the few characters who cannot survive on worlds other than Earth are "handicapped" and called "apes" and "throwbacks."

In *X-Men*, Cyclops is forced to wear specially made visors/glasses every minute of every day. These also render him colorblind. Telepathic characters exert a lot of energy shutting out people's thoughts and emotions, if they're able to do so at all. Sookie from Charlaine Harris's The Southern Vampire Mysteries outright refers to her telepathy as a disability.

---

1 http://disabilityinkidlit.com/

Sometimes, characters' actual disabilities intersect with magical abilities, such as characters with narcolepsy or epilepsy whose episodes link into the ability to see into other worlds, into people's minds, or into the future. Other times—such as in my own *Otherbound*—characters with certain abilities or curses are misdiagnosed with medical conditions because the people around them don't know the truth.

In the above examples, the authors clearly drew conscious parallels. That's not always the case, though. In SFF, where you're dealing with fantasy creatures—each with their own strengths and limitations—as well as magic and technology, accidental parallels are inevitable.

Take for example characters who are magically mind-wiped; who are brainwashed; who are under supernatural influence; who are artificially created (Frankenstein, clones, androids)... heck, take *zombies*. Many zombie stories come down to a kill-or-be-killed situation, but in others, zombies can be restrained and made harmless relatively easily. This is used as a gag at the end of *Shaun of the Dead*. In that film and John Ajvide Lindqvist's novel *Handling the Undead*, zombies retain elements of their previous selves; in the British TV series *In the Flesh* and Jaclyn Dolamore's recent YA release *Dark Metropolis*, zombies can be "restored" to their former selves by means of medication.

Yet, I rarely get the impression that authors are conscious of how those characters relate to the perception of—for example—intellectually disabled, mentally ill, or otherwise neuroatypical people. Let's be clear: I am no way saying "disabled people are just like zombies" or "it's sort of like mentally ill people are mind-wiped." We're dehumanized often enough as is. I *do* want to point out that characters in the above categories are often stripped of agency and identity for reasons that are frightfully similar to the reasons given for dehumanizing disabled people in real life.

SFF features countless heart-wrenching scenes featuring protagonists who decide to "mercy kill" a loved one who underwent a terrible ordeal. It's meant as a poignant, tragic show of compassion and mercy. The characters will give reasons like: "They can't even talk." "They're drooling." "They're not the same person they used to be." "They wouldn't have wanted this." "They can't even look after themselves." "It's unnatural keeping them alive like this."

What does that imply about the millions of disabled people who fit those descriptions?

Similar problems arise with other parallels. Characters may be disrespected, treated as burdens, or wallow in their own misery in ways that echo problematic portrayals of disabled people. For all the interesting questions tackled in SFF, I wish I saw more questions of informed consent. Or questions of treatment, of assistive tools, of accommodations, of community. Characters rarely adapt to their situation and move on with their life to the best of their ability.

While I don't think disability metaphors are sufficient disability representation, I *do* think that they'll come up naturally in many texts, and that they're relevant to the discussion of disability in SFF. For authors, it's important to be true to their plot, their world, and their characters... but it's also important to consider how their narrative may resonate with and impact disabled readers.

Note: titles in this article are merely examples. Inclusion doesn't reflect my opinion of the title or the handling of the disability parallel, whether good or bad.

This article first appeared on *SF Signal* on October 28, 2014.
www.sfsignal.com/archives/2014/10/corinne-duyvis-on-minding-your-metaphors/

COLLATERAL DAMAGE

Kari Sperring

First of all, I'd like to thank everyone who has commented, and is still commenting, on my piece yesterday about SFnal futures and women. I'm reading. I'm nodding and thinking. I'm finding it hard to reply, but I am listening.

A number of people have asked what has been going on with me, that I wrote this (and my long twitter rant, which you can find storified here).[1]

It's this. Lately, I've been feeling like all I am is collateral damage. I seem to have been fighting to be allowed to exist, to be a person and not just a thing, almost my entire life. It's exhausting and draining and endless and I never seem to make any lasting gains. Indeed, as I age, the amount of space I'm permitted to occupy gets smaller and smaller and my sense of existence is shrinking.

And it's not just me. On all sides I see other people facing the same thing. I see brilliant women writers like dancinghorse (Judith Tarr) and scifi-writir (Carole McDonnell) dismissed from the narrative of fantasy and SF because they're older, or because their books have fallen out of print, or some variation and combination of those, because genre history continues to belong to men. I see the same thing happening to QUILTBAG writers and writers of colour and writers with disabilities. On all sides there are wonderful initiatives like the Geekfest Nine Worlds, anthologies and projects promoting the work of writers who are not white westerners, anthologies of queer fiction, blog series on ableism and othering in SF. I love all of this. It's a step forward.

But what I'm also seeing is that in almost all of these, there's a group that's consistently left behind. I'm seeing collateral damage.

I'm seeing older women—whether women of colour or white women, lesbian, bi or straight, trans or cis forgotten, or only considered relevant once they're dead or long out of print and the limelight (if they ever had any share of the latter to begin with). I'm seeing women writers who debut later—and women writers, along with writers of colour and writers with disabilities often face additional challenges which mean that they are more likely to debut later—being written off with no or few reviews, dismissed unread as predictable.

It's the pattern we seem unable to see when we fight for change. It's the pattern we just reproduce without thinking—and then excuse, usually on the grounds that we—that insidious, apparently collective SFF "we" which masquerades as all of us but all too often means only those with more privilege—that we need to attract more new blood, more "young fans."

I have never once heard or seen anyone suggest that "young fans" won't want to see established older male writers. Every single convention, including Nine Worlds, has its roster of established male pros over 40. Whenever I

1 https://storify.com/KariSperring/calling-out-the-men-who

hear this line about attracting the young, my heart sinks. Not because I don't want to see new people in fandom—of course I do.

Because the people who are asked to stand aside, the people whose work is deemed of little or no interest, are almost entirely older women. The older men go sailing merrily on.

Now, older men of colour are also victims in this: I would never deny that. It infuriates me that our genre is still talking about Robert E Howard but never mentions Charles Saunders, who wrote and is still writing some of the best swords-and-sorcery out there.

What it comes to is this: most women who are now over about 40 have been told their whole lives to be good, to keep their heads down, to keep on working away quietly and to wait their turn. And now, within SFF, at the point when their male contemporaries are celebrated, these same women are being told, No, it's too late for you, you don't matter enough; that space is needed. Get out of the way.

We're collateral damage. If we debut later, we may well find ourselves declared over, irrelevant, not worth reading even before the print is dry on our 1st book. If we've been in the industry for years, we find ourselves forgotten or dismissed and our innovations and talents and insights attributed to others (all too often male others).

I've been making a rough list of writers who were big names in the 80s, male and female, and looking at where they are now. The biggest women writers of that period, in my memory, anyway, were Barbara Hambly, R A McAvoy, C J Cherryh, Katherine Kurtz, Judith Tarr, Julian May, Mary Gentle, Lois MacMaster Bujold, Tanith Lee, and Connie Willis.

Only three of those women are still being published regularly by major publishers (and one of those—Cherryh—is largely ignored). Most of the others are still writing, but in other genres, for small presses, or via kickstarter.

The big name men, though. Guy Gavriel Kay, David Brin, William Gibson, Bruce Sterling, Greg Bear, Larry Niven, Michael Swanwick, George R R Martin, Samuel R Delany, Charles de Lint...

They're pretty much all still there. They're famous, their books get inches of review space, they're talked about and promoted and cited as influences.

Now, I'm not saying there aren't male writers who have fallen out of contract or seem to be being unjustly neglected. Gary Kilworth springs to mind, along with Graham Dunstan Martin (whose work I love) and the great, great Walter Jon Williams, who does not get the recognition he deserves.

On every side, I see people telling most of those women I listed to step aside. (The exceptions are Bujold and Willis.) I see their books go unreviewed. I see their influence marginalised. Those are some wonderful, wonderful writers, writers you should be reading. There are more established women writers than Le Guin (great though she is). They deserve to be celebrated, too. They deserve their place in genre. So does Charles Saunders.

They deserve better than to be pushed aside while their male peers sail merrily on.

Women over 40, whatever our colour, our sexuality, our ability should not just be Collateral damage.

I call foul.

Edited to add: This isn't about expecting younger women to step aside, either. It suits our patriarchal culture to try and play the dis-privileged off against each other and to pretend that there's only enough space for a few. This isn't about women gaining at the expense of other women. This is about a system that builds in barriers for everyone who doesn't conform to that straight, white, able-bodied, male norm.

This article first appeared on *livejournal.com/la_marquise_de_* on June 17, 2014.
users.livejournal.com/la_marquise_de_/365312.html

WISCON 38: GUEST OF HONOR SPEECH

N. K. Jemisin

[ETA 3/28/14: Added markup; text is still the same. Also, please note a discussion here about a line in the Delany quote that concerned some people.][1]

Thanks to all the WisCon volunteers, members, and other supporters, who have given me the opportunity to speak to you now.

Trigger warning: I'm going to refer to rape, harassment, racism, and other forms of bigotry and abuse in this speech. Also, profanity warning. That's sort of standard with me.

I'm going to start this off with a quote from Chip Delany, writing in the essay "Racism and Science Fiction" which was published in NYRSF in 1998.[2] It's online, you can look it up.

> Since I began to publish in 1962, I have often been asked, by people of all colors, what my experience of racial prejudice in the science fiction field has been. Has it been nonexistent? By no means: It was definitely there. A child of the political protests of the '50s and '60s, I've frequently said to people who asked that question: As long as there are only one, two, or a handful of us, however, I presume in a field such as science fiction, where many of its writers come out of the liberal-Jewish tradition, prejudice will most likely remain a slight force—until, say, black writers start to number thirteen, fifteen, twenty percent of the total. At that point, where the competition might be perceived as having some economic heft, chances are we will have as much racism and prejudice here as in any other field.

> We are still a long way away from such statistics.

> But we are certainly moving closer.

I'm tempted to just stop there, drop the mic, and walk offstage, point made. Chip's a hard act to follow.

But it has been almost twenty years since his prophetic announcement, and in that time all of society—not just the microcosm of SFF—has ratcheted toward that critical, threatening mass in which people who are not white and not male achieve positions of note. And indeed we have seen science fiction

---

1 http://nkjemisin.com/2014/05/a-note-on-my-wiscon-speech/
2 http://www.nyrsf.com/racism-and-science-fiction-.html

and fantasy authors and editors and film directors and game developers become much, much more explicit and hostile in their bigotry. We've seen that bigotry directed not just toward black authors but authors of all races other than white; not just along the racial continuum but the axes of gender, sexual orientation, nationality, class, and so on. We've seen it aimed by publishers and book buyers and reviewers and con organizers toward readers, in the form of every whitewashed book cover, every "those people don't matter" statement, and every all-white, mostly-male BookCon presenters' slate. Like Chip said, this stuff has always been here. It's just more intense, and more violent, now that the bigots feel threatened.

And it is still here. I've come to realize just how premature I was in calling for a reconciliation in the SFF genres last year, when I gave my Guest of Honor speech at the 9th Continuum convention in Australia.[3]

For those of you who don't stay on top of the latest news in the genre, let me recap what happened after that speech: I was textually assaulted by a bigot who decided to call me a "half-savage" among other things.[4] (Whoops, sorry; he calls himself an "anti-equalitarian", because why use a twelve-cent word when you can come up with a $2 word for the same thing? Anyway.) He did this via the Science Fiction and Fantasy Writers of America's official Twitter feed, which meant that he was using the organization as the tool for a personalized, racist, sexist attack; because of this he was later expelled from the organization.[5] He was just the inciting incident, though; the really interesting thing is what surrounded this whole affair. I got the expected rape and death threats from this man's supporters and others, which I duly reported to various authorities, for whatever good that did. During the month or so that it took SFWA to figure out what it wanted to do with this guy, a SFWA officer sat on the formal complaint I'd submitted because she thought I had "sent it in anger" and that I might not be aware of the consequences of sending something like that to the Board. A SFWA affiliate member posted a call for civility on his website; in the process he called me "an Omarosa" and a "drama queen", but of course he didn't mean those in a racialized or gendered way.[6] In a semi-secret unofficial SFWA forum there was intense debate—involving former SFWA presidents and officers, and people who weren't members at all—about why it was desperately important that SFWA retain its harassers and assaulters, no matter how many members they drove off, because their ability to say whatever they wanted was more important than everyone's ability to function in genre workspaces, and SFWA's ability to exist as a professional association.

Let me be clear: *all* of these were racist and sexist attacks, not just one on the SFWA Twitter feed. And let me emphasize that I am by no means the only woman or person of color who's been targeted by threats, slurs, and the intentional effort to create a hostile environment in our most public spaces. People notice what happens to me because for better or worse I've achieved a high-enough profile to make the attacks more visible. But I suspect every person in this room who isn't a straight white male has been on the receiving

3 http://nkjemisin.com/2013/06/continuum-goh-speech/
4 http://fozmeadows.wordpress.com/2013/06/14/reconciliation-a-response-to-theodore-beale/
5 http://www.locusmag.com/News/2013/08/beale-expelled-from-sfwa/
6 http://www.pretty-terrible.com/2013/06/19/how-not-to-have-a-conversation/

end of something like this—aggressions micro and macro. Concerted campaigns of "you don't belong here."

This is why I say I was premature in calling for a reconciliation. Reconciliations are for *after* the violence has ended. In South Africa the Truth & Reconciliation Commission came after apartheid's end; in Rwanda it started after the genocide stopped; in Australia reconciliation began after its indigenous people stopped being classified as "fauna" by its government.[7] Reconciliation is a part of the healing process, but how can there be healing when the wounds are still being inflicted? How can we begin to talk about healing when all the perpetrators have to do is toss out dogwhistles and disclaimers of evil intent to pretend they've done no harm?

(Incidentally: Mr. Various Diseases, Mr. Civility, and Misters and Misses Free Speech At All Costs, if you represent the civilization to which I'm supposed to aspire then I am all savage, and damned proud of it. You may collectively kiss my black ass.)

Maybe you think I'm using hyperbole here, when I describe the bigotry of the SFF genres as "violence." Maybe I am using hyperbole—but I don't know what else to call it. SFF are dedicated to the exploration of the future and myth and history. Dreams, if you want to frame it that way. Yet the enforced SWM dominance of these genres means that the dreams of whole groups of people have been obliterated from the Zeitgeist. And it's not as if those dreams don't exist. They're out there, in spades; everyone who dreams is capable of participating in these genres. But many have been forcibly barred from entry, tormented and reeducated until they serve the status quo. Their interests have been confined within creative ghettos, allowed out only in proscribed circumstances and limited numbers. When they do appear, they are expected to show their pass and wear their badge: "Look, this is an anthology of NATIVE AMERICAN ANCIENT WISDOM from back when they existed! Put a kachina on the cover or it can't be published. No, no, don't put an actual Navajo on the cover, what, are you crazy? We want the book to sell. That person looks too white, anyway, are you sure they aren't lying about being an Indian? What the hell is a Diné? What do you mean you're Inuit?"

But the violence that has been done is more than metaphysical or thematic. Careers have been strangled at birth. Identities have been raped—and I use that word intentionally, not metaphorically. What else to call it when a fan's real name is stripped of its pseudonym, her life probed for data and details until she gets phone calls at her home and workplace threatening her career, her body, and her family? (I don't even need to name a specific example of this; it's happened too often, to too many people.) Whole subgenres like magic realism and YA have been racially and sexually profiled, with discrimination based on that profiling so normalized as to be nearly invisible. How many of you have heard that epic fantasy or video games set in medieval Europe need not include people of color because there weren't any? I love the Medieval PoC blog for introducing simple visual evidence of how people like me were systematically and literally excised from history.[8] The result is a

---

7 http://www.aljazeera.com/indepth/features/2014/04/rwanda-genocide-survivors-back-reconciliation-20144215732338738.html and http://en.wikipedia.org/wiki/Australian_referendum,_1967_%28Aboriginals%29
8 http://medievalpoc.tumblr.com/

fantasy readership that will defend to the death the idea that dragons belong and Those People don't.

Incidentally, the person who runs the Medieval PoC blog estimates she has received something on the order of 30 death threats in recent months.

And let's talk about the threats—including the ones I'm likely to get for this speech. The harassment. The rapes. The child abuse. Let's talk about how many conventions have been forced to use disturbingly careful language to basically say, Don't assault people. Let's talk about how much pushback statements like that have gotten from people whining, "Aw, c'mon, can't I assault someone just a little?"

Worst of all, the violence has at this point become self-perpetuating. I can't tell you how many times I was told, with great vehemence and hostility, that there was no chance of me having a career in SFF—by other people of color. Yeine, the protagonist of THE HUNDRED THOUSAND KINGDOMS, was almost a white man because I listened to some of what these people were saying. (Imagine if I'd listened to all of it.)

I have no idea what to do about all this. Just keep doing what I've been doing, I guess—just write, and try to improve my writing, and publish, and try to stay published. Every few months, pause to deal with some bigot's bullshit. Then get back to writing. For the first time in my life I was diagnosed with high blood pressure earlier this year. It's back down to normal, now, but bigotry kills, you know. Gotta be more careful of my physical and psychological health. Gotta survive. Because that's all anyone can do, if we're ever to make it to the point that reconciliation is possible. We aren't there yet.

There are some signs of hope, I guess: SFWA did throw that one bigot out, though plenty more remain. Chip Delany's been honored as a SFWA Grandmaster some fifty years after one of his novels was rejected for serialization in ANALOG because its editors didn't think anyone could relate to a black protagonist. WisCon invited me here to be one of its Guests of Honor, five years after I ragequit the Concom over the Elizabeth Moon affair. We are talking about what's happening. We are fighting back. But I am desperately afraid that Delany's prediction will continue to prove true, and that the violence will escalate as more of us step up and demand that our contributions be recognized, our personhood respected, our presence acknowledged. If that's the case, then we haven't seen the worst of it yet. And we need to prepare.

So. If they think we are a threat? Let's give them a threat. They want to call us savages? Let's show them exactly what that means.

Arm yourselves. Go to panels at Wiscon and claim the knowledge and language that will be your weapons. Go to sources of additional knowledge for fresh ammunition—histories and analyses of the genre by people who see beyond the status quo, our genre elders, new sources of knowledge like "revisionist" scholarship instead of the bullshit we all learned in school. Find support groups of like-minded souls; these are your comrades-in-arms, and you will need their strength. Don't try to do this alone. When you're injured, seek help; I've got a great list of CBT therapists, for any of you in the New York area. Exercise to stay strong, if you can; defend what health you have, if you can't. And from here on, wherever you see bigotry in the genre? Attack it. Don't wait for it to come directly at you; attack it even if it's hitting another group. If you won't ride or die for anyone else, how can you expect them to ride or die for you? Understand that there are people in this genre who hate you, and who do not want you here, and who will hurt you if they can. Do not tolerate their intolerance. Don't be "fair and balanced." Tell them they're unwelcome. Make them uncomfortable. Shout them down. Kick them out. Fucking fight.

And maybe one day, when the fighting's done, then we can heal. On that day, all of us will dream freely, at last.

Thank you again.

This article first appeared on *nkjemisin.com* on May 25, 2014.
nkjemisin.com/2014/05/wiscon-38-guest-of-honor-speech/

EMIC, ETIC, AND THE DEPICTION OF OTHERNESS IN SFF

Tade Thompson

Over the last decade or so there have been a number of disagreements within the SFF community in relation to ethnicity, gender, and otherness in general. In particular, real problems appear to arise around the depiction of minorities and the reception and writing of critical reviews of books and stories that attempt this.

By "Other" I refer to differences in gender, ethnicity, religion, sexuality, neuronormativeness, ability, mental health and other conditions that may cause deviation from a society's consensus norm. By SFF I mean the widest definition of speculative fiction including science fiction, fantasy, slipstream, horror, interstitial, magical realism and any other artificially divided sub-genre.

Few would argue with the statement that there is a problem with the depiction and treatment of the Other in SFF. Consider cover art whitewashing, for example LeGuin's *A Wizard of Earthsea*, Hurley's *Bel Dame* sequence or Larbalestier's *Liar*, all of which feature characters of colour within the books depicted as light-skinned on early or released covers. Consider Racefail 2009 with all its complexities. Consider the entry on Race in the Encyclopedia of SF. There are many examples, but I do not wish to review them as there are other sources for this, more detailed, better researched, better thought out.

We've seen recently that this problem of depiction can lead to psychological harm and real life consequences. People are stalked, they are threatened with physical harm, and they are bullied. There are examples of people being hounded out of online spaces and removing themselves from all SFF community interaction.

It is not necessarily laziness, racism or xenophobia that leads to poor depiction of otherness. Golden age SF, for example, may not have been directed towards minorities. The audience was presumed to be white males, therefore the idea of investigation of the Other to any degree of rigour was perhaps seen as unnecessary. The stereotypes served the story so why bother? Nobody from, say, West Africa was ever going to read it, so anybody could make up whatever they wanted.

The depiction of a culture other than one's own will always have a degree of subjectivity, no matter how objective the author or observer wishes to be. Even in anthropology, the casual reader will note a gradual increase in objectivity over the decades. Challenge and counter-challenge over data and methods is the norm. Margaret Mead's work in Samoa (formerly Western Samoa) was once considered seminal. Having lived there myself, and having read other ethnographies, the most charitable thing I can say is that the work is of its time. Napoleon Chagnon's view of the Yanomamö as warlike is equally open to challenge. Eriksen said the manner of describing a social/cultural system must depend on one's interests.

The rub in SFF is how the writer who has privileged status can write about otherness, both in terms of creating authenticity and not perpetuating negative stereotypes. There are some activists who argue about the intentionality of a writer, talking about deliberate reinforcement of colonial values. I cannot read anybody's mind, but I will say that in any struggle for equality there are many kinds of people, from both extremes and all points in between. Even the shrill, anarchic-types have a part to play in reaching the goal, even if that part is to draw attention to the issue or to stimulate the emergence of more erudite actors in the field. The fact is, any writer who delves into otherness should expect to be scrutinized. No research, no participant observation, no perusal of ethnography or history, no consultation will ever be enough.

No fictional portrayal of any community is ever going to be accurate, including those by members of said community. The best we can hope for is some degree of concordance with lived experience. For example, the stereotype of the obedient Asian wife will have poor concordance while a more nuanced, complex character will have higher concordance. This has to do with the complexity of real life. One thing that becomes obvious from reading anthropology and history is the inability of anyone to capture the entire essence of a culture in words or images. We can try, but it is impossible, and not just to the observer from without. Outsiders cannot see everything and have biases; insiders cannot see everything and have biases.

> When authenticity is prized and imagination becomes suspect, a novelist's right to portray anyone outside of his experience is questioned...When the literary culture at large tries to impose an answer by insisting that "authenticity" resides in the sex or the ethnic or national origin or biographical experience of the author, it kills the very thing that makes the literary culture vibrant, which is the sense of freedom, vitality, and power the author feels while he is creating his work.[1]

Nobody (no single body or body of people within a group) can be the arbiters of what is or is not an accurate fictional portrayal of their community.

When describing the Other the creator must of necessity use anthropological approaches, whether or not the creator realizes this, and whether the Other forms a part or the whole of the narrative. What is known about this group? What has my direct experience been? What more information can I find about this group? I would suggest that the quality of the answers to these three questions will have a drastic effect on the acceptability of depiction.

The answers will change depending on the creator's position in time, their own diligence and attention to detail, their politics, their socio-cultural placement, their privilege, their mental state, and their personal philosophy.

---

1 Smiley, J (2006). *13 Ways of Looking at the Novel*, pp 151-152.London: Faber and Faber.

This difference can, at best, bring flavour and nuance to works of art, but also holds the risk of perpetuating negative experience in the other.

In anthropology, emic refers to life as experienced by the members of a society, while etic refers to explanations, analyses, descriptions and writings by a researcher. The concepts were derived from the linguistic ideas of phonemics and phonetics. We can say that generally, the anthropologist wishes to portray life as lived by the "native", but an observer can never achieve an emic description because of translation between languages/meaning, reproducing experience via writing, and the fact that the observer can never become identical with what she writers about.

SFF writers depict aliens and fairies in loving detail, giving them whole histories and complex societies and yet casually dismiss the Others in their midst with stereotypes, tired tropes that do not stand up to even casual scrutiny. This recursive, ouroboros-type, self-perpetuating mythology makes it obvious that the writer has been watching TV as research.

Entertainment and escapism is important because leisure reading can reinforce or change worldview. The content can either restate the status quo or improve complex understanding. Framing is everything, and the framer is affected by personal, family, and cultural influences.

Some SF writers try to avoid the problem by saying they don't see race, and by creating societies that have only one race. To say you do not see race is either patronizing, dishonest, or ignorant, and perhaps all three. It is also a symptom of privilege. To write without reference to the Other is to be ignorant of how ANY society works. To do so deliberately is cowardice. Art, writing, entertainment, whatever you call it, is about the human condition, which, in turn, is a heterogeneous and complicated mess.

Writing Otherness is an iterative process, not a binary, yes-no activity. You are not going to write it and get a pat on the head. Some will like what you have done; some will hate it.

Interrogating your text for Otherness

More than any other time in history information is available to people with the will to find it. That means any creator must expect challenge and interaction with critics on some level.

Borrowing a format from Madden (1988) I'd like to suggest 10 questions that might be useful for the purposes of revision of a work that features Others.

1. Does my plot rely upon the Otherness either wholly or partially? (e.g homosexuality as the punchline.)

2. Have I used the presence of others to add "spice" or exoticness (e.g. orientalism)?

3. Do the Others exist in the narrative only to support the viewpoint character or do they have agency of their own?

4. Does my narrative inadvertently contribute to discrimination?

5. Am I reflective of my own privilege and have I examined my

depiction of others through this prism?

6. Am I using real-world observation and examples as the source material or have I recycled tropes from media?

7. Have I made reasonable attempts to test my portrayal within the groups portrayed?

8. Have I avoided depicting others in order to avoid controversy (e.g. the gender-neutral or race-neutral fallacy)?

9. Have I maintained my own creative vision?

10. Having done all the above, am I prepared to receive the inevitable criticism of my portrayal of otherness post-publication? Am I willing and able to learn from this?

Where to from here?

The problems of Otherness within SFF need to be addressed, but not in a manner that stifles creativity. Nuanced depictions take hard work and will never be a hundred per cent accurate, opening the creators up to criticism. Looking away from the issue will not make it go away. Interrogating both ourselves and our work might provide useful insight.

Bibliography

- Chagnon, N (1983). *Yanomamö: The Fierce People*. 3rd Ed. New York: Holt, Rinehart & Winston.

- Eriksen, T (2001). *Small Places, Large Issues: An Introduction to Social and Cultural Anthropology*. 2nd ed. London: Pluto Press.

- Mead, M. 1978. *Coming of Age in Samoa*. Harmondsworth: Penguin.

- Madden, D (1988). *Revising Fiction: A Handbook for Writers*. New York: Plume/Penguin.

- Smiley, J (2006). *13 Ways of Looking at the Novel*, pp 151-152. London: Faber and Faber.

- SFE: The Encyclopedia of SF, 2014. Race in SF.[2] [Online] (Updated 26 August 2014) [Accessed 19/11/2014]

This article first appeared on *Safe* on December 2, 2014.
sffpoc.wordpress.com/2014/12/02/emic-etic-and-the-depiction-of-otherness-in-sff/

---

2 http://www.sf-encyclopedia.com/entry/race_in_sf

THE UNBEARABLE SOLITUDE OF BEING AN AFRICAN FAN GIRL

Chinelo Onwualu

Being an African fan girl is a strange, liminal thing. You're never quite sure that you exist, you see. A part of you is rooted in your culture and its expectations for how a woman ought to behave—church, family, school—but another is flying off into the stars carrying a samurai sword and a machete. Not one thing or another, you're both at the same time.

It doesn't help that you're invisible. In all the representations of geek culture, in all the arguments for inclusion, it doesn't seem like your voice can be heard. After all, shows like *The Big Bang Theory* which are supposed to be modern representations of geeks and their culture seem entirely populated by white people with plenty of free time and disposable income. If you don't look like that, don't have that kind of money or time, are you still a geek? If a tree falls in the forest... Even in the niches that have been carved for ourselves on the continent, you are still a strange, semi-mythical beast—the only woman at Lagos Comicon who wasn't working or attending with her significant other.

And what of those pop culture representations that have given you your identity? The books, movies, television shows and comics that formed the language of your childhood and helped you understand notions of heroism and virtue? Even in them your reflection is distorted.[1]

The mutant Storm who you discovered in middle school is an African woman, certainly. But her tribe is made up. And remember that episode of the cartoon that took us back to her childhood in her village? Remember how you noted that her snow white hair was straight even then, and you wondered where on earth she had found the time and money to relax her hair? And don't forget your horror when you rewatched *Conan the Destroyer* and realised that Grace Jones' Amazon, whom you'd long cherished for her fierceness, her beauty and her strength, was a racist stereotype.

You look on in anger and despair as the black female characters on your favourite shows are too often written as stereotypical or one-dimensional. They aren't allowed to grow or learn and are too quickly dispatched to make way for someone or something deemed more interesting. Their bodies—and by implication yours—are the site for the unconscious racism and sexism of the writers and their fans.[2] You wonder: "If people hate Tara from *True Blood*, or Gwen from *Merlin*, and Martha from *Dr. Who*—black women who are

1 http://www.socialjusticeleague.net/2011/09/how-to-be-a-fan-of-problematic-things/
2 http://www.racialicious.com/2011/10/18/fandom-and-its-hatred-of-black-women-characters/

smarter, more beautiful, and far more interesting than I am—so much, then how much more will they hate me?"

You watch as your entire continent is reduced to a black man yodelling nonsense and white children dressed in feathers and face paint in an "Africanised" version of a popular song and you seethe.[3] Quietly, for among your people it is not seemly for a woman to make too much noise.

You understand that geek culture is supposed to be the refuge of the misunderstood. All of us were at one point the kid who stayed inside during recess reading in the library rather than playing with the others. We were the ones pretending to have lightsaber battles when the other kids were playing soccer. Your Barbie dolls never played house; they were too busy exploring the alien landscapes of your bedroom floor and befriending the monsters under your bed. None of us fit into the easy boxes of our societies—you know this. But when you see that the self-appointed gatekeepers of the world you claimed before you knew it existed have erected walls to keep out members of your sex and race, it can't fail to hurt.[4]

So you turn away.

After all, you have always existed in isolation. Your favourite books were not ones you could discuss with your friends who always gave those puzzled, pitying looks when you mentioned them. You watched your favourite shows in your bedroom, laughing into the silence while your family avidly discussed the latest Nollywood film in the next room. You go to see your favourite superhero summer blockbusters by yourself, aware that you may be the only woman in the audience who has actually read the comic book that the movie is loosely based on.

You make sure to defend your beloved characters when they are denigrated, but you do so in your heart.[5] You don't have the unlimited bandwidth that your peers in richer countries do and in the empty spaces of the internet you're never quite sure anyone is listening anyway. You pore over pictures of conventions far away, admiring cosplays you can't afford to imitate and reading recaps of panels that you wish you could have attended.[6] There are no libraries from which you can borrow the sci-fi and fantasy books being written today and you can't really afford the few online portals which will accept transactions from your country and deliver to it, so you trawl e-zines for short stories. And in the eerie quiet of the early morning, you write your own. Worlds browner than the ones on screen, filled with women just like you who are torn between two identities.

You know you are not alone. There are thousands of women just like you all over the continent. They have fought to forge their unique identities outside of the prescribed roles they were expected to fill. They have kept that childhood sense of wonder and aren't ashamed to squeal like schoolgirls when they get excited. They run when they are in a hurry and they take the stairs two at a time. Like you, they are still curious and aren't afraid to ask questions, but they scattered like magic beans across a vast farm. They are

3 http://www.youtube.com/watch?v=DAJYk1jOhzk
4 http://journal.transformativeworks.org/index.php/twc/article/view/473/353 and http://fozmeadows.wordpress.com/2012/12/08/psa-your-default-narrative-settings-are-not-apolitical/
5 http://irresistible-revolution.tumblr.com/
6 http://www.racialicious.com/2012/06/07/race-fandom-when-defaulting-to-white-isnt-an-option/

growing into their own twisted shapes and no one around them can understand why.

So you call to them. You ask them to come and pour their hearts and stories into this space you've helped to create. You assure them that they are not alone, that in the vast spaces on the worldwide web, there are others like them. Like a song in the darkness you have put out your own story and you hope that they recognise its notes, and that they respond. For you may not have any answers; you may not have any original insights. But you know your own experience and you hope that that's enough.

This article first appeared on *Omenana* on November 30, 2014.
omenana.com/2014/11/30/the-unbearable-solitude-of-being-an-african-fan-girl/

CONVENTIONS, HIERARCHIES AND FORCED DIVERSITY

Bertha Chin

This past weekend, I was at Worldcon in ExCel London. Despite my love of scifi TV and film, my taste in books/literature tend to veer towards crime, horror and however else one chooses to classify Haruki Murakami's books so I've never given Worldcon much thought (and have generally aimed towards San Diego Comic Con instead).[1] Worldcon—or Loncon 3, as it's known this year, also has an academic track: a conference within a convention.[2] And this is the first time I've ever experienced Worldcon, as well as attending a convention which has an academic track running through it. I was contacted by a friend and colleague who asked if I would be interested in submitting a pre-consituted academic panel to celebrate the 10th year anniversary of the re-imagined *Battlestar Galactica*. Our panel was accepted, and I was also asked to speak in several of the fan panels. I thought it would be interesting, given my research has always been centred on online fandom; that this is a wonderful opportunity to be surrounded by fans who frequent conventions and to learn new things. I was put into panels on social media and celebrity/fan interactions, and on researching fans, all of which made sense given my research. There were a couple of initial panels that I said no to as I didn't really understand why I would be assigned them in the first place (given the exhaustive volunteer form we had to fill in detailing our interests and expert knowledge). But, it's a big convention, and I don't envy the organisers the momentous task of assigning everyone into panels they were all suited for. So I appreciate the complexity of the work, even when I was hearing from numerous participants (as well as throughout the different panels during the convention) about being placed into panels they have no expert knowledge of.

Granted, I was only there for 2 days out of the 3 I had originally planned due to personal reasons. But what follows is a personal experience of Worldcon, and I think it prudent that I should reflect on what some of the exchanges made me feel. As an academic, as a fan, and as someone who is obviously non-white.

One of the panels I was initially asked to moderate, and later to speak on was a panel on racial representations and whitewashing. It was scheduled to be on a day I wasn't going, so I had declined anyway. I had also declined

1 http://fanlore.org/wiki/Worldcon
2 http://www.loncon3.org/

because I'm usually someone who engages with media texts more socially and culturally rather than say, "racially." So as an academic, I didn't think I have anything constructive to add to the panel, when I feel it should be reserved for other speakers more knowledgeable and more passionate about the subject than I. But when I had to reject being on the panel *three* times, I can't help but think that the only reason why I was continually persuaded to be on the panel was because my surname is Chin instead of Smith. That, by virtue of my skin colour and "exotic" name, I then MUST HAVE something to say about racial representations and whitewashing in the media. Because, how dare I do not?!

I did get out of the panel eventually, but not without it leaving a bad taste in my mouth. As if I'm now confined by how I appear to others, so if I want to make a valuable contribution, to be listened to, then by god, I need to talk about issues that has been decided for me to be important. Because at the end of the day, who's interested in my research and in what I have to say because I haven't been given permission to speak about that! And this coloured (no pun intended) my anticipation of the convention, which wasn't helped by a separate incident that occurred. I was with fellow academics on Saturday evening, and after obtaining drinks, had proceeded to one of the "fan tents" manned by a big, fan organisation for a bit of a wind down after a long day. Upon walking in, our party was immediately asked if we were there for the "Asian meeting" (and bear in mind, this was a party of 1 Asian, 1 half-Asian, 2 Welsh and a Dutch). Granted, there was a scheduled "Asian meeting" at the time (which I found out after the fact) but at that point, I wasn't sure if I was supposed to feel offended or included.

For that matter, are we (as Asians) so stereotypically shy and intellectually starved that special efforts have to be made to make me feel welcome into the strange new world of science fiction conventions? Or for that matter, the strange new world of arts and humanities? Because, you know, being stereotypically Asian, I should only be skilled in science and mathematics (I failed my way through maths class, by the way, thanks for asking). I have been to many academic conferences around the world (and a couple of comic and scifi conventions in the UK), and more often than not, I'm usually the only Asian/East Asian person in the group but never have I felt more discriminated against more than at a convention that was promoting diversity as its theme. My ability and desire to say something, to speak up, should have no bearing whatsoever on the fact that some people suddenly decide I'm less privileged and suddenly need rescuing. Or worse, have a path cleared for me in order to be able to speak! I do not need permission to speak, and you can turn around and accuse me of having the privilege to be able to have that voice because I have accrued enough social, cultural and educational capital but I do not need anyone's permission to do anything!

And this was something that appears to be continually driven through over the weekend, or at the very least the panels that I've sat and spoken in: the ageism, sexism, racism, anti-academic-ism, hierarchism and various other -isms. I have no doubt Worldcon means a lot to the people who have been going to the convention throughout the decades it has been running and has forged a community there. I even understand the protectionism that they feel when hordes of media fans invade, because yes, sometimes we haven't read the book or appreciate the fight to be legitimised back in the day but does that make our experience less valid, and therefore devalued? I mean, truth be told? If you're wondering why your attendees/supporters are aging when younger fans are heading to other conventions, then it's time to take a step back and do a little bit of navel-gazing. Over the course of the time I was there, I've witnessed:

- A young female panelist, a professional like every other speaker on the panel talked over and mocked because she was young and did not have the "40 years worth of experience of being in fandom."

- A panelist—an author from *Star Trek* fandom who had turned pro, callously disregarding LGBT issues by calling it "LGB what-ever". So much for Infinite Diversity in Infinite Combinations, or perhaps she's not a fan of the Vulcan philosophy...

- A panelist being called a racial slur, threatened and stalked but organisers did not remove the offender from the convention itself (which still perplexes me).

- One of the panels I was speaking in, an audience member snapped their fingers at the speaker to get her to stop talking because she wanted to disagree.

Frankly, I did not pay a considerable sum of money to voluntarily speak at a convention only to be yelled at, have fingers snapped at me or have disdain shown me when I introduce myself as an academic. I'm pretty sure younger con-goers aren't interested in going to a convention where they don't feel welcomed, when the insinuation that their objects of fandom are moronic and inferior are thinly veiled. Bad behaviour is bad behaviour. And I know organisers can't control how the audience reacts in a panel, but perhaps the Code of Conduct should also include a clause that says panelists shouldn't be hurled abuse or shouted at. As with everything—and I remember saying this at my panel on social media and celebrity/fan interaction to a question on celebrities with problematic politics—you can always choose to walk away and not engage. Especially when you know nothing good or productive can come from it. I know, empty words, seeing as this is how flame wars always happen.

As for the diversity thing? I don't know. As I said, no one can control how other con-goers behave. I can only reflect on how I felt about the matter, and if you know me well, you'd know I'm usually the last person to be offended at something. So take it as me being unusually sensitive over nothing or just me being a jerk. But I would have appreciated that my reasons for saying no to a panel are respected, because anything more was going to be unnecessarily awkward.

This was my first Worldcon. It will very likely be my last (not because I had a bad experience; just that I don't foresee myself flying to a specific location to attend it).

Although, thank you for ensuring that the observations I made on fan hierarchies in my PhD thesis is still extremely valid though.

This article first appeared on *The 13th Colony* on August 18, 2014.
the13thcolony.wordpress.com/2014/08/18/conventions-hierarchies-and-forced-diversity/

WITH GREAT POWER COMES GREAT RESPONSIBILITY: ON EMPATHY AND THE POWER OF PRIVILEGE

Kameron Hurley

had the questionable delight of hanging out with a 3 year old for the last week, and at some point, when I hauled off his pants so he could go "Pee-pee in the potty" he proceeded to sit on said toilet for a solid five minutes having an argument with me because I'd said "Hey!" when he tried to hit his mother.

"You YELLED at me!" he yelled. "We don't yell in this house."

"We don't hit our mom, either."

"We don't YELL. You HURT my FEELINGS."

At some point, this child will understand the difference between a feeling of guilt for being called out when he does something bad and actual hurt feelings, but today is not that day.

"And you hurt your mom's feelings," I said. "You don't hit your mom."

"We don't YELL IN THIS HOUSE."

"We don't hit our mother."

About this time, I realized I was standing in a bathroom arguing with a half naked 3 year old child, and I needed to cut my losses and walk away, because I was the adult. I would never convince him that his feeling of guilt was not as serious as him having almost hit his mother; I'd get stuck in a toddler logic loop. Because what one *almost* does to someone one sees as so far outside the self when one is 3 is not something that's ever going to compute. What's going to register is YOU hurt MY feelings.

What almost happened to his mom is moot.

I was reminded of this particular exchange the last couple of days listening to folks rage—both on Twitter and in mainstream media, now—about what idiots folks in fandom are for rising up in rage against having the Jay Leno of Britain (or whatever), Jonathan Ross, host the Hugo Awards.[1]

Because in all the rage about how fandom must be full of crazy idiots who no longer have a Great White Hope to Save their Genre From Obscurity, what nobody seems to remember is that the actual pushback on Twitter was not raised fists to hit him, but expressions of fear that Ross *was going to hit their mom*. It was the internet yelling, "HEY!" and asking for reassurance that they wouldn't be diminished, spat on, ridiculed, or raged at in their own house.

---

1 http://www.bleedingcool.com/2014/03/01/when-jonathan-ross-was-presenting-the-hugo-awards-until-he-wasnt/

(EDIT: for a sample of some of the "abuse" hurled at Ross, there's an abbreviated storify thread here).[2]

In fact, folks like Farah Mendlesohn spoke up pretty clearly about this early on, before the statement was made public (her post about resigning her committee position over the issue has since been made private) and Seanan McGuire bravely stated her fears point blank on Twitter, fears which, if I was a Hugo nominee and attendee, I would also share.

Farah and Seanan are both people I respect highly, and I take their concerns seriously. But others did not. So there was no accompanying statement, no reassurance from either Ross or those who chose him, just "Here he is YOU SHOULD BE GRATEFUL YOU UNWASHED MASSES."

And in response, two highly respected women's concerns were shrugged off like "Bitches must be crazy."

When you play the "Bitches must be crazy" card, the Internet won't be far behind you, my friends.

I'm a fat nerd. I've been bullied my whole life. When the kids in school stopped, there was the wider world out there to tell me I was too big, too loud, too smart, too brash. I got used to being hit. I saw it happen all the time.

What we want when we say "HEY!" to someone—and someone, in this case, who has vastly more power than we do—is reassurance. We're looking for an explanation, a statement, that this person gets where we're coming from, and despite our fears, isn't going to raise his fist to hit us. This is not rocket science. It's not a tough thing to figure out if you apply a little empathy.

EMPATHY, JOURNALISTS. Try it some time.

Sadly, empathy is the one thing that a lot of the mainstream pieces covering the incident seem to be ignoring. I haven't seen one piece that actually took the concerns of the community seriously. Instead of a concert of concerned, formerly bullied geeks looking for reassurance, it was a "twitter mob" with pitchfolks and torches banging on some rich dude's door, baying for blood.

I realize that "angry twitter mob" makes for a more compelling click bait story, but casting Jay Leno, or Howard Stern, or the cast of SNL as victim because a few dozen or a few hundred people on Twitter said, "HEY DON'T HIT ME I'M AFRAID YOU'LL HIT ME THE WAY YOU DID PERSON X" would be fucking absurd, and we'd call it out as such.[3] When did the privileged become victims? Did somebody send the dude a rape threat? Did he have to get a restraining order against somebody on Twitter? Because these are things that happen to the people who spoke up, these are things that happen to us all the time, and are probably happening to many of the women who said, "HEY I'M AFRAID YOU'LL HIT ME!" either to or about Ross publicly. And unlike the rich with big voices, we don't have as many resources we can set in motion to protect ourselves when those threats do come in.

We speak out because we are brave, not because we're baying for blood. We speak out because we're tired of being hit, and we need to know that if you're coming into our house, you're not going to act like an asshole. We went to school with that dude. We deal with that dude on the internet everyday.

2 http://storify.com/infamousfiddler/the-hugos-and-wossy
3 http://storify.com/infamousfiddler/the-hugos-and-wossy

We are fucking tired of that dude.

So instead of snarking back at people on Twitter and calling them nut-jobs and invoking Neil Gaiman's name as a ward of protection, it would have behooved the privileged person to stand back and say, "Hey. Wow. I'm so sorry! I didn't realize so many of you had that impression. Let me assure you that I love and support this community and I take this gig seriously. I respect and love every single one of you and please be assured I'll be respectful and welcoming, just as I hope you will be respectful and welcoming to me as a host."

Yeah, that's a tough thing to do when you're being yelled at. Trust me. I've been there. But it's the adult thing to do. It's the thing the person with the most power needs the guts to be able to do. It comes with the job.

Because when somebody says, "I'm afraid you'll hit me," and you say, "FUCK YOU WHY WOULD I HIT YOU YOU THINK I'M A MONSTER OR SOMETHING YOU FUCKING IDIOT!" is going to achieve exactly the opposite impression of what you purport to intend.

The truth of the matter is that raising my voice in the pizza place, me saying "HEY!" prevented the 3 year old from hitting his mom. Oh, you can say all you like that maybe he was just raising his arm to hit her and wouldn't have carried through, but I'd seen it before. I knew I'd see it again. And somebody needed to say "HEY!" and prevent it.

Yes, I raised my voice. And to a self-involved toddler, raising one's voice, especially when everyone tells you not to, can seem liked the gravest of crimes. But the truth of the matter is that a few dozen people yelling "HEY!" on the Internet at a public figure with a global following and three million Twitter followers is even less of a threat or mob or grave insult than an adult raising their voice to a toddler, because as an adult telling a kid to be quiet, I have the privilege of being an adult. A few dozen or even a few hundred people on Twitter are just random joe-blows shouting on Twitter. They have no privilege or power.

The person with the privilege is the public figure. The person who has to take a step back and consider their words carefully is the one with the most privilege.

In this case, that's not angry fans or even pros on Twitter who are fearful of being hit.

It's the public figure with the power to hit.

And if the public figure can't show empathy, or respond cordially, as befitting their place of power, but instead snarks at people on Twitter and walks off in a huff without even trying, I can't help but wonder if they were really such a good fit in the first place.

So please stop sharing those annoying articles that call bullied nerds a bunch of idiots who want to keep their genre in the ghetto. They don't. What they want is to feel they're marginally more safe among their people than they are in the wider world, even if, as recent sexist meltdowns have shown us, that's not really true. We want to believe it. We want to believe things are getting better. We've been hit before, and when we see a raised fist now—or even a potential raised fist—we react in the way that survivors do, with caution that, from the outside, to those without empathy, may look nuts, but to us are born out of sheer self-preservation.

Nobody likes how the Ross thing went down. But let's not heap this on Twitter's shoulders, but the shoulders of those with the most privilege, who should have stepped back, applied empathy, and responded accordingly.

I'll remind folks that it wasn't long ago when a pretty well-known writer got into it on Twitter for a tweet taken out of context, and after a harrowing beginning, apologized publicly and graciously, and then individually to each person who may have felt harmed by the exchange.[4]

That's how people with perceived power and privilege act when the shit goes down: they grit their teeth and bear it, with grace.

I've done it myself, though I often *feel* powerless, because it's not my own perceived power that matters. It's the power other people give me.

With great power comes great responsibility.

Prove you know what to do with it.

It may not be too late.

This article first appeared on *kameronhurley.com* on March 5, 2014.
www.kameronhurley.com/with-great-power-comes-great-responsibility-on-empathy-and-the-power-of-privilege/

---

4 http://www.beverlybambury.com/2014/01/how-to-handle-social-media-missteps.html

ESSAY: BIGOTRY, COGNITIVE DISSONANCE, AND SUBMISSION GUIDELINES

Charles Tan

First off, before I start, I wanted to say I didn't want to write this blog entry. Not because it needs to be said, not because it's another controversy in the speculative fiction field, and not because I'm probably the least qualified person to talk about it, but rather because it's another case of a privileged White Anglo-Saxon Male who posts something problematic on the Internet, and marginalized groups get to respond.

So instead of starting off with what's wrong, let me begin with what's right. When talking about diverse anthologies and submission guidelines, here are some books that fit the bill:

- *Long Hidden: Speculative Fiction from the Margins of History* edited by Rose Fox & Daniel Jose Older

- *Diverse Energies* edited by Tobias S. Buckell & Joe Monti

- *Mothership: Tales from Afrofuturism and Beyond* edited by Bill Campbell and Edward Austin Hall

- *The Sea is Ours: Tales of Steampunk Southeast Asia* edited by Jaymee Goh and Joyce Chng

- *Kaleidoscope: Diverse YA Science Fiction and Fantasy Stories* edited by Alisa Krasnostein and Julia Rios (**disclosure**: I work for Twelfth Planet Press)

With that aside, I want to point out two Guest of Honor speeches from the recently-concluded Wiscon 38. One from Hiromi Goto and another from N.K. Jemisin. Here's an excerpt:

> "How important, then, that published stories come from diverse sources; from the voices, experiences, subjectivities and realities of many rather than from the imagination of dominant white culture. For even as we've been enriched and enlightened by tales from Western tradition, stories are also carriers and vectors for ideologies. And the white literary tradition has a long legacy of silencing, erasing, distorting and misinforming." - Hiromi Goto[1]

---

1 http://www.hiromigoto.com/wiscon38-guest-of-honour-speech/

> "We've seen that bigotry directed not just toward black authors but authors of all races other than white; not just along the racial continuum but the axes of gender, sexual orientation, nationality, class, and so on. We've seen it aimed by publishers and book buyers and reviewers and con organizers toward readers, in the form of every whitewashed book cover, every "those people don't matter" statement, and every all-white, mostly-male BookCon presenters' slate." - N.K. Jemisin[2]

I want to home in on a specific passage from Jemisin's speech:

> A SFWA affiliate member posted a call for civility on his website; in the process he called me "an Omarosa" and a "drama queen", but of course he didn't mean those in a racialized or gendered way... And let me emphasize that I am by no means the only woman or person of color who's been targeted by threats, slurs, and the intentional effort to create a hostile environment in our most public spaces. People notice what happens to me because for better or worse I've achieved a high-enough profile to make the attacks more visible. But I suspect every person in this room who isn't a straight white male has been on the receiving end of something like this—aggressions micro and macro. Concerted campaigns of "you don't belong here."

On the very same day Jemisin made her speech, a call for submissions for an anthology titled *World Encounters* went up (you can find the screenshot from Pretty Terrible of the edited submission guidelines as of 2014/05/27), from the same editor who called Jemisin an "Omarosa" and "drama queen" (the original post has been deleted as of 2014/05/28).[3]

Now there are two points I want to tackle: the submission guidelines itself, for the Formalists out there, and the editor. Why does the latter matter? Because as someone whose culture has been marginalized, to quote Hiromi Goto, I don't want to be part of "a long legacy of silencing, erasing, distorting and misinforming." And when you're a writer, your immediate gatekeeper is your editor. You want your editor to be someone informed, someone you can trust. Imagine, for example, if the editor of an LGBT anthology was Orson Scott Card.[4] Wouldn't you, either as a writer or a reader, find that problematic?

Also, to clarify, I don't think there will be a "perfect" editor or anthology. There will always be something that people will complain about, or find problematic. But on the other, that's no excuse for cultural appropriation (especially from people of privilege), and it's easy to screw things up. Case in point, Wil Wheaton's non-apology when using the term "spirit animals," even when it's explained to him why it's wrong.[5]

2 http://nkjemisin.com/2014/05/wiscon-38-guest-of-honor-speech/

3 http://bryanthomasschmidt.net/call-for-submissions-world-encounters, http://www.pretty-terrible.com/2014/05/26/cognitive-dissonance/, http://www.pretty-terrible.com/wp-content/uploads/2014/05/BTS-Call-for-Subs1.png and http://www.pretty-terrible.com/wp-content/uploads/2013/06/bryanthomasschmidt.net-a-week-under-siege-.png

4 http://www.salon.com/2013/05/07/sci_fi_icon_orson_scott_card_hates_fan_fiction_the_homosexual_agenda_partner/

5 http://wilwheaton.tumblr.com/post/76188837092/hi-wil-im-not-trying-to-be-antagonizing-you-seem-to

I. The Submission Guidelines

> What if aliens landed on Earth right next door? How would your neighbors react? What about you? What if they landed all over the world? How would people of different cultures respond? What about Earth explorers encountering aliens on their own planets far from home?

The premise is fine. It sounds generic, but nothing problematic yet.

> Submissions outside these dates and parameters will be summarily rejected and cannot be resubmitted. I reserve the right to close submissions at any time if the slush pile is too big and I have what I need. No money is promised or contracts offered until the Kickstarter funds. No simultaneous submissions.

> *Also, people who are living or have lived in NonWestern cultures, especially the ones they write about, will absolutely have a leg up as authenticity is really important to me.*

Here, there is an attempt to reach out to marginalized groups, although this would immediately be contradicted by the editor's succeeding paragraph (see below). Also, it assumes that:

1. The authors will actually write about the culture they've interacted with ("especially the ones they write about") because there's always a possibility that I, a Filipino, might write about Japan, and what do I really know about Japan?

2. That the authors will automatically be familiar and understand the culture, because the possibility that they are "cultural tourists" couldn't possibly happen, and

3. As a reader, the authenticity that I care about is what's written on the page, not the author's biography; a knowledgeable person might not necessarily be able to adeptly convey their experiences for example.

> *Multi-award winner Mike Resnick will be writing a new Africa story for this, and there will be other headliners with reserved slots, including Kay Kenyon and Jack McDevitt,* but I will be looking for 10-15 stories from the open call.

Wait, wait, a privileged Western white writer writing about Africa? This hasn't been done before!

And Mike Resnick has written about Africa before. He must get it right, right?[6]

In many ways, the editor's oversight of this fact is part of a larger, arguably unconscious, racism on his part. Take for example his blog entry

6 https://fozmeadows.wordpress.com/2013/06/02/old-men-yelling-at-clouds-sfwa-lunacy/http://www.haikasoru.com/tag/mike-resnick/

titled Broadening The Toolbox Through Cross Cultural Encounters: On Resnick, Africa & Opportunity.[7] Instead of talking about writers from the continent of Africa (and it's a large continent, so there's a large pool of writers like Chinua Achebe, Lauren Beukes, and Joan De La Haye), we get Mike Resnick. Nnedi Okorafor gets mentioned but only as an off-hand comment, rather than the focus of the article.

So when talking about an anthology that's diverse and inclusive, neither Mike Resnick, Kay Kenyon, or Jack McDevitt are what I'd consider the examples you should be touting as a contributors. Because to many, it appears that you are favoring the already privileged writers instead of those marginalized.

I won't even comment that an author that was touted in the original version was eventually rescinded in the edited version, after it was brought up to the said author's attention.[8]

> The goal is to have stories by a few known and upcoming Western writers but also include some up and coming foreign natives writing from their own cultural view as well to give exposure to SF from outside the Western world as long as it matches the theme. I will be limiting the number of Western writers included to be sure we get those outside voices.

Words matter. Here, we have a contradictory paragraph. On one hand, it claims that it wants to give "foreign natives" a chance. First off, you don't call writers of other cultures foreign natives. It's foreign *to you* and they are natives *to you* (when was the last time people referred to themselves as natives?). It already tips the editor's hand that the book is from a Western paradigm. On the other hand, it's also the Western writers that seem prioritized here. I mean that's why we have guaranteed authors like Mike Resnick, Kay Kenyon, and Jack McDevitt (none of which are, ahem, "foreign natives").

> Stories can be Past, Future, Present, on Earth or off, let your imagination run. But I don't want a bunch of alien POV stories.
>
> I'd like varied POV from different cultures, so I want 1 or 2 from alien POV but not half the anthology or a third. I want some set on Earth and some off. Some could be on starships, too. But I don't want all. So if you are setting them on Earth and if you are using American POV or Alien POV, please let me know so I can encourage balance.
>
> I would accept a really good story longer than 7 k, but contact me and it will be under much more scrutiny. 3-5k is my sweet spot, honestly. 5-7 is okay but, again, not ideal because I have so many great people wanting in and I'd love to have as many stories, authors and cultures represented as possible. Of course I will take the best stories. If it works out at 12 instead of 20, so be it. But I'm

7 http://bryanthomasschmidt.net/broadening-the-toolbox-through-cross-cultural-encounters-on-resnick-africa-opportunity/

8 http://www.pretty-terrible.com/wp-content/uploads/2014/05/BTS-Call-for-Subs-Google-Cache.png

just telling you what I'm shooting for.

This is just horrible writing. This can be summed up "I want X, but not too much of X, or too little of X." That's not to say you won't be making these decisions as an editor, but it's usually made *after* you've received all the submissions, not before.

I want this to reach a broad audience, including education uses, so if you use foul language, humorous setting is going to be easier sell than serious and if you drop more than two F-bombs in a story, you are lessening your chances. Same goes for "goddammits," "shit," "asshole,""mf," and you get the picture. I am not trying to be a prude or force my beliefs on you.

I just want to balance an audience because people need to learn about cultures and perspectives and that has educational value. To quote the description at the top: "we'd like this to be a collection parents and kids can read and discuss to learn and encourage interest in SF and other cultures."

This means I also don't want political stories. No bashing other people groups, cultures or belief systems/parties. *This is not to be divisive but uniting, because my experience has taught me there are a lot of other viewpoints in the world we Westerners can learn from, but hearing them won't happen if we turn people away.*

First, all stories are political. In fact, the paragraph banning "goddammits," "shit," "asshole," etc. is a political decision. When someone says they're not political, what they really mean is that their politics belongs to the status quo, and they don't want to challenge that. One example is Nintendo's recent statement regarding same-sex marriage in a their video game, *Tomodachi Life*: "Nintendo never intended to make any form of social commentary with the launch of *Tomodachi Life*."[9]

What they really mean by "no social commentary" is "we are against homosexual partnerships."

Second, we go back to the dominance of the Western paradigm in the anthology. That's why words like "we Westerners" are used. What is the point of soliciting stories from Non-Western writers, if inevitably, their stories will be Westernized to cater to a perceived Western audience?

I love action but I'd also like a bit of levity so humor is good. I don't want all humor. And I don't want all action but I do need some of both. (How's that for being specific.) That being said, sex and graphic violence also should be kept out. Pretty obvious. Enough said. *Smatterings of foreign words for flavor are fine, but we should be able to interpret it in context. You can play with (translations in parenthesis too) but too much of that just increases word count and makes it harder to read.*

---

9 http://www.salon.com/2014/05/08/nintendos_anti_gay_cop_out_why_its_demented_same_sex_ban_is_no_game/

Again, more bad writing (I want X, but not too much...). With the bolded part, the editor betrays their lack of understanding of other cultures and the craft of writing.

First, for great writers, foreign words are included in the text not necessarily because they're flavor, but because they're essential to the story. Second, if an author chooses (or does not choose to) translate a word and place it in parenthesis, there's a reason for it, and it's not due to extending the word count. Third, if it's harder to read, that's because the author doesn't condescend to the reader.

> As I am expecting an Africa story from Mike Resnick, seek authenticity. *He's famous for his Africa stories and I have no doubt whatever he does will be brilliant.* After all, he's got Nebula and Hugo nominations and awards for these stories. *Which means, if you write Africa, expect to be compared.*

First, writers are only as good as the work they submit. No competent editor would blindly accept a story that hasn't been written yet. Because it could be crap, and that's regardless of your politics.

Second, some would argue Resnick's stories are inauthentic. And it doesn't also mean that another writer, say one hailing from South Africa, will write an inferior South African story.

> *This editor has been to Africa, Mexico and Brazil and studied the cultures, countries and religions extensively, for example, so please research any culture you choose.* Do not write what you think they are. Do not write stereotypes.

Africa is a continent. Mexico and Brazil are countries. To equate the two is an inability to understand their cultural nuance, especially from someone who proclaims they have studied the culture, countries, and religions extensively.

> I am inviting a few Western writers whom I know have traveled and have strong cultural knowledge, sensitivity and passion for places they visited.

Translation: because despite my previous claims that this anthology is for writers outside of the Western world, this is really for my Western writer friends (because we don't have enough of those!).

> *Not every Mexican is the same, for example, but please have it so your Mexicans are real enough my actual Mexican friends would tell me you got it right.* (I do have friends around the world who will read for cultural authenticity before I make final selections, so I want authentic.)

Here we have a contradiction. On one hand, the editor is making a claim that Mexicans are diverse. On the other hand, he also wants a Mexican archetype that will ring true to every Mexican (or at least his friends, because his friends represents Mexico). Which is faulty because you can't please everyone in a culture, because that's the definition of diversity. I can write about my own Filipino experience, and it might ring true to some Filipinos, but will sound faulty for others.

Also, it seems the barometer for cultural expertise is "they are my friends from around the world", which honestly isn't very methodical.

In a Bingo card from The Angry Black Woman, there's a space relevant to this situation: "'knows something about POC, because her POC friend told her so."[10]

> What are the odd little cultural quirks people exhibit which would strike outsiders as odd but insiders as perfectly normal? Use those in your story for humor, confusion, etc.

Yes, because we should pander to our Western audience. And not because cultural quirks are essential to the story.

> Must be willing to respect the editor's editing requests. No assholes allowed. Seriously. Also, if you have slandered my name or resent me for not sharing your views, don't bother. I guarantee I won't.

To borrow an image from Pretty Terrible.[11]

> Truthfully, these people, Luhrs, Gates, Hines, Saus, Fox, etc. are like rotting meat looking for a place to stink. To quote a friend. - @BryanThomasS

I guess the editor can slander and resent other people, but not the other way around.

II. The Editor

> Never heard of me? Never read my work? Never interacted with me, yet you know who I am, huh? That sounds quite reasonable to me. Since I have not said or done anything racist or sexist in my entire life, and since we don't know each other, that's unfortunate. There's really no basis for that association. But I am sure my life and work will more than disprove your theory over time far more than anything I might argue here, because facts always triumph over speculation, so God Bless.

So Thomas Bryan Schmidt claims that "[he] has not said or done anything racist or sexist in his entire life."[12] Despite in the same blog post, he labels N.K. Jemisin as an Omarosa. Or, you know, his history of name calling, whether it's due to a person's gender or race.[13]

Look, full disclosure. I've said lots of racist and sexist things in my life. I've screwed up, horribly.[14] So I wouldn't make any attempt to claim that

---

10 http://theangryblackwoman.com/2009/09/22/the-bingo-project/

11 http://www.pretty-terrible.com/2014/05/27/flapping-my-rotting-meat/

12 http://www.pretty-terrible.com/wp-content/uploads/2013/06/bryanthomasschmidt.net-a-week-under-siege-.png

13 http://www.pretty-terrible.com/2013/06/19/how-not-to-have-a-conversation/

14 http://deepad.dreamwidth.org/50595.html

I'm not racist or sexist. But I'm willing to tackle, to change, and to correct my-self. I don't always succeed.

Bryan Thomas Schmidt isn't that person. He has two main problems: 1. He never blames his own writing for conveying the wrong message. For example: "I should apologize to them that THEY misconstrued and misinter-preted my words?"[15] Or statements like this:[16]

> Folks, this practice today of taking people at what you assume they mean, not face value of words, is rude, selfish and arrogant. #stop #fb - @BryanThomasS

Regardless of your politics, that's just a bad policy for someone whose profession is writing and editing. People don't need to *know* you. They can only read the words you use.

> @damiengwalter Then you'd be assuming wrong and clearly don't know me at all. - @BryanThomasS

> @anneleonardauth And the fact they don't know me or my past makes it all the more assumption without basis in fact. - @BryanThomasS

And 2. When people try to explain, educate, or address his points, he ignores them. If he hasn't heard of you, you get banned. If he has and you're famous, he'll try to placate you.

> @BryanThomasS Perhaps, if that many people are reading rac-ism/sexism into what you say, it might be worthwhile to consider - @mouseferatu

> @BryanThomasS the possibility that something in your phrasing is conveying a message you don't intend? - @mouseferatu

> @BryanThomasS No. I don't know Gates & Saus, but Jim Hines and Rose Fox are not "like rotting meat looking for a place to stink." - @gregvaneekhout

> @BryanThomasS I saw people WTFing at your anthology guide-lines. Did you self-critique and examine them? Did you ask what the problems were? - @jakedfw

> @BryanThomasS At least you aren't being called rotting meat, like several authors I respect. - @RevBobMIB

Disregard, disregard, disregard, ban.

---

15 http://www.pretty-terrible.com/2013/06/24/update-on-the-recent-unpleasantness/
16 https://twitter.com/BryanThomasS/status/470752347724206081

III. My Experience

As far back as 2012, I witnessed an exchange between Bryan Thomas Schmidt and a friend.[17] The former had an ambiguously-worded tweet that could be interpreted as defending Save the Pearls.[18] Bryan then wrote a blog post condemning my friend. I replied, in private and politely, why I thought his blog post was wrong, and informed him that I would be posting a rebuttal on my blog. He then took down the post, called me a bully, and banned/blocked me.

I told this and showed the transcripts to an author/editor friend of mine, and he told me neither he nor his wife would support bullies. So back in 2012, I shut up.

Maybe posting this account makes me a bully. But by not speaking out back then, it's paving the way for injustice. In 2013, Bryan posted about #SFF-Civility.[19] In 2014, it's the Submission Guidelines mentioned above. Because I have no doubt, some people will submit.

And it goes beyond those projects.

I love SF Signal. I was a contributor. I stopped contributing after 2012. It's not because Bryan Thomas Schmidt was also a contributor to the site, but that fact wasn't encouraging either. I don't know how the current members of SF Signal feel about him. [**2014/05/30 Edit:** He was no longer a contributor to SF Signal since the last quarter of 2013.][20]

Adventures in Sci-Fi Publishing produced interesting podcasts before 2012. After that year? I wouldn't know. I stopped listening by then. Bryan Thomas Schmidt was a sponsor of the show, and guested a few times.

#sffwrtcht is also run by Bryan Thomas Schmidt. It's been consistent and a valuable venue for authors or publishers looking for some publicity. Bryan claims that it's inclusive, but how can it be inclusive when the owner calls people names like rotting meat, deletes tweets/comments/posts, and immediately bans people unless they're famous?[21] So yeah, it's not a venue for me. [**2014/05/30 Edit: The hashtag was apparently appropriated by Bryan from a female creative and was never acknowledged.**][22]

I'll just be here, with the rest of #TeamRottenMeat.

This article first appeared on *Bibliophile Stalker* on May 28, 2014.
charles-tan.blogspot.com/2014/05/essay-bigotry-cognitive-dissonance-and.html

---

17 https://storify.com/charlesatan/101-and-importance-of-being-clear

18 http://www.theguardian.com/books/2012/aug/21/racism-row-novel-coals-pearls

19 http://www.pretty-terrible.com/2013/06/24/update-on-the-recent-unpleasantness/

20 http://bryanthomasschmidt.net/for-immediate-release-sffwrtcht-on-twitter-will-end-in-2014/

21 http://www.pretty-terrible.com/2014/05/27/flapping-my-rotting-meat/

22 http://www.associatedgeekery.com/2014/05/29/associated-geekery-episode-51/

OF AWARDS ELIGIBILITY LISTS AND UNBEARABLE SMUGNESS

Amal El-Mohtar

We need to have a serious talk about awards and eligibility and the awkward eggshell-dance people feel obligated to do every time this year.

Recently I went on a tear on Twitter because I saw women for whom I have tremendous admiration and respect speak up about how difficult they find it to overcome shyness and low self-esteem enough to talk about their work, and what an ongoing struggle it is for them to find value in their art, to think of it as in any way contributing anything to the world.[1]

> Women agonizing over whether or not to post your award-eligible work? You don't need this but: I give you permission. I want your lists. - @tithenai

> It's not obnoxious or rude or self-aggrandizing to state what you had published last year. It's useful for people making nominations! - @tithenai

This is an old story. This is most of my friends.

John Scalzi has views on posting eligibility lists.[2] So does Adam Roberts.[3] The former says hooray, lists! The latter says boo, lists! Mysteriously, both of them really want to see more recognition and lauding of writing by commonly marginalized people, but while Scalzi offers the use of his Comments space for anyone to share their eligibility, Roberts decries the practice as "making it easier for the guy with the loudest megaphone to shoehorn his way onto the shortlists."

Scalzi has also responded to Roberts' post, but neither of them state what bothers me the most in this folderol: *nothing will stop the guy with the megaphone.*[4] No hand-wringing or tut-tutting about reading widely or behaving with dignity or integrity or what have you is going to end the practice of brash, confident people telling other people, often and obnoxiously, to vote for them. But, crucially, the hand-wringing and tut-tutting does have an effect: it discourages the people who already feel silenced and uncomfortable from ever talking about or taking pride in their achievements.

1 http://storify.com/tithenai/awards-eligibility-and-lists
2 http://whatever.scalzi.com/2014/01/06/on-letting-people-know-about-your-award-eligible-work/
3 http://sibilantfricative.blogspot.co.uk/2014/01/award-season-2014-on-me-not-pimping-my.html
4 http://whatever.scalzi.com/2014/01/08/adam-roberts-on-sff-award-awareness-posts/

You cannot with one breath say that you wish more women were recognized for their work, and then say in the next that you think less of people who make others aware of their work. You cannot trust that somehow, magically, the systems that suppress the voices of women, people of colour, disabled people, queer people, trans people, will of their own accord stop doing that when award season rolls around in order to suddenly make you aware of their work. You MUST recognize the fact that the only way to counter silence is to encourage speech and *make room* for it to be heard.

It breaks my heart to read post after post of (mostly women) saying "well I usually wouldn't do this but so-and-so" (OFTEN ME) "goaded me into doing it so here it is", or to participate in discussions where women—extraordinary, talented, accomplished, *incandescent* women—confess how terrified they are by the prospect of talking about their publications during award season because what if assholes start treating them like they treated Seanan McGuire.[5]

There's a peculiar, unbearable, vicious smugness in sitting back and talking about how tacky it is of people to list their publications and that of course YOU won't do so because while winning awards is nice naturally YOU don't really care about them. I find that behaviour several orders of magnitude more repellent than asking for votes. Requests for votes I can ignore; what I can't ignore is the real toll taken on brilliantly talented people by this kind of rhetoric—brilliantly talented people who already think themselves unworthy of any kind of positive attention.

Can we please just accept—and make widespread the acceptance!—that making lists during Awards season is fine? That it's standard? That there is a vast difference between stating one's eligibility and campaigning for votes? That lists are *extremely helpful* to nominating parties who are rigorous in their reading and want to see conversations in fandom expand and diversify? And that rolling one's eyes about the whole process helps precisely no one while in fact hindering many?

Because this is something for which I'll certainly campaign.

This article first appeared on *amalelmohtar.com* on January 9, 2014.
http://amalelmohtar.com/2014/01/09/of-awards-eligibility-lists-and-unbearable-smugness/

---

5 http://seanan-mcguire.livejournal.com/506585.html

WHY I THINK AUTHOR ELIGIBILITY POSTS ARE SELFISH, DESTRUCTIVE AND COUNTER-PRODUCTIVE

Martin Petto

Today is the last day of nominations for the BSFA Awards.[1] Members can nominate as many times as they wish (I'm on my third set) and here are some things I'd particularly like to see make it onto the shortlist:

- Best Novel: *iD* by Madeline Ashby
- Best Short Fiction: 'Spin' by Nina Allan
- Best Artwork: Yuko Shimizu's cover for *The Melancholy Of Mechagirl* by Catherynne M Valente
- Best Non-Fiction: Jared Shurin on the Gemmell Legend Award shortlist.[2]

Unfortunately, along with the positives of award season (talking about great books) there now comes an inevitable negative (authors posting their eligibility). I thought I'd written my definitive position on this two years ago but sadly things have worsened since then.[3] So here are five beliefs I hold that together explain why I think author eligibility posts are selfish, destructive and, for the majority of authors, counter-productive.

1. Posting your eligibility is lobbying for awards

This should be blindingly obvious. The only possible effect of posting about the eligibility of your work is to change the number of people who nominate that work. This is, after all, why authors do it. Yet the fact that this is lobbying is mysterious elided in most conversations about eligibility posts which instead subsume it into the broader issue of self-promotion or couch it in the neutral terms of increasing voter information.

The brilliant thing for authors is that they don't need to say "nominate me" or even "my work is worth nominating" (which strangely they recoil from) for the lobbying to be effective. But to claim there is no connection is about as sophisticated example of sophistry as the famous "and if you get hit, it's your own fault" scene from The Simpsons.[4]

1 http://www.bsfa.co.uk/its-the-final-countdown-2-days-to-go-for-the-bsfa-award-nominations/
2 http://www.pornokitsch.com/2013/09/david-gemmell-legend-awards-summary.html
3 https://everythingisnice.wordpress.com/2012/01/11/how-come-china-mieville-never-blogs-about-his-award-eligibility/
4 http://imgur.com/r/TheSimpsons/pE95U

2. Reader voted awards are for readers, not authors

Perhaps this is a more understandable bit of confusion as speculative fiction has always had a very permeable barrier between fan and pro. So in the Hugos we have fans (some of whom are pros) voting for fan categories (for which pros are eligible), for pro categories (for which fans are eligible) and even, bizarrely, for industry categories that it is impossible for them to know anything about.[5] But regardless of whether you are a fan or a pro or somewhere in between, when it comes to nominating fiction, you are acting in a specific capacity: as a reader.

A helpful analogy might be to reviews. An author might review another author but they must do so with their reader hat on and whilst a positive review might benefit the author receiving it, that is a side effect of its main purpose to inform other readers of the quality of the text. The same is true of awards where the purpose of voting is for readers to form a critical consensus around the best fiction of the year. Authors "helping" voters to complete their ballots are no more neutral than authors "helping" reviewers to interpret their work.

Authors have more power than readers and it is easy for them to unintentionally poison reader spaces, whether that is reviews or awards. Yet whilst the social norms preventing this still apply quite strongly to reviews, they have been stretched to breaking point with respect to awards. This year, we have seen authors accelerate the trend of taking ownership of the space by actively erasing readers. Take, for example, this quote from author Amal El-Mohtar's widely discussed post about author's publishing their eligibility: "There's a peculiar, unbearable, vicious smugness in sitting back and talking about how tacky it is of people to list their publications and that of course YOU won't do so because while winning awards is nice naturally YOU don't really care about them."[6] The conversation has entirely shifted from readers to authors, from voting for awards to winning awards.

3. Eligibility posts don't help readers to make their ballots more diverse

A new argument made this year—and the key thrust of El-Mohtar's justification for such posts—is that if all authors publish their eligibility then this will increase diversity in award shortlists by correcting the tendency of women and minorities to be less comfortable at self-promotion. The first thing to say is that self-promotion ("please read my book") is not the same as lobbying ("please tell people that my book is one of the best of the year") and it is perfectly possible to want people to be more comfortable in promoting their work without wanting them to lobby for it.

This brings us to the arms race argument where authors might concede that perhaps in an ideal world they wouldn't need to lobby but since some people do (and white men are more likely to do it) then others need to do it or they risk being drowned out. As a point of principle, a vote for yourself can never be a noble act; as a point of practicality, eligibility posts are an incredibly poor way of making your voice heard. If you are worried that someone has

5 https://everythingisnice.wordpress.com/2012/02/21/abolish-the-hugo-best-editor-categories/
6 http://amalelmohtar.com/2014/01/09/of-awards-eligibility-lists-and-unbearable-smugness/

got a megaphone, cupping your hands together and shouting is not going to get you far. More than that, complaining about those people asking both of you to keep it down is just going to entrench the existing problem.

4. Readers are not employers

Part of the problem, I think, is two related issues intersecting in an unhelpful way. The first is that women are systematically disadvantaged in the workplace due to patriarchal culture, both visible (women remain the default carer and earnings never recover if you leave the workplace to become a carer) and invisible (the way women have been taught to act and the way people perceive the way women act). The second is that women are equally disadvantaged in the arts. This later point is set out by Coffee & Ink in this post in favour of eligibility posts but the trouble with the intersection is set out in the comments:[7]

> There has been a recent study showing pretty conclusively that in businesses that tout their culture as being one of meritocracy, so therefore, you know, no pesky diversity issues need to be considered, white men are rewarded much more [...] And while the study may have looked at businesses, writing and publishing and all that...is a business.

The problem is suggesting that awards are rewards equivalent to bonuses or promotions. Readers aren't authors' employers, publishers are authors' employers; readers are at the bottom of the power differential, not the top. This is not to say that readers should abdicate all responsibility for ensuring that reader spaces are diverse, merely that it is most appropriate for readers themselves to address the issue. The need for the employee to be assertive to secure a deserved performance reward does not map across to literary awards (and where it does map across—for example, contracts—it needs to be directed at publishers). Rather there is a need for a collective discussion about what readers want from their awards, a discussion made harder by authors attempting to take ownership of it.

5. Literature is not a business

Yes, publishing is an industry but literature is an art. From my perspective, speculative fiction increasingly seems to be losing sight of this and we are moving to a situation where reviews and awards are viewed simply as publicity material. Worse, at any sign of push back to this cultural shift, authors play the victim. Slowly it is becoming the new norm for readers and authors alike.

I find it very sad. I don't want to live in a world where books are the same as toothbrushes and readers are just consumers. I want awards to be about readers recognising and discussing exceptional work. At its best, eligibility posts would be irrelevant to this process since authors are uniquely poorly placed to assess the quality of their own work. But the ubiquity of such posts and their vociferous defence means they become actively harmful.

---

7 http://coffeeandink.dreamwidth.org/1195737.html

So I would like authors to be honest. If, on the one hand, you think your story is one of the six best published last year then say so. If, on the other hand, you don't think your story is that good but, for what ever reason, you still want the kudos of an award then say that. If you can't or won't say either, perhaps you shouldn't say anything at all. Or, even better, do what readers do: talk about someone else's work.

This article first appeared on *Everything Is Nice* on January 13, 2014.
everythingisnice.wordpress.com/2014/01/13/why-i-think-author-eligibility-posts-are-selfish-destructive-and-counter-productive/

ON MERIT, AWARDS, AND WHAT WE READ

Joe Sherry

Since the Hugo Award nominees were announced on Saturday, I have read whatever I came across that talked about the nominees. I love the conversation and getting the pulse of what people are thinking and saying about the awards. This isn't specific to the Hugo Awards, I do it for the Nebula and World Fantasy Awards, I pay attention to other non-genre awards, and I plan to get more involved in reading about one or two other annual awards. This is what I'm interested in.

When I wrote about my Preliminary Thoughts on the Hugo Awards, I did mean what the title implied: those were my preliminary thoughts.[1] Not quite a snap decision, but without yet having read deeply into the short list of nominees. I mentioned at the time that I wished to follow what John Scalzi had said about judging the individual works on their own merits.[2] It made sense to me and still does. Regardless of how a particular story is viewed to have on the ballot, and regardless of one's personal views of any author who has a story on the ballot, the story is on the ballot. If we are to do honest justice to the process, to respect the award, we should fairly evaluate the story and the story alone and then compare that to the other stories nominated in a particular category. That makes sense to me.

Since then, however, I have read more and more commentaries on the nominees and the more I have read, the more I have had to think about—to the point that I am writing this in an effort to work out my own thoughts.

There are a couple of controversies which have come out of this year's Hugo short list. The first seems to me to be the lesser controversy. For the past several years, Larry Correia has been running a small campaign to get himself and others of his esteem nominated for a Hugo Award. This year it began with a comic he drew, it continued with several update posts, and ended with the slate of who he was nominating with his membership.[3] Not a huge deal, ultimately, though it has been construed that Correia has been exhorting his readers to purchase memberships and follow his lead in nominating that particular lineup. One author, Vox Day, likewise endorsed what Correia was doing, and then added his own recommendations.[4]

While I feel there is a subtle difference between this and authors simply listing what works they have that are eligible, where the difference is in the

1 http://joesherry.blogspot.com/2014/04/preliminary-thoughts-on-hugo-award.html
2 http://whatever.scalzi.com/2014/04/19/quick-2014-hugo-nomination-thoughts/
3 http://monsterhunternation.com/2014/01/14/sad-puppies-2-the-illustrated-edition/, http://monsterhunternation.com/2014/02/20/sad-puppies-2-the-debatening/ and http://monsterhunternation.com/2014/03/25/my-hugo-slate/
4 http://voxday.blogspot.com/2014/01/the-huggening.html and http://voxday.blogspot.com/2014/03/the-sad-puppy-hugo-slate.html

tone and the explicit goal of Correia, I concede that the difference may not be much more than semantics. While it may be considered unseemly to talk about how much one wants an award or to campaign for such, because the cost of a supporting membership to Worldcon is relatively low and so few people actually nominate, it doesn't take all that many nominating votes to make the final ballot. All it takes if 5% of the vote, and to be in the top five (except for ties) of those receiving nominations. In the of the Novelette category, there were 728 ballot submitted, so a minimum of 36 or 37 nominations is all that is required (depending on rounding). A motivated group of fans could (and did) easily secure enough nominations to place their choices on the ballot. Hopefully, that motivated group is also acting with integrity and selecting only those they felt were truly the best. But, that is almost besides the point. In the corner of the internet which I sit, that is coming across poorly, but I see it as less of an issue because this was also a possibility based on how the rules are set up.

The real issue and controversy at hand is that of Vox Day and his nomination. This is less so because of the relative quality of the story, and much more so about the quality of the man. Vox Day is the pseudonym for Theodore Beale. I missed this when it went down in mid 2013 when I was much less plugged in to what was going on inside this genre that I love, but the abbreviated version is that N.K. Jemisin was Guest of Honor at Continuum in Australia and she gave a powerful speech dealing with racism and in which she also called out, not by name, Theodore Beale for being "a self-described

misogynist, racist, anti-Semite, and a few other flavors of asshole."[5] Amal El-Mohtar details the response Beale, writing as Vox Day, had for Jemisin. It was disgusting and it was racist.[6] El-Mohtar called for the expulsion of Beale from the SFWA, something which eventually occurred.[7] Foz Meadows had an

angry, but well reasoned (in my opinion) response to Vox Day.[8]

There were numerous other responses to this, as there tends to be, but to a large point, the story would have ended there except that in part due to the mobilization of the fans of Larry Correia and Vox Day, a story by Vox Day is on this year's Hugo ballot.

This is where the conversation changes. This is where I have run into a number of essays which have led to my confronting my opinions on evaluating based on merit. Rachel Acks writes "There is a point at which I can no longer separate the art from the living artist. I cannot escape the fact that my support of their art, however miniscule in relative scale it may be, implicates me in what they then use their platform to do and say. It makes me complicit, if only peripherally, in the harm they choose to do."[9] Rose Lemberg, however, takes a different perspective than Acks, though both end up in the same place.[10]

5 http://nkjemisin.com/2013/06/continuum-goh-speech/
6 http://amalelmohtar.com/2013/06/13/calling-for-the-expulsion-of-theodore-beale-from-sfwa/
7 http://www.locusmag.com/News/2013/08/beale-expelled-from-sfwa/
8 http://fozmeadows.wordpress.com/2013/06/14/reconciliation-a-response-to-theodore-beale/
9 http://katsudon.net/?p=2953
10 http://roselemberg.net/?p=762

> It is my opinion that such conciliatory voices from prominent personae who are 1) power brokers in our communities and 2) considerably less marginalized than the diverse fans and authors they are championing—are not helping the cause of marginalized and othered Diversity Age authors and fans. In these statements there is often an embedded tone argument, an entreaty to Diversity Age fans to play nice with people who explicitly or implicitly dehumanize and more yet, threaten violence against them. Such conciliatory language from power brokers suggests story lines for the whole community to align with—storylines whose buzzwords are "reason," "respectability," and "merit."

Natalie Luhrs, who after expressing her opinion that Correia and Day gamed the spirit of the awards with how they ended up on the ballot was attacked in the comments of her blog, had this to say in a follow up post:[11]

> After that, there was an insistence from both the trolls and other parties that I should judge the nominated works on their merits alone. These works do not exist in a vacuum and the context in which they are produced is, for me, relevant. The personal is political. I am not going to waste my time reading books written by people who hold me, my friends, and my family in contempt—and Larry Correia and Vox Day do. They have made this abundantly clear through their own discourse as well as through the discourse they allow and encourage to flourish in their comments.

All of this is reasonable. All of this makes sense. It is also a personal decision because I want to extend this a little bit beyond Vox Day and into a more general thought. Also, I believe where a line is drawn will depend both on the reader as well as on who the writer is and how the two intersect. How much does who the artist is matter in our enjoyment or appreciation of the art? How much should it matter? Does time and distance matter?

Can we watch a Woody Allen movie knowing the credible accusations of molestation against him?[12] Do we view Annie Hall or Manhattan differently, or do they remain major works of art? Does it change how view his new work? Is Ender's Game a lesser work because Orson Scott Card is openly homophobic?[13] Rachel Acks can no longer read Card's work, despite having admired it deeply before she learned of his homophobia. Does reading a particular work suggest support for the personal views of the artist even if those views are not evident in the work itself? Does it matter if the artist is still living?

I don't have a good answer to those questions. I can still read and recommend Ender's Game even though I abhor Card's stance on homosexuality. I often do not think about Card the man when I read his book, I just enjoy

11 http://radishreviews.com/2014/04/21/do-i-dare-disturb-the-universe/
12 http://www.vanityfair.com/magazine/archive/1992/11/farrow199211, http://www.vanityfair.com/hollywood/2013/11/mia-farrow-frank-sinatra-ronan-farrow and http://kristof.blogs.nytimes.com/2014/02/01/an-open-letter-from-dylan-farrow/
13 http://www.nauvoo.com/library/card-hypocrites.html

the book. But then, am I expressing tacit support for Card the man when I support *Ender's Game*?

Vox Day is only the latest in this conversation, the latest bigot to make the rounds into my small corner of the world and show a contemptible side of humanity. I understand what Acks and Lemberg and Luhrs and so many others are saying about taking ownership of what we want the Hugos to be about, and that regardless of the relative merits of his story, if we are able to separate our personal thoughts of the author from the story and find the story to be of sufficiently high quality to move to the top our ballots, what, if anything, does it say about the Hugo Awards and this small part of science fiction and fantasy fandom that would recognize *that* author who was removed from the SFWA because of the combination of the ugly things he said and the way he used SFWA social media to broadcast those words. Can we, in considering the winners, separate that a worthy story may have won from the fact that an unworthy person won?

Does it matter who creates the art?

Am I writing from a place of privilege when I ask that question? I am a heterosexual cisgendered white male. I am not a writer, and I don't have a professional stake in this. I feel that I am a member of one small part of a larger community, and I want to think through this, but my perspective will always be shaped by who I am and where I sit, and that perspective can be significantly and substantially different because there are all sorts of things that I just don't have to deal with in my life. My privilege.

The only possible answer that I have, which is not much an answer at all, is that the individual must decide what is acceptable and if they are able to separate art from the artist and in what circumstances they are able to do so. It is a completely valid position to take that, in the case of Vox Day, the hate is too virulent and it cannot be tolerated and that any art is irrevocably lessened by the who the artist is. Or, in the case of Woody Allen, Orson Scott Card, or anyone else.

Examining art is ultimately a personal act and if it has long been my opinion that half of reading and interpreting a story is in what the reader brings to the table, then part of what the reader brings to the table is how they view the artist and in many cases, it cannot be separated. Nor should it be.

I do still plan to analyze each story and novel as they are presented (as much as what I do could be construed as analyzing), but I fully accept and understand that others are not able to nor find it desirable to consider the art without also considering the artist. What I don't know is if, in this case, I will be able to do so myself.

It is possible that I will read the nominated story from Vox Day and find that it is so good that I would need to find a new way to talk about it, to figure out how to get across that the story is utterly brilliant that I expect it will still be read in fifty years and will be included in anthologies covering the best science fiction stories ever written. It's possible, but right now I am stuck in the position that no matter how I may feel about the story in the future, what I know about how the man conducts himself online and, as such, in public, is so disgusting, off-putting, and worthy of censure that I am finding it difficult to reconcile the idea of merit as fully independent from the artist. On the other hand, perhaps it won't matter in the end. The only way to find out is to try.

This article first appeared on *Adventures in Reading* on April 24, 2014.
joesherry.blogspot.com/2014/04/on-merit-awards-and-what-we-read.html

ON THE PITFALLS OF "MERIT"

Rose Lemberg

As I see it, there is currently a split in the fandom. I tentatively think of it as a split between Golden Age fans and Diversity Age fans. This is not about age, as I've written before, but about storylines: who gets to write stories, who gets to be a protagonist of stories, who gets to consume stories and express their opinions as authoritative. There is a certain correlation between demographic variables, and the Golden Age vs Diversity Age split in fandom, but it is far from absolute, and this imperfect mapping often creates dissonance in the way we speak about fandom, the works within it, and personalities who generate and consume these works.

It is not surprising that there is a demographic correlation with regard to these fandoms, as many people like to see protagonists who are like themselves. It is also no big secret that Golden Age works often tend to other, exclude, and dismiss Diversity Age Fans. Nevertheless, there is an overlap between these fandoms. Perhaps instead of talking about a binary split, we can talk about a continuum between these two axes; a continuum of values and interests that maps loosely but not precisely onto demographics. Some people can hold positions that overlap with both axes. A white, cisgendered, heterosexual man can certainly be a Diversity Age fan.

However, the position of a white, cisgendered, heterosexual man is a demographic position of privilege and power both in fandom and without it. Within the Golden Age umbrella, this demographic has been the one primarily fronted through narratives, power structures, promotion through mainstream presses, and other venues of power. This demographic position of power is not automatically dismantled or disappears within Diversity Age fandom—on the contrary, we see a flow of social capital from fans, in form of sales, praise, and support, towards such powerful fans who side with Diversity Age positions.

Such powerful fans are, not surprisingly, in a position to powerfully promote Diversity Age voices, which are, in many cases, still building their influence and earning social power and fanbase. While speaking out, up and coming diverse writers and fans often become targets of ridicule and scorn due to their demographic and social positioning—when they get any attention at all. In that way, white, cisgendered, heterosexual men (and often women, though there is a notable social and power difference) who are power brokers in our communities can—and get—to do a lot of good for Diversity Age fandom.

However, the temptation is strong to use this power not just to do ally work, but to self-build through the struggle of marginalized Diversity Age writers and fans—through campaigning for Diversity positions which incurs increased social capital, as well as increased financial capital. Few are the voices that rise to openly criticize such powerful fans if their work happens to be less than clueful, because they are in power positions to grant and withdraw favors, as well as grant and withdraw considerable social capital in our communities. It is exactly the risk that I am taking here.

Now I will speak about conciliatory voices. Some of the people on Hugo ballot this year—regardless of how they got there—spoke openly and vociferously against personhood and agency of Diversity Age authors and fans, to an extent that many Diversity Age authors and fans felt and continue to feel threatened emotionally and at times physically. At the same time, certain conciliatory voices of prominent fandom people have been raised to ask fandom to judge Hugo-nominated works on their literary merit.

The suggestion that we read solely for "merit" fronts the idea of "objectivity", i.e. that a view which considers a given work in a vacuum, without social context in which the work has been created and disseminated, is somehow desirable and superior to other ways of reading. Fronting "objectivity" has a long and problematic history within academia and beyond. The fallacy is that what gets to be objective gets to be again defined by power brokers, thus effectively silencing and disenfranchising the marginalized.

This suggestion also carries within it a value judgment: "objectivity good, anger bad"—which slides yet again into the old and tired tone argument.

It is my opinion that such conciliatory voices from prominent personae who are 1) power brokers in our communities and 2) considerably less marginalized than the diverse fans and authors they are championing—are not helping the cause of marginalized and othered Diversity Age authors and fans. In these statements there is often an embedded tone argument, an entreaty to Diversity Age fans to play nice with people who explicitly or implicitly dehumanize and more yet, threaten violence against them. Such conciliatory language from power brokers suggests story lines for the whole community to align with—storylines whose buzzwords are "reason", "respectability", and "merit."

But these "voices of reason" may not speak fully for Diversity Age fans, because the very notion of such reason and its objectivity is a Western ideal (and by extent white, male, and historically entrenched ideal within the power structures of the West) which we are thereby encouraged to adopt. The ideal of objective merit might seem desirable at first glance, because we are socialized to desire it. In fact, the adoption of this ideal is dangerous: it suppresses non-Western, non-cisgendered-male modes of thinking and communicating, and imposes a mainstream, power paradigm upon the marginalized—it often has, in short, a silencing effect.

Also, conciliatory statements often have the effect of diverting the attention yet again (along with the accompanying social praise and support) from the marginalized voices to the power brokers, thus increasing the social capital of those who already have it, while marginalized voices go unpromoted and unsupported—unsupported often in context of vicious attacks from those who deny Diversity Age fans their personhood.

This is not about Golden Age vs Diversity Age split, but about lending one's ear to white supremacists and their allies. For many of us, who are well-versed in surviving violence of various kinds, knowing the context is crucial for survival. This is why we cannot divorce the work from its author, or from the social context within which these authors operate. A context in which a given author is actively dangerous—emotionally, physically—is crucial.

It is within this context that many of us will judge such works, and many of us may feel angry, uncomfortable, disenfranchised, dismissed, and silenced when the paradigm of "merit" is suggested by power brokers—even when they are powerful allies in other contexts.

This article first appeared on *roselemberg.net* on April 22, 2014.
roselemberg.net/?p=762

DON'T ATTACK REVIEWERS

Jonathan McCalmont

Last weekend, the Guardian published an astonishing piece by Kathleen Hale about her experiences tracking down someone who spoke ill of her and her books online.[1] According to Hale, the negative reviews spiralled out into a more generalised form of online vitriol that motivated Hale to trace her reviewer's real identity, travel to confront them and then write an article about it in the Guardian that paints Hale as the (moderately self-critical) victim of things like "trolling" and "catfishing" rather than a petulant and intimidating online presence. Anyone who has published a negative review online will read this article and shiver, particularly at the manner in which Hale presents the silencing of her critic as a signifier for personal growth:

> I'm told Blythe still blogs and posts on Goodreads; Patricia tells me she still live tweets Gossip Girl. In some ways I'm grateful to Judy, or whoever is posing as Blythe, for making her Twitter and Instagram private, because it has helped me drop that obsessive part of my daily routine. Although, like anyone with a tendency for low-grade insanity, I occasionally grow nostalgic for the thing that makes me nuts.

It's nice that Hale was afforded the privilege of writing about her experiences in a venue as visible and respected as the Guardian and it's nice that she was able to transform her defeated and diminished critics into stepping-stones on the road to personal self-improvement. I am genuinely glad that she is feeling better but the bulk of my sympathies still lie with her critic.

I feel quite close to this issue because, for the past ten years, I have been hanging out on the margins of science fiction fandom occasionally writing about books and commenting on the state of the field. In that time I have seen a partisan dislike for negative reviews of favourite books broaden into a more generalised taboo against negative reviewing and a related dissolution of the taboo against authors confronting their critics and responding to reviews. Given that Hale frames her encounters with critics in strictly psychological terms, I think it appropriate that I should begin by doing the same.

The **first** time I took a step back from genre culture was as a result of being stalked for daring to publish negative reviews. The stalking was limited to some creepy comments and a rather cack-handed attempt to run me out of town on a rail by posting a long diatribe in the comments of a number of widely-read blogs but It did give me pause for thought and a reason for cutting back on my reviewing.

---

[1] http://www.theguardian.com/books/2014/oct/18/am-i-being-catfished-an-author-confronts-her-number-one-online-critic

The **second** time I took a step back from genre culture was a number of years later. Alienated from the field, I had set up this blog as a means of encouraging myself to write about a wider array of things but I had been slowly drifting back towards the field because of a number of decent friendships that made me feel as though I was welcome. After a sudden change in circumstances left me with a good deal more spare time, I decided to increase my output and so started volunteering to review a wider range of books and generally chasing the field by reviewing stuff that was already being widely discussed.

In February 2009, I reviewed Ellen Datlow's anthology *Poe* for Strange Horizons.[2] I liked some of the stories but not all of them and was largely unimpressed by the anthology as a whole. A few days later, the Hugo-winning editor Ellen Datlow appeared in the comments to take issue with things that I had said. She was later joined by the author Anna Tambour whose contributions make little sense even upon re-examination. Curious as to where these authors and editors were coming from, I backtracked and came across a discussion of the review on Datlow's blog.[3] I later commented in public about Datlow's willingness to go after her critics and she responded by saying that she didn't believe that I had actually read her work.

In hindsight, this type of stuff seems like weak beer. In the past five years, online discussion has grown considerably more hyperbolic and an editor linking to a negative review on their blog would most likely result in 110 comments rather than 11. However, I started reviewing under the principle that a reviewer's right to express their opinion about a book was sacrosanct and when you realise that this right has suddenly been taken away it cannot help but make you feel alienated from your culture (*am I *that* out of touch?*) and just that little bit more careful when choosing which books to review (*does this author have a history of going after their critics and do I think that my review might prompt such a response?*).

A couple of years later, I took it upon myself to review Jo Walton's Hugo Award-winning novel *Among Others*. By that point, I was aware of the growing willingness of authors to go after their critics and so had fallen into the habit of publishing my reviews on an external site rather than my blog. However, when I posted a link to the piece on my blog, I made the mistake of expanding upon some of my points to the extent that this provoked a link directly to my blog as well as to the review.[4] This time, the link prompted 82 comments. Later that summer, Jo Walton appeared on a panel at Worldcon and reportedly discussed my review at some length. I still don't know what was said at that panel but I do know that Jo Walton later wrote me an email in order to apologise.

It was around this time that my genre reviewing output began to decline. I stopped chasing the conversation and when *Strange Horizons* stopped sending me emails inviting me to review, I never bothered to chase them. The community had spoken and I didn't belong. I even spoke out online about how I was completely done with genre reviewing and I didn't even think about

2 http://www.strangehorizons.com/reviews/2009/02/poe_edited_by_e.shtml
3 http://ellen-datlow.livejournal.com/163670.html
4 http://ruthlessculture.com/2011/03/29/review-among-others-2011-by-jo-walton/ and http://papersky.livejournal.com/2011/03/31/

reviewing another work of genre fiction until I encountered Tim Maughan's short-fiction collection *Paintwork*. While I am now closer to genre spaces than I was in 2011 and 2012, I'm no longer a regular reviewer and most of my writing takes the form of either columns published in a magazine or cultural commentary that I consider fan-writing rather than literary criticism.

Having written all of this out, I now realise that it seems extraordinarily petty. In hindsight, I wonder what I was worried about but that anxiety did sour me on the genre community and was directly responsible for my "career" as a genre reviewer coming to a rather ill-tempered end. I sympathise with Kathleen Hale's critics because I received far less intense blow-back for my reviewing and collapsed like a house of cards. These days, I consider anyone who dares to post a negative review to be heroic because I know what it's like out there and I know that I probably don't have another dog-pile in me.

In order to get a feel for what it can be like to be a genre reviewer in the current climate, I invite you to take a look at the comments to this overview of Ben Aaronovitch's *Peter Grant/Rivers of London* series by the Book Smugglers as well as the column by Renay that those comments inspired.[5] Aaronovitch also responded to the column and when the fight eventually spilled out onto Twitter and into the wider genre blogosphere, Renay found herself on the receiving end of some very unpleasant threats. When asked not to impose his intended interpretation upon his fans' readings, Aaronovitch got angry, started insulting people and later claimed that the term "fan" was itself problematic and promptly resigned from fandom for about as long as it took for him to be invited to be a guest at a convention.[6]

I think that the *Strange Horizons* blow-up neatly demonstrates the power dynamics involved in choosing to express yourself in genre spaces: If a fan says something and gets into trouble, they can rely upon their friends to back them up. When an author says something and gets into trouble, they can rely upon their friends, their fanbase, their publisher and their agents to provide support. Some of whom will have a financial interest in the author's career. When Renay popped her head above the parapet and dared to say that maybe we should think about our cultural spaces in a different light, she was attacked and threatened to the point where her later columns were noticeably more personal and less likely to attract attention. When Ben Aaronovitch went for a fan, people with ties to the industry bent over backwards to make him feel welcome.

The power imbalance is so pronounced that I find it difficult to believe that anyone could write something as privileged and insensitive as that which recently appeared on Robert Jackson Bennett's blog:[7]

> In my experience, artists aren't the powerful ones in this situation. We're vulnerable, powerless, and desperately exposed, and it's assumed that we'll stay that way. Granted, we chose to be in this situation—we've put ourselves out there before the world—but the increased anonymity of the internet means we catch a lot more

5 http://thebooksmugglers.com/2013/07/smugglers-ponderings-on-the-peter-grant-series-by-ben-aarnovitch.html and http://www.strangehorizons.com/2013/20130909/renay-c.shtml
6 http://web.archive.org/web/20130927005004/http://temporarilysignificant.blogspot.co.uk/2013/09/splattered-with-shit.html and http://www.dwcon.org/pages/52/ben-aaronovitch
7 http://www.robertjacksonbennett.com/blog/whats-the-difference-between-criticism-and-harassment

tomatoes in the face than we used to, and it's assumed we'll grin and bear it.

I don't even want to know what kind of corrupted and malformed neural pathway might lead you to look at my history as a reviewer or the reaction to Renay's column and conclude that we were the people who had the power in those situations. Was Kathleen Hale's critic the one who had the power when a manifestly troubled writer decided to turn up on her doorstep? Was Kathleen Hale's critic the one with the power when an article was written about her in a national newspaper? Was Kathleen Hale's critic the one with the power when she decided that she felt unsafe with unlocked accounts? No.

Setting my own experiences and feelings about authors responding to critics aside, I think that much of the discussion surrounding Hale's piece ignores the structural causes for these types of confrontation.

The reason that authors are starting to "catch a lot more tomatoes in the face" is that the publishing industry has royally *fucked* them. Step back a single generation and you will find that most of an author's PR was handled by their publishers. Sure... an author would have to do the occasional interview and maybe the odd public appearance but when a publishing house decided your work was worth publishing they put their weight behind it allowing you to spend your time writing rather than hustling for PR and managing your brand. What has happened over the last ten years is that authors have been forced to become so involved with their own PR that there is no longer any distance between them and the people discussing their work. The reason the taboo against authors responding to reviewers has been replaced with a taboo against negative reviews is that there is a world of difference between having your PR people turn a blind-eye to the things being said about you in another room and being expected to sit quietly in front of a bunch of people discussing your failings.

The changes in the social protocols surrounding reviewing show how the lack of distance between authors and fans has put fan spaces under pressure to conform to the requirements of the modern publishing industry: A literary culture built to meet the needs of fans naturally encourages robust criticism because robust criticism encourages fans to talk amongst themselves and a negative review is no bad thing (whether you agree with it or not) because it aims to prevent fans from spending money on books they won't enjoy. Conversely, a literary culture built to meet the needs of literary professionals has no interest in protecting people from bad purchasing decisions. This type of literary culture emphasises not only positive reviews that help to sell (sometimes terrible and offensive) books but also coverage of the types of things that publishers want. Why encourage fans to find their own areas of interest when you can drive them towards the blogs of people who review the right type of book in the right type of way and at the right time? A literary culture built to suit the needs of literary professionals has no need for independent or idiosyncratic voices and absolutely no need for reviewers who dare to point out that the hot novel of the moment is a waste of money. However, a literary culture built to suit to needs of its bourgeois professionals may feel the need to set out a set of rules that the lower classes would be wise to follow, hence Robert Jackson Bennett laying down the law as to where and when it is acceptable for critics to express their own opinions:[8]

> In other words, when you leave your platform, your own personal space of the internet, and go to someone else's, or even to a community platform, it requires a different code of behavior. This isn't your space anymore, so you need to act differently. And remember, you've had your say back on your own platform. That's the place to speak your mind.

What has changed in the last generation is that the book publishing industry has been bought out by corporations who see the literary world as nothing more than another domain from which to extract money. Thus, the infamously sloppy and old-fashioned publishing industry was put under pressure to perform and in order to perform, belts had to be tightened and resources squeezed including authors who could no longer be allowed to sit around writing when there was marketing to be done. I understand when people like Robert Jackson Bennett say that they're feeling vulnerable and exposed but it is capitalism and not fans who put them in this position.

Many of the writers who are now compelled to interact with fans in fannish spaces were not members of those spaces prior to becoming authors. Having been told by agents and publishers to set up a Twitter account and get branding, they arrive in fannish spaces expecting the cultural equivalent of an eBay account: Put effort in here, extract money there. Brought to these spaces for entirely selfish reasons, it is not surprising that these authors should find themselves alienated from a set of cultural values devised and maintained by people intent upon using those spaces for different reasons. Faced with a disconnect from the cultural values they have and the cultural values that benefit them financially, some authors choose to either lobby for a new set of rules (as in the case of Robert Jackson Bennett) or lash out at reviewers (as in the case of Kathleen Hale and Ben Aaronovitch) who refuse to act according to the rules that many new authors were lead to expect by publishers who don't have the time to promote the books they themselves chose to publish.

As an occasional critic and commentator on the world of science fiction literature, I am concerned about the changing attitudes towards fan spaces. I am concerned not only because I have become more and more conscious of how scary it can be to express a dissenting opinion in genre culture but also because I wonder whether these types of business practices are sustainable in the long term.

My views on diversity and inclusivity in fandom rest upon a vision of

society that might be described as Darwinian if that didn't invoke images of Richard Dawkins shouting at Muslims or libertarian plutocrats blaming the poor for being the victims of economic oppression.[9] In my view, everyone who decides to "do" cultural stuff makes a decision as to which cultural spaces are deserving of their attention. The more attractive a cultural space

8 http://www.robertjacksonbennett.com/blog/whats-the-difference-between-criticism-and-harassment
9 http://ruthlessculture.com/2012/07/10/sub-cultural-darwinism-some-thoughts-on-the-rise-and-fall-of-fandoms/

is to potential members, the more that cultural space will grow and benefit from their continued emotional and financial investment. In a sense, all of a culture's fandoms and spaces are "competing" for resources in the form of new members. A literary culture built to service the needs of fans will develop values that protect fans and allow them enough space to find themselves and do what they want to do. Conversely, a literary culture built to service the economic needs of a professional literary class will seek to restrict fans' agency to the point where they are merely passive recipients of PR and economic resources to be exploited by those deemed worthy of entry to the professional classes. Is a literary culture that emphasises the passive nature of its non-professional participants really more "competitive" than a literary culture that allows non-professionals the space to express themselves freely? Would a 14-year old version of you rather invest in a cultural space where they are expected to sit still, pay up and help to sell stuff or a cultural space that allows people to find their own voice regardless of what it might have to say? I am not convinced that a literary culture built to service the needs of a professional literary class is as viable as a literary culture built to service the needs of book readers everywhere. I think that frowning on negative reviews whilst turning a blind eye to attacks on reviewers silences voices and makes it much less likely that fandom will attract new voices to replace those who have been silenced in the past. I am sympathetic to writers who feel overwhelmed and horrified by readers' refusal to be passive economic resources but the answer is never to intimidate, ostracise and occasionally stalk those fans that refuse to conform to their professional requirements.

Authors (like Ben Aaronovitch or Kathleen Hale) who attack reviewers are not freak occurrences but a direct result of increased commercial pressure being placed on cultural spaces. The more international capital requires profit, the more corporations squeeze their publishing arms and the more the publishers squeeze their writers, the more writers wind up attacking reviewers who dare to disrupt their branding strategies. The rising pressure on our cultural ecosystems mirrors the increased pressure on real-world ecosystems and shifting to a set of values that discourages negative reviewing whilst turning a blind-eye to attacks on reviewers is really no different to shifting to a set of values that turn a blind-eye to fracking, clear-cutting forests and strip-mining mountainsides. Like all cultural spaces, fandoms are valuable resources but apply too much pressure to those resources and you risk destroying them not just for yourself but for the authors and fans that come after you.

This article first appeared on *Ruthless Culture* on October 24, 2014.
http://ruthlessculture.com/2014/10/24/dont-attack-reviewers/

MEDIA COMMENTARY

THE INESCAPABLE GOODNESS OF 'TEEN WOLF''S SCOTT MCCALL

Deborah Pless

If you're not currently watching *Teen Wolf*, then I'd like to take a minute and suggest that you start. Not because it's an amazing show and you're missing out on world-class storytelling, or even because the shirtless dudes are really that amazing. I mean, they're nice, but they're not quite enough to compensate for the plot-holes, marginalized characters, and frequent tonal shifts that plague the series. The reason I think everyone and their mother should watch *Teen Wolf* has very little to do with the show itself, and everything to do with a single character: Scott McCall.

Now, this might seem super obvious to state, since Scott (played by Tyler Posey) is the nominal protagonist of *Teen Wolf*. I mean, he is the "teen wolf" that the show's title is referring to. It's Scott's life that's transformed when he's bitten by a crazed werewolf, it's Scott who has to man up and learn how to be a supernatural creature in a banal world, and it's Scott who has to do all of this while trying not to fail all of his classes or lose sight of what makes him human.

It's all about Scott.

But the real reason why Scott makes the show work isn't because he's the main character. At this point that role is largely in name only—Scott has been the central character but not the "main" one for a few seasons now. No, the reason everyone should watch *Teen Wolf* and marvel at Scott McCall is actually a lot simpler than that. Simply put, Scott McCall is a really, really good person. Like a really, really, really, *really* good person.

Scott is the kind of person that Sunday school teachers coo over and little old ladies know by name. He's a Disney prince of a guy, and he's so incorruptibly wonderful that the entire arc of this most recent season dealt with the fact that you literally cannot make him a bad guy.

He is also, and I feel like this is where the show gets really interesting, a biracial teenager from a "broken home" living with his Hispanic mother in a house where the power gets shut off because they can't pay their bills and where he has to take extra hours at his after-school job so they can buy groceries. This kid is basically the werewolf messiah, and he's not an upper-middle class white boy. He's from the exact demographic that we would consider "at risk youth." Scott's a lot closer in socioeconomic status and cultural image to Mike Brown and Trayvon Martin than he is to the original Scott McCall of the *Teen Wolf* movie. And that? Makes the show worth watching.

Now, I really shouldn't give Jeff Davis, the show creator, too much credit here. Or really any credit. From what I've been able to tell, Davis has been ambiguous at best and downright irritated at worst regarding Scott's racial and economic background. The majority of this development has actually come because of the actors. Tyler Posey is biracial, and very open about the fact. After finally being confronted one too many times about having cast a non-white actor in the lead role, Davis decided to make it an intentional choice, but Scott's race actually remained a non-topic for the first few seasons of the show.

Additionally, one gets the impression that Scott was not always intended to be the best boy ever. In the first season, it seems like the show is going to make Scott heroic, but complicated, like the usual television heroes. It wasn't until the second season (the agreed upon worst season) that the show started to build Scott up as a great person, and it was in the third season that everyone just sat down and agreed that Scott is basically the best person to ever live. So it's been a long process.

And don't get me wrong. When I say that Scott is, on this show, pretty much the best person to ever live, I don't think I'm exaggerating.

So far he has somehow managed to become the Alpha of a werewolf pack simply by being a really good leader and inspirational and pure of heart (something so rare that there is literally a plot where another werewolf pack tries to steal him), as well as being the kind of guy who doesn't just stay friends with his ex-girlfriend, he stays *best* friends with his ex-girlfriend.

There are scenes where Scott tells his friends how much they mean to him and how much he loves them. There are scenes where Scott tells his enemies how much they mean to him and how much he loves them. There is literally a scene where Scott breaks through a magic spell with the power of love. Actually there are a bunch of scenes where he does that. Because Scott McCall is magic.

And it's not just that he's sappy and cute and magically gifted. Scott McCall would be an angel if he didn't have any supernatural powers, and from what I can tell, that's the point. He's like Steve Rogers that way. What happens if you give superpowers to a person who has a weak constitution (interesting because both Steve and Scott have debilitating asthma for most their lives), but an infinite ability to care for others? Well, it appears that you get Captain America and True Alpha Scott McCall. Becoming a werewolf didn't make Scott a good person, it just gave him the power to be the best good person he could be.

I cannot emphasize enough how much I love Scott. In the first season he's a little annoying, sure, but honestly I blame the writers for that. They didn't yet know how to write him, and they were portraying his defining feature (his ineffable goodness) as a liability and frustrating weakness. Once they realized that Scott's actual flaw is that he's pretty much incorruptible, the show really picked up and got more interesting. They doubled down on Scott's niceness, and the result is awesome.

Which is why it's all the more important to note that Scott? Not your average white teenager. Not a white teenager at all. While the circumstances of Scott's life are actually probably the result of the writers trying to create a scenario where it's plausible for a sixteen year old boy to spend most of his nights running around the woods fighting monsters, the facts remain the same.

Scott's parents are divorced, and at the start of the show at least, his father is completely out of the picture. It is implied several times that his father was an alcoholic, and borderline abusive. Scott's mother, on the other hand, is a genuinely amazing and wonderful woman, but she's busy providing for her teenage son (and the occasional love-starved foster kid that her son literally brings home to live with them because that is an honest to goodness plot point). Melissa (played by Melissa Ponzio) is a fantastic mother, but she's not around a lot, because she's always working.[1] She's a nurse, and while it's a profession that pays pretty well, it's clear that it doesn't pay well enough.

And, I mean, I just can't get over how interesting Scott's background is from this perspective. Because his father, who we later discover is an FBI agent, is a codedly upper-middle class white man, but Scott chooses to live with his working class Hispanic mother. Nursing, though an important (very) and difficult job, is generally considered a lower-class profession. It's something working class people do. Higher income people with the same interests become doctors.

It's hard to think of a more positive representation of a Hispanic teen in pop culture. It's hard to think of a more positive representation of any teenager in pop culture. Scott's one of a kind. Because while he is a rather static character (he is good and he stays good), Scott isn't by any means boring, nor is he a bad character. Like I mentioned earlier, he's a lot like Captain America. Just because he's good doesn't mean everyone else is, and a great deal of really interesting conflict can come from Scott and his idealism butting up against the world.

This one quirk, too, pretty much saves the show. Without Scott and his magical werewolf amazingness, the show would quickly disintegrate into a series of teen trauma tropes. I mean, the other characters are great and all (Allison was amazing, Malia is hilarious, Lydia is a gem, Derek is my squishie), but Scott is the reason why the show is worth watching.[2]

So even if you don't like Teen Wolf, and think it's cheesy or bad or kind of offensive sometimes (all of those being perfectly reasonable things to think), remember Scott McCall. Remember that one time that he asked, in perfect earnestness because Scott is never not earnest, why his mother hadn't kept her maiden (Hispanic) last name. He wanted to know so he could understand, and made it clear that he would support her no matter what. Remember the time that Scott took time away from hunting the supernatural creature of the week to help his best friend who was going through a rough time.

Remember the time that Scott risked his life to save his high school bully from being hurt. Repeatedly. Even when it became clear that said high school bully was a real and honest threat. Remember that time that Scott allowed himself to be tortured in order to save someone who wasn't even technically in his pack.

1 http://www.kissmywonderwoman.com/2014/04/strong-female-character-friday-melissa.html
2 http://www.kissmywonderwoman.com/2013/08/dereks-whole-storyline-is-rapey-stop.html and http://www.kissmywonderwoman.com/2014/07/strong-female-character-friday-malia.html

Remember all of the times that Scott has proved he has a pure heart, and then remember the way that the media usually shows us Hispanic (non-white in general) teenagers. *Teen Wolf* does a lot of things wrong. A *lot*. But this is one thing that they do consistently right.

Remember Scott McCall.

This article first appeared on *Kiss My Wonder Woman* on September 10, 2014.
www.kissmywonderwoman.com/2014/09/the-inescapable-goodness-of-teen-wolfs.html

WHY DO FANBOYS ALWAYS MAKE THEM FIGHT?

brownbetty

There's a post that was making the rounds on my tumblr dashboard about a week ago with the title "Why do Fangirls Always Make them Gay?" which sounds confrontational, but is actually various ways of answering that question, and the link discusses well, why *might* fictional gay men be meeting the erotic fantasy needs of women?[1]

And it's a discussion we've had a million times, and you may or may not find something new there, but it happened to pop up only a little before this post, artwork depicting Marvel and DCU big hitters at a pool hall, and Captain America has just knocked over Superman's drink with his cue.[2] The original poster has captioned it "Beginning of the most EPIC barfight ever!"

And of course, by the time it showed up on my dashboard, it had devolved into a discussion of Bucky and Jason Todd having sex, which brings it neatly back to "Why Do Fangirls Make them Gay?" but is not actually where I was going.

Because the thing is, if you've read much superhero comics, you know that whenever two characters from separate titles meet, they are more or less required to spend two pages having a fight over a misunderstanding before they can get down to the business of whatever the story is supposed to be about. These encounters have an almost ritual quality; on the one hand, there is a supposed justification for the fight, but on the other hand, no one is ever seriously injured in these fights, and they generally end quickly, with handclasps, and seem to be a means of engendering mutual respect.

And yet, let me come back to my insistence that these fights are *so stupid*. Go back to my second link. As the second comment down points out, Superman and Captain America fighting over a spilled drink? If you were to come up with two comics characters *less likely* to get in a fight over a spilled drink, *more capable* of settling their differences with words, I do not know who they would be. (Okay, maybe um... Martian Manhunter, and... Pepper Potts. There you go. But it took me a moment.)

Both of these are, we are supposed to believe, grown adult men deeply committed to the building of just societies and of civil institutions, and respected moral leaders of their respective circle of friends and acquaintances. And yet, I assure you, each of them has resorted to fisticuffs on first acquaintance with nearly everyone they know, or at least, everyone they know who wears a tight-fitting costume. And comics asks us to believe that this is consistent with their character.

---

1 http://neverbalance.tumblr.com/post/91338849949/why-do-fangirls-always-make-them-gay/mobile
2 http://dsudis.tumblr.com/post/91753015819/feanorinleatherpants-brokentoyinlalaland/mobile

Superman and Captain America are about to get in a fight, in this art, because it is a scene the artist wants to see.

And *yet*. *Fangirls* are being asked to explain why we "make them gay" and told we must justify "making them act out of character."

No one ever asks, "Why do fanboys always make them fight?" Because fanboys write the comics.

(And okay, I'm not sure it's objectively better to make them fuck on first acquaintance than fight on first acquaintance, maybe it's bonobo vs. chimpanzee methods of social regulation, or maybe it's something simpler, but it's definitely not better to fight than fuck. C'mon.)

This article first appeared on *Sturdy and Serviceable* on July 15, 2014.
brownbetty.dreamwidth.org/632553.html

I'M THE TYRANNY OF EVIL MEN

thingswithwings

''ve been thinking a lot about *Captain America: The Winter Soldier*. Quite a lot, really. And about the different interpretations I've seen of the film, and why people are able to see two very different films in it. I wanted to sort through all my thoughts and try to pull on these threads, about the philosophy of the film, what it critiques and what it fails to critique.

HYDRA and SHIELD

After reading a lot of Cap2 reaction posts, I think the thing I most want to talk about is Hydra and Shield (I know, it should be HYDRA and SHIELD, but I can't allcaps through this whole post, so let's not shout) and how intertwined or opposed they are.

Because I've seen some posts talking about how Cap2 is a surprisingly on-point, progressive, political critique, and specifically that it's critiquing the contemporary surveillance state, drone killings, etc. And I've seen posts saying that Cap2, while it may gesture at those things, doesn't seem to put any blame on Shield, instead shifting the blame to Hydra, which seems to imply that Shield spying on us and killing people isn't a problem, and it's only a problem when Nazis get involved. As in the first Iron Man film, the problem isn't making weapons—it's weapons falling into the wrong hands.

So which is it?

I don't think either of these readings are wrong; in fact, I think they're both right, because they're both pulling on threads that exist in the film. I think that Cap2 is in some ways a deeply ambivalent text—ambivalent in the sense of "going in all directions", not the sense that it doesn't care. In the end, it's very easy to watch the film and see a pro-transparency, anti-drone, anti-surveillance, the-people-have-a-right-to-know kind of text; it's also very easy to watch the film and see a Hollywood-typical shifting of American atrocities onto the backs of other, more comfortable villains (WWII era Germans, represented by Hydra, and Cold War era Russians, represented by Bucky). Given the politics of the circles I hang out in, arguing for the former vs the later means arguing in praise of the film or arguing in order to blame the film. We would like to believe that the film is actually coming out for politics that are, in America at the moment, somewhat radical.

[[And it's important, I think, to note that asshole American conservatives are seeing the film as a blatantly moralistic pro-Snowden prop piece (see: dude from the Washington Post who told everyone not to see it on account of its pro-Snowden politics). That, to me, indicates that there is something in this film that works against American conservatism or makes that conservatism uncomfortable, no matter how much the ending may be reifying American exceptionalism.

I actually think that the film deserves both praise and blame, but I really hate reading texts and looking for reasons to praise or blame them; what I'd rather do is try to figure out how those critical and anti-critical elements are working together or against each other. What are the desires of this film, and what are its anxieties?

I think that this film desires to be anti-surveillance, anti-drone, anti-American exceptionalism, and pro-transparency.

I think that this film is also anxious about appearing to be any of those things, and that it is anxious about the consequences of taking those positions.

In interviews, the Russo brothers, who wrote and directed, have explicitly said that they were thinking about Snowden, they were thinking about the NSA, that they modelled Project Insight off of Obama's kill list. It's clear, from interviews, that this is what Chris Evans, Scarlett Johannson, Anthony Mackie, and Samuel L. Jackson were working with as well. That's the desire. But the anxiety is: if we critique exceptional power, how can we continue to make superhero films about people who have—and deserve—exceptional power? The Russos have also said that they had in mind the 70s-era political thriller as a genre on which to base this story; so the question becomes, how do you blend that genre with the genre of the superhero action film? Are they even compatible? The hero of the political thriller is often the investigative journalist who exposes the truth to the masses; and while this film's ending rests heavily on a revelation of truth, it also rests heavily on, y'know. Punching.

So, okay, let's think about the elements that pull this film in one direction or another: either the film is critical of Shield, or it's only critical of Shield-with-Hydra-in-it. If the former, it's much more radical and interesting than if the latter.

Cap2 Is Critical of Shield, and, by Extension, America

1. Fundamentally, the film breaks Shield. Our heroes say there's nothing in it worth salvaging, that the whole structure is corrupt. But is that because it contains Nazis, or because it was corrupt to begin with? This is big, and I don't want to underplay it: superheroes commit treason in this film. Natasha reveals government secrets while Steve and Sam crash government spy planes. They do this not only because Hydra has control of that information and that technology, but also because they think that no one should have control of that information and that technology. This is explicit and is a big point in favour of this reading.

2. The film is actually interestingly careful to complicate who the villains are. This happens twice: someone calls Zola a German scientist, and computer-Zola responds, "I'm Swiss, actually."

Pierce, talking to the World Security Council, clarifies that Batroc is Algerian, not French. I noticed it because it happened twice, and in both cases seemed to be about complicating the comfortable, conventional map of the world, as seen in many shitty American action films: America good, Germany bad, etc. Zola's status as a Swiss WWII Hydra/Nazi scientist makes us think about the complexities of Switzerland's involvement with Germany during that period, the politics of so-called neutrality, and the various ways in which the Allies allowed the right kind of enemy to escape prosecution. This is reinforced again in the Zola scene, by:

3. Natasha's mention of Operation Paperclip. Zola as a beneficiary of Operation Paperclip has been done in comics before, but I was kind of shocked to see it in an MCU film. American complicity in the war, willingness to shelter war criminals, and willingness to get rich and build their empire based on scientists whose work started in concentration camps. This is an acknowledgement of real instances in American history of America being foundationally unethical (as were all the Watergate references, of course).

4. Zola's presence in the heart of Camp Lehigh, the place where Steve was made. They walk past those portraits of Peggy Carter, Howard Stark, and, uh... Tommy Lee Jones... and it's like seeing their seal of approval, their complicity, their willingness to compromise the most important principles. Zola is literally in the foundations of Shield, and Shield opened the door willingly, knowing exactly what he was. I find this whole scene actually deeply critical of Peggy, Howard, and Tommy Lee Jones, which is significant of course because they're Steve's mentors in the first film. Steve begins to see that the system in which he is working is, and *has always been*, filled with horrors. The question is, is Zola the cancer that infected the "healthy body" of Shield from the start, or is he the only way in which Shield can exist in the first place? Like Hydra, is he the foundation of the organization, or is he a contaminant?

5. Of course, Natasha's big moment, when she makes transparent all of Shield's secrets. This is the moment that is most likely to make people think of Wikileaks or other whistleblowing, Snowden etc., and it is a strong moment in which the transparency of information is valued. Our heroes destroy Shield by destroying its secrets and exposing its methods. (I actually have another whole rant about how beautiful this is as a sacrifice for Natasha to be making; I want to vid that moment when her fin-

gers hesitate on the keyboard SO HARD. My girl. She's willing to see regimes fall, we knew that already, but she destroys herself and everything she's built when she destroys Shield's secrets.) But this is the aspect of the film that people are connecting most directly to contemporary American politics, and with good reason.

6. Pierce isn't Red Skull. This is huge, okay: PIERCE ISN'T RED SKULL. I went into the film assuming that Pierce would be Red Skull. I've seen this Cap story, where he meets with a politician who's deep in American business and Shield business, who ends up connected to Hydra, and dudes it is always the Red Skull, come back again. But Pierce was exactly what he said he was: an American politician who learned about expediency from Nick Fury. The fact that the villain was American, the head of Hydra in this film was American, was really important. Also important to note that Brock Rumlow (Crossbones) was American, and stayed that way. Sitwell and Senator Stern were American, and stayed that way. This wasn't brought in from outside... except in the obvious way that it's brought in from outside? But to me it's like American skinheads and neo-Nazis who've created their own vile version of Nazi philosophy.

7. Robert Redford's casting, of course. Other people have been talking about this, how the film reads a lot like the 70s political thrillers that Redford starred in, *All the President's Men* and *Three Days of the Condor*, Nixon-era thrillers in which the government and CIA are corrupt, but of course Redford himself isn't. But when Redford, who looks like he should be the hero—who has the same all-American (white) good looks that Steve Rogers has, who's hearty and folksy and all about getting our boys home safely—when Redford's the villain, I feel like that's another thread pulling us towards the idea that Shield is what's evil, not just Hydra.

8. Nick Fury specifically says that the Greatest Generation did some nasty stuff, compromising their principles. Unfortunately, Steve then says "yes but b/c FREEDOM" which flattens the critique and drowns it in patriotic gibberish. I love how this film acknowledges that Steve isn't a saint or a pacifist—the opening scene where he unflinchingly kills people or throws that knife into that dude's hand is explicit about that—but I think this is a moment when the film doesn't quite know how to deal with that, and it shies away from it. I would've infinitely preferred it if Steve had said, "Yeah, we made compromises, some that didn't make us sleep so well at night. And we shouldn't have." This is

one of the moments where you can really see the film going in for a punch and then pulling it due to its many anxieties.

9. Nick Fury stops being Nick Fury. Pierce learned what he knows from Nick Fury, and then Nick Fury stops being Nick Fury. More on that later.

Cap2 is Critical of Hydra, not Shield, and Promotes American Exceptionalism

1. Natasha's testimony in the hearing at the end of the film seems to contradict a lot of what she does earlier—which, again, feels like punch-pulling. She sets information free, trusting the world to be able to deal with it and make rational, ethical decisions about it, but then in the hearing she says "Hydra was selling you lies, not intelligence," which seems to imply that intelligence would've been okay, and that it's only Hydra's interference with Shield's operations that created a problem.

2. The rest of Natasha's final speech at the hearing, my god. "You're not going to put me in prison. You're not going to put any of us in prison. You know why? Because you need us. Yes, the world is a vulnerable place, and yes, we all make it that way. But we're also the ones best qualified to defend it. So if you want to arrest me, arrest me. You know where to find me." To me this is straight out of the opening scenes of *Iron Man 2*: other people aren't qualified to make the world safe, but I am. This is pure exceptionalism, American exceptionalism grafted onto superheroes, whose ability to defend America (or, I guess, "the world,") put them outside the law. In a way, this film is the spiritual successor of *Iron Man 2* (which I, for the record, like a lot more than *Iron Man*) and it's torn by the same conflicts, trying awkwardly to marry the superhero genre to an acceptable political philosophy. Natasha won't go to prison, and Steve won't go to prison, and Sam won't go to prison, for the same reasons that the engineers of the 08 financial crisis and contemporary American war criminals don't go to prison: America declares them necessary for the world to function, and so they are unaffected by the law. This is also, of course, the rationale for Shield itself. (I do like "you know where to find me," though—Natasha making herself vulnerable and available to the eyes of the law is really interesting as a character note).

3. Sharon Carter gets a job working for the CIA, as if that's somehow better than Shield????????? This three seconds of film is to me super-damning evidence. I mean, it's fine for someone who worked for Shield to think it's cool to work for the CIA, but if

we're meant to see this as a morally safe choice, as opposed to the morally dubious nature of Shield... ???? Similarly, while I love Maria applying for a job at Stark Industries and smiling through her lie detector test and having incredibly self-satisfied and athletic sex with Pepper, the idea that SI is the moral post-Shield choice is also suspect. I mean, SI in the MCU at this point is supposed to be a non-evil corporation (I doubt that it could be, but we can pretend I guess), but just the idea that the employees are all going to go to places like the CIA and huge corporations like SI seems to give lie to the idea that we won the war against what Hydra represented within Shield. If you don't think that the CIA and real-world corporations like SI (Haliburton, for example) are complicit in unconstitutional surveillance, drone strikes, etc, then... well. I guess what I'm saying is, I don't see how a film can be purely critical of Obama's kill list or the NSA or anti-Snowden factions, how it can be pro-transparency and anti-drone and anti-surveillance when it's also happy to give a thumbs-up to the CIA and big American corporations.

4. Zola in the basement of Shield again, per point 4 above. In this reading he's the cancer that's afflicted Shield, rather than the foundation on which it is built and from which its principles emerge. A subversion of what Peggy, Howard, and Tommy Lee Jones fought for. A gross contrast to their vision. A Zola-free all-powerful military agency that spies on every single cell phone and computer on the planet and kills people who are presumed enemies would be absolutely fine. I always think about that moment in Avengers when Coulson explains that he's looking for Loki via every cell phone and computer on the planet. I have to assume that Steve didn't understand what that meant at the time, because my Steve Rogers would never, ever, think that was okay.

5. All the Heil Hydra bullshit, with the secret society stuff and the ACTUALLY SAYING Heil Hydra, it's just too far removed from the comfortable and familiar homegrown atrocities that the film would like to critique. In fact it's too comic-book-y for the 70s political thriller, I think. It removes us from the uncomfortable idea that we, our paranoia and fear and hatred and will to power, that we might be what's wrong with this picture. And can I just also mention that I find it super fucked up that a Latino dude and a Jewish dude are the ones Heil Hydra-ing each other? because it's fucked up. Almost as fucked up as the idea that current American security-state paranoia has anything in common with an old black dude in a bad neighbourhood carrying a gun to walk home.

6. The simple fact that it's a film full of cool Shield agents/military people doing cool things with cars and mechanical wings and big guns and such... the fact that it's an action film, and has an action film's tendency to glorify and sanction violence, and dehumanize the victims of that violence, makes it harder for the film to make the argument that drone strikes... dehumanize the victims of glorified, sanctioned violence. Am I supposed to be horrified by drone killings when the rest of the film looks like an FPS video game, and indeed will probably spawn a tie-in FPS video game?

Hydra and Shield: Where Do We End Up?

I think of this as a film that wanted to make a bunch of harsh, timely critiques of the American apparatus of war and surveillance, but ended up pulling back from that in several crucial ways. There's an in-universe problem, where if Natasha, Sam, Steve, and Nick ARE just taking down Shield, and there's no Hydra to blame, then they're just guilty of treason/terrorism and have sabotaged billions of dollars of American military equipment. This, of course, also makes Natasha's speech in the hearing at the end suspect—perhaps she's giving them what they want to hear—but since the film is making such a point about her now being honest/transparent (putting her hand on the Bible and swearing to tell the whole truth and all), I don't think so. But anyway, in-universe, they need to be fighting someone who isn't an international but heavily US-led military/spy organization. You need Hydra to keep Natasha, Sam, Steve, and Nick out of prison at the end. But the in-universe cop-out is also an extra-universe cop-out; the Watsonian excuse also functions at a Doylist level. Hydra prevents viewers of the film from seeing Shield as the enemy, prevents the film from functioning at the critical level that it may want to function at. Hydra gives us a great excuse to not see ourselves in Shield. Which of these levels of cop-out comes first (Watsonian or Doylist) doesn't really matter, because the overall effect is that viewers are given an easy out.

I would also say that a lot of the critique that happens throughout the film is backpedalled upon by the ending: that's Natasha's hearing, Sharon working for the CIA and Maria for SI, Nick saying that "all the rats didn't go down with the ship" and he's going to go get rid of them. Endings of things are often where they express their deepest anxieties and retreat into conservatism, where the questions put into the air by the earlier parts of the text have to be put to rest in one way or another; the ending of the film cuts us off from the actually somewhat interesting critique that the rest of the film begins to make.

Nonetheless, I do think it's an interesting film for the ways in which it attempts to engage these questions, and it's an interesting film BECAUSE I'm able to make these lists... it's ambivalent, pulling in multiple directions, but it's wrestling with them, and I like that a lot. To further discuss this, I want to talk about Nick Fury's journey through the film and how he represents Shield and Hydra simultaneously.

Nick Fury, Nick Fury, and Steve Rogers

I was very interested to see how much depth and complexity was given to Nick Fury in this film, because I never felt like any other Marvel film managed to do that at all. The best we get is in Avengers, when he's a perfect but uninteresting encapsulation of the Shouty Black Police Captain. I loved his character in this, and his character arc, and wanted to talk about how important it is for the film as a whole.

When we first see Fury in this film, he's trying to access a file. He uses his authorization: "Fury, Nicholas J." Access is restricted, however. By whom? "Fury, Nicholas J." Right away we are presented with the idea of a Fury working against himself—with the idea that there are two different Nicholas J. Furies, and that they are in conflict. This is how far the "compartmentalization" of Shield goes: Nick has compartmentalized some things so that he himself isn't able to see them. Nick—who is always called Nick by everyone in the film, which I was very happy to see—is divided against himself. Nick wants access to information, and Nick wants to deny access to information. He is the desire for knowledge and the desire to keep that knowledge hidden.

It's not going too far to say that, in Nick's character arc, we see the entire thematic structure of the film laid out.

Because here's what happens to Nicholas J. Fury: he sides, at the end, with Steve Rogers.

Nick is, in a way, Alexander Pierce's mentor, and teaches him that expediency is better than due process or authorization, and that you yourself should be the arbiter of what requires expediency. Nick is proud to show off the new helicarriers, which can take out "1000 hostiles per minute"—*hostiles*, that horrifying and dehumanizing language that allows people to be proud of being able to kill so many humans at once. Nick calls Steve "the greatest soldier in history", and Steve points out that soldiers trust each other—"that's what makes it an army, not a bunch of guys running around shooting guns." Nick, the greatest spy in history, replies: "the last time I trusted someone, I lost an eye."

Nick, who doesn't trust Steve (he has his apartment bugged) and who trusts Steve more than anyone (he's the person Nick goes to when he's on the run) eventually has to make a choice, in this film, about whether to be a soldier or a spy, whether to be a guy running around shooting guns or a guy who's willing to trust others. These are the two Nicholas J. Furies: the one who shares, who trusts, who is horrified by Pierce's actions, and the one who kills hostiles, compartmentalizes, and is part of Pierce's supervillain origin story.

I'm not wild about "soldier" being such an unproblematically positive term in this film—Sam uses it too, at the end, when he calls himself "more of a soldier than a spy"—but I do like the way Nick's character arc foregrounds and problematizes the issue of trust.

Because "soldiers trust each other" isn't just something Steve says because it helps unit cohesion: it's part of what makes Steve a good person. He's not stupid, and he's not naive, but he does trust people, even when he doesn't know if his trust is well-placed. Steve telling Natasha that he trusts her is one of the key moments between them, and is about him seeing that she's got her own set of principles that she follows, even if they're not the same as his. Steve's big speech on the helicarrier is about trust: about giving the Shield agents all the information he has, and trusting them to take the right action. It's about trusting that one terrified agent, the one with his finger on the button: trusting him to make the right decision. Steve throws himself off of high places and he trusts that he's going to land soft: this is not because he's never landed hard, but because he needs to trust in order to be able to function in the world and make it better. In this context, Steve's trust is what drives the whistleblowing/anti-surveillance plot at the end: Natasha is going to give the information to the world, rather than treating human beings like stupid, naive cattle. She trusts people to make rational decisions based on that information, rather than keeping it from them "for their own good" or "in order to avoid mass panic" or whatever the usual superhero reasons are. Natasha Romanov, that one guy with his finger on the button, every citizen on Earth: Steve Rogers gives his trust to all of them.

Steve and Nick are together at the beginning of the film, arguing; Steve tells Nick that he needs to trust, and Nick tells Steve that he has to get with the program, and Steve's response does for both of them: "Don't hold your breath." But at the end of the film, they both have to decide whether to trust, or whether to strike out in anger and fear. Steve's test is with Bucky, and it absolutely breaks my heart, because it's clear that Steve is willing and able to kill Bucky if he has to, to save millions of lives. He'll do it if he has no other choice. But as soon as his obligation is fulfilled, as soon as he's got the microchip thing doing whatever, Steve refuses to fight. Steve is both the good soldier who does his duty and sacrifices himself—sacrifices his best friend—and the conscientious objector, who lies passively and refuses to fight, because once it's his choice, he can't bear to kill Bucky. He trusts Bucky instead, and his trust saves Bucky just as it saves everyone else. Steve doesn't force you to do what he wants: he asks you to make the right choice, and is willing to die to give you that choice.

Meanwhile, Nick Fury's ability to trust is tested as well, and he too has to choose between anger and fear and trust and sacrifice. Pierce asks him if he has the courage to take the next step, and Nick says no, "I have the courage not to." And Nick chooses to give up on compartmentalization and de-encrypt the file to give it to the world.

Nicholas J. Fury, as it turns out, is still capable of trust. We thought he had lost his trust, as we thought he had lost his eye, but it turns out that they're both still there, and that Nick is still willing to expose that part of himself, to be vulnerable enough to trust, to remove his eyepatch. The last time I trusted someone, I lost an eye, Nick says, except it's not really true. His trust, like his eye, is damaged but intact. And thus Nick has two retinal scans, because he is a Nicholas J. Fury divided against himself, but when he moves his eyepatch away and exposes his second eye, his second self, he chooses to be the Nicholas J. Fury who can trust, who can throw himself off of high places and hope he lands soft. Who doesn't compartmentalize. Who, we hope, sees the utter horror in building a machine that can kill up to 1000 human beings per minute.

And in the end, that's the Nick who burns it all down.

At the end, Nick's eyepatch is gone: he's not compartmentalized anymore, an outer cynical Nick and a hidden trusting Nick. He's resolved that conflict within himself, become part of a team with Natasha, Steve, and Sam, and the Nick we saw at the beginning of the film—the Nick who hasn't trusted anyone since that time he lost an eye—is dead. Seriously, he's dead, and we go to his graveside. "If anyone asks for me," Nick tells Steve and Sam, "tell them I'm right here." And he points to his grave: Nicholas J. Fury, "The path of the righteous man..." Ezekiel 25.17. This is a hilarious reference to Samuel L. Jackson's role in *Pulp Fiction*, of course (and I just read an interview with Sam Jackson a couple weeks ago where he talks about how he still does that speech once or twice a week, just because nobody believes that he still knows the whole thing). So, it's a funny reference, a cute little intertext for the sharp-eyed fan, like the light-saber at the end of the car chase scene. But, for reals, let's look at Samuel L. Jackson's speech in *Pulp Fiction*, the speech his character gives before he kills someone, then reconsiders at the end:

> Ezekiel 25:17. 'The path of the righteous man is beset on all sides by the inequities of the selfish and the tyranny of evil men. Blessed is he who, in the name of charity and good will, shepherds the weak through the valley of the darkness. For he is truly his brother's keeper and the finder of lost children. And I will strike down upon thee with great vengeance and furious anger those who attempt to poison and destroy my brothers. And you will know I am the Lord when I lay my vengeance upon you.' I been sayin' that shit for years. And if you ever heard it, it meant your ass. I never really questioned what it meant. I thought it was just a cold-blooded thing to say to a motherfucker before you popped a cap in his ass. But I saw some shit this mornin' made me think twice. Now I'm thinkin': it could mean you're the evil man. And I'm the righteous man. And Mr. .45 here, he's the shepherd protecting my righteous ass in the valley of darkness. Or it could be you're the righteous man and I'm the shepherd and it's the world that's evil and selfish. I'd like that. But that shit ain't the truth. The truth is you're the weak. And I'm the tyranny of evil men. But I'm tryin, Ringo. I'm tryin' real hard to be the shepherd. He became the shepherd instead of the vengeance.

And that is, seriously and truthfully, the story of Nicholas J. Fury: he's trying real hard to be the shepherd, to become the shepherd instead of the vengeance. To become Nick—what everyone, very carefully, calls him all through this film—rather than Fury (great vengeance and furious anger). He's trying to recognize himself as a force for tyranny, and change himself into a force for compassion, and it's a hard road. For me, this lends a lot of strength and credence to the idea that Shield—and, by extension, America—is the real villain in this film, because Fury's journey encourages us all to see ourselves for tyrants and shape ourselves into shepherds, rather than pretending that the tyrants always come here from outside.

It's a cute little reference, but it's also, really, the entire film.
I'm the tyranny of evil men.

This article first appeared on *hypothetically speaking* on April 9, 2014.
thingswithwings.dreamwidth.org/213279.html

PAIN, PERSONHOOD, AND PARITY: THE DEPICTION OF BUCKY BARNES IN THE MARVEL CINEMATIC UNIVERSE

Sara L. Sumpter

This essay contains multiple spoilers for the ending of *Captain America: The Winter Soldier*. If you have not yet seen the film, please proceed at your own risk.

Prologue

The day before I went to see *Captain America: The Winter Soldier* for the fifth time, I spent an afternoon in the park with one of my closest friends and her two-year-old son, Son'eu. As we wandered the pathways of the vast gardens of the Hama Rikyū Park, my friend and I took turns running herd on Son'eu—who at two is a bundle of seemingly unlimited energy and endlessly varied short-term interests. Over and over again, we chased him away from steep precipices, pulled him back from the water's edge, and got him down from an assortment of dangerously high (for a two-year-old) places. We also spent a considerable amount of time picking up after him.

It was this act of picking-up-after that stuck with me during my viewing of *The Winter Soldier* the following day. The behavior of the Winter Soldier character reminded me strongly of Son'eu; for Son'eu is at that stage in life when anytime he finishes with something (in the case of our most recent outing, a partially-drunk mango smoothie), he drops it on the ground and walks away. It does not matter if the thing in question has been finished; if he is finished with it, he drops it on the ground and walks away. And we pick up the pieces.

Throughout the film, the Winter Soldier displays this pattern of behavior. He drops every single weapon that comes into his hands, and it does not matter if the weapon itself retains its usefulness. It does not matter if the gun's clip is empty or still loaded with bullets; if the Winter Soldier is done with it, he drops it and moves on to something else. He picks up or pulls out a weapon, uses it for as long as it engages his attention, and tosses it aside in favor of something new. It is an exceptionally childlike action.

There has been a lot of commentary written about the Winter Soldier/Bucky Barnes in the month since the film was released in the US, and much of it has characterized his actions as those of a dog or an animal, but I believe that what he really is is a child caught in the formative stages of personality development.[1] A number of his exhibited behaviors suggest this: his habit of dropping things when he no longer needs or wants them—child; his tendency to become frustrated and erratic when something does not go as he expects—child; his kneejerk rejection of Steve Rogers' attempts to help him (even though deep down he senses that Steve is committed to, and working for, his best good)—child.

The Winter Soldier is a dangerous child having a lethal temper-tantrum all the way through this film. He is a two-year-old dropping half-empty mango smoothies on the ground when he is done with them. He is a little boy trying desperately not to cry.

Part One: Pain and Personhood

The emotionally regressed state of the Winter Soldier is understandable in light of how often he is implied to have undergone repeated mental conditioning. According to the original comics (and supported by the hints given in the film), the Winter Soldier was given a memory wipe to ensure compliance every single time his handlers woke him up out of cryo-sleep. He then spent a few days awake on a mission and was immediately put back to sleep after the completion of that mission. That sleep was presumably not restorative. After all, the cryo-stasis prevented his body from aging; it also therefore probably prevented his brain from doing the necessary mental repair-work that only happens while the body is in a true, deep sleep. When we consider that the Winter Soldier had his memory wiped before every mission, and that he had at least twenty-five missions that the intelligence community knew of, that is a serious, serious number of mental reconditioning procedures over a relatively short—from the Winter Soldier's perspective—period of time. It is little wonder then that his emotional baseline is that of a small child.

The artificially-induced childlike quality of the Winter Soldier's personality gives a whole new meaning to the micro-expressions of actor Sebastian Stan—particularly during the bank vault scene with Alexander Pierce (portrayed by screen-legend Robert Redford). The way the Winter Soldier zeroes in on Pierce after Pierce sits down in front of him is reminiscent of the way a child will focus on a teacher or parent during story hour, and the manner in which he presses his lips together after his second assertion that he knew Steve Rogers ("But I knew him!") recalls a child fighting back tears because he knows that if he wants to cry, Pierce will give him something to really cry about. However, the emotional state that has been produced in the Winter Soldier by the repeated experience of mental and physical pain goes far beyond regression to childhood and into the realm of near-personlessness.

In her book *The Body in Pain: The Making and Unmaking of the World*, literary theorist Elaine Scarry argues that pain—both physical and mental—has the power to destroy the human capacity for speech.[2] Humans scream,

---

1 For the purposes of this essay, I will distinguish sharply between the Winter Soldier and Bucky Barnes—for while it is true that the Winter Soldier is Bucky Barnes, Bucky Barnes *is not* the Winter Soldier, and this dichotomy lies at the heart of the characters' emotional struggle.

2 Elaine Scarry, *The Body in Pain: The Making and Unmaking of the World* (Oxford: Oxford University Press, 1985).

shriek, or shout rather than speak when they suffer severe bodily or emotional pain because that experience of pain has eradicated their ability to respond verbally. This description perfectly summarizes the situation of the Winter Soldier, who through his repeated mental conditioning is in a constant state of pain, and this aspect of the Winter Soldier's character is expressed in three different ways in the film: through his silence, through his use of (to an English-speaking audience) a foreign language, and through the presence of a specific musical cue in the film's score.

The Winter Soldier is a person whose identity has been obliterated by pain—a pain that has destroyed almost every last vestige of his personhood. It is for this reason that he almost never speaks. His lack of speech is emblematic of his lack of personhood, and this is reiterated a) by the fact that no one in the film—other than Alexander Pierce and Steve Rogers—speaks to him, and b) by the fact that he does not speak in English (his body's native tongue) to anyone in the film—other than Alexander Pierce and Steve Rogers. Furthermore, the Winter Soldier's lack of personhood—grounded in an intense internalized emotional pain—is symbolically expressed through Henry Jackman's brilliant "Winter Soldier Theme", which is primarily characterized by the reoccurring presence of a piercing, metallic scream—a scream that is positively visceral, expressive of a tremendous amount of pain, panic, and fear. Brutal and brutalizing, the theme impacts the listener on a palpable, instinctive, organic level, giving sonic form to the blank, numbness inside the Winter Soldier's mind.

This wordless wail—sometimes shrieking, sometimes droning—plays every time that the Winter Soldier is present on screen and functions as an articulation of the Winter Soldier's status as a person whose self has been so fundamentally damaged by pain that he cannot and does not speak, or cannot and does not speak in a language that is not inherently othering.[3] Thus, the moments when the Winter Soldier speaks in Bucky Barnes' native tongue—even when he speaks in anger—are those when the personality of Bucky Barnes is most present.

All of the conversations that the Winter Soldier has in the film are about self. When the Winter Soldier tells Alexander Pierce that he knew the man on the bridge, he is not just seeking to have a suspicion confirmed—he is asking Pierce to affirm his personhood. He is asking to be acknowledged as an identity—as a self. He is begging Pierce for this, and Pierce will not give it to him. Pierce will not affirm his personhood, as allowing the Winter Soldier personhood would directly conflict with HYDRA's project of using him as a weapon. By contrast, Steve Rogers consistently affirms his personhood, referring to the Winter Soldier by name—as opposed to referring to him as an object or a pronoun—and speaking to him of specific shared past experience. It is this treatment of the Winter Soldier as a person, as Bucky Barnes, that directly contributes to his recovery of a sense of identity—both during the fight in the street and during the fight on the helicarrier. Over and above what the Winter Soldier feels for Steve Rogers is what Steve makes him feel about himself—namely, that he has a self that must be found.

---

3 It does not, however, play when Bucky Barnes is present and attempting to manifest.

In a film that is all about choice, the characterization of the Winter Soldier as a person made devoid of self through the infliction of pain drives home the idea that choice is not possible without identity.[4] As a person denied personhood, the Winter Soldier cannot choose anything, and the moments when he attempts to do so constitute the heart and soul of the film—functioning as an emblem of the stolen choice that HYDRA plans to foist upon the world in its entirety through the implementation of Project Insight.

Part Two: Mirroring and Inversion

The droning iteration of the "Winter Soldier Theme"'s wordless wail can be heard at several key points in the film: during the introduction of the character when he attacks Nick Fury on the streets of Washington, D.C.; during the rooftop confrontation between him and Steve Rogers after Fury's "assassination"; during the bank vault scene when he sits in a stupor while recalling fragments of his past life; and—significantly—during Steve Rogers' apprehension by Brock Rumlow and the HYDRA S.T.R.I.K.E. team after Steve has realized for the first time that the Winter Soldier is Bucky Barnes. Here again, the music functions as a symbolic articulation of internalized pain that is now expanded to include the pain that Steve Rogers feels and which has become so extreme that he, too, is temporarily rendered speechless—an emotional state interpreted with beautiful subtlety by Chris Evans, who shines in this moment.

The parity between the internalized pain of the Winter Soldier and Steve Rogers is no accident. Indeed, it is one of the many examples of the ways in which their experiences mirror, or function as inversions of, one another. Obvious inverted parallels can be found in the manner in which both Steve Rogers and Bucky Barnes have been transformed into super soldiers—one because of a willing sacrifice and the other because of a coerced participation—and in the way they each represent two sides of the same war-torn coin. While Steve Rogers stands as the shining ideal, Bucky Barnes skulks as the seedy, though pragmatic, reality—a reality taken to horrifyingly efficient extremes in the Winter Soldier—and this mirroring between the two characters was clear even in *Captain America: The First Avenger*.

The inverted parallels of Steve Rogers and the Winter Soldier/Bucky Barnes' experiences unfold across a vast expanse of time, serving as a frame for their interactions. Bucky's exit from the narrative of *The First Avenger* begins during the mission to capture Zola, when he fails to deflect a power blast fired by a HYDRA operative with Steve's shield and is thrown from a compartment of the moving train where the mission is taking place. Not coincidentally, the Winter Soldier's entrance into the narrative of *The Winter Soldier* effectively begins when he, a HYDRA operative, fires a grenade whose impact Steve fails to deflect with his shield, thus resulting in his being thrown from the overpass where the assault is taking place.[5] Though Steve cannot

---

4 The theme of choice is so central to the storyline that composer Henry Jackman created a motif to symbolize the moments when a character faces a choice and orchestrated the motif differently depending on the emotional tenor of the situation surrounding the choice. It can be heard during "Fallen," "Taking a Stand," "Natasha," "Time to Suit Up," and—most strikingly—"The End of the Line," when the Winter Soldier makes the choice to pull Steve Rogers out of the Potomac River and thus save his life.

5 I consider the overpass battle sequence to be the effective entrance of the Winter Soldier into the narrative

know it at the time, his mirrored reiteration of the fall of Bucky Barnes marks the starting point of a cyclical journey, in which Steve and the Winter Soldier will ultimately be forced to relive the circumstances of their past tragedy—the moment in time where one of them falls to their "death" while the other one watches, helplessly, until they cannot watch any longer.

The final confrontation of *The Winter Soldier* does not, however, merely culminate in an inverted parallel of Bucky and Steve's physical falls. It also culminates in an inverted reenactment of an even earlier, psychological fall—Steve's descent into depression and loss over the death of his mother. It is highly significant that the memory that comes to Steve's mind in the moments before the assault on the helicarriers is the memory of Bucky's support of him through the death of his mother. It represents a time in his life when Steve was in a dark place—so dark and so alone that he did not want Bucky's help. But Bucky would not back down. Bucky was there for him even when he could not bring himself to reach out for the help that he desperately needed. This is what Steve meant when he remarked, in the S.T.R.I.K.E. team transport after confronting the Winter Soldier face to face for the first time, that even when he had nothing he had Bucky. He was thinking about that specific moment in time, and he was thinking about it because it was a defining moment in their friendship. Now the situation is reversed, and it is Bucky in the dark place—so dark and so alone that he does not want (or cannot accept) Steve's help, though he desperately needs it. And Steve cannot back down because this is another defining moment in their friendship.

Though the roles of Steve Rogers and the Winter Soldier/Bucky Barnes have been reversed—with Steve now reaching out to pull his friend up from the darkness of emotional isolation—in their final moments, as the remnants of the Insight helicarriers crash down around them, it is both men who act to save one another. The Winter Soldier does not understand it, but Bucky Barnes has always been the person who waded into the water to pull Steve Rogers out when he got in too deep, and he cannot do anything less in this moment. Recalled to his sense of self through Steve's consistent linguistic affirmation of his identity and faced with a set of circumstances that he has lived through before more than once, the Winter Soldier can at last choose to act upon the information he has been given—not because he has been ordered to, but because he *himself* wants to. It is his complementary act to save Steve—reflective of the same bravery that Steve has shown to him—that marks the first step on the path to the reclamation of his personhood and agency. Reunited with a sense of self, the Winter Soldier is at last free to act selflessly.

Epilogue

Much has been made of the fact that Bucky Barnes is one of the few people to recognize the greatness in Steve Rogers before his transformation into Captain America. Much has also been made of the fact that, in *The First Avenger*, Bucky demonstrably feels conflicted about that transformation. Less noted, however, is how Bucky's sense of conflict and resentment—and

of the film. Though he appears briefly in scenes prior to this one, and though he has previously been discussed in the abstract by other characters, he does not—in my opinion—have a concrete, effective role until this point.

the way he dealt with those feelings—reveals the kind of person he truly is. The narrative motif of the man who can recognize greatness in another but not attain it himself, and who is therefore corrupted by his resentment, is a classic trope. It appears in such literary masterpieces as Dumas' *The Count of Monte Cristo*, Melville's *Billy Budd*, and Schaefer's *Amadeus*. However, the story of Bucky Barnes is one of a man who recognizes a greatness he cannot himself achieve and is not corrupted by that recognition. Unlike the villains of the above-mentioned tales, Bucky Barnes comes to terms with the situation, choosing friendship over envy—and heroism over villainy—something that suggests a greatness within Bucky Barnes that Bucky himself is not aware of. But Steve Rogers, of course, is. Just as Bucky is one of the few people to recognize Steve's greatness; Steve is one of the few people to recognize Bucky's. Both of them know each other better than they know themselves, and it is that parallel knowledge that ultimately saves them both.

In our last glimpse of the Winter Soldier, in the final post-credits scene, he both does and does not look different. He wears civilian clothing, having no doubt dropped his old uniform somewhere, but he remains cloaked in a mantle of silence. He is still caught in the throes of his experience of pain as he stares—dumbfounded—at an museum exhibit about the life of Bucky Barnes. As he stares, the musical motif of the mechanical scream builds once more into a high-pitched frenzy, shrieking out in a final burst of dissonant noise that signals to the audience that—in spite of the fact that the Winter Soldier ultimately decided to save Steve Rogers' life—Bucky Barnes has not yet recovered from his mental conditioning, and the Winter Soldier is at a loss as to what to do as a result. The Winter Soldier has dropped everything on the ground and walked away, and it is up to Bucky Barnes—and those who love him—to pick up the pieces.

This article first appeared on *Sara Reads* on May 11, 2014.
sechan19.blogspot.com/2014/05/pain-personhood-and-parity-depiction-of.html

EVERY REVIEW OF BLACK WIDOW IN 'CAPTAIN AMERICA' IS WRONG

Gavia Baker-Whitelaw

As a pop culture fan, you get used to the fact that mainstream critics are rarely going to share your glowing adoration of trashy entertainment. Justin Bieber albums may sell like hotcakes, but that's not because they get good reviews.

For me, it's superhero movies. The genre may have come a long way over the past decade or so, but most film critics are still less than thrilled to evaluate the latest installment of Wolverine Punches the Bad Guy. Luckily, it's no skin off my back if some middle-aged dude at the *New York Times* can't tell the difference between Quicksilver and The Flash.

The divide between fans and critics only becomes a problem when I notice professional reviewers making judgments based on their own preconceptions, rather than what actually took place onscreen. There is no better example of this than the ongoing coverage of Scarlett Johansson's role as Black Widow in *The Avengers* franchise. Regardless of what ScarJo says, does, or wears while playing this character, countless well-respected film critics continue to mistake her for a vacuous 1960s Bond Girl.

According to the *Guardian's* early review of *Captain America: The Winter Soldier*, it's the first time Black Widow has got to be an "actual character" rather than a "voluptuous female mascot."[1] Unfortunately, chief *Guardian* critic Peter Bradshaw's follow-up was a little less sure of this, with Black Widow then being described as a "leather-clad [...] ass-kicking ex-Soviet adventuress whose auburn hairstyle is matched by her distinctive fake tan-type maquillage and restrained ochre lipstick."[2]

I'm glad he told us about her makeup routine, because otherwise that description would teach us next to nothing about her character.

In the *Independent*, Black Widow is a "sultry femme fatale", although the *Telegraph* gives her the inaccurate but far more positive rating of "the most (the first?) complex female role in the *Avengers* franchise to date."[3] Apparently he failed to notice Pepper Potts (40-year-old tech company CEO), the four central female characters of the *Thor* movies, Peggy Carter (World War II intelligence agent), Maria Hill (deputy director of an international spy agency), and half the main cast of *Agents of S.H.I.E.L.D.*

1 http://www.theguardian.com/film/2014/mar/20/captain-america-the-winter-soldier-first-look-review
2 http://www.theguardian.com/film/2014/mar/27/captain-america-the-winter-soldier-review-marvel
3 http://www.independent.co.uk/arts-entertainment/films/reviews/captain-america-the-winter-soldier-film-review-a-dramatic-shakeup-for-marvels-big-boy-scout-9220052.html
http://www.telegraph.co.uk/culture/film/filmreviews/10712254/Captain-America-The-Winter-Soldier-review.html

This is just a casual look at some of the newspaper reviews in the UK, where *Captain America: The Winter Soldier* has already been out for a week. When the movie is released in the U.S. on April 4, you can expect more of the same from American reviewers. The general consensus so far is that Black Widow, a character who receives almost as much screentime as Captain America himself, is only worth describing in terms of her appearance, and then only for about one sentence in a multi-paragraph review.

Just for kicks, I took a look at the top reviews for *The Avengers*, to see what America's most acclaimed and respected cinema critics thought of Black Widow back in 2012. Bear in mind that most of these quotes are the only description of Scarlett Johansson's performance in the entire review.

In the *New Yorker*, Anthony Lane wrote, "not to be left out, Black Widow repels invading aliens through the sheer force of her corsetry," while the *Wall Street Journal*'s Pulitzer-winning Joe Morgenstern complained, "Black Widow spends lots of time looking puzzled or confused."[4] *New York Times* reviewer A.O. Scott referenced the 1960s British spy series *The Avengers* (no relation), writing, "those poor souls who cherish old daydreams of Diana Rigg in leather will have to console themselves with images of Scarlett Johansson in a black bodysuit."[5]

The *Chicago Tribune*'s Michael Phillips went for that old favorite, "leather-clad", while *Salon*'s Andrew O'Hehir didn't even bother to beat around the bush, describing, "Scarlett Johansson in a catsuit [...] cocking her head just so as if to acknowledge that she's the idealized fetish object of the 11-year-old boy within every so-called adult male."[6] *Idealized fetish object.*

Time Out didn't even bother referring to Black Widow by name, joking that Johansson's superhero persona was "Distracting Catsuit."[7] By comparison, the comments from the *Hollywood Reporter* ("a sultry, scarlet-haired assassin") and *Village Voice* ("ass-kicking all-purpose Girl Friday") seem positively feminist.[8]

If you feel like playing film critic misogyny bingo when America's first round of *Winter Soldier* reviews are published this week, I recommend looking out for the phrases "leather-clad" and "ass-kicker." These are an easy way to weed out any reviewers who weren't paying attention to the movie, because neither phrase describes Black Widow's actual role.

For one thing, Black Widow is not "leather-clad." Not unless you're talking about the casual leather jacket she wears in a handful of scenes, anyway. Her official uniform is no tighter than Captain America's was in *The Avengers*, and is similar to S.H.I.E.L.D.'s artificial fabric jumpsuits.[9] By comparison, the Winter Soldier's signature look involves leather body armor, '90s grunge hair, smudged eyeliner, and a black rubber mask.

4 http://www.newyorker.com/arts/critics/cinema/2012/05/14/120514crci_cinema_lane and http://www.wsj.com/news/articles/SB10001424052702303916904577378881752158826
5 http://www.nytimes.com/2012/05/04/movies/robert-downey-jr-in-the-avengers-directed-by-joss-whedon.html and http://en.wikipedia.org/wiki/The_Avengers_%28TV_series%29
6 http://www.chicagotribune.com/entertainment/movies/sc-mov-0501-avengers-20120502,0,2194875.column and http://www.salon.com/2012/05/02/the_avengers_will_superhero_movies_never_end/
7 http://www.timeout.com/us/film/the-avengers
8 http://www.hollywoodreporter.com/movie/avengers/review/314291 and http://www.villagevoice.com/2012-05-02/film/superheroes-bump-superegos-in-joss-whedon-s-all-star-avengers/
9 http://www.digitalspy.co.uk/movies/i397875-8/the-avengers-rolling-gallery-hawkeye-captain-america-black-widow.html

Spider-Man's spandex costume is probably more salacious, but I'm pretty sure he doesn't wind up being described as an *homme fatale* by anyone with a Pulitzer.

Honestly, this kind of catsuit-focused review says more about the reviewer than the film itself. Apparently the mere concept of Scarlett Johansson in a tight outfit is so dazzlingly erotic that it bypasses some male reviewers' conscious minds and causes them to ignore everything she says and does for the rest of the movie. The result is a series of reviews from highly respected film critics who, given the opportunity to describe each Avenger in a single sentence, replace Black Widow's summary with the announcement, "I AM A HETEROSEXUAL MAN AND SCARLETT JOHANSSON'S BOOBS ARE AWESOME."

Captain America, Thor, and the Winter Soldier have all filmed shirtless scenes (in Thor's case, purely for eye candy purposes on both occasions), and Cap's everyday outfit of choice is a white T-shirt several sizes too small for his bulging torso. Yet oddly enough, reviewers somehow manage to discuss those characters on their own terms, rather than reducing them to their component body parts and costumes.

This unrelenting focus on Scarlett Johansson's appearance, coupled with the assumption that her only non-decorative role is that of an "ass-kicker", indicates a fundamental inability to see Black Widow as the well-rounded character she actually is.

While Johansson's first Marvel appearance in *Iron Man 2* may have relied somewhat upon sex appeal, this was quickly nixed in favor of characterizing her as the most cerebral Avenger. Her most important scenes in *The Avengers* relied upon her intelligence and skills as a spy, to the extent that she even managed to outwit Loki, the God of Lies. At the end of the movie, she's the one who closes the portal that let all the aliens into New York. Then in *Winter Soldier* she's given second billing to Captain America, a meaty role that showcases a wide-ranging skillset that stretches far beyond just "kicking ass." At no point during any of these movies does she seduce anyone, by the way.

Sadly, there's very little sign of this character in the most easily accessible reviews of both *The Avengers* and *Winter Soldier*. Judging by the *Guardian*, *WSJ*, or *New Yorker*, Black Widow is more like a blow-up doll with a black belt. By their logic, if she's wearing a tight outfit, then she must be a sexy ass-kicker, meaning that she must be the token female character, and therefore is little more than eye candy.

With that thought process in mind, it must make perfect sense to relegate Black Widow to a single sniggering comment about her catsuit, because obviously Scarlett Johansson is just there for decoration. And if you've read in the *New York Times* that Black Widow is a token female character, then chances are you'll have internalized that opinion before you even buy a ticket. The feedback loop of misogynist preconceptions continues on, and in the end, we all lose out.

In geek culture circles, Marvel Studios is known for producing the most progressive of summer blockbuster franchises, coming out ahead of DC adaptations (*Batman* and *Superman*), the *Star Trek* reboot series, and Sony's

Spider-Man movies.[10] They've achieved this status on the comparatively unimpressive grounds that each Marvel Studios movie includes at least one three-dimensional female character who isn't a damsel in distress or the dreaded leather-clad ass-kicker. Yet the prevailing assumption among professional critics is still that any woman in a superhero movie falls into one of those two categories.

Pepper Potts is only seen as Tony Stark's "equal" once she puts on the Iron Man armor in *Iron Man 3*. Black Widow is a "voluptuous mascot" because Scarlett Johansson is an attractive woman. Natalie Portman's Jane Foster got relatively good reviews for *Thor* because she's a scientist who wears plaid shirts and sensible shoes, but then she wound up being heavily criticized in *Thor: The Dark World* for fainting while terminally ill, because fainting is for damsels.[11] If you're a woman in a superhero movie, you're shit outta luck.

Marvel has spent several years teasing fans with the possibility of a Black Widow solo movie, which Scarlett Johansson has already said she'd be very happy to do.[12] Luckily, she's already well prepared for the inevitable influx of reviews that will expend a paragraph describing her body and "leather" catsuit before moving onto the substance of the film.

In an interview with *Esquire* magazine in 2006, Johansson was already grimly amused by being awarded the dubious honor of being Sexiest Woman Alive.[13] "You work hard making independent films for fourteen years and you get voted Best Breasts," she said. "What about my brain? What about my heart? What about my kidneys and my gallbladder?"

The interviewer, apparently unaware of the irony, followed this up by writing, "There is, no doubt, a fetish Website devoted to Scarlett's gallbladder—which, by the way, fellas, is all natural."

You just can't win.

This article first appeared on *The Daily Dot* on April 2, 2014.
www.dailydot.com/fandom/black-widow-reviews-wrong-captain-america/

---

10 http://www.dailydot.com/opinion/star-trek-into-darkness-too-many-dcks/
11 http://www.nytimes.com/2013/11/08/movies/thor-the-dark-world-brings-back-marvels-alien-superhero.html
12 http://www.dailydot.com/fandom/marvel-black-widow-movie-release-date/
13 http://www.esquire.com/women/the-sexiest-woman-alive/scarlett-johansson-pics

WE ARE SANSA

Anne C. Perry

A few years ago I was on a *Game of Thones* fan panel. The moderator started by asking a pretty standard question—our favourite characte. The answers were pretty standard, too: Tyrion, Arya, Arya, Jon... and then I opened my mouth and I said it. My favourite character is Sansa Stark.

In my memory the room drew back with a collective hiss, but I know it wasn't that bad. A couple did, definitely, but a few others nodded. I wasn't surprised. Sansa's not enormously popular and, at the time, only the first series had aired in the UK; although Sansa had evolved into a much more nuanced and interesting character in the books, many people still only knew her as stuck-up Series 1 Sansa. (And Sansa in the first book/series *is* awful; that's part of what makes her interesting. But we'll get back to that.)

Things took a turn for the worse later, when we were discussing why we like the characters we'd chosen. I argued that Sansa is strong, interesting and well-characterized. The rest of the panel, and some of the audience, took issue with my claim. "She's bitchy! She's spoiled! She just sits around and waits for stuff to happen! She's scared! She's a coward!", came the responses.

"She's *thirteen years old*," I said. "What would *you* have been like in her situation, when *you* were thirteen?"

Someone in the audience bit back. "Arya's only *eight* and *she* doesn't act like that."

And there it is. Fiery independent Arya does the right thing, the heroic thing, the expected thing (for a main character in a fantasy series): she escapes, she vows revenge, she fights back. She does the thing we like to think we'd do, in the same situation. We want to be Arya.

But we aren't Arya.

We are Sansa.

In a way, that audience member proved one of my points for me: the difference in Arya's and Sansa's responses to everything that happens to them is huge, and significant. It's primarily significant of good writing and good characterization. Sansa and Arya two different people who respond to their situations in different ways. And they respond in ways that are *consistent with their characters as previously established*.

To begin with, we can never forget that both characters are the indulged daughters of an *incredibly powerful nobleman*. Sansa is more or less fine with the system because it's set up to benefit her in a way it doesn't and can't benefit 98% of Westeros. Arya may rail against the status quo, but she has the privilege of doing so without serious repercussions. The system, as such, benefits *both* characters, in ways they do and do not immediately appreciate.

Arya, from the beginning of the series, is constantly fighting against that status quo. She doesn't care about pretty dresses and doesn't want to spend her free time learning to embroider. She hasn't got the patience for such activities, much less the desire. She also doesn't want her future to be defined by her role as wife and mother, which are the only viable options she's presented with. And she's *eight* when the book opens; it is entirely believable that an eight-year-old girl wouldn't care about dresses or embroidery, about marriage and family.

Sansa begins the series at age 13, an age when lots—by no means all, but many—young women *do* begin to care about boys and clothes, and start thinking seriously about the future. Importantly, Sansa has no real issue with the status quo. She—being the elder daughter of one of, again, one of the most powerful noblemen in her country—is a beneficiary of the status quo, and she more or less recognizes that fact, and she's content with it.

And Sansa in the first book really *is* difficult. She's established as having an uneasy relationship with Arya to begin with; her decision to side with Joffery following the fight with Mycah drives a wedge between the two that might never be repaired. But she's punished for her decision with Lady's death (which is in itself a significant act) and paid in full for it by the end of *A Game of Thrones*. If indeed one were even tempted to blame her for what she did. Which, of course, any reader *might* be; Arya is so clearly in the right and Sansa so clearly in the wrong that it's easy to forget that a) they're both very young, and b) Sansa is doing *what she believes is right*. But it's also worth noting that Sansa's trying to find a safe middle ground between Arya's position and Joffrey's; to say she can't remember what happened is not an unreasonable effort at compromise.

Sansa takes the side of the man she's going to marry—the future king of Westeros—at her sister's expense, without understanding that Joffrey's behavior during the incident is significant of a deep-seated and dangerous sadism and without knowing that the consequences of her decision will impact her directly. And how could she? How could she know that, by trying to negotiate a middle ground between Joffrey and Arya, her prospective future mother-in-law would demand the death of her own, well-behaved wolf? The incident isn't just the first indication of the danger that Joffrey (and Cersei) pose for Sansa, because they—unlike Sansa—are willing to use the system in which they've been raised to further their own ends. It's significant of the shifting of the balance of power that will follow in further books.

***

A Song of Ice and Fire is, in part, a series of books devoted to examining what happens when systems break down. Arya, who was never comfortable with the Westeros status quo to begin with, is *slightly* better set up to deal with immediate consequences of Ned's execution and everything that follows. Sansa, on the other hand, becomes a prisoner of the chaos that develops around her. She has no coping mechanisms and no fallback position because she's been raised to trust the system that is failing her.

Sansa is regularly told through the first book (and which she tells herself in later books) that "courtesy is a lady's armor." The significance of this single line is enormous; she, as introduced in *A Game of Thrones*, has been trained to operate within a system that encourages and rewards certain behaviour by women. Over the course of the novels, her defences are stripped away—beginning with her dire wolf protector, Lady—(get it? Get it?) and moving deeper and deeper through her family and friends and into her psyche until only a calamitous ruin remains.

A girl who expected to marry a handsome prince, rule a gentle court and be beloved as a kind and generous queen is reduced to a prisoner in a tower, beaten and tormented by her husband-to-be, used as a pawn by everyone else. No prince comes to save her, her eventual husband—to whom she is unwilling married—is the damaged dwarf uncle of her father's murderer. Her knightly protectors are a psychotic monster and a mercenary drunk. The man who masterminds her rescue from King's Landing is a scheming murderer with disturbingly unpaternal feelings for her. Her mother's sister is consumed with irrational jealousy of her. Her parents and one brother are dead, her sister and two brothers have vanished (and are apparently dead), her last brother is stationed an impossible distance from her, her childhood home has been razed to the ground. She's engaged to marry a murderous narcissist, the child of another murderous narcissist, who are between them responsible for the death of everything she's ever known and loved. She is trapped by her circumstances as surely as if she'd been locked in a dungeon. Until she learns to use her history and her knowledge of the system that constrains her, she can have no hope of escaping it.

Arya is well suited to manipulate the system from without, considering her established character, her history and her status as outsider. Sansa is exceptionally well-suited to do the same from within, again considering her character, her history and her status. Every time the system seems to fail Sansa, Sansa survives and adapts. Her survival is passive, especially at the beginning of her story, but her adaptation becomes conscious.

What's fascinating about Sansa's character is how easy she is to underestimate. Although most (if not all) of the characters—and most of the audience—write Sansa off as a victim of circumstances, a not-particularly-clever girl with little agency and no power, she has the potential to become one of the series' more significant characters. Sansa is in the unique position of being completely familiar with the system and therefore has the perspective to operate within—and succeed within—its confines. Only a handful of other characters in the series have a similar perspective and agency; they include Cersei, Tyrion and Littlefinger. All of whom Sansa has spent a significant amount of time with, and all of whom are themselves powerful players in the competition for control of the iron throne because they themselves have been consistently underestimated, and because they themselves consciously manipulate a society that underestimates them.

Sansa is in a precarious, vulnerable position throughout most of the series, both books and television. The tv show emphasizes her vulnerability through the careful manipulation of symbols—her jewellery depicts insects, her clothing is covered in flowers.[1] And not Margaery Tyrell's golden rose belt; no, Sansa's flowers are cloth roses sewn to her neckline, flowers and

---

1 http://clothestomidnight.blogspot.co.uk/2013/06/sansa.html

leaves embroidered on her dresses. Martin employs a different device in the novels to emphasize Sansa's vulnerability; he attaches a number of recognizable fairytale tropes to her, from the princess in the tower to the wicked stepmother to the unnatural father. And then, over the course of the series, he carefully subverts each and every one. In both the television show and the novels, Sansa eventually takes control of her identity and her agency; in the books the process is largely internal as she constructs a new identity for herself, while in the show she finally learns to lie—and does so very effectively—and trades in her delicate fabrics and insect jewellry for a new, more confident and mature personhood.

***

All of which brings me back to my original point. Arya's journey throughout the series—both books and television—is fascinating, and well worth its own explorative essay. But her character is more traditional, and more traditionally escapist, than Sansa's. From the beginning Arya has a strong sense of self, and rails against the same social injustices we'd like to believe we would, in her situation. She rebels against a status quo that doesn't offer her the same opportunities it offers her brothers, despite her desire and her worthiness. When the system breaks down she abandons it entirely. She is the character upon which thousands of epic fantasies have been built. She is the character we want to be.

But Sansa's journey is no less fascinating. She's changing herself from the inside-out, and evolving into a character with the ability and opportunity to effect change from her position within the system. It's unfair of us to compare her to Arya, because they've been very ably developed *from the very beginning* as entirely different characters, who want different things and respond to their situations in very different ways. Where Arya's impulse is to abandon the system that mistreats her, Sansa's is to hide within it, to take what protection from it she can. As Arya begins to understand the power she has as an outsider, Sansa develops an appreciation for the kind of power she has on the inside. Eventually, both will come to learn how to use the system for their own ends.

One of the great fascinations of the series (both iterations) is its yearslong tracking of a number of characters who are trying to reform themselves following a calamitous and ongoing breakdown of the social order. The noble children of Ned and Catlyn Stark are the nearest analogues to our comfortable middle-class selves in the series, which is why they're so important as point-of-view characters: they're the most like us. Their responses track most closely to how we'd like to respond, should our own society begin to fail. If our father was killed by a cruel king, we'd vow revenge, wouldn't we? We'd teach ourselves to fight, wouldn't we? We'd start a war, wouldn't we?

Wouldn't we?

Honestly, probably not. Because we are not Arya.

We are Sansa.
And that's no bad thing.

This article first appeared on *Pornokitsch* on August 6, 2014.
www.pornokitsch.com/2014/08/we-are-sansa.html

WHY IS RUE A LITTLE BLACK GIRL?—THE PROBLEM OF INNOCENCE IN THE DARK FANTASTIC

Ebony Elizabeth Thomas

Author's Note: This post contains racist images and language. Reader discretion is advised.

Part of my job as a children's and young adult literature scholar is to keep up with the best new reads. I began reading Suzanne Collins' Hunger Games books while a graduate student in 2009. I found Katniss' story compelling but familiar. As an avid reader of fantasy and science fiction trilogies, I find that generally the first book hooks me, the second book becomes my favorite, and the finale rounds off the story. *The Hunger Games* was no exception.

When the movie series' first installment premiered, I was not as engaged on social media as I am now. I was facing surgery for a rapidly detaching retina. I was performing the delicate political dance of leaving one tenure track position for another. And I was wrestling with the emotional angst of moving away from my hometown—and almost everyone I knew—for the first time in my life.

I don't remember much about the spring of 2012. However, I do remember when certain corners of social media collectively decided that it wasn't exactly okay for Rue to be a little Black girl.[1]

First, I begin with a confession: I was bewildered that some readers and fans of *The Hunger Games* didn't pick up on the textual clues that Rue would probably be considered (and treated as) Black if she lived in the contemporary United States. Perhaps it's because I am so used to searching for traces of myself any way that I can in a story (including reading White characters described as "dark" as dark-skinned when I was a child!). I have long been clued into science fiction and fantasy writers' myriad ways of signaling non-White characters, many of them problematic. So I was thrilled to see Collins' attempts to subvert these troubling conventions. Of course, there's a fine line between subversion and creating a magical Negro character, but I felt that the author walked it better than some when it came to Rue.[2]

Many read Katniss, the protagonist of the series, as the symbolic mockingjay. In the larger narrative, she evolves into the symbol of the rebellion

---

1 http://www.newyorker.com/books/page-turner/white-until-proven-black-imagining-race-in-hunger-games
2 http://tvtropes.org/pmwiki/pmwiki.php/Main/MagicalNegro

against the Capital. However, in a very real sense, Rue was, and is, the mockingjay.

I can't help but hear echoes of Harper Lee's essential *To Kill a Mockingbird* in the name Collins created for her fictional avian symbol. Apparently, I am not alone.[3] Birds in religion, myth, and folklore can symbolize any number of things: the soul, paradise, metamorphosis or transformation, beauty, vulnerability, dreams and the afterlife, omens, flight or escape—just to list a few. Some birds are considered noble and majestic (the eagle), while others are are silly or absurd (usually the flightless ones, like the extinct dodo). Still others symbolize peace (doves), humility (sparrows), predation (hawks), fear (ravens and owls), or opportunism (vultures).

> Atticus said to Jem one day, "I'd rather you shot at tin cans in the backyard, but I know you'll go after birds. Shoot all the blue jays you want, if you can hit 'em, but remember it's a sin to kill a mockingbird." That was the only time I ever heard Atticus say it was a sin to do something, and I asked Miss Maudie about it. "Your father's right," she said. "Mockingbirds don't do one thing except make music for us to enjoy. They don't eat up people's gardens, don't nest in corn cribs, they don't do one thing but sing their hearts out for us. That's why it's a sin to kill a mockingbird." - Harper Lee, *To Kill a Mockingbird*

The mockingbird is a symbol of innocence for all the reasons that Atticus Finch states. Notice that the mockingbirds, who sing sweetly, are contrasted with blue jays, whose calls are more jarring. Just as the doomed mockingbird, Tom Robinson, is the central symbol of Harper Lee's classic, Rue from District 11 *is* the doomed mockingjay of the Games.

So if Rue is the mockingjay, what is the problem?

The problem with innocence in the dark fantastic is that in the collective popular imagination, a dark-skinned character can't be innocent on his or her own. Harvard professor Robin Bernstein traces the origins of racial innocence to before the Civil War in her award-winning book *Racial Innocence: Performing American Childhood from Slavery to Civil Rights.*

> In the late eighteenth and early nineteenth century... a competing doctrine entered popular consciousness. In this emergent view, children were innocent: that is, sinless, absent of sexual feelings, and oblivious to worldly concerns... Childhood was then understood not as innocent but as innocence itself; not as a symbol of innocence but as its embodiment... This innocence was raced white (Bernstein 4).

I strongly recommend Bernstein's book, in which she traces repertoires of performed racial innocence to the first instances where "angelic white children were contrasted with [black] pickaninnies so grotesque as to suggest that only white children *were* children" (Bernstein 16). If this is quite shocking to you, and you are under 50, please realize that quite a bit of the children's

---

3 http://www.philly.com/philly/blogs/entertainment/movies/To-Kill-a-Mockingjay-Was-Suzanne-Collins-Hunger-Games-dreamed-up-while-watching-Gregory-PeckHarper-Lee-classic.html

and young adult literature you know has been carefully edited and chosen since the 1960s to reflect changing social sensibilities. When I became a kidlit scholar, I was quite horrified to learn about the original Oompa-Loompas from Roald Dahl's *Charlie and the Chocolate Factory.*[4]

Roald Dahl was one of my favorite children's authors growing up, but speaking with some of those who worked with him and edited him, his views on people of color and women were problematic.[5] Even Dr. Seuss, as Philip Nel has recently written, was not immune.[6]

No matter how progressive, liberal, or politically and socially astute we think we have become, everyone living in the United States (and elsewhere, for Dahl was certainly not American) has been affected by ideas about *which* children can be—and cannot be—viewed as innocent. Of course, in the Enlightenment, and afterward, there are examples of dark-skinned peoples being viewed as noble savages. However, the prevailing cultural script that has been handed down over the generations is that *some children are more innocent than others*. We notice this, but we are not encouraged to speak it aloud, because **the construction of childhood innocence on foundations of race is something that is implied but never spoken**, lest we offend others. As Robin DiAngelo and Ozlem Sensoy note:

> "...When confronted with the history of colonialism and racism and its effects on racialized people, Whites tend to claim racial innocence and take up the role of admirer or moral helper... Challenging White innocence often ignites anger" (DiAngelo and Sensoy 109).[7]

Other scholars have analyzed how racial innocence (and by extension, racial guilt) gets constructed through discourses of schooling, including Michael Dumas, Zeus Leonardo and Ronald K. Porter, and Dorothea Anagnostopoulos, Sakeena Everett, and Carleen Carey.[8] However, I want to extend this empirical work to speculate critically on what might happen as young people read and view narratives of the fantastic.

I believe that Collins' construction of Rue as *the* symbol of innocence meant that some readers automatically imagined her as White. After all, in what universe is an older Black tween innocent? Certainly not in American schools, with the often noted discipline gap.[9] Certainly not in contemporary

---

4 Thomas refers to Faith Jaques' Oompa Loompa illustration for the 1977 British edition of Charlie and the Chocolate Factory, which featured caricatures of Black pygmies in stereotypical "primitive garb." See http://www.roalddahlfans.com/articles/char.php.

5 http://www.philnel.com/2010/09/19/censoring-ideology/

6 http://www.philnel.com/2014/06/22/blackcat/ The line also refers to a 1930s advertisement for Flit, an insect repellant, which was drawn by a then relatively unknown Theodore Seuss Geisel. The ad featured a cartoonishly big-lipped, grass skirt-wearing Friday in conversation with a shipwrecked Robinson Crusoe about the "fearful" flies found on the island. The advertisement was sourced from Business Insider (http://www.businessinsider.com/before-dr-seuss-was-famous-he-drew-these-sad-racist-ads-2012-3?op=1), which acquired the image from UC San Diego's website on Dr. Seuss' advertising artwork (http://libraries.ucsd.edu/speccoll/dsads/).

7 http://www.tandfonline.com/doi/abs/10.1080/13613324.2012.674023#preview

8 http://www.tandfonline.com/doi/abs/10.1080/13613324.2013.850412#preview, http://www.tandfonline.com/doi/abs/10.1080/13613324.2010.482898#preview, http://das.sagepub.com/content/24/2/163.short, http://das.sagepub.com/search?author1=Dorothea+Anagnostopoulos&sortspec=date&submit=Submit

9 http://www.npr.org/templates/story/story.php?storyId=5169996

children's literature, where Black kids and teens are underrepresented... and when they do appear, are sometimes viewed as "unlikeable" or "unrelatable."[10]

Collins also makes the grave mistake of stating from Katniss' point of view that Rue reminds her of her younger sister, Prim. Prim is a much more familiar figure in children's literature—the guileless, golden girl child often is the counterweight that balances the evil that the protagonist must overcome, and *The Hunger Games* is no exception. What is different is that while trapped in the Game, Rue becomes Katniss' Prim, a younger companion who shares in the existential threat until she is overcome by it.

This was too much for some readers to take.[11]

I was pumped about the Hunger Games. Until I learned that a black girl was playing Rue. - @johnnyknoxIV

And for the record, im still pissed that rue is black. Like you think she might have mentioned that...? Is that just me, or... - @LexieBrowning

After watching the hunger games preview 6 times in a row, I realized Rue is black. Whaaaat?! #shocked - @nikki_eggers14

@EmmaAintQuick I know, rue is too black for what I pictured. But Peeta IS nomworthy #nom - @abimaxwell

why is Rue a little black girl? #sticktothebookDUDE @TheHungerGames - @FrankeeFresh

to all my hunger games readers out there: Did anyone picture Rue as being black? No offense or anything but I just didn't see her like it - @lexipaden

HOW IN THE WORLD ARE THEY GOING TO MAKE RUE A FREAKIN BLACK BITCH IN THE MOVIE ?!?!?!???! lolol not to be racist buuuuut.... I'm angry now ;o - @freakinej

@HG_Tweets nah, I just pictured darker skin, didn't really take it all the way to black - @JBanks56

Sense when has Rue been a nigger - @Clif_Ford_Kigar

It gets worse.[12]

"why does rue have to be black not gonna lie kinda ruined the movie."

10 http://www.nytimes.com/2014/03/16/opinion/sunday/the-apartheid-of-childrens-literature.html, http://cynthialeitichsmith.blogspot.com/2013/10/guest-post-sarah-aronson-on-its-okay-if.html and http://www.xojane.com/entertainment/are-black-people-really-not-relatable
11 http://jezebel.com/5896408/racist-hunger-games-fans-dont-care-how-much-money-the-movie-made
12 http://uptownmagazine.com/2012/03/some-racist-hunger-games-fans-are-pissed-the-movie-included-black-people/

> "Kk call me racist but when I found out Rue was black her death wasn't as sad."

> "why did the producer make all the good characters black"

And worse.[13]

> @HausOfCaitlyn some ugly little girl with nappy add hair. Pissed me off. She was supposed to be cute and at least remind her of Prim! - @GagasAlexander

> Awkward moment when Rue is some black girl and not the little blonde innocent girl you picture @EganMcCoy - @sw4q

But Collins' text just doesn't give these young readers a way out. During the heat of reader and fandom debates, Adam of the Hunger Games Tweets Tumblr, the helpful fan who originally compiled some of these responses helpfully screen-capped places in *The Hunger Games* where the physical features of the District 11 tributes (Rue and Thresh) are explicitly described.[14]

> *The boy tribute from District 11, Thresh, has the same dark skin as Rue, but the resemblance stops there.* He's one of the giants, probably six and a half feet tall and built like an ox, but I noticed he rejected the invitations from the Career Tributes to join their crowd. Instead he's been very solitary, speaking to no one, showing little interest in training. Even so, he scored a ten and it's not hard to imagine he impressed the Gamemakers. He ignores Caesar's attempts at banter and answers with a yes or no or just remains silent. If only I was his size, I could...

I am just at the beginning of this side of my work, but after more than 15 years of teaching, writing, and interacting online and in various fandoms, I have found a few things to be true. One of them is the dire consequences that a person of color—or even *a character of color*—faces when he or she steps outside of his or her assigned place, or flips the script in any way.

Another thing that I have found to be true is that essential qualities such as goodness, beauty, innocence and truth have been so often racialized as White in literature and media that ascribing them to other groups is seen as transgressive even when White people are not part of the conversation, the art, or the representation.[15]

Unfortunately, the effects of this racial innocence and threat are not just textual. When Collins' Panem was transmediated from page to screen, young Amandla Stenberg and her costars were targets of this threat.[16]

The idea of Rue as the slain mockingjay—the symbol of purity and innocence—was likely strange, even alien, to some young readers conditioned by the scripts of our society. However, there *is* another tradition where counter-stories of other dark birds have long been told.

13 http://www.businessinsider.com.au/the-hunger-games-were-you-upset-rue-was-black-because-a-lot-of-other-people-are-2012-3
14 http://hungergamestweets.tumblr.com/
15   http://thedarkfantastic.blogspot.com/2014/07/asieybarbies-i-am-beautiful-campaign_6.html
16   http://www.themarysue.com/sad-amandla-stenberg-responds-hunger-games-racism/

In one of these stories, enslaved Africans sprouted wings and flew back to Africa.[17]

In a beloved poem from the most dire years of the nadir period, a caged bird elicited sympathy... and inspired one of the greatest American poets and teachers of the 20th century.[18]

And then, there was a song, a song from a time of freedom, new hopes, and dreams of peace, that imagined what the bird's eye view of one who "soars to the sun and looks down at the sea" might be like.[19]

Finally—for I could go on and on—there is the Sankofa bird, originating with the Akan people of Ghana, and now sacred to people of African descent all over the world—as a poignant reminder of the link between the past and the future.20

I close with the words of Zeus Leonardo and Ronald Porter:

> As Nishitani Osamu observes, race dialogue in mixed-race company works to maintainthe Western distinction between 'anthropos' (the inhuman) and 'humanitas' (the human). Osamu points out, "*anthropos* cannot escape the status of being the object of anthropological knowledge, while *humanitas* is never defined from without but rather expresses itself as the subject of all knowledge." Put another way, race dialogues often maintain the status of whiteness as being both natural and unchanging in the white imaginary... Whiteness is the immovable mover, unmarked marker, and unspoken speaker (Leonardo and Porter 149).[21]

Leonardo and Porter explode the myth that it is possible to be safe in cross-racial dialogues, yet many studies (including my own) have shown the asymmetry of such conversations. As Bernstein notes, "Whiteness [...] derives power from its status as an unmarked category" (Bernstein 7). In order to deconstruct it *and* the role of race in the imagination, lists of multicultural fantasy and science fiction, while extremely important, are not enough. This is why I have not limited my analyses to works by writers of color, although I understand the necessity of promoting underrepresented authors, have done so in other projects, and will continue to do so. In *The Dark Fantastic*, I am interested in the the ways that children's and young adult literature, media, and culture—especially science fiction, fantasy, and fairy tales—inscribe the racial scripts of the world we know onto each generation's collective imagination.

If we don't want our children and teens to automatically assume that Rue is White in spite of a text that states otherwise...

If we find racist Tweets and posts by young people born long after the 1960s to be untenable...

Then we can no longer shrink away from uncomfortable conversations about race in literature, schooling, and society.

We must name, deconstruct, and rethink the very meanings of white and black, light and dark, innocence and evil, human and inhuman in our

17   http://www.scholastic.com/teachers/book/people-could-fly#cart/cleanup
18   http://www.poetryfoundation.org/poem/175756, https://www.goodreads.com/work/quotes/1413589-i-know-why-the-caged-bird-sings
19   http://www.bbc.com/news/magazine-25834460
20   http://www.berea.edu/cgwc/the-power-of-sankofa/
21   http://www.tandfonline.com/doi/abs/10.1080/13613324.2010.482898#preview

imaginations before we can experience true liberation and equality in the realms of the real world.

In Suzanne Collins' *The Hunger Games,* Rue, as the mockingjay, became a symbol of innocence, freedom, equality, and justice for the fictional world of Panem.

Perhaps someday Rue will be universally viewed in the same way in ours.

This article first appeared on *The Dark Fantastic* on July 28, 2014.
thedarkfantastic.blogspot.com/2014/07/why-is-rue-little-black-girl-problem-of.html

NOSTALGIA AS A WEAPON: THE 'SAILOR MOON' RENAISSANCE IS A FEMINIST MISSION BEHIND THE LINES OF POP CULTURE

Juliet Kahn

ailor Moon did not enter my life so much as consume it. I was eight, and in the space of a few weeks I learned all the attack names, bought the first two issues of the manga, went through three different understandings of how to pronounce "Takeuchi", and developed a tiered list of my favorite characters. I spent hours spelunking the MIDI-laden cave that was Geocities, learning the language of dub-versus-sub wars, exploring webrings, indulging in awful pidgin Japanese, and realizing that I was not actually the only person in the world that loved this show. I filled the drawer of my nightstand with printouts of art book pages (I never did anything with them, but they were the most beautiful things I had ever seen and I needed to possess them somehow). I scraped up a special outfit—a white turtleneck and blue pleated skirt, with my hair in pigtails—just to wear while watching the show. Opinions crowded my head, the first ones I'd ever really developed on my own: on translation choices, best and worst story arcs, ideal romantic pairings. I didn't just write Sailor Moon fanfiction—I wrote Sailor Moon *poetry*. It was, by far, the most vivid and vital part of those last few playground years.

Today, *Sailor Moon* is inescapable. There's the new anime of course, and the new musicals, the merchandise, and the retranslation of the manga. But it's the emblem of a wider renaissance as well, a resurgence of love for *mahou shoujo*, or magical girl anime and manga—a movement led by women well out of their childhood years. A quick stroll through Tumblr reveals Sailor Moon cupcakes, punky Sailor Moon jackets, heartfelt essays about what the portrayal of lesbianism in *Sailor Moon* meant to the reader, dozens of artists working together to reanimate an episode of the anime, Sailor Moon nail art tutorials, cats named Luna, Beryl, Haruka and everything in between, hand-sculpted figurines, ornate embroidery projects, and an endless avalanche of fanart. Sailor Moon as an *Adventure Time* character. Sailor Moon cheekily clutching a Hitachi Magic Wand. Sailor Moon as a vicious biker chick.[1] Sailor Moon protesting the Supreme Court's Hobby Lobby ruling.

---

1 http://comicsalliance.com/best-cosplay-ever-this-week-babs-tarr-inspiration-edition-interview/

Sailor Moon fans have not so much rediscovered their love for Naoko Takeuchi's sword-and-sparkle epic as they have elected her queen mother of their imaginations and ultimate aspirational self. She is, simultaneously, symbol, cause, and leader.

This resurgence is animated by more than typical fannish passion. This is a need to return to a world where young women are in charge. This is an anger at the pabulum of Good Role Models for Girls, at boob windows and "fridging" and "tits or gtfo."[2] This is 15-year-olds covering their notebooks in "MERMAIDS AGAINST MISOGYNY" stickers, yet also gravely serious grad students applying bell hooks to Takeuchi's use of Greco-Roman myth.[3] This is a collective invoking of spirits, made more potent in their absence—Usagi Tsukino and all her friends as saints and saviors, carrying the light of childhood optimism to an adulthood in sore need of it. This is nostalgia as a weapon. "Pretty soldiers" indeed.

But why *Sailor Moon?*

Takeuchi's greatest strength as a creator is characterization, and it is this to which fans primarily rally today. *Sailor Moon's* cast is massive—and they are nearly all female, from the heroes to the villains to the sidekicks. This manifold nature removes the burden of representation from any one or two female characters as is the case in most media: Usagi can be emotional, flighty, and boy-crazy, and still a wonderful heroine because *she doesn't stand for half the population.*

In this way, watching *Sailor Moon* as a woman is like suddenly realizing you've been drowning and taking a big gulp of air—the female characters can just *be.* You don't cringe internally when one of them becomes a love interest, or is grievously injured, or fails. It is so *relaxing* to indulge in, so genuinely escapist to put aside that tally one keeps in their head of deaths, rapes, and de-powerings.

To a young girl, *Sailor Moon* is a fantasy she didn't know she wanted; to a woman, it is mental and emotional respite. How often do we find stories by, and almost entirely about women? A few contemporary works spring to mind—*Orange is the New Black, The Joy Luck Club* and other works cubbyholed as "women's fiction", plus a few lucky classics—but they are thin on the ground, and quite frankly, you're sh*t out of luck if you don't click with them for whatever reason. How could we not long to return to a world where women are free to be hero, villain, and every variation thereupon?

It is here that Takeuchi's work clearly shines—her characters are warm and wonderful, far livelier than those typically found in consciously-created "girls' entertainment." Sailor Jupiter, the brawniest of the cast, is never the Tomboy, nor is Sailor Venus, who dreams of stardom, ever the Bimbo. Their friendships feel real and valid and drawn from life, full of conflict and genuine love. In characters like Sailor Mars, Takeuchi broke ground that has since lain untouched: from the beginning to the end, she maintains her devotion to Shintoism, her "weirdness", despite the fact that it intimidates others, and above all, her disinterest in men.

2 http://en.wikipedia.org/wiki/Women_in_Refrigerators
3 http://en.wikipedia.org/wiki/Bell_hooks

It cannot be overstated how remarkable this is—Mars is never portrayed as just needing to meet the right boy, as being frigid or bitchy or in any way possessing a defect in need of correction. Her understanding of herself, as a *teenage girl* who prefers to be alone, is respected and treated as correct.

Takeuchi's heroines are fallible, but never shamed, brave with both feet on the ground, and loving without ever having to be chastened. They are avatars of death, as with Sailor Saturn, whose power is to bring about the apocalypse. They are elegant, thrill-seeking race car drivers like Sailor Uranus, in love with world-class violinists like Sailor Neptune. They are ace students like Sailor Mercury. And they are lovable flibbertigibbets like Sailor Moon, who ascends to the level of creation goddess by the end of the series. Picking a favorite character is serious work for a young fan, but never frustrating for lack of choice.

Here's the thing that struck me most, though, upon adulthood re-reads: without delivering big fat speeches about it, the women of *Sailor Moon* deal with some pretty intense issues. Never in the frantically postured manner of Grim n' Gritty Comix, but Takeuchi never shies away from death and conflict. The third arc of the series centers around Uranus and Neptune's efforts to kill Saturn before she can destroy the world, and the last arc is predicated on the deaths of every single main character besides Usagi.

Even sex, the final frontier of children's entertainment, is a part of the series.[4] It is more than clear to an adult reader that Usagi and Mamoru, the flagship couple, have a sexual relationship. Takeuchi loved drawing them artfully naked together, often in bed, culminating in the penultimate scene of the manga where they wake up together amidst rumpled sheets and mussed hair. In the anime, Haruka and Michiru tease each other about what they'll do "later, when [they're] alone." It's never something Takeuchi highlighted to make A Point about teenage sexuality, good or bad. No one is ever punished for it—Usagi never stops being the most pure hearted wielder of love and justice around just because she is not "pure" in the archaic sense. It just *is*.

Sailor Moon, like all truly great children's stories, never shields children from the more serious and even unpleasant realities of life, nor does it use them to bludgeon readers into a certain point of view. It trusts them to face these issues and handle them like thinking, emotional human beings. Like most children, I knew when I was being lied or preached to, and I resented it. *Sailor Moon* wove its honesty into a grand flying carpet of story and whisked me away so skillfully that I never noticed that I was engaging with Adult Topics—only human ones.

And it is those stories, those adventures, that stay with me. Because on top of the female characters and the social consciousness and all that grown-up business, there's the simple fact that *Sailor Moon* is *really goddamn fun*. Really goddamn fun in a way that girl-centric stories with adult lessons to impart rarely are. Totally awesome team-ups happen between powerhouse characters! Hidden abilities are revealed at climactic moments! Villains become heroes! Heroes become villains! Alternate future selves return to the past to warn of timelines gone wrong! The scope of the story increases with

---

4 http://comicsalliance.com/kate-or-die-leth-all-ages-lgbt-comics-cartoons/

each arc, revealing a vast intergalactic sisterhood of senshi with different outfits, customs, and struggles.

The final battle of the manga takes place between Sailor Moon and *the force of chaos itself*, on the lip of the origin point of all existence—which is subsequently destroyed. It's a sprawling, thrilling saga of a story, something a fan can commit to for years. You can take *Sailor Moon* very, very seriously—I speak as someone who has staked her reputation on it. But you can also just squeal over that one time when Usagi was losing against Queen Beryl in the final battle, and all was totally lost until *oh my god,* the ghosts of the dead senshi came back and helped her win. Over a wailing guitar riff. At the north pole. On a giant tower made of magical moon crystal.

It is these things—compassion, characters, consciousness, and scope—that make *Sailor Moon* the *grande dame* of the magical girl genre and a generation's formative influence. Women stand by *Sailor Moon* today because it respected them, enriched them, *and* entertained them when others refused to—others that have not changed much in the 23 years since the manga debuted.

It is unlikely that *Sailor Moon Crystal* will do much of anything different when it comes to the classic tale, which has already been interpreted half a dozen ways. It will be a story about a group of young women who learn of their magical powers, become friends, and save the world. It will be cute and funny and mostly lighthearted. It will be massively popular, because it remains necessary. And for a while, it will make us forget how frustrating that truly is.

This article first appeared on *Comics Alliance* on July 14, 2014.
comicsalliance.com/sailor-moon-feminism-renaissance-nostalgia-women-role-models/

GENDER, 'ORPHAN BLACK' & THE META OF META

Foz Meadows

Recently, my husband and I burned through S1 of *Orphan Black*, which, as promised by virtually the entire internet, was awesome. But in all the praise I'd seen for it, a line from one review in particular stuck in my mind. The reviewer noted that, although the protagonist, Sarah, is an unlikeable character, her grifter skills make her perfectly suited to unravelling the mystery in which she finds herself. And as this was a positive review, I kept that quote in mind when we started watching, sort of by way of prewarning myself: *you maybe won't like Sarah, but that's OK.*

But here's the thing: I fucking *loved* Sarah. I mean, I get what the reviewer was trying to say, in that she's not always a *sympathetic* character, but that's not the same as her actually being *unlikeable*. And the more I watched, the more I found myself thinking: why is this quality, the idea of *likeability*, considered so important for women, but so optional for men—not just in real life, but in narrative? Because when it comes to guys, we have whole fandoms bending over backwards to write soulful meta humanising male characters whose actions, regardless of their motives, are far less complex than monstrous. We take male villains and redeem them a hundred, a thousand times over—men who are murderers, stalkers, abusers, kinslayers, traitors, attempted or successful rapists; men with personal histories so bloody and tortured, it's like looking at a battlefield. In doing this, we exhibit enormous compassion for and understanding of the nuances of human behaviour—sympathy for circumstance, for context, for motive and character and passion and rage, the heartache and, to steal a phrase, the thousand natural shocks that flesh is heir to; and as such, regardless of how I might feel about the practice as applied in specific instances, in general, it's a praiseworthy endeavour. It helps us to see human beings, not as wholly black and white, but as flawed and complicated creatures, and we *need* to do that, because it's what we are.

But when it comes to women, a single selfish or not-nice act—a stolen kiss, a lie, a brushoff—is somehow enough to see them condemned as whores and bitches forever. We readily excuse our favourite male characters of murder, but if a woman politely turns down a date with someone she has no interest in, she's a timewasting user bimbo and god, what does he even *see* in her? Don't get me wrong, I've seen some great online meta about, for instance, the soulfulness and moral ambiguity of Black Widow, but I've also seen a metric fucktonne more about what that particular jaw-spasm means in that one GIF of Cumberbatch/Ackles/Hiddleston/Smith *alone*, and that's before you get into the pages-long pieces about why Rumplestiltskin or Hook or Spike or Bucky Barnes or whoever is really just a tortured woobie who needs a hug. Hell, I'm guilty of writing some of that stuff myself, because see above: plus, it's meaty and fun and exactly the kind of analysis I like to write.

And yet, we tend overwhelmingly not to write it about ladies. It's not just our cultural obsession with pushing increasingly specific variants of the Madonna/Whore complex onto women, such that audiences are disinclined to extend to female characters the same moral/emotional licenses they extend to men; it's also a failure to create narratives where the women aren't just flawed, but where *the audience is still encouraged to like them when they are*.

Returning to *Orphan Black,* for instance, if Sarah were male, he'd be unequivocally viewed as either a complex, sympathetic antihero or a loving battler with a heart of gold. I mean, the ex-con trying to go straight and get his daughter back while still battling the illegalities of his old life and punching bad guys? Let me introduce you to *Swordfish, Death Race*, and about a millionty other stories where a father's separation from a beloved child, whether as a consequence of his actual criminal actions, shiftless neglect, sheer bad luck or a combination of all three, is never couched as a reason why he might not be a fit parent. We tend to accept, both culturally and narratively, that men who abandon their children aren't automatically bad dads; they just have other, important things to be doing first, like coming to terms with parenthood, saving the world, escaping from prison or otherwise getting their shit together. But Sarah, who left her child in the care of someone she trusted absolutely, has to jump through hoops to prove her maternal readiness on returning; has to answer for her absence over and over again. And on one level, that's fine; that's as it should be, because Sarah's life is dangerous. And yet, her situation stands in glaring contrast to every returning father who's never been asked to do half so much, because women aren't *meant* to struggle with motherhood, to have to *try* to succeed: we're either maternal angels or selfish absentees, and the idea that we might sometimes be both or neither isn't one you often see depicted with such nuance.

Which isn't to say that we never see mothers *struggling*—it's just seldom with their desire to *actually be mothers*. Maternal angels struggle with the day-to-day business of domesticity: how to deal with teenage chatback and those oh-so-hilariously forgetful sitcom husbands, how to balance the bills and keep everyone fed, how to find time for themselves amidst all their endless finding time for others. By contrast, selfish absentees are usually career-oriented single mothers in high-stress jobs, either unwilling or unable to find the appropriate amount of time for their children. Looking at the gender disparity in the characterisation of TV detectives who are also parents is particularly interesting: not only are the men more likely to have wives at home (to begin with, at least), they're also more likely to be granted reconciliation with their children later. Contrast obsessive, depressive detective Kurt Wallander, who slowly rebuilds his relationship with his daughter, with obsessive, depressive detective Sarah Lund, who steadily destroys the possibility of a relationship with her son.[1] Compare single fathers like Seeley Booth and Richard Castle, whose ability to parent well is never implied to be compromised by their devotion to the job, with single mothers like Alex Fielding and Glo-

1 http://en.wikipedia.org/wiki/Kurt_Wallander and http://en.wikipedia.org/wiki/Sarah_Lund

ria Sheppard, whose characterisation is largely defined by the difficulties of striking a balance between the two roles.[2] *Orphan Black*'s Sarah is a rare creature, in that she falls outside the usual boxes for maternal categorisation, and in so doing forces us to re-examine exactly why that is.

In fact, though their respective shows and stories are utterly dissimilar in every other respect, in terms of her approach to motherhood, the character Sarah most reminded me of was Laura Gibson, the protagonist of *SeaChange*, an Australian show about which I have previously waxed lyrical, and which I cannot recommend highly enough.[3] Though ostensibly subject to the same stereotyping outlined above—Laura was a high-flying corporate lawyer and newly single mother whose decision to move to a small town and reconnect with her family constituted the titular sea-change—she was written with such complexity and feeling as to defy the cliché. She was eager and well-meaning, but just as often selfish and oblivious. Though she learned to slow down and listen to others over the course of three series, she never became a domestic goddess or a motherly martyr; nor did she magically lose her flaws or suddenly develop a perfect relationship with her children. Instead, she remained a prickly, complex character, quick to both give and take offence, but also introspective, passionate, sly and caring. Like Sarah, she wasn't always sympathetic, but that didn't stop me from loving her, flaws and all.

But what of female villains? Perhaps I'm just not reading the right meta, but it's always seemed a bit glaring to me that, whereas (for instance) there are endless paeans to the moral complexity and intricate personal histories of the Buffyverse's Spike and Angel, their female counterparts, Drusilla and Darla, never seem to merit the same degree of compulsive protection. I've seen a bit of positive/sympathetic meta surrounding *Once Upon A Time*'s Regina, but otherwise, I can't think of many overtly antagonistic female characters whose actions and motives are viewed as complex, and therefore potentially redemptive, instead of just as proof that they're bad women. We think of men as antiheroes, as capable of occupying an intense and fascinating moral grey area; of being able to fall, and rise, and fall again, but still be worthy of love on some fundamental level, because if it was the world and its failings that broke them, then we surely must owe them some sympathy. But women aren't allowed to be broken by the world; or if we are, it's the breaking that makes us villains. Wronged women turn into avenging furies, inhuman and monstrous: once we cross to the dark side, we become adversaries to be defeated, not lost souls in need of mending. Which is what happens, when you let benevolent sexism invest you in the idea that women are humanity's moral guardians and men its native renegades: because if female goodness is only ever an inherent quality—something we're born both with and to be—then once lost, it must necessarily be lost forever, a severed limb we can't regrow. Whereas male goodness, by virtue of being an acquired quality—something bestowed through the kindness of women, earned through right action or learned through struggle—can just as necessarily be gained and lost multiple times without being tarnished, like a jewel we might pawn in hardship, and later reclaim.

2 http://en.wikipedia.org/wiki/Seeley_Booth, http://en.wikipedia.org/wiki/Richard_castle, http://en.wikipedia.org/wiki/Wire_in_the_Blood#Characters and http://en.wikipedia.org/wiki/The_Protector_(TV_series)
3 http://www.imdb.com/title/tt0138785/ and https://fozmeadows.wordpress.com/2011/09/20/seachange/

Throughout history, women's legal status and protections have been tied to the question of whether or not they're seen to be virtuous, whatever that means in context. The sworn virgins of Albania were granted equal status with men—indeed, were allowed to live and act as men—provided they never had sex, owing to a specific legal stricture which ascribed female virgins the same financial worth as men, while valuing women less.[4] The big three monotheisms—Judaism, Christianity and Islam—all boast scriptures and/or religious laws that have, both historically and in the modern day, allotted specific legal privileges to women provided they remain virtuous; privileges which are invariably retracted should the woman in question be seen to have strayed, or become tarnished, or to have otherwise lost her virtue. We see this echoed in modern rape culture, which puts the onus for self-protection on women to such a degree that, far too often, if a woman is raped, her victimhood is viewed as a consequence of poor character—because if she really *was* innocent, then how did she let it happen? Why was she dressed that way, or out late, or drinking? Why, if she wasn't already lacking in virtue, would she have been in the company of a rapist?

And so, our treatment of morally ambiguous female characters ends up paralleling some truly toxic assumptions about gender and morality. Women cannot act to redeem themselves independently, because under far too many laws, our need of redemption voids our right to try and reacquire it. Good women can redeem broken men, but good men can't redeem broken women, because once we're broken, we lose our virtue; and without our virtue, we're no longer women, but monsters, witches and viragos.

Which is why, to come full circle, I fucking *love* the fact that *Orphan Black*'s Sarah Manning isn't always sympathetic; isn't always traditionally likeable. She is, rather, an antiheroine in the most literal sense: and with all the Madonna/Whore bullshit we're still caught up in imposing on women, that's a class of character we desperately need to see more of.

(Note: I've only talked about men and women here, rather than third gender, genderfluid and other gender non-conforming persons, because it's men and women we usually see depicted in stories, and whose narratives therefore form the bulk of our cultural stereotyping. The absence or elision of narratives concerning other genders, however, along with their own highly stereotyped portrayals when they do appear, is a problem in and of itself, and a contributing factor in the way men and women are stereotyped: because when we view gender purely as a fixed binary phenomenon, whether consciously or unconsciously, we make it harder to see beyond the rules that binary has traditionally imposed on our thinking, repeatedly foisting "masculine"/"feminine" values onto successive new characters without ever stopping to think that actually, we might challenge or subvert those norms instead, a blindness which only helps to further perpetuate the problem.)

This article first appeared on *Shattersnipe: Malcontent & Rainbows* on May 9, 2014.
fozmeadows.wordpress.com/2014/05/09/gender-orphan-black-the-meta-of-meta/

---

4 http://en.wikipedia.org/wiki/Albanian_sworn_virgins

WE'RE LOSING ALL OUR STRONG FEMALE CHARACTERS TO TRINITY SYNDROME

Tasha Robinson

DreamWorks' *How To Train Your Dragon 2* considerably expands the world introduced in the first film, and that expansion includes a significant new presence: Valka, the long-lost mother of dragon-riding protagonist Hiccup, voiced by Cate Blanchett.[1] The film devotes much of its sweet, sensitive middle act to introducing her, and building her up into a complicated, nuanced character. She's mysterious and formidable, capable of taking Hiccup and his dragon partner Toothless out of the sky with casual ease. She's knowledgeable: Two decades of studying dragons means she knows Toothless' anatomy better than he does. She's wise. She's principled. She's joyous. She's divided. She's damaged. She's vulnerable. She's something female characters so often aren't in action/adventure films with male protagonists: She's *interesting*.

Too bad the story gives her absolutely nothing to do.

There's been a cultural push going on for years now to get female characters in mainstream films some agency, self-respect, confidence, and capability, to make them more than the cringing victims and eventual trophies of 1980s action films, or the grunting, glowering, sexless-yet-sexualized types that followed, modeled on the groundbreaking badass Vasquez in *Aliens*. The idea of the Strong Female Character—someone with her own identity, agenda, and story purpose—has thoroughly pervaded the conversation about what's wrong with the way women are often perceived and portrayed today, in comics, videogames, and film especially.[2] Sophia McDougall has intelligently dissected and dismissed the phrase, and artists Kate Beaton, Carly Monardo, Meredith Gran have hilariously lampooned what it often becomes in comics.[3] "Strong Female Character" is just as often used derisively as descriptively, because it's such a simplistic, low bar to vault, and it's more a marketing term than a meaningful goal. But just as it remains frustratingly uncommon for films to pass the simple, low-bar Bechdel Test, it's still rare to see films in the mainstream action/horror/science-fiction/fantasy realm in-

1 http://thedissolve.com/reviews/865-how-to-train-your-dragon-2/

2 http://eschergirls.tumblr.com/ and http://www.washingtonpost.com/news/act-four/wp/2014/06/12/of-course-it-takes-work-to-build-female-video-game-characters-companies-should-do-it-anyway/

3 http://www.newstatesman.com/culture/2013/08/i-hate-strong-female-characters and http://harkavagrant.com/index.php?id=311

troduce women with any kind of meaningful strength, or women who go past a few simple stereotypes.[4]

And even when they do, the writers often seem lost after that point. Bringing in a Strong Female Character™ isn't actually a feminist statement, or an inclusionary statement, or even a basic equality statement, if the character doesn't have any reason to be in the story except to let filmmakers point at her on the poster and say "See? This film totally respects strong women!"

Valka is just the latest example of the Superfluous, Flimsy Character disguised as a Strong Female Character. And possibly she's the most depressing, considering *Dragon 2*'s other fine qualities, and considering how impressive she is in the abstract. The film spends so much time on making her first awe-inducing, then sympathetic, and just a little heartbreakingly pathetic in her isolation and awkwardness at meeting another human being. But once the introductions are finally done, and the battle starts, she immediately becomes useless, both to the rest of the cast and to the rapidly moving narrative. She faces the villain (the villain she's apparently been successfully resisting alone for years!) and she's instantly, summarily defeated. Her husband and son utterly overshadow her; they need to rescue her twice in maybe five minutes. Her biggest contribution to the narrative is in giving Hiccup a brief, rote "You are the Chosen One" pep talk. Then she all but disappears from the film, raising the question of why the story spent so much time on her in the first place. It may be because writer-director Dean DeBlois originally planned for her to be the film's villain, then discarded that idea in later drafts.[5] But those later drafts give her the setup of a complicated antagonist... and the resolution of no one at all. (Meanwhile, the actual villain gets virtually no backstory—which is fine, in a way—but it leaves the film unbalanced.)[6]

And Valka's type—the Strong Female Character With Nothing To Do—is becoming more and more common. *The Lego Movie* is the year's other most egregious and frustrating example.[7] It introduces its female lead, Elizabeth Banks' Wyldstyle, as a beautiful, super-powered, super-smart, ultra-confident heroine who's appalled by how dumb and hapless protagonist Emmet is. Then the rest of the movie laughs at her and marginalizes her as she turns into a sullen, disapproving nag and a wet blanket. One joke has Emmet tuning her out entirely when she tries to catch him up on her group's fate-of-the-world struggle; he replaces her words with "Blah blah blah, I'm so pretty." Her only post-introduction story purpose is to be rescued, repeatedly, and to eventually confer the cool-girl approval that seals Emmet's transformation from loser to winner. After a terrific story and a powerful ending, the movie undermines its triumph with a tag where WyldStyle actually *turns to her current boyfriend for permission to dump him* so she can give herself to Emmet as a reward for his success. For the ordinary dude to be triumphant, the Strong Female Character has to entirely disappear into Subservient Trophy Character mode. This is Trinity Syndrome à la *The Matrix*: the hugely capable woman who never once becomes as independent, significant, and exciting

4 http://bechdeltest.com/
5 http://www.latimes.com/entertainment/movies/la-et-mn-dragon-director-dean-deblois-20140613-story.html%23page=1
6 http://thedissolve.com/news/1426-op-ed-ban-the-backstory/
7 http://thedissolve.com/reviews/531-the-lego-movie/

as she is in her introductory scene. (Director Chris McKay sorta-acknowledged the problem in a *DailyMail* interview presented as *"The Lego Movie* filmmaker promises more 'strong females' in the sequel," though his actual quotes do nothing of the sort.)[8]

And even when strong, confident female characters do manage to contribute to a male-led action story, their contributions are still more likely to be marginal, or relegated entirely to nurturer roles, or victim roles, or romantic roles. Consider Tauriel in *The Hobbit: The Desolation Of Smaug*, a wholly invented Strong Female Character ostensibly created to add a little gender balance to an all-male adventure.[9] She's capable of killing approximately a billion spiders and orcs with elven archery kung-fu, but she only shows any actual personality when she's swooning over the dwarf Kili, and being swooned over in return by Legolas, in a wearyingly familiar *Twilight*-esque love triangle. Consider Katee Sackhoff's Dahl in *Riddick*, introduced as a tough second-in-command who proclaims early on that she's no man's sexual object—unlike the movie's only other woman, a brutalized, chained rape victim, casually killed to make a point—but given no particular plot relevance.[10] Despite what Dahl says, she's just sexual spice for the film: She strips for the camera, fights off a rape attempt, smirks through the antihero's graphically crude come-ons, then decides at the end that she *would* like to be his sexual object.[11] Consider Alice Eve's Carol Marcus in *Star Trek: Into Darkness*, introduced as a defiant, iconoclastic rules-breaker exactly like James Kirk, but ultimately winding up in the story largely so she can strip onscreen and present herself as an embarrassingly ineffectual hostage.[12] Rinko Kikuchi's Mako Mori in *Pacific Rim* is weak next to Charlie Hunnam's Raleigh—her past trauma blocks her from being effective in mecha combat, and endangers everyone around her—but even when she proves her strength, he still has to assert himself by knocking her out and dumping her limp body as he heads off to save the day at the end.[13] Ditto with Tom Cruise's Jack in *Oblivion*, who pulls the same move on Julia (Olga Kurylenko), his capable partner.

It's hard for any action movie to have two or more equal heroes, and the ensemble approach doesn't work for every story. It's understandable that for a Hero's Journey plot to entirely resolve, the hero sometimes has to take the last steps alone. For male heroes, that often means putting independence and self-sacrifice before any other consideration. But for decades, action movies have found ways to let male sidekicks drop back at the climax of a story without dying, disappearing, or waiting at home to offer themselves to the hero to celebrate his victory. Female characters don't have to dominate the story to come across as self-reliant, but they do have to have some sense of purpose. Valka's is, apparently, to deliver some heartening information and a little inspiration to Hiccup, and nothing else. It's a bafflingly piddly role for

8 http://www.dailymail.co.uk/tvshowbiz/article-2597511/The-Lego-Movie-filmmaker-Chris-McKay-promises-strong-females-sequel.html

9 http://thedissolve.com/reviews/429-the-hobbit-the-desolation-of-smaug/

10 http://thedissolve.com/reviews/186-riddick/

11 http://www.empireonline.com/empireblogs/empire-states/post/p1399

12 http://thedissolve.com/features/one-year-later/591-one-year-later-star-trek-into-darkness/ and http://geekleagueofamerica.com/2013/05/25/star-trek-into-misogyny-and-sexism/

13 http://thedissolve.com/reviews/51-pacific-rim/

someone whom the narrative seems to care about passionately... until it's time for her to *do* something.

So here's a quick questionnaire for filmmakers who've created a female character who isn't a dishrag, a harpy, a McGuffin to be passed around, or a sex toy. Congratulations, you have a Strong Female Character. That's a great start! But now what? Screenwriters, producers, directors, consider this:

After being introduced, does your Strong Female Character then fail to do anything fundamentally significant to the outcome of the plot? Anything at all?

If she does accomplish something plot-significant, is it primarily getting raped, beaten, or killed to motivate a male hero?[14] Or deciding to have sex with/not have sex with/agreeing to date/deciding to break up with a male hero? Or nagging a male hero into growing up, or nagging him to stop being so heroic? Basically, does she only exist to service the male hero's needs, development, or motivations?

Could your Strong Female Character be seamlessly replaced with a floor lamp with some useful information written on it to help a male hero?

Is a fundamental point of your plot that your Strong Female Character is the strongest, smartest, meanest, toughest, or most experienced character in the story—until the protagonist arrives?

...or worse, does he enter the story as a bumbling fuck-up, but spend the whole movie rapidly evolving past her, while she stays entirely static, and even cheers him on? Does your Strong Female Character exist primarily so the protagonist can impress her?

It's nice if she's hyper-cool, but does she only start off that way so a male hero will look even cooler by comparison when he rescues or surpasses her?

Is she so strong and capable that she's never needed rescuing before now, but once the plot kicks into gear, she's suddenly captured or threatened by the villain, and needs the hero's intervention? Is breaking down her pride a fundamental part of the story?

Does she disappear entirely for the second half/third act of the film, for any reason other than because she's doing something significant to the plot (besides being a hostage, or dying)?

If you can honestly answer "no" to every one of these questions, you might actually have a Strong Female Character worthy of the name. Congratulations!

But there are exceptions to every rule. *Edge Of Tomorrow* features Emily Blunt as Rita, an ultra-tough female character who dies to motivate the male protagonist.[15] (Repeatedly!) She starts off as the biggest bad-ass in her world, but is eventually surpassed by hero William Cage (Tom Cruise), who starts off as a bumbling fuck-up. She mostly exists in the story to provide Cage with information and cheer him on, and eventually validates him with a brief romantic moment. And yet the story doesn't degrade, devalue, weaken, or dismiss her. It sends the hero on without her at the end—but only at the *very* end, after she's proved her worth again and again. She's tough. She's confident. She's desperate. She's funny. In short, she's aspirational and

14 http://tvtropes.org/pmwiki/pmwiki.php/Main/StuffedIntoTheFridge
15 http://thedissolve.com/features/the-conversation/606-the-day-after-the-edge-of-tomorrow/

inspirational, and just as exciting at the end of the movie as she is at the beginning.

So maybe all the questions can boil down to this: Looking at a so-called Strong Female Character, would you—the writer, the director, the actor, the viewer—*want to be her*? Not want to prove you're better than her, or to have her praise you or acknowledge your superiority. Action movies are all about wish-fulfillment. Does she fulfill any wishes for herself, rather than for other characters? When female characters are routinely "strong" enough to manage that, maybe they'll make the "Strong Female Characters" term meaningful enough that it isn't so often said sarcastically.

This article first appeared on *The Dissolve* on June 16, 2014.
thedissolve.com/features/exposition/618-were-losing-all-our-strong-female-characters-to-tr/

WHY 'HOW TO TRAIN YOUR DRAGON 2' IS A RADICAL FEMINIST TRIUMPH

Aja Romano

Last week, the Dissolve issued a widely-circulated takedown of what it called the "Trinity Syndrome" specifically in relationship to the main female character in DreamWorks' *How to Train Your Dragon 2*.[1] According to Dissolve, the Trinity Syndrome, named after the iconic character from *The Matrix* series, manifests itself in Hiccup's mother Valka as follows:

> She's wise. She's principled. She's joyous. She's divided. She's damaged. She's vulnerable. She's something female characters so often aren't in action/adventure films with male protagonists: She's interesting.

> Too bad the story gives her absolutely nothing to do. ... Valka is just the latest example of the Superfluous, Flimsy Character disguised as a Strong Female Character.

The essay goes on to allege that Valka is weak at several crucial moments in the plot. Specifically it paints her as a damsel who needs rescuing in the third act. It also goes on to give a list of other characters who fail by this standard, including the much-loved *Pacific Rim* character of Mako Mori. Tumblr user quigonejinn has a compelling post explaining how important Mako Mori is from a cultural perspective, written in response to the existence of the Mako Mori test.[2]

In responding to the Dissolve essay specifically, Tumblr user apocalypsecanceled rephrased Dissolve's argument:[3]

> [H]ow DARE this woman of color have the unmitigated gall to show vulnerability and make mistakes and be supported by other people?...

> how dare she not be an invincible dragon lady who nevertheless sacrifices herself to rescue her white dude savior???

It's important to recognize the way the Dissolve has reframed the narrative of *Pacific Rim* in order to recognize that that's also what it has done to the

---

1 http://thedissolve.com/features/exposition/618-were-losing-all-our-strong-female-characters-to-tr/
2 http://quigonejinn.tumblr.com/post/59672477502/the-mako-mori-test-pacific-rim-inspires-a-bechdel and http://www.dailydot.com/fandom/mako-mori-test-bechdel-pacific-rim/
3 http://apocalypsecanceled.tumblr.com/post/89103034923/this-is-what-yall-sound-like-when-you-call-mako-a-weak

191

narrative of *How to Train Your Dragon 2*. Ironically, it's *HTTYD 2*'s reframing and rejection of die-hard sexist Hollywood tropes—specifically the one about "fridged women" being used as fodder for manpain and male-centered violence—that makes it unique in the pantheon of children's films.[4]

There are full spoilers for *HTTYD 2* from this point on, so be warned.

Five minutes into this film, which opens with Hiccup rejecting his father's wish for him to be the new village chief, I was muttering, "Make Astrid the new chief, make Astrid the new chief," under my breath. I mean obviously that would be the best possible solution to everyone's lives, right?

But because this is *Dragon Rider*, not *Whale Rider*, we got a standard narrative about Hiccup's expanding heroism—sort of. The unique thing about Hiccup's character in this film is that it doesn't actually undergo any, well, development. While the narrative stresses that people can change, Hiccup himself doesn't actually change all that much. But that works for this film, because *How To Train Your Dragon 2* is less a traditional coming-of-age arc about a single character learning to accept responsibility and find his place, and more a collective arc about an entire community evolving and changing together.

As a character, Hiccup is, perhaps, one of the most feminist and progressive male heroes in film history. He's a character who consistently rejects, over and over again, the idea that violence is ever a solution in situations of conflict. He's a character who actively practices empathy and, of course, active conservationism. He's a disabled character who not only adapts to his disability without ever losing anything that makes him amazing, but sees it as a thing to be *proud of*, to celebrate as something that makes him special and gives him more in common with his best friend.

Meanwhile, while Hiccup is going on a discovery quest, his female counterpart Astrid is busy rejecting orders and doing her own thing. After Hiccup's failed first *and* second attempts to try to find the villain Drago, he gets sidetracked by his encounter with his mother and lapses into inaction. Meanwhile, Astrid makes the totally independent decision to enlist the dragon trappers' help and/or follow them to Drago. Without that action, Team Peace might never have actually encountered Drago, the plot's third act might never have gotten underway, and Eret would never have switched sides to help free the dragon riders and defeat the bad guy.

As an aside: how much chemistry did Astrid and Hiccup have together? When was the last time you saw a romantic couple in an animated film have that much casual touching and body interaction that wasn't a deliberate setup for a meet-cute? Maybe *Shrek*? Maybe never. It was great.

There's also the glorious casual onscreen display of Ruffnut's sexuality.

Female sexuality is never shamed or repressed in *HTTYD 2*. Additionally, as ladygeekgirl points out in her smart take on the film, the women of DreamWorks, unlike the women of *Frozen*, actually have faces that are different from one another.[5]

---

4 http://en.wikipedia.org/wiki/Women_in_Refrigerators
5 http://ladygeekgirl.wordpress.com/2014/06/16/so-how-was-how-to-train-your-dragon-2/ and http://www.dailydot.com/entertainment/disney-frozen-animating-female-characters/

The women of *Frozen*—mother and two supposedly non-identical daughters—were differentiated only by change of hair and eye colors, while the women of *HTTYD* were are physically distinct.

Not only do each of these women have individual faces, they also each get their own promotional movie poster for the film—another "when was the last time...?" moment for DreamWorks.

This brings us to the film's treatment of Hiccup's mother.

In absolutely every other Hollywood version of the *HTTYD 2* narrative, Hiccup's discovery of his mother's two-decade-long absence would have resulted in an explicit shaming of her choices and a prolonged "how could you abandon me?" confrontation that would probably have ended with her breaking down in tears and Hiccup's eventual acceptance and forgiveness of her inexplicable absence all this time.

Instead, Hiccup instantly and immediately recognized that his mom's choices *were her own choices*, and that they were obviously valuable and important. At no point did the narrative shame Valka for rejecting her role as a mother and a housewife. Instead, she not only got to make the coolest entrance, but basically was presented as the most unbelievably cool character we've seen in an animated film in ages.

Additionally, the film totally validated her life choices by making her caretaker of the coolest free-range dragon park ever, and presenting the choice to rejoin her family as a choice that would validate all of her earlier choices to leave them behind.

In absolutely every other Hollywood version of the *HTTYD 2* narrative, Hiccup's mother would have been briefly united with her husband and son, only to die tragically in the next big battle, thereby giving them extra manpain and creating more fuel for their ultimate avenging of her death.

In absolutely every other Hollywood version of the *HTTYD 2* narrative, it would have been Valka sacrificing her life for that of her son instead of Stoick. Let's call it the Lily Potter Syndrome.

But instead, the film actually showed how damaging the trope of killing off the dead woman for more manpain really is, by using her earlier presumed death as the catalyst for all Stoick's misplaced vengeance against dragons. We know *how* wasteful and wrong that misplaced anger is because the first film worked through it at length.

Additionally, instead of going on a vengeance quest after Stoick's death, we see Valka *and* Hiccup both rejecting the idea that such a motivation for violence would do anything but bring them and their homeland of Berk more pain. To the very last scene they're in together, Hiccup is trying to reason with Drago; every one of his actions is done from a position of non-violent communication.

That recognition is absolutely central to any kind of effective reading of *How to Train Your Dragon*. This is literally a franchise which has taken the most notoriously war-mongering stereotype in existence, Viking culture, and gradually transformed it until the characters not only refuse to use violence as a solution, but proudly proclaim that they are a "land of peace." That's an unbelievably radical and transformative narrative for a Hollywood film to deliver, much less a Hollywood children's film. The *HTTYD* franchise now joins *Avatar: The Last Airbender* as one of the only animated franchises to commit this deeply to such a polarizing political stance.

Dissolve's essay seems to completely overlook this aspect of *HTTYD 2*. At *no point* are the male characters aggressors against Drago. Although they talk about it, they never actually act violently except to defend their home from capture. In fact, the only person to attack Drago first is Valka, who hits him weakly out of anger after watching her giant bewilderbeast get killed. And despite what the Dissolve essay speculates, it seems evident that Valka has never really physically fought with Drago herself. When the time comes to actually physically attack, she gets no further than poking him with her stick a few times.

Valka was never intended to be a serious physical match for Drago, nor should she have been, because the whole point of her character aligned with her son's is to personify the Viking nation's progressive anti-violence stance. Sorry that Valka was too busy working as a zoologist to become the vaunted warrior-hero-soldier that apparently makes a female character strong enough for you, Dissolve. Instead, she spends years subversively rescuing dragons from capture like a radical Greenpeace activist, and she is the one who leads the enormous dragon army into battle against Drago.

And come to that, when was the last time you saw a mother and son riding side-by-side into battle together? Another point for you, DreamWorks.

While it's true that she gets rescued by her husband, so does everyone else in her family. They spend the movie running around trying to protect each other: Stoick saves Hiccup, Valka, and Hiccup again; Valka saves Toothless, Toothless saves Hiccup, and then Hiccup and Toothless save everyone.

Even more significantly, while it's true that she doesn't get to do much in the third act, she doesn't have to. She doesn't have to because unlike 90 percent of other Hollywood films, *HTTYD* is a universe with more than one woman in it. And as a result, it gets to have a variety of women who do a variety of different things. Valka doesn't *have* to be an all-powerful warrior-soldier, because Astrid and Ruffnut are out there dumping flaming sulfur on the enemy and generally proving that women can be badasses on the battlefield. Valka proves that women can be badasses as activists and scientists and even, yes, as moms, too.

Dissolve's reading of *HTTYD 2* completely misses the multiple ways in which the film is trying to avoid the reductive trope that the only strong characters are the characters who fight. By insisting that Valka is weak because she falls down and has to be rescued by her husband, Dissolve is failing its own measurement of strength, considering she's the only character who actually is the aggressor against Drago at any point. But moreover, it's failing to consider the film's *entire point,* which is that violence is not the way forward, and that humans and dragons need to rescue each other.

Ultimately, what expands in *How to Train Your Dragon* is not the central character's growth and understanding, but that of the entire world. Hiccup shifts from exploring and mapping out the physical world of the film to actively uniting the people who live in it. His mother, who by all narrative trope standards should have been killed off in an act of self-sacrifice at the end of act two, instead finishes the film seeing her life's work come to fruition in ways she never thought possible.

As a narrative of female empowerment, we find this pretty damn satisfying.

This article first appeared on *The Daily Dot* on June 22, 2014.
www.dailydot.com/opinion/how-to-train-your-dragon-2-is-feminist/

ONE HUNDRED YEARS OF WEIRD FEAR: ON H.P. LOVECRAFT'S LITERATURE OF GENEALOGICAL TERROR

Daniel José Older

Ooze, Seep and Trickle

I was on a train going through Connecticut once, sort of writing a short story but really eavesdropping on a conversation between an excruciatingly proper old woman and an eager young reporter. "What," the reporter wanted to know, "is the main emotion that inspires you to write the books you write?"

The woman paused; I wondered who she was, if I'd read any of her books. The reporter leaned in. I stopped even pretending to be in my notebook and listened.

"Disgust," she finally croaked. "Disgust."

If any writer can be described as rooting his work in the inspiration of disgust, it is Howard Phillips Lovecraft. Here he is in a letter written during his traumatizing and highly inspiring stay in Brooklyn during the mid-1920s:

> The organic things inhabiting that awful cesspool could not by any stretch of the imagination be call'd human. They were monstrous and nebulous adumbrations of the pithecanthropoid and amoebal; vaguely moulded from some stinking viscous slime of the earth's corruption, and slithering and oozing in and on the filthy streets or in and out of windows and doorways in a fashion suggestive of nothing but infesting worms or deep-sea unnamabilities. They—or the degenerate gelatinous fermentation of which they were composed—seem'd to ooze, seep and trickle thro' the gaping cracks in the horrible houses ... and I thought of some avenue of Cyclopean and unwholesome vats, crammed to the vomiting point with gangrenous vileness, and about to burst and inundate the world in one leprous cataclysm of semi-fluid rottenness. From that nightmare of perverse infection I could not carry away the memory of any living face. The individually grotesque was lost in the collectively devastating; which left on the eye only the broad, phantasmal lineaments of the morbid soul of disintegration and decay ... a yellow leering mask with sour, sticky, acid ichors oozing at eyes, ears, nose, and mouth, and abnormally bubbling from monstrous and unbelievable sores at every point...

The paragraph is worth mentioning in its entirety both for its sheer racist bombast and for how strikingly reminiscent it is of his fiction. Lovecraft, the ornery, peculiar literary godson of Edgar Allen Poe and Bram Stoker, is widely considered to be the father of the subgenre "weird fiction." Weird fiction could be placed somewhere between fantasy, horror, and science fiction—a pulpy combination of the three that generally is grounded in the real world. Between 1917 and 1935, he published an almost encyclopedic array of short stories, mostly in the pulp magazine *Weird Tales*, that grow from general morbid absurdity to dreamtime hyperballads to detailed, collage-like dispatches of our crooked world's disastrous run-ins with the tentacled elder gods of a vast, highly conceptualized alternate universe. The mythos he created persists to this day in the movies, comic books, novels, video games, RPGs, and, most recently, a Thanksgiving struggle plate that went viral.[1]

That Lovecraft was racist beyond even the excessive racism exhibited by other white writers of his time is not in question. The above paragraph is far from an aberration among his over 100,000 pages of letters, and he populates his fictional universe with slithering, swarthy-faced mongoloids and idiot, infanticidal black men (he almost never wrote about women of any race—an erasure that warrants an essay unto itself). As writer Phenderson Djèlí Clark points out in his excellent essay on Lovecraft, "It's always perplexing to watch the gymnastics of mental obfuscation that occur as fans of Lovecraft attempt to rationalize his racism."[2] Responses tend to write off his racism as a product of his times and then be paradoxically surprised that it didn't hinder his success. "In spite of […] his overt racism," biographer Donald Tyson tells us, "he created a mythic world that continues to captivate the imagination of millions of readers." The phrase "in spite of" comes up a lot, as well as allusions to a vaguely presumed-to-be anti-racist, first-person plural that is of course appalled by such bigotry.

"Paradoxically," writes French critic Michel Houellebecq in one of the more head-on takes on the H.P. Lovecraft racism issue, "the character of Lovecraft fascinates us partly because his system of values is entirely opposed to ours. Fundamentally racist, openly reactionary, he glorifies puritan inhibition." It is the presumptive *we* that bothers me most here. This was written in 1991, the year of Rodney King, when black income in the U.S. was 57% of white income and race riots exploded in Crown Heights, Brooklyn, as well as the Parisian suburb Val-Fourré. Ten years later, Houellebecq himself will be brought up on charges of inciting racial hatred by the French Human Rights League and a variety of mosques for his novel *Plateforme*; what magical post-racial *we* are we dealing with?

Here we have the one hand correctly contextualizing Lovecraft within a society that was founded on and thrives on racism, while the other hand is shocked that such an overt racist could endure in the collective imagination. The subtext here is, "anyway, moving on to brighter topics." Meanwhile, the only modern myths that have captivated the imagination of millions of white readers have been crouched in white supremacy. The "in spite of" phrase is a

1 http://lubbockonline.com/local-news/2013-12-17/lubbock-mans-lovecraft-inspired-turkey-goes-viral#.UremdGRDvbA
2 http://pdjeliclark.wordpress.com/2013/05/03/hp-lovecrafts-madness/

myopic, ahistorical fallacy. The Cthulhu Mythos endures not in spite of Lovecraft's racism but because of it.

Lovecraft wrote weird racist fiction in a racist time, and he did it extremely well. Of course it took hold. As a country, a planet even, we've still never truly reckoned with this past. But in the glossy white-empowered rewrite of modern times, racism becomes something that happened and then ended except for a few irritating little incidents in flyover states and the occasional massacre.

No Sleep Since Brooklyn

Writing pulled Lovecraft from the agoraphobic mire of a nervous breakdown. He hadn't written much until that point, a few short stories, though he always showed signs of an active imagination. In the early 1910s he became involved with some amateur writers associations, eventually putting pen to paper—he abhorred the typewriter—to contribute his own stories and then rising to prominence among his peers. His first submission letter to *Weird Tales* could be used as a tip sheet on what not to do when approaching editors: He's self-deprecating, and not humorously so; he's demanding, he's fussy, and everything is handwritten. When he got rejections he would immediately shelf the story and never send it out again. He felt that getting paid was beneath him, even as he slid into abject poverty toward the end of his life. He never wrote about sex or money in a corner of the industry where the magazine covers were splattered with naked women and hidden treasures. In spite of all this (yes, in this case, in spite of), Lovecraft got himself published regularly in the pages of *Weird Tales* and several other major pulp magazines.

These early and mid-career stories, "The Music of Erich Zann" and "Herbert West - Reanimator" for example, already show a masterful commitment to the sinister crossroads of imagination and the modern world, a quirkiness beyond the average pulp writer. But the experience of living in Brooklyn was a painful turning point. Lovecraft came to New York in 1922 with a swoon of "aesthetic exaltation" at the "innumerable lights of the skyscrapers, the mirrored reflections and the lights of the boats bobbing on the water, at the extreme left the sparkling statue of Liberty, and on the right the scintillating arch of the Brooklyn bridge." His seemingly loveless marriage disintegrated and his attempts to find a job failed at every turn. Lovecraft ended up alone and miserable in a boarding house on Clinton Street, not far from Red Hook, surrounded by the very immigrants he already harbored deep prejudices against.

Brooklyn is where Lovecraft's literature of disgust becomes rooted in something much closer to the human heart: fear. Aristotle says the two main emotions of drama are fear and empathy. In his seminal essay, "Notes on Weird Fiction", Lovecraft simplifies it to one:

> Fear is our deepest and strongest emotion, and the one which best lends itself to the creation of nature-defying illusions. Horror and the unknown or the strange are always closely connected, so that it is hard to create a convincing picture of shattered natural

law or cosmic alienage or "outsideness" without laying stress on the emotion of fear.

His stories had always been creepy, but in Brooklyn all the writer's inner neuroses take human shape, outnumber him, interact with him on a daily basis and occasionally, steal his shit. Having lived fear, this intense, creeping claustrophobia and slow-gathering terror take new life in the later works. Lovecraft's melodramatic few years in Brooklyn are equivalent to Dante's first sighting of Beatrice: The writer has a vision; the vision is transformative, it does something to him on the inside. The writer will never be the same.

Lovecraft wrote "The Horror at Red Hook" in a fevered all-nighter after having his favorite overcoat lifted from his room. It's almost universally disliked; Lovecraft said it was "rather long and rambling. And I don't think it is very good," and critics don't include it in the final phase of his "major works", but here we have the seeds of the Cthulhu Mythos, even if the old gods themselves are not mentioned by name. I actually found this one of his more compelling works; the sinister plot unravels in a noir-like, slow-building frenzy. A burned-out Brooklyn detective with a "Celt's far vision of weird and hidden things, but the logician's quick eye for the outwardly unconvincing" looks into the suspicious doings of an eccentric millionaire and discovers an underground network of immigrants worshiping the goddess Lilith. There are nods to Stoker and the gumshoe masters and it all climaxes with a horrific mass slaughter of women and children in a Red Hook basement, which burns down, sparing only the deeply traumatized Detective Malone. It is appallingly racist, the "swarthy" immigrant cult members are preparing a massive child sacrifice to their devilish god, and the precursor to supernatural sleuths like Harry Blackstone and Dirk Gently.

But if we really want to get a sense of Lovecraft's complex relationship to New York, we have to look at "He" (1925). (I don't normally like to make assumptions about what an author's work says about their personal opinions, but Lovecraft himself said: "If you want to know what I think of New York, read 'He.'") A dull, intimidated poet wanders the midnight streets of the West Village, tantalized and inspired by its crumbling, cyclopean architecture. (And why… why why why does this word recur in damn near every Lovecraft story? What image are we to take from this? Buildings with a single window at the top? Buildings built by one-eyed giants? It means nothing to me visually, yet it's clearly one of Lovecraft's favorite adjectives.) He meets a stranger dressed in nondescript clothes that later turn out to be from another century. He follows the stranger through the (cyclopean) streets and into some quirky inner garden area, up some stairs to a creepy little room. Why does he follow the stranger? We never really know, but this unnamed, almost suicidally passive poet will find much like-minded company in the cadre of mild-mannered, ill-fated intellectual Lovecraft semi-heroes to come.

What follows is a peculiar scene so full of tension it is *almost* erotic. The stranger does a little magic and transforms the stunning cityscape out the window into New York of the distant past, then rattles off an alarming monologue about poisoning an entire tribe of Native Americans (he may have escaped from a Faulkner plotline), all the while getting closer and closer to our freaked-out narrator, finally grabbing his hand as he works himself up into a frenzy. Meanwhile, some unfathomable clamor makes its way up the stairs toward them and begins knock knock a-knocking, Raven-style, and then demands entrance. At the climax of the stranger's story, the unfathomable clamor reveals itself to be the very deceased tribe he'd spoken of. Since no one opens the door for them, they tomahawk their way into the room. "I did not move, for I could not; but watched dazedly as the door fell in pieces to admit a colossal, shapeless influx of inky substance starred with shining, malevolent eyes." They collect the stranger, who has himself depleted into an amorphous cloud, and continue on their way, theoretically exercising their vengeance on more otherwordly colonials.

There is so much wrong with this story, narratively speaking: It's basically a weird idea, vaguely dramatized. There is no real conflict, just a gathering tension that only kind of resolves into not much meaning. The protagonist is useless to us, a nervous witness to an event entirely unrelated to him, and when it's over not much has changed; he tears out into the night and is found the next day, bedraggled but otherwise unharmed. His only actions are to follow, watch, and then run.

Still, there is something here that gets to the heart of why Lovecraft resonates. Supernatural fiction, at its best, puts us in conversation with the tension-fraught relationship between history and the present. Ghosts are the personification of the idea that the past didn't go anywhere, we live with it on a daily basis. Lovecraft deploys his supernatural beings across the streets of New York, where they continue to play out the genocidal wars that our country was built on.

Has Lovecraft written himself in here as the uneasy witness to a terrible history, the passive poet and newcomer to the big city? Perhaps. But he also cultivated the appearance of one from another time: He fabricated a British accent reminiscent of his colonial ancestors and wore old-fashioned clothes. He certainly leads us, the readers, through darkened streets and demands we bear witness to supernaturally transforming cityscapes while diatribing maniacally about deep down xenophobic tragedies. So let's say he's both: awkward witness and phantom tour guide. Either way, he places himself at the embattled crossroads of history. And what is New York if not that very crossroads, alive and teeming with victories and tragedies with each new day? The city is always a crossroads—of the future and past, a mash-up of class, race, and gender dynamics all bumping mercilessly against each other, falling in love and committing mass murder—and so few urban fantasies today grasp that in any way beyond background noise. But here, in all its abhorrent messiness, is history and race, front and center.

The Writer As Elegant Demonic Archivist

"One can never produce anything as terrible and impressive as one can awesomely hint about," Lovecraft wrote to fellow science-fiction writer James Blish. And indeed, most of what he offers up are tantalizing clues, that creeping sense of horror. In one of his final stories, "The Whisperer In Darkness" (1930), a professor from Lovecraft's invented New England school Miskatonic University is lured to the Vermont cabin of a crazed conspiracy theorist. During an all-night conversation with what turns out to be the decomposing body of his host, animated by alien beings, the professor learns presumably the entire mystery of this other realm, a thing we the readers never get a chance to fully know. In typical Lovecraft fashion, the knowledge nearly drives our protagonist mad: "Never was a sane man more dangerously close to the arcane of basic entity—never was an organic brain nearer to utter annihilation in the chaos that transcends form and force and symmetry."

Other stories such as "Pickman's Model" (1926), "The History of the Necronomicon" (1927), and "The Case of Charles Dexter Ward" (1927) offer up the evidence we might find in the archaic archives of an unsolved crime: journal entries from unfortunate souls who fell afoul of the transdimensional monsters and their devotees, police reports, witness statements. Here is exhibit B, a most unusual and otherwordly item of jewelry on display at the Miskatonic University museum. Here in their locked-away collection you'll find the feared Necronomicon, written by the "mad Arab" Abu Aziz, a name that Lovecraft took on during his elementary school fascination with Middle Eastern lore. Here's the testimony of a heartbroken father whose son was possessed by an ancient worshipper of the demonic Yog Soggoth and then disintegrated.

There is something of Stoker in this collage of firsthand documents and local lore told with thick, regional accents. But Lovecraft and his denizens were never as lusty or glamorous as the count. The elder gods simply want to wipe the Earth clean so they can restart their own tentacled civilization, and the protagonists give nary a damn about love or money; their forward fire is lit by the deep desire for knowledge. Something is very, very amiss in the world and these mild-mannered college professorly types will stop at nothing to find out what.

But it's not from some heightened sense of justice or the need to save the world that compels them so much as a haunting, inexplicable desperation. They are afraid, and remain so throughout entire stories, right up until they meet their grisly end or, occasionally, outwit the demon gods and their worshippers and make it away only bruised and distraught. Lovecraft offers up no heroes, although we get several noble bands of vigilantes risking it all to lay waste to the odd gigantic invisible menace. Rather, we have the passively curious observer, usually doomed. Lovecraft's philosophy has been (hilariously) described as cosmic indifference, in part because he doesn't seem invested in the survival or nobility of his characters, but rather serves them over to get chomped up in ignoble, useless deaths.

Even when told without the use of firsthand accounts, Lovecraft's prose can take on a cautious, reportorial quality. This is the crouch. You get the sense he's only exercising such restraint to earn the inevitable rhetorical and conceptual explosions later on.

When he pounces, there is a palpable release of tension. Lovecraft is an overwriter, and when he gets excited the adjectives do tend to pile on. And what is exciting in the twisted world of elder gods and comely intellectuals? Usually, architecture. Cities and quaint New England townships shine in brilliant effervescence in the waning sun, horrific towers glare down on twisted inner sanctums of terror as unseemly denizens shuffle and ooze beneath.

Even in his personal writings, biographer Donald Tyson points out, the height of Lovecraft's breathless prose is reserved not for his wife but the first time he glimpses the snow-covered roofs of Marblehead, Mass., a moment which he describes as "the most powerful single emotional climax experienced during my nearly forty years of existence."

Amid this world of cyclopean towers and quiet, sunlit steeples, Lovecraft deploys his self-destructively curious professors, poets, and anthropologists. They brave horrific, gut-wrenching situations, keep coming back for more, but the greatest terror, the final Lovecraftian reveal is often one that turns inward, reaching back to the depths of family genealogy.

"In climbing towards the goal of making robots appear human," Japanese roboticist Masahiro Mori wrote in 1970, "our affinity for them increases until we come to a valley, which I call the uncanny valley."[3]

The uncanny valley is that slim in-between stage, where characters look very real indeed but not quite real enough. The resulting weirdness has an unsettling effect on the audience—we don't know how to process these mutant neither here nor there monsters. As Mori states, "One might say that the prosthetic hand has achieved a degree of resemblance to the human form, perhaps on a par with false teeth. However, when we realize the hand, which at first site looked real, is in fact artificial, we experience an eerie sensation. For example, we could be startled during a handshake by its limp boneless grip together with its texture and coldness. When this happens, we lose our sense of affinity, and the hand becomes uncanny." Animators soon learned the hard way that movies whose characters fell within the Valley (notably, *The Polar Express*) inevitably tank.

Lovecraft pitches a tent in the Uncanny Valley and releases more than a few of his unfortunate inbetweeners from there. *Facts Concerning the Late Arthur Jermyn and His Family* chronicles several generations of explorers: "The Jermyns never seemed to look quite—something was amiss." Indeed. After a sprawling enumeration of the various Jermyns, which keeps us intrigued only by virtue of occasional freakish details—Grandpa Jermyn killed an explorer who told him about a mysterious African city ruled by white apes, then killed two of his own children; the surviving son Alfred Jermyn became a circus trainer, had an unusually close relationship with a white haired ape, attacked it and was killed—we find Arthur Jermyn, who quickly sets himself on fire after receiving a mysterious package that turns out to be a mummified white ape that turns out to by his grandmother!

The Shadow Over Innsmouth begins as a travel log. It's restrained, matter of fact, almost bland but again stays afloat by way of masterful deployment of eerie details. As is typical of Lovecraft, we know from the opening lines that something horrible happens later: There's a government raid, folks barely make it out alive, chaos will come, he promises: "Results, I am certain, are so thorough that no public harm save a shock of repulsion could ever accrue from a hinting of what was found by those horrified raiders at Innsmouth." So we read on: Robert Olmstead, our mild-mannered narrator is fascinated by archeology and ends up in Innsmouth, this creepy little town that not even the residents of nearby Arkham, also a creepy little town, will ven-

3 http://spectrum.ieee.org/automaton/robotics/humanoids/the-uncanny-valley

ture to. The Innsmouth folks have a strange, fishlike quality to them: "Some of 'em have queer narrow heads with flat noses and bulgy, stary eyes that never seem to shut, and their skin ain't quite right. Rough and scabby, and the sides of their necks are all shriveled or creased up. Get bald too, very young." By accosting the town drunk—the exceptionally named Zadok Allen—our narrator gets a lecture on the whispered ancient origins of these Uncanny Valley dwellers. It's all pretty standard horror story fare: Things get worse and worse and the possibility of escape bleaker and bleaker until all out chaos erupts and our hero is dashing through the midnight Innsmouth streets, enacting the curious hobble-walk of its fishlike inhabitants until he can make it out of town just as the FBI swoops in to tear the place up.

But the story doesn't end there. Lovecraft's value system for horror isn't satisfied by a mere chase and escape motif when there are deeper levels of disgust for which to reach. Having escaped Innsmouth, Olmstead's fascination, like Jermyn's and, in fact, Lovecraft's, turns to his own family history, which he eventually traces back to the very aquatic monsters he'd barely gotten away from. He doesn't just come to accept this fact; Olmstead embraces it. "I shall plan my cousin's escape from that Canton madhouse," he plots as the story draws to a close, "and together we shall go to marvel-shadowed Innsmouth. We shall swim out to that brooding reef in the sea and dive down through the black abysses to Cyclopean and many columned Y'ha-nthlei, and in that lair of the Deep Ones we shall dwell amidst wonder and glory for ever."

Both of Lovecraft's parents died in an asylum and it's easy to imagine a line between this horror of genealogy and his fear of inheriting their mental illnesses. His characters, confronted with the slow-building horrors of supernatural mayhem, routinely call into question their own sanity as dream world and real world intermingle deliriously. Fortunately, the narratives themselves rarely leave ambiguous what really happened, even if the characters themselves get lost in their own inconceivable situations. The monsters are real; another world is not only possible, it's alive and tentacled, breathing menacingly in our neighbor's basement.

But Lovecraft's rabid xenophobia also seethes through this narrative of mutant family trees. As Robert Price points out, "what Lovecraft found revolting in the idea of interracial marriage [is] the subtextual hook of different ethnic races mating and 'polluting' the gene pool." The brainy, awkward Olmstead, besieged by half-breeds in this dilapidated Northeastern city by the sea is of course Lovecraft himself, surrounded by "swarthy" Syrians in that hated boarding house near Red Hook. The horror master knows that the self is the one thing we can never escape, we carry the victories and fuckups of our ancestors everywhere we go, like it or not, and once again history comes crashing into the present tense: The ultimate in fear is that which you fear being inside you, a part of you. It is inescapable so one can either embrace it and lead a secret aquatic life or set one's self on fire.

Lovecraft wrote in a time when *Pace v. Alabama* still allowed states to punish interracial marriage with two to seven years of hard labor. He was all for it: "There will be much deterioration, but the Nordic has a fighting chance of coming out on top in the end." Attempts to federalize the illegality of miscegenation looked like this:[4]

> That intermarriage between negroes or persons of color and Caucasians or any other character of persons within the United States or any territory under their jurisdiction, is forever prohibited; and the term 'negro or person of color,' as here employed, shall be held to mean any and all persons of African descent or having any trace of African or negro blood.

And in 1922, the Cable Act passed, retroactively stripping citizenship from anyone marrying an "alien ineligible of citizenship." The United States didn't fully legalize inter-racial marriage until 1967.

Lovecraft's inward-looking horror endures, stands out, persists, because it reflects white America's own tortured conversation with itself. Here, coded in legalese and legitimized by the mechanisms of the state, we have the same rippling fear of lineage that sends Arthur Jermyn into his self-immolating frenzy and Olmstead into an underground life of crime. In the opening years of the 20th century, white America was looking back at its own twisted history; *The Birth of a Nation* (1915) places the Klan as the heroic saviors of the South, protecting its maidenly virtue from lusty mulattos. Enter Lovecraft with his literature of the genealogical terror. Of course it endures.

Allow me to further contextualize: In the second decade of the 21st century, a hundred years after Lovecraft wrote his first short story, "The Tomb", in the age of Trayvon, Rinisha and Marissa, the troubled world of science fiction and fantasy is only beginning to come to terms with people of color being among its ranks. Sci-fi conventions and online forums continue to be in the thrall and fallout of one racist/sexist incident or another. Major publishing houses still whitewash characters of color on the covers; racial coding still rules the day and mainstream slavery narratives in fantasy literature still revolve around the mythical white savior. This is the legacy we're left with by not fully confronting the racism of our own literary lineage.

The World Fantasy Award, one of the industry's most prestigious honors, is a statue of Lovecraft, and one of the most honest and challenging angles on this is the dialogue between fantasy authors Nnedi Okorafor and China Miéville over their discomfort at receiving it.[5] "I put it out of sight," Miéville writes of the bust, "in my study, where only I can see it, and I have turned it to face the wall. So I am punishing the little fucker like the malevolent clown he was, I can look at it and remember the honour, and above all I am writing behind Lovecraft's back."

Indeed. As writers, consumers of weird literature, creatures of imagination and insight, lovers of justice, can we face Lovecraft head-on, taking in his atrocious bigotry, and still find value in his work? We don't have a choice. The mythos endures, its legacy reaches into the heart of modern speculative fiction; the world we live in is complicated and imperfect, beset by tragedy and weighed down with lies powerful people have told us about ourselves. So we call it what it is, unflinchingly and not for the sole purpose of moving on but

4 http://civilliberty.about.com/od/raceequalopportunity/tp/Interracial-Marriage-Laws-History-Timeline.htm
5 http://nnedi.blogspot.com/2011/12/lovecrafts-racism-world-fantasy-award.html

to sit with the painful resonance of this truth and proceed humbly, cautiously, with sharpened knives.

This article first appeared on *BuzzFeed* on January 7, 2014.
www.buzzfeed.com/danieljoseolder/one-hundred-years-of-weird-fear

WRITING IN INK TO SAMARKAND

Paul Weimer

You can hear a distant thunder of hoofbeats, steadily growing louder as it approaches. It is a stratum of secondary world fantasy that looks beyond the boundary, the Great Wall of Europe. Secondary world fantasy that is inspired by Byzantium and the Silk Road, all the way to the western borders of China. Characters, landscapes, cultural forms derived from the Abbasid Caliphate, the Taklamakan Desert, and the Empires of Southeast Asia much more than Lancashire.

Thanks to the rising popularity of fantasy fiction, riding, in part, on the wave of *Game of Thrones'* massive success, many of science fiction and fantasy's old paradigms and forms of have gotten a new look by virtue of new and diverse styles and varieties of stories, new and formerly inhibited voices (primarily women, genderqueer, and minorities), and new or formerly under-utilized wellsprings of inspiration. Elizabeth Bear, one of the many authors at the center of this paradigm shift, calls this "Rainbow SF." As Science fiction readies its generation ship to move beyond the white-heteronormative-males-conquer-the-galaxy pastiche, popular fantasy is beginning to look beyond the faux-medieval western European that remained so popular throughout the genre's formative decades. And this doesn't even include the rise of World SF, as fiction from markets and voices beyond North America and England begin to be heard in the field.

I call such books "Silk Road Fantasy."

Silk Road Fantasy is hardly a new idea, and can be traced to the works of early 20th century writer Harold Lamb, and even more specifically to Khlit the Wolf, the Cossack, who wanders from China to Russia in the course of his adventures in the 1600s. Stories like *"Tal Taluai Khan"* set Khilit on the road to adventure, and bring him traveling companions and temporary allies ranging from Afghanistan to China. Most notable of these, Abdul Dost, a Muslim in contrast to Khilit's Eastern Orthodox Christianity, himself becomes the narrator of several of the stories. Those who champions Lamb's fiction, like Harold Andrew Jones, have done excellent work in introducing a new generation of readers to these classic, formative novels. However, in my opinion, the real genesis of Silk Road Fantasy as well as the term itself, comes from the works of Susan Shwartz and Judith Tarr.

In the late '80s and early '90s, Shwartz wrote several series of novels exploring the Silk Road. In the *Heirs of Byzantium* trilogy, an alternate magical Byzantium is the base setting for intrigue and adventure. *Empire of the Eagle* follows the imagined adventures of the survivors of the defeated Roman Legions of the battle of Carrhae, sent further and further east, far away from the world they knew. *Imperial Lady*, co-written with Andre Norton, explores the other end of the Silk Road, featuring a former princess of the Han Court as its protagonist, exiled to the steppes. And, notably, *Silk Roads and Shadows*, the trope namer, wherein a princess of Byzantium heads east in search of the secret of silk.

Judith Tarr's role skews slightly more historical in flavor than Shwartz, and with slightly different interests and locations, focusing on the diversity of Silk Road Fantasy in terms of geography and ethnogeography, and a strong focus on the Crusades. *A Wind in Cairo* features a protagonist transformed into a stallion during the wars between Saladin and the Christian Crusaders. Similarly, *Alamut* (and its sequel *The Dagger and the Cross*) revolve around a prince of Elfland who gets caught up in events like the battle of Hattin and falls for a deathless fire spirit. The cultures, societies and vistas of her *Avaryan* novels, too, range from the Mediterranean to Tibet in their inspiration and wellsprings.

However, as wonderful as their work was (and still worth tracking down decades later), Tarr and Shwartz were among only a few lonely voices in a field not yet ready for exploration. The '80s and '90s were fascinated with faux-medieval worlds—the Four Lands, Midkemia, Osten Ard, and endless celtic fantasy trilogies—meant that the voices drawing on the Silk Road were few and far between. Drowned out. Nearly forgotten.

In the last few years, with the rise of other diversity in fantasy, Silk Road fantasy has returned to prominence. Among the foremost explorers of this long dormant sub-genre is the aforementioned Elizabeth Bear and the *Eternal Sky* trilogy. In his review of the first volume, Aidan Moher, editor of A Dribble of Ink, said, "*Range of Ghosts* is wonderful and compelling, a truly great novel that moves the genre forward by challenging and embracing its history all at once." Bear brings a stunning variety of cultures, terrain, and indelibly memorable characters to Silk Road Fantasy, illustrating the potential for fantasy liberated from the strict terrestrial and historical influences embraced by a large portion of the genre, and fully embracing the potential for secondary world fantasy.

Elizabeth Bear may be the leading light of Silk Road Fantasy, but many others are beside her as she explores a ethnic and geographical history that remains elusive and unknown to many western readers. Mazarkis Williams' *Tower and Knife* trilogy borrows on the Middle East and Central Asia in the sensibilities of the Cerani Empire. K.V. Johansen explores the deep, expansive history and mythology of a world inspired by landscapes and peoples of central Asia and Siberia, complete with a trade road that connects them all. Chris Willrich's second *Gaunt and Bone* novel, *The Silk Map*, takes his heroes west out of a China-like realm onto a Central Asian-like deserts and steppe in a poetically intimate story of family in the midst of looming conflicts and events to shape the future of the world, with magical guardians, trade cities, and and airship flying steppe nomads.

As alluring as the idea of fantasy inspired by lands outside Europe is, there is, as always, the danger of cultural appropriation when dealing with cultures, peoples and societies far outside one's own. Taking merely a veneer or slapdash borrowing of the hard-won heritage of people with a history and concerns of their own is more than just impolite, it's a real problem. Just as the '80s and '90s had a torrent of fantasy novels whose careless borrowings of Celtic mythology and culture frustrate historians and experts in that field, readers must be wary of encouraging Silk Road Fantasy that uses similar appropriations to give its world and air of mysticism and otherliness. Approached with respect, care and careful research, these settings and histories provide wonderful and fresh things for fantasy.

Is Silk Road Fantasy the next big thing? Some upcoming releases certainly indicate that its a booming sub-genre of secondary world fantasy. Ken Liu is publishing his first novel, *The Grace of Kings*, and Elizabeth Bear is working on three more novels set in her *Eternal Sky* universe. The vast potential of fantasy's creative potential, Silk Road Fantasy and beyond, remains full of limitless potential. Consider a sword and sorcery novel set in a city inspired by Samarkand, or a secondary world road trip fantasy novel in the vein of Michael Chabon's *Gentlemen of the Road*. How about more novels that are inspired by the Mongols, the Tibetan Empire, the shamans of the Siberian steppe, the Moghuls, and others along the branches of that fabled trade route. I look forward to many other writers exploring the Silk Road, with careful respect and care to the source cultures, and writing in ink to Samarkand.

This article first appeared on *A Dribble of Ink* on July 14, 2014.
aidanmoher.com/blog/featured-article/2014/07/writing-ink-samarkand-silk-road-fantasy-paul-weimer/

NOTES ON OCTAVIA BUTLER'S 'SURVIVOR'

Matthew Cheney

After reading Gerry Canavan's essay on two newly published short stories by Octavia Butler, one of which is a prequel to her 1978 novel *Survivor*, I decided it was time for me to read *Survivor*, since though I'd read most of Butler's books, and repeatedly assigned a couple of them in classes, I'd never gotten around to this one.[1]

The problem, however, is that *Survivor* is a book Butler disavowed and, once she had the ability, she prohibited it from being reprinted. Used copies tend to sell for at least $65 (although one just sold on E-Bay for $15. Alas, I discovered it only after the sale!).

However, I figured I might be able to get a copy through interlibrary loan, and that's how I discovered my university library had a copy. (You can also find a bootleg PDF online if you search for it. But I didn't tell you that.) I went to the library fully expecting that the book did not exist—that it had disappeared off the shelf without anyone noticing, or that for some reason the catalogue was mistaken. But no. It was there: a hardcover without a dustjacket, in pretty bad condition, its mustard-yellow boards scratched and torn, its corners crushed and frayed, its binding broken. I will be returning it with a note, something to the effect of: "Please take care of this book. It might not look like much, but it is rare. It is valuable. We need it to be preserved."

Having now read *Survivor*—or, more accurately, having compulsively devoured the novel in two days, which for me is very fast, indeed—what I find myself most wanting to say is exactly that, to whoever will listen: *We need this book to be preserved.*

After reading/devouring *Survivor*, I went looking for reviews of it and articles about it. I read every interview with Butler that I could find where she mentioned it. I wanted to know why she had gone out of her way to keep this book from us, because for me it was not just a satisfying read, but a far more satisfying ending to the Patternist series than *Patternmaster*, her first-published novel, a novel I like well enough, but which feels thin: a book for which Butler had considerable vision, but not yet the skill to bring that vision to vivid life.[2] *Survivor* is certainly not as skilled as many of Butler's later novels, even the later-published novels of the Patternist series (as novels, I think both *Wild Seed* and *Clay's Ark* are more accomplished)—but it's at least the equal of *Mind of My Mind*, and in some ways superior to it: I found the ending quite moving, for instance, while for me the most interesting sections of *Mind* are in the middle. *Survivor* also provided a certain sense of closure to

---

1 https://lareviewofbooks.org/review/knowing-ones-listening-octavia-e-butlers-unexpected-stories and http://en.wikipedia.org/wiki/Survivor_%28Octavia_Butler_novel%29
2 http://en.wikipedia.org/wiki/Patternist_series

the Patternist series that *Patternmaster* didn't for me, perhaps because *Survivor* is about some of the last remnants of humanity, the ones who escape Earth and don't end up the "mute" slaves of the Patternists.

Butler's public statements about *Survivor* are not especially illuminating. In an interview with Amazon.com, she said:[3]

> When I was young, a lot of people wrote about going to another world and finding either little green men or little brown men, and they were always less in some way. They were a little sly, or a little like "the natives" in a very bad, old movie. And I thought, "No way. Apart from all these human beings populating the galaxy, this is really offensive garbage." People ask me why I don't like Survivor, my third novel. And it's because it feels a little bit like that. Some humans go up to another world, and immediately begin mating with the aliens and having children with them. I think of it as my Star Trek novel.

One of the central elements of *Survivor* is the ability of humans to have children with the natives of a far-off planet, and this biological improbability seems to be a part of the problem she sees with the book. Elsewhere, she spoke of publishing *Survivor* too soon, as if she wished she'd given it another draft or two, maybe to at least gesture toward some justification for the ability of humans to procreate with the Kohn, the native people of the planet (a common ancestor, for instance).

The biological improbability isn't the main thing. Though no explanation would make it highly scientifically sound, there are improbabilities in Butler's other novels, and this one is hardly a reason to condemn a book to the memory hole.

The main reason she gives there is that of, we might say, the colonial gaze, something common to science fiction from its beginning.[4] In this, though, I think Butler underestimated the richness of her own writing. While certainly the Kohn could have been portrayed more complexly, the novel is not as simple as she makes it out to be, and the humans are often portrayed negatively—they are unprepared, deeply prejudiced, almost suicidally stubborn, and sometimes just stupid.

Why, I wondered, would Butler have apparently come to perceive her novel as simplistic colonialist tripe? Some of the academic writing on Butler has given it good analysis and not come to that conclusion. (The best article I've seen is "Negotiating Genre and Captivity: Octavia Butler's *Survivor*" by Maria Holmgren Troy, which looks closely at one of the genres that I thought *Survivor* was most closely in conversation with when I read it: the captivity narrative.)[5] Then I thought to look up some of the original reviews, and I read Cherry Wilder's from the January 1979 issue of *Foundation* and Geraldine Morse's from the July 1978 issue of *Galileo*.[6] They were illuminating.

3 http://www.amazon.com/exec/obidos/tg/feature/-/11664/
4 http://books.google.com/books?id=xnKLj4mrZjMC&lpg=PP1&dq=colonialism and the emergence of science fiction&pg=PP1#v=onepage&q&f=false
5 http://muse.jhu.edu/journals/callaloo/summary/v033/33.4.troy.html and http://en.wikipedia.org/wiki/Captivity_narrative
6 http://www.isfdb.org/cgi-bin/pl.cgi?293933 and http://www.isfdb.org/cgi-bin/pl.cgi?180781

The Wilder review begins:

> It is interesting to see female fantasies emerging in science fiction; it is also important to perceive them for what they are, because a fantasy—one of the persistent, satisfying day-dreams of mankind—is not a good story. This has been amply demonstrated by hundreds of male fantasies masquerading as science fiction or sword and sorcery. ...
>
> The female fantasy that is currently gathering momentum seems to run as follows: "I was the chosen mate of a large, alien-looking male." There is a treatment of this in Floating Worlds by Cecelia Holland and an interesting variant in Octavia Butler's new novel Survivor. In both cases, with Holland's six and a half foot black Styth and Butler's giant, blue-furred Tehkohn Hao, the aliens are distantly human and the union is blessed with issue.

The Morse review begins:

> If you enjoyed Mandingo, that titillating tear-jerker about the lust of a white plantation mistress for her black slave, you'll probably enjoy Survivor, which raises the tension at least theoretically by introducing a pleasant bestiality in the male partner, who would closely resemble a six foot tall blue gorilla if such a thing existed.
>
> Survivor isn't a bad book, and the ploy of miscegenation perks up an otherwise uneventful story, but with apologies to the gorilla, there's no real meat in it.

Oh my.

I don't know if Butler read these reviews, but if she did, I can see them causing her to rethink her novel. She might have thought that if she had failed so spectacularly as to elicit such responses from reviewers of, presumably, at least a modicum of intelligence and literacy, then she must not have written the book she thought she wrote. Because though of course I'm just speculating here, I'm pretty confident that Octavia Butler did not set out to write a hot-and-heavy interspecies romance fantasy. (I would also suggest that Morse is misreading Mandingo, but lots of people did.)[7]

Survivor is not a fantasy about how much fun it would be to be ruled and dominated by a big furry blue guy. But I can see where readers' discomfort comes from. Diut, the leader of the Tehkohn, is at first repulsed by Alanna, but then works through his repulsion until it becomes a kind of attraction, and he takes her on as a kind of project. He then decides she'd be a great wife for him, and he takes her to his bedroom. She fights him. He says the Tehkohn do not have a tradition of forced mating, but he also doesn't offer her much choice. She gives in when he tells her that if she mates with him, she will be free to live how she wants. At first, it causes her pain ("'I always give pain before I give pleasure,' he said. 'Your body will accustom itself to me.'" [100]),

---

7 http://mumpsimus.blogspot.com/2010/01/mandingo.html

but Alanna finds his fur pleasant and an attraction for him grows. She comes to value him and eventually to love him.

Butler's purpose, it seems to me, was to show how repulsion can become attraction. Humans and Kohn find each other's bodies at best alien, at worst utterly repulsive. They see each other as animals and savages. Alanna is a perpetual outsider, though—on Earth, her parents were killed by Clayarks (humans mutated by the disease brought back on the *Clay's Ark* starship) and she roamed feral for a while until she was adopted by the religious missionaries who soon take her with them to the new planet. She does not share their very strict religion, though, and plenty of the missionaries thought she should be cast out—not only because she wasn't of their faith, but also because of her ancestry.

Here's an important passage from early in the novel:

> "Neila, I've been talking to some of the others and they agree. If we're going to keep the girl in the colony, surely she'd be happier with her own kind."

> There had been a moment of silence, then Neila spoke quietly. "Her own kind? Who are you suggesting I give my daughter to, Bea?"

> The older woman sighed. "Oh, my. I knew this was going to be difficult. But, Neila, the girl isn't white."

> "She's Afro-Asian from what she says of her parents. Black father, Asian mother."

> "Well, we don't have any Asians, but one of our black families might..."

> "She has a home, Bea. Right here."

> "But..."

> "Most of the blacks here are no more interested than the whites in adopting a wild human. The ones who are interested have already been here. Jules and I turned them down."

> "...so I'd heard."

> "Then why are you here?"

> "I thought that after you'd had a few days with the girl, you might... reconsider."

> There was the sound of Neila's laughter. "Come to my senses, you mean."

"That's exactly what I mean!" snapped the older woman. "Several of us feel that you and Jules ought to be setting a better example for the young people here—not encouraging them to mix and…" [31]

A fear of mixing, a fear of impurity and contamination, carries through the whole novel, again and again leading characters toward decisions and actions that harm them. One of the pleasures of reading even Butler's earliest books is that many things which seem straightforward and even obvious are complicated by something else within the story. She doesn't just show us that the fear of mixing and contamination is a hindrance and even a danger to various characters—she shows that sometimes it's a justified fear. The other group of Kohn, the Garkohn, kidnap and seem to plan to inseminate some of the humans because within their ethical system, this means the humans are then bound by Garkohn laws and dictates. In all of her novels, Butler is fascinated by the ways that power is wielded, and even when she seems to show power to be a necessary and perhaps benevolent tool, it is never unambiguously so.

This reminds me of something Dorothy Allison wrote in a 1989 essay on Butler for the *Village Voice* (collected in *Reading Black, Reading Feminist* ed. Henry Louis Gates):[8]

I love Octavia Butler's women even when they make me want to scream with frustration. The problem is not their feminism; her characters are always independent, stubborn, difficult, and insistent on trying to control their own lives. What drives me crazy is their attitude: the decisions they make, the things they do in order to protect and nurture their children—and the assumption that children and family always come first.

…While acknowledging the imbalances and injustices inherent in traditional family systems, Butler goes on writing books with female characters who heroically adjust to family life and through example, largeness of spirit, and resistance to domination make the lives of those children better—even though this means sacrificing personal freedom. But she humanizes her dark vision of women's possibilities by making sure that the contradictions and grief her women experience are as powerfully rendered as their decision to sacrifice autonomy […] Homosexuality, incest, and multiple sexual pairings turn up in almost all her books, usually insisted on by the patriarchal or alien characters and resisted by the heroines, who eventually give in. Her women are always in some form of bondage, captives of domineering male mutants or religious fanatics or aliens who want to impregnate them. Though the men in Butler's novels are often equally oppressed, none is forced so painfully to confront the difference between surrender and adjustment. Women who surrender die; those who resist, struggle, adjust, compromise, and live by their own ethical stan-

8 http://www.worldcat.org/title/reading-black-reading-feminist-a-critical-anthology/oclc/21375690

dards survive to mother the next generation—literally to make the next world. Maybe if this world were not so hard a place, butler might be writing less painful fiction.

I think the patterns that Allison sees in Butler's novels are sometimes more nuanced than she describes here, and this description doesn't really show the way that Butler's interest in the idea of family is an interest in the idea of a chosen family, or at least a family less of blood than convenience. Her families often become communities. Her interest in power (and power struggles), though, leads her to depict families and communities where not everyone has the equal power to choose whether to be a member. Again and again, people are pulled into communities against their will. They may come to see the community as the best place for them, but usually it is some person of power who brings them in. (For more on family, communities, and kinship in Butler's work, see some of the references in Susan Knabe and Wendy Gay Pearson's "'Gambling Against History': Queer Kinship and Cruel Optimism in Octavia Butler's *Kindred*" in *Strange Matings: Science Fiction, Feminism, African American Voices, and Octavia E. Butler*.)[9]

Nonetheless, Allison gets at the peculiar frustration, discomfort, and even discombobulation that reading Butler can cause. I struggled with this myself when I read my first Butler novel, *Parable of the Sower*, somewhere around 1996 or so. I *hated* it. Viscerally and vehemently. Mostly because I thought Butler was trying to write a book about how wonderful the protagonist Lauren Olamina was, and how much we should all worship and admire her. As a novice to reading Butler, I didn't yet understand the complex stance her books take toward their protagonists, particularly the ones like Lauren who become the leaders of a group or community. Yes, there is attraction, but the attraction can also be a trap, and that was the trap I fell into: I legitimately liked Lauren through much of *Sower*, but I was also put off by her confidence in her, I thought, insipid spirituality. (Again, I was reading it shallowly. The text is quite ambivalent about that spirituality, if "spirituality" is even the right word for it.) In Butler's work, power always corrupts. But sometimes, there's just no better option.

It also counters the power fantasies so prevalent in SF and popular culture in general. Cherry Wilder was, I think, spectacularly wrong about the "female fantasy" of *Survivor*. In various interviews, Butler noted that as a child she was an avid reader of comic books, and the influence is clear—indeed, the Patternist series sometimes feels like a version of the X-Men. But Butler's take on the power fantasies inherent to both superhero comics and a certain strain of science fiction is not an uncritical one. She knows the seductive power of such fantasies, and she's more than aware of the terrors that seduction can lead to. (As I, perhaps prejudicially, read her, she sees similar seductions in religion. Sometimes I think a basic theme of Butler's work could be stated as, "The power fantasies of comic books, sci-fi, and religion are not all that different...")

Along similar lines, a clever idea that Maria Holmgren Troy proposes is that *Survivor* can be read as (among other things) an allegory of science fiction itself:

9 http://www.aqueductpress.com/books/StrangeMatings.php

Interestingly, in the context of science fiction, it is possible to see Alanna—and by extension Survivor—as a child of Butler's imagination, and the name "Jules Verrick" as a reference to Jules Verne, who is sometimes considered to be the "father of science fiction." Verne is regarded as one of the most important "pioneers of the tale of the extraordinary voyage into outer space, the most typical of all science-fictional themes" (James 16), which ... is one of the premises of Survivor.[10] Verrick's wife is called Neila, which if the letters are reversed spells "alien." Thus, in this allegorical reading, Octavia Butler's wild child is adopted by the white science-fiction tradition with its domesticated aliens, a tradition which her transgressive work challenges; consequently, the genre and its audience's generic expectations are forced to expand in order to contain Survivor. Butler stated in an interview in the late 1970s that what she would really like her novels to accomplish is to "make people feel comfortable with characters who are not all male, who are not all white, and who just don't fit. Who are not middle class, who don't fit the stereotype" ("Butler Interviewed" 31).[11]

Of all of Butler's books, Survivor may be the one most clearly in dialogue with much of the science fiction that came before it. While reading it, I thought repeatedly of some of the novels of John Brunner, perhaps because Butler cited them as an influence in a 1997 interview with Joan Fry for Poets & Writers (collected in Conversations with Octavia Butler):[12] "The writers who influenced me most tended to be those who were the most prolific. John Brunner was very prolific—my favorites are Polymath, The Whole Man, and The Long Result." (The influence of those three books on the Patternist series seems pretty clear, with Polymath the closest to Survivor.) One of the things I find notable in the two original reviews of Survivor that I was able to dig up is their determination to read the book within the standard science fictional frame, and thus to see it as unoriginal and thin and perplexing; whereas it's a much more satisfying novel if read as an at least somewhat skeptical outsider to the conventional conversation, the standard narrative.

I have moved away from so much of what I thought I'd be writing here, and I haven't written much in detail about Survivor itself, but perhaps that's for the best. I need to read it again. I am very torn about many of its elements and implications. But I am not torn about one thing: no matter how much Butler regretted the book, no matter how embarrassed she was by it, it is, I think, a perfectly respectable part of her oeuvre, and vastly better than the work of many, many writers.

With that in mind, I think it's worth considering whether Butler's literary executor(s) should consider re-releasing Survivor. The question should be considered carefully, because it was Butler's wish that no-one read the book. (In Strange Matings, Nisi Shawl says the first Butler novel she read was Survivor, and so eventually she asked Butler to sign it for her. Butler did, but wrote: "Nisi, I wish you didn't have this one.") Any new edition should of course make

10 http://www.worldcat.org/title/science-fiction-in-the-twentieth-century/oclc/185500987
11 http://sf3.org/history/janus-aurora-covers/aurora-14-vol-4-no-4-table-of-contents/
12 http://www.worldcat.org/title/conversations-with-octavia-butler/oclc/320196636

Butler's disavowal clear. My own desire would be for an academic/critical edition, a book where the text of the novel was accompanied by some essays about it (and not just fawning ones). With the release of the new short stories, it seems especially valuable to have *Survivor* available again. But I don't know. It's entirely a selfish desire on my part—I'm fascinated by the book and would like to own it, and I'd like to be less worried that my library's copy is going to disintegrate and be impossible to replace.

In any case, if you happen to find a copy of *Survivor*, don't be afraid of it. It's worth reading. It's not Butler at her best, by any means, but it's at least a worthy companion to *Patternmaster* and *Mind of My Mind*, and it's not nearly as bad as she thought it was. Indeed, when I think of *Survivor* now, it's with some sadness, because I don't like to think of Butler disliking her own work so much that she would want it to disappear, especially when that work is more complex and thoughtful than much of what's out there.

This article first appeared on *The Mumpsimus* on August 7, 2014.
http://mumpsimus.blogspot.com/2014/08/notes-on-octavia-butlers-survivor.html

REVIEWS

FLESH AND BONES

Nina Allan

"Kevern, look. I don't know when your mother did these, but they are of another time. Art has changed. We have returned to the primordial celebration of the loveliness of the natural world. You can see there is none of that in what your mother did. See how fractured her images are. There is no harmony here. The colours are brutal—forgive me, but you have asked me and I must tell you. I feel jittery just turning the pages. Even the human body, that most beautiful of forms, is made jagged and frightful. The human eye cannot rest for long on these, Kevern. There is too much mind here. They are disruptive of the peace we go to art to find." (*J* 272)

When the longlist for the Man Booker prize was announced two months ago, I expressed delight that David Mitchell's *The Bone Clocks* had been selected—a choice that could only, I suggested, be good for speculative fiction's relationship with the Booker—and surprise at the inclusion of Howard Jacobson. Not that the choice of Jacobson himself was anything out of the ordinary—he's won the prize once already—but that in *J* he had produced a work that everyone seemed to agree was science fiction. I felt curious about that, to put it mildly, and thought it might be interesting in the run-up to the prize to read both works and compare them, to discover how two such outwardly dissimilar writers had chosen to approach speculative themes, to see which—if either—eventually made it through to the shortlist.

We now know the answer to that last—Jacobson's *J* made the cut, Mitchell's *The Bone Clocks* didn't. But what of the books themselves? Mitchell's novel was the bookies' favourite right through the longlist period, with both mainstream and SFF critics expressing strong opinions about it, and its disinclusion came as something of a shock. Conversely, no one seemed to be talking much about *J*, and the previously Booker-crowned Jacobson appeared something of an outsider. At the time of the shortlist announcement I was about halfway through *The Bone Clocks*, and planning to move on to *J* as soon as I'd finished. Having now read them both, I think it's safe to say that my opinions coming out of this particular reading experience are pretty much the opposite of what I expected. That in itself has made this mini-project worthwhile.

I went into *The Bone Clocks* from the position of having read all Mitchell's previous works bar one (*The Thousand Autumns*) and considered them all well above average, both in terms of the writing itself and in terms of what Mitchell was trying to achieve with it. I had a particular fondness for *Black Swan Green*, and thought both the concept and execution of *Cloud Atlas* close to miraculous. I was expecting big things of *The Bone Clocks*, especially given that it had been widely tagged as Mitchell's most openly speculative novel to date.

That is true—it is—but that goes no way towards mitigating the fact that in my opinion it is also Mitchell's weakest novel by quite some distance. The mainstream critics who thought the novel was let down by its "plunge" into fantasy in the fifth segment pointed to the rest of the novel—its five real-world sections—as proof of Mitchell's gifts as a storyteller and a wordsmith. If only he'd ditch all this awful genre nonsense, they seemed to be saying, we might actually have a decent writer on our hands. Many of those same critics have pointed to Mitchell's characterisation—and his portrayal of his central character Holly Sykes in particular—as the chief strength of the novel, but for me it felt patchy at best, bland for the most part, and dire at worst. Far from being a brilliantly realised creation Holly is something of a cipher, acting out the roles Mitchell requires for her rather than taking on any discernible life of her own. We learn little, if anything, of Holly's interests or ambitions. As she appears in "A Hot Spell" (the novel's first long segment) she is deliberately set up to be a "typical" fifteen-year-old girl, enamoured of the wrong boyfriend and looking for any excuse to cut loose from her parents. I found Mitchell's realisation of the teenage mind unconvincing. He deliberately sets out to make Holly as "average" as possible, scattering her speech with contractions and causes, but his portrayal of her is inconsistent—he has Holly referencing Radio 4's Thought for the Day at one point, and her stroppiness and decision to become a runaway feel like bolt-on elements, exercises in youthful alienation rather than the real deal. In contrast with the beautifully evoked, deeply felt ambience of *Black Swan Green*, the whole of this part one seems strangely flat, a recapitulation stripped of weight and personal investment. The checklist of references to contemporary politics and music has all the verisimilitude of stage decoration for a 1980s theme party. As the book progresses Holly becomes even less her own person, dragooned into action first as a winning waif pursued by an amoral serial seducer, then as the pissed-off partner of an obsessive war reporter (some of the dialogue that is given to Holly in that section is just awful) and as "mysterious other" for a morally bankrupt author later on. We are asked to see Holly as "special"—yet aside from the fact that she hears voices, we know nothing about her specialness, because we know next to nothing about her. We are interested in her because our attention is caught by the way she keeps cropping up throughout the book—but shorn of the forward momentum granted to her by the plot, there is remarkably little substance to Holly Sykes. She is wooden throughout, a narrative placeholder. When you consider the wonderful characterisation we saw in *Cloud Atlas*—the Sixsmith/Frobisher section contains some of the finest writing Mitchell has yet produced—and the brilliant portrayal of the teenager Jason in *Black Swan Green*, this is still more of a pity.

The most consistent character-building we find in *The Bone Clocks* comes in "Myrrh is Mine, its Bitter Perfume" (the novel's second segment) and "Crispin Hershey's Lonely Planet" (its fourth). The "hero" of the former is Hugo Lamb, who gave a cameo appearance as Jason's loathsome cousin in *Black Swan Green* and who appears here as an even more loathsome Cambridge undergraduate and amateur-soon-to-turn-professional-sociopath. Hugo's attitudes and behaviours are worse than vile, and he is brilliantly written. Equally so is Crispin Hershey, an embittered novelist who takes his revenge on a literary critic with appalling results. (In a recent interview on Radio 4's Front Row, Mitchell insisted that the character of Hershey was not based on Martin Amis. *Dessicated Embryos*, he reminded us, was the title of a piano work by Erik Satie, not a backhanded reference to one of the younger Mr Amis's early successes. But *Red Monkey*? Hal "The Hyena" Grundy?? Come on.) Both Lamb's portion of the narrative and Hershey's are dynamic and vigorous, enlivened by moments of genuine comedy and, in Hershey's case, pathos. A shame then that "The Wedding Bash", part three of the novel and potentially just as interesting as the two sections that bookend it, turns out to be another misfire. Its protagonist Ed Brubeck was interesting in 'A Hot Spell'—intelligent, mature beyond his years and a bit of a loner, he came off the page far more forcefully than Holly. But when he reappears as a war journalist in "The Wedding Bash", it seems to be for the sole purpose of expounding Mitchell's views on Western intervention in Iraq and Afghanistan. It is not that one disagrees with Ed's views—indeed the section might have been a lot more interesting if one had—but that they would appear to have zero importance to or impact on the novel as it progresses. I initially believed that Mitchell was playing a long game, that he would be bound to link this realworld war in some ingenious way with the "secret history" that is revealed two hundred pages later. As it turns out, no—Ed Brubeck is just the author having a go at Tony Blair. Not a bad thing in itself, but not relevant to the story either.

Which brings us to the crux of this novel, or its downfall, depending on your point of view. In "An Horologist's Labyrinth", part five of the novel and its longest section, we learn that Holly has been a pawn in a larger game all along, a centuries-long battle between two opposing groups of immortals, the Horologists (the goodies) and the Anchorites (the soul-sucking baddies). It is these meddlesome demigods who variously "stole" Holly's brother, co-opted her lover to the dark side, helped her to find her missing daughter and plagued her with invisible voices from the age of seven. Now is the time of final reckoning, a fight to the death between the Blind Cathar and his Forces of Evil and our plucky band of Scoobies, outmanned in numbers but not in moral strength.

Where do we even start?? In his review for The New Yorker, the critic James Wood stated the following:[1]

> As soon as the fantasy theme announces itself [...] the reader is put on alert, and is waiting for the next visitation, which arrives punctually. Gradually, the reader begins to understand that the realism—the human activity—is relatively unimportant.

I earlier wrote a lengthy criticism of Wood's essay, because it seemed and still seems to me that to equate "the human activity" solely with the realist mode is to denigrate a mode of literature—the fantastic—whilst remaining

1 http://www.newyorker.com/magazine/2014/09/08/soul-cycle

ignorant of its capabilities.[2] I stand by that assertion, and would go further in saying that Wood's main purpose in this essay seems to lie in using *The Bone Clocks* as a proof of the inherent crapness of speculative fiction generally. I think he's got it the wrong way round—one bad book is no proof of anything, and he doesn't go anywhere near far enough in putting a rocket up *The Bone Clocks* for the direness of that fantasy section.

It is the imbalance that is so embarrassing, the use of the kind of broad brush gestures and clichéd dialogue that would and should not be taken seriously in any literary context. Contrary to what Wood says in his review, the best speculative fiction works precisely because the writer sees no inherent difference, in fictional terms, between the quotidian realm and the fantastical, and approaches the writing of each—characterisation, sense of place, the use of language—with equal care and weight. In terms of a story's seriousness, whether the "human case" to be examined resides in a fictional Glasgow or a fictional Gormenghast should be of little importance. Mitchell himself clearly understands this—even if some of the science fiction in *Cloud Atlas* feels a little clunky, there can be no doubt that Mitchell fought hard for the soul of that book and won. The central SFnal sections feel as integral to the whole as the outer, realworld sections, and in formal as well as plot terms each thread of the story leads logically and elegantly from one to the next. In ambition and execution, *Cloud Atlas* as a novel project more than measures up to Mitchell's formidable talent as a storyteller.

Why then is "An Horologist's Labyrinth" so rife with genre cliché—decades-old genre cliché at that? Why does Hugo Lamb, so brilliantly realised in part two, reappear speaking like a badly-written Bond villain in part five? Why does Holly suddenly start bellowing about FAHMLY in upper case? I sought desperately for some ironical, authorial awareness of just how ham-fisted this section is, but failed to find it. It felt like being trapped in a particularly dreadful episode of *Doctor Who*.

The sixth section, "Sheep's Head", is not much better. We're into science fiction territory now, so of course everyone starts capitalising their nouns: Convoy, Cordon, Village. Then someone says: "There's a link between bigotry and bad spelling, I've met it before" (542), the Chinese are blamed for slaughtering the last elephant herds for the luxury goods market, and Holly wonders what it's going to be like for her granddaughter Lorelei, being raped by born-again Christians and forced into servitude in some even-worse version of Saudi Arabia. The novel's eventual denouement is so lazy and so—I hate to use the word of a writer like Mitchell—trite it barely merits discussion. One reader review I happened upon suggested that the Horologists are ciphers for writers, that the novel's ending is a wishful rewriting of "the Script." This could have been an interesting idea, but there is little evidence that this is what Mitchell intended, and if it is, then he has fumbled the execution so badly that it scarcely matters. Ian McEwan performed that trick better at the end of *Atonement*, and I say that as someone not keen on praising McEwan at the best of times.

I think the best word to describe my feelings about *The Bone Clocks* is baffled. Here we have six loosely linked novellas struggling to find a core

2 http://www.ninaallan.co.uk/?p=1693

narrative. Here we have a use of genre tropes so hackneyed and two-dimensional they would feel out of place and old hat even in a more conventional core genre urban fantasy. What is Mitchell trying to tell us here, what was he trying to *do*? Was it simply that he struggled with this book for so long that it finally overmastered him? I can empathise with that situation, one-hundred percent. But no amount of fellow feeling, or admiration for the talent that still bursts suddenly and unexpectedly to life in parts of even this book, will prevent *The Bone Clocks* from being anything other than a baggy, directionless mess.

I fully expected to love *The Bone Clocks*. I thought this might be the year Mitchell won the Booker. I came away thinking that he'd have to pull something pretty special out of the bag to make me trust him again. Howard Jacobson's *J* was another matter entirely. Jacobson is one of those writers whose flagrant self-regard seems so unwieldy it is almost comedic. I went into the book assuming I would hate it, that it would be both useless at being SF and so up itself as to be more or less unreadable. I was prepared for almost anything but what I actually found: a work that is unlike anything else I have ever read, a book that has nothing do to with science fiction but that is nonetheless fascinating in the way it approaches speculative materials, a novel that will remain with me long after the discussion of the current Booker Prize shortlist is over and no matter what the result.

J has been widely described as a dystopia, bearing comparison with classics of the subgenre such as *1984* and *Brave New World*. I personally think this is misleading, and anyone picking up *J* expecting a gory slice of police brutality and the perils of being a subversive in an authoritarian State with a capital S is going to find him or herself confounded almost immediately. No doubt there will be complaints in some quarters—indeed I've already encountered a few—that Jacobson shows no interest in what I would reluctantly describe as worldbuilding, in constructing a quid pro quo equivalent of a fully realised dystopian universe complete with depleted landscapes, alternate technologies and carefully delineated chart of alternate history. I would argue that Jacobson's scattershot attempts at worldbuilding—there is a thing called a utility phone that will only accept local calls, the internet has been deconstructed or abolished, the names of places and people have been rearranged—are kept deliberately vague, because worldbuilding was the last thing on Jacobson's mind (he has probably not even heard of the concept and would doubtless sneer at it if he had). Unlike other mainstream dabblers, Jacobson does not fail at science fiction, because he wasn't trying to write science fiction in the first place. Where mainstream writers trying their hands at SF so often go wrong is in concentrating so hard on reconstructing what has already been done that they lose control of the central thrust of their idea—or else discover that they never had one (see above). The resulting texts often feel pallid, an emotional or intellectual void. Gutless. Once the second hand trappings of dystopia or post-apocalypse or whatever have been stripped away, there is nothing to see. Jacobson has provided us with something to see, a thought-experiment so effective and so original that there is only one way to read this book: forget SF, forget dystopia, forget any preconceived ideas you might have about Jacobson and read the book for what it is.

In steep contrast with *The Bone Clocks*, *J* is not an easy reading experience. I don't just mean the content, I mean the style, which is terse, undramatic, frequently wordy, sometimes opaque. It is, as they say, hard to get into. But if there is a secret to reading *J*, it is not to try to get into it, but instead to let it get into you. Let it possess you. See what happens. Although evasion—not saying things, not clarifying, not noticing—forms the very fabric of *J*, the novel is not in the end evasive, and its central characters, though rendered elliptically in muted tones and without any of Mitchell's gestural *verismo*, become insistent in their reality, terrifying in their vulnerability. They linger in the mind. In the very best sense of the word they are *durable*. For all Jacobson's reticence in revealing her, Ailinn Solomons turns out to be just about a hundred times more convincing and important than Holly Sykes.

Another misconception about *J* is that it is "about" the Nazi Holocaust. Although the fictional event at the centre of the novel—referred to throughout as WHAT HAPPENED, IF IT HAPPENED—concerns the massacre of Jews, Jacobson has said in interview that *J* is not about antisemitism or the Holocaust specifically:[3]

> The Jews happen to be the group that I know about, so it is informed by antisemitism, but the point is that if you get rid of 'the other' you then have an absence; an absence of irony, an absence of disputatiousness. No argument should ever win that completely.

To "write what he knows" has been a sound decision for Jacobson, because the sense of quietly determined, indeed passionate personal investment that permeates this text allows it to be transformed all the more forcibly into the universal. In essence, *J* is about *all* othering—scapegoating, politicised hatred, the corruption of a whole society by the sense that there are "some people" who it is all right to ostracise, blame, dispose of because they don't really belong, who are "not like us." What *J* does most effectively is to deprive us of the "just obeying orders" defense, as put forward by concentration camp functionaries and SS officers at Nuremberg. *J* shows us a society sanctimoniously in mourning for itself, even while the cells of resurgent hatreds—hatreds that have never in fact gone away—bubble like septic sores just beneath the surface. The atmosphere of unease, of dread—especially in the more openly fantastical "Necropolis" section of the book, which reads like a half-remembered nightmare—is palpable. The complacency of individuals—the bland smiles, the bland music—becomes ever more chilling as the book progresses. In the end you realise—as our protagonist has suspected all along—that you are standing on ground that looked solid, but that has been fatally undermined and is about to collapse:

> 'What will it take? The same as it has always taken. The application of a scriptural calumny...to economic instability, inflamed nationalism, an unemployed and malleable populace in whom the propensity to hero-worship is pronounced, supine government,

3 http://www.theguardian.com/books/2014/sep/13/howard-jacobson-man-booker-interview

tedium vitae, a self-righteous and ill-informed elite, the pertinaciousness of old libels... Plus zealotry. Never forget zealotry, that torch to the easily inflamed passions of the benighted and the cultured alike. What it won't take, because it won't need—because it never needs—is an evil genius to conceive and direct the operation. We have been lulled by the great autocrat-driven genocides of the recent past into thinking that nothing of that enormity of madness can ever happen again, not anywhere, least of all here. And it's true—nothing on such a scale probably ever will. But lower down the order of horrors, and answering a far more modest ambition, carnage can still be connived at—lesser bloodbaths, minor murders, butchery of more modest proportions.' (*J* p 292)

In his New Yorker review, James Wood argues that the fantasy element of *The Bone Clocks* is so overbearing it renders its human protagonists impotent—in fact the central issue with Mitchell's novel is that the fantasy element is actually meaningless, a paper tiger, a bit of cheap decoration pinned on to a story that doesn't have a clear idea of what it's trying to do. The novel wears its fantasy on its sleeve like a row of brass buttons polished to mirror brightness but does nothing with it. *The Bone Clocks* is easy and often enjoyable to read, but when you ask yourself what it is *about*, you are forced to conclude: not a lot. By contrast, *J* takes those elements of speculative fiction that make it so versatile and so important—the idea of disjuncture, of discomfiture, of *imagining*—and fashions from them something that is both remarkable in terms of its concept and vital in terms of what it is saying. The novel is meticulously crafted, a concentrated amalgam of thought and emotion that entirely repays the effort of getting to grips with it. It is a resolute book, a tough book. Is it valuable as literature? Yes. Should Jacobson feel proud of what he has achieved here? Certainly.

This article first appeared on *The Spider's House* on
September 22, 2014.
www.ninaallan.co.uk/?p=1710

"NEVER GIVE A SWORD TO A WOMAN WHO CAN'T DANCE"

Aidan Moher

Ann Leckie can dance.

When her debut novel, *Ancillary Justice*, released in 2014, nobody expected it to hit the science fiction community like a nuclear bomb. But it did. And Leckie was dancing the whole way through.

It was a firecracker of a novel—small and intense—but the unusual narrative structure and Leckie's bold take on gender might have limited the audience to the most passionate and feminist-minded readers. Instead, the exact opposite happened: *Ancillary Justice* wasn't a small *snap, crackle, pop* in a corner of fandom, it was a conflagration of love and adoration heard 'round the community.

Ancillary Justice won almost every major literary award for science fiction and fantasy in 2014, including the Hugo and Nebula Awards for Best Novel, and has sold over 30,000 copies to date, proving that not only is there a market for progressive, thoughtful space opera, there's a thirst for it among readers. *Ancillary Justice* was a huge critical and commercial success, but with that success comes a lot of pressure for a sequel that lives up to its predecessor and satisfies its many fans. Writing under that sort of pressure can be the first stumbling point for many first time novelists, but Leckie never misses a beat.

From genderless characters to the concept of ancillaries (human conduits for advanced AI), Leckie surprised readers with many aspects she introduced in *Ancillary Justice*. With those set pieces established, however, *Ancillary Sword* is forced to rely less on subversion and unsettling reader biases, and more on its ability to deliver the things that readers want from a space opera. Does it succeed? Yes. And No.

Ancillary Sword flies on different wings than its predecessor. *Ancillary Justice* was a frantic roller coaster of a novel, leaving readers out of breath as they followed Breq on her quest for vengeance. *Ancillary Sword* features a more straight forward narrative. Gone is the complex split narrative, and in its place is a plot that trades structural complexity for approachability without sacrificing nuance.

In so many ways, *Ancillary Sword* is less a space opera and more a languid exploration of ideas that were passed by in *Ancillary Justice*'s mad rush to its climax. *Ancillary Sword* features no big space battles, very little in the way of physical danger for the protagonists, and only the barest hint of a threat from the mysterious Presger (who would be smack bang in the middle of the conflict in most other space operas.) By avoiding the trap of trying to write the same novel over again, Leckie allows *Ancillary Sword* to nurture its own success, and to be as compelling and interesting as its predecessor without feeling stale.

At the centre of many of the novel's most central themes are the ancillaries and Breq's growing discomfort with her own history and the uneasy truce she has formed with the Lord of the Radch, Anaander Mianaai. Early in the novel, Breq ponders the twisted physical reality of the 3,000 year old emperor:

> Each of her thousands of brains had grown and developed around the implants that joined her to herself. For three thousand years she had never at any time experienced being anyone but Anaander Mianaai. Never been a single-bodied person—preferably in late adolescence or early adulthood, but older would do in a pinch—taken captive, stored in a suspension pod for decades, maybe even centuries, until she was needed. Unceremoniously thawed out, implant shoved into her brain, severing connections, making new ones, destroying the identity she'd had all her life so far and replacing it with a ship's AI.
>
> If you haven't been through it, I don't think you can really imagine it. The terror and nausea, the horror, even after it's done and the body knows it's the ship, that the person it was before doesn't exist anymore to care that she's died (21).

"We ourselves are actually made up of different parts that are all, so far as we know—acting as one." Leckie said in a recent AMA on /r/sciencefiction, in response to a reader's question about the technological intersect between ancillaries and their humaninty.[1] "Or when they're not, we tell ourselves a story about our actions that makes it seem like we are, and smooths over conflicts or inconsistencies. But it doesn't take much to disrupt that, and maybe it's an illusion to begin with. I think of ancillaries as working kind of the same way, only on a larger scale."

Breq is an ancillary who gains freedom by sacrificing her connections to the individual pieces that Leckie references above, an aspect that Leckie uses ably examine themes of individualism, societal obligation, and human rights. Breq directly confronts many of these issues through her narrative and some of the novel's most introspective and philosophical moments. One such passage occurs when Breq considers the changes in her psyche as she continues to struggle with the loss of her ship and her ancillary bodies:

> When I had been a single ancillary, one human body among thousands, part of the ship Justice of Toren, I had never been alone. I had always been surrounded by myself, and the rest of myself had always known if any particular body needed something—rest, food, touch, reassurance. An ancillary body might feel momentarily overwhelmed, or irritable, or any emotion one might think of—it was only natural, bodies felt things. But it was so very small, when it was just one segment among the others, when, even in

---

1 http://www.reddit.com/r/sciencefiction/comments/2ige0f/im_ann_leckie_the_author_of_ancillary_justice_ama/cl2e4sh

the grip of strong emotion or physical discomfort, that segment knew it was only one of many, knew the rest of itself was there to help (138).

Considering the parallels between the ancillary bond and the fierce loyalty of close knit and insular communities, such as the Valskaayans that Breq encounters on Athoek, Leckie is able to focus on the great gulf between the haves (those willing to bend to the Radch definition of being "civilized") and the have nots (those still fighting to keep the identity of their cultures and society intact) and ponder the many different definitions for "freedom" and "justice" Is it heavy handed at times? Yes. But the questions Leckie asks are nuanced and give new perspective to all the various characters in the novels and the societies from which they're raised.

Breq desperately yearns the return of her ancillary network, is haunted by the limits of her single body, but struggles to reconcile her individual yearnings with her bitterness towards the threat that the hive-like ancillary technology poses to humanity. Breq's anger, so explosive when it was focused in on her fight-or-flight quest for vengeance against Anaander Mianaai in *Ancillary Justice*, takes a back seat to her struggles to understand the nature of justice—a word central to Radch society, but also at the root of many of its problems—and finding peace in imperfect solutions.

As a result of the slower narrative, readers are treated to more of Leckie's humor throughout the novel. This levity provides another layer of depth as Breq herself navigates the intricacies of human social behaviour.

"Fleet Captain is pretty fucking badass." The vulgarity, combined with Seivarden's archaic, elegant accent, set them laughing, relieved but still unsettled (35).

These sweet moments are balanced by biting social commentary and verbal swordplay that keeps the reader on their toes. *Ancillary Sword* is full of tense and interesting confrontations, but unlike the spaceborne battles in *Ancillary Justice*, these social conflicts are often more labyrinthine and delicate in nature. Breq is, in many ways, a savant at reading human emotion and nuance from an objective perspective, but lacks some of the subjective instincts inherent to non-ancillary humans. Watching Leckie slowly pick apart these barriers within Breq is fascinating.

Leckie herself has stated that she "actually know the genders of most of the characters in the all-Radchaai scenes," which provides an interesting perspective on her approach to writing characters in a genderless society while still catering to readers that naturally try to assign gender labels to all characters.[2]

There's one moment when Breq is speaking to another character in a non-Radchaai language that uses gendered pronouns, and so sheds light on the gender of a character named Raughd that was opposite what I had posited in my visualization. This immediately sent my mind scrambling as it analyzed the relationships that Raughd had with other characters, and, in turn, what effect that had on my perception of their gender. This mad scramble helped me to recognize the biases that I was trying to apply to characters,

2 http://www.tor.com/blogs/2014/10/ann-leckie-reddit-ama-ancillary-justice-ancillary-sword

the boxes my mind wanted to place them into, and recognizing this provided me with an added layer of perspective unique to Leckie's narrative. It allowed me to parse the characters by characteristics other than their gender and to accept their relationships at face value.

Where *Ancillary Sword* really succeeds, perhaps better than its predecessor, is in those relationships that are developed throughout the novel. Between its breakneck pace and the orientation required to understand the complexities of Leckie's narrative style/pronoun usage, it was often difficult to find time to breathe while reading *Ancillary Justice*; whereas *Ancillary Sword* gives the reader welcome opportunity to sidle up alongside Breq and her companions and adversaries.

Tisarwat, a young lieutenant aboard Breq's ship, Mercy of Kalr, is full of secrets, and it's difficult not to fall in love with her earnestness and heart. Seivarden, one of the highlights of *Ancillary Justice*, is sadly sidelined, but is replaced by the equally brooding Sirix. Kalr Five, whose enthusiasm for antique dishware is amusing and ultimately relevant to the plot, also endears herself to the reader in her limited screentime. *Ancillary Sword* breathes life and personality into a setting that could at times be very sterile and difficult to empathize with in *Ancillary Justice*. While the emotions never run quite so high as they did while experiencing Breq's final hours with Lieutenant Awn, the various characters in *Ancillary Sword* are motivated by believable desires and remain interesting even when Breq is only watching them from afar.

Building on the impressive groundwork laid by *Ancillary Justice*, *Ancillary Sword* might be a surprising departure from its predecessor, but it's clear than Leckie understands the delicacy necessary to handle the follow-up to one of the most beloved novels of the past decade.

Ancillary Sword is one of the year's finest novels and a terrific follow-up to *Ancillary Justice*. Breq's story of vengeance and redemption takes several turns that add to an already conflicted and labyrinthine narrative, proving that Leckie's no one trick pony. The Imperial Radch trilogy continues to be one of the most impressive science fiction narratives of recent years.

This article first appeared on *A Dribble of Ink* on October 8, 2014.
aidanmoher.com/blog/review/2014/10/review-ancillary-sword-ann-leckie/

MICROREVIEW [BOOK]: 'CITY OF STAIRS' BY ROBERT JACKSON BENNETT

The G

I once said that the hardest reviews to write are of the books you love the most. But I was wrong—the hardest reviews to write are of the books that feel the most important. And Robert Jackson Bennett's genre-busting novel *City of Stairs* is a must-read for anyone who cares about fantasy fiction. Why? Because fantasy is, far more than its cousin science fiction, slave to its conventions; few works genuinely challenge those conventions as dramatically or effectively as *City of Stairs*. And for that alone, you should read this novel.

But it also happens to be a really good story. *City of Stairs* takes place in the city of Bulikov, which was once the capital of "the Continent", a large landmass made up of multiple, vaguely Slavic societies, who at one point united to conquer the known world. They were able to do so because the gods (or "Divinities") favored them and empowered them with powerful, reality-bending magics. Until, that is, the day when a leader—called the Kaj—rose from the subjegated, vaguely South Asian Saypuri. With a terrible (and largely unexplained weapon), the Kaj and his army killed the Divinities, which instantly destroyed everything that depended upon their magic (include the actual buildings people lived and worked in). Vast destruction followed. Now the Saypuri have subjugated the Continent, maintaining Their hegemony through technological superiority and the banning of both magical artifacts and open discussion of the Continent's magical past.

City of Stairs centers, superficially at least, on the murder of Efrem Pangyui, a Saypuri scholar engaging in research on the Continent's magical past—the exact thing Continentals cannot do themselves. Enter Shara Thivani, a Saypuri agent and friend of the murdered Pangyui, who is determined to find his killers. She is joined by Sigrud, a massive Dreyling who acts as her muscle and advisor—think Sigurd/Siegfriend mixed with Beowulf, but updated for the video game set. We learn that resentment of Saypuri repression runs deep, and that a committed group of Continentals are ready to use violence in order to restore the Continent to its former glory. But that's not all they find...

City of Stairs covers the basics of genre storytelling effectively. The plot is fast-paced and engrossing, the characters deep and well-rounded and there's a good mix of investigation, action and contemplation. The narrative structure is complex but not gimmicky, with Bennett weaving Shara's and Sigrud's backstories, as well as the political history of Continent and Saypur, into the foregrounded mystery without infodumping (i.e. the bane of my literary existence). And genre readers will delight in Sigrud, who may be a millennia-old trope, but somehow manages to feel fresh and exciting. The scene where he fights the sea monster is just... wow. Simply put, *City of Stairs* is on one level a fun book that can appeal to a broad cross-section of fantasy readers. But it's much, much more than that.

Fantasy is, like the romance novel or police procedural, a fundamentally conventional genre, with all its attendant sub-genres defined by laundry-lists of expected ways of doing things. And if something unconventional comes around, given that it's sufficiently popular, it simply spawns a new convention. So it's unexpected and delightful to read a novel that simply refuses to be categorized: it's epic but not medieval, so it's not epic fantasy; there are cars but no guns, so it's not flintlock fantasy; there are dirigibles but no Victorianisms, so it's not steampunk; it takes place in one city but in a second world, so it's not urban fantasy; etc. Instead it's a world where magic and technology coexist, where technologies from various historical time-periods coexist, where architecture is central to the story being told and where no place or people is based off of English or Anglophone archetypes.

Of course, whenever breaking with fantasy convention comes up in the discourse, the argument breaks down like this:

A: Why is fantasy so damned conventional/risk-averse?
B: "Because REALISM."
A: "If there are dragons and/or wizards, 'realism' is already out the window."
B: "Yes, but if everything is unrealistic, readers won't have anything to hold on to."
A: "That's what I call 'a lack of imagination.'"
B: "Boo 'message-fiction!'"

Now, I read (and enjoy) a lot of conventional fantasy, but eh... I find the lack of boundary-pushing more than a little frustrating. Still, the argument that messages or agenda can overshadow fundamentals has some merit, in the sense that they shouldn't but they can. So it's notable that *City of Stairs* breaks fundamentally with convention in ways that never feel less than wholly intuitive, fully realized and deeply integrated into the DNA of the novel. Everything is internalized into character perspective, nothing is infodumped and the result is a rich, vibrant and incredibly exciting fantasy world like no other I've ever encountered.

City of Stairs is also a fundamentally political novel, but one that eschews clear metaphor for more ambiguous explorations. Some reviewers (for example Nisi Shawl) have situated *City of Stairs* within postcolonial discourses, in the sense that it presents a world at least partially defined by historical oppression of dark-skinned peoples (the Saypuri) by light-skinned peoples (the Continentals).[1] But I don't think that's quite what Bennett is getting it. Though the historical oppression of Saypur is quite disturbing, Saypur is now the colonial overlord, and book takes place in what is in essence a captive city. Indeed, over time Shara grows more and more troubled by the

---

1 http://seattletimes.com/html/books/2024505109_citystairsbennettxml.html

colonial regime she represents—even as she works to stop those who would seek to restore the old order. The effect is to argue that oppression is simply what power differentials lead to, and to argue that such behavior is unacceptable regardless of whether it is justified in terms of "divine right", historical grievance or material "superiority."

Yet this also leads the reader to focus on Bennett's cultural choices. The Continentals are pseuso-Slavic, the Saypuris pseudo-South Asian—but why? It's refreshing to read a fantasy novel where the default categories are neither pseudo-Anglophone nor pseudo-Celtic, but where the subjects are not exoticized either. At the same time, considering how little these cultural choices mattered, I was never clear why anyone needed a pseudo-Slavic or pseudo-Sanskrit name to begin with—or, for that matter, a pseudo-Angophone or pseudo-Celtic one. (Sigrud is a different story, of course, but the Dreylings are the cultural group with with the least impact on the narrative.) The effect isn't bad, per se; rather, it just feels underdeveloped.

Finally, the one negative—the ending. I won't spoil it, and I'll note that it isn't all bad, but it nevertheless felt a bit too network TV for a novel that was HBO-plus 95% of the way to the finish line. Regardless, *City of Stairs* is a dazzling, sophisticated and thoroughly modern fantasy, and stands in contrast to the staid medievalisms that dominate the genre. Imagine China Miéville and George R. R. Martin stuck in an elevator, with only a laptop to keep them company, and you're almost there. It is a monumental work of fantasy that does more to push the genre forward than anything I've read in years, and will likely go down as the best fantasy novel of 2014. Robert Jackson Bennett is a name to remember and a talent to behold.

This article first appeared on *Nerds of a Feather, Flock Together* on October 8, 2014.
www.nerds-feather.com/2014/10/microreview-book-city-of-stairs-by.html

REVIEW: 'THE GOBLIN EMPEROR' BY KATHERINE ADDISON

Memory Scarlett

Maia, the youngest son of the Emperor, has spent most of his life relegated to a backwater estate since his elven father would rather not see a constant reminder of the goblin lady he regrets marrying. Maia expects his exile to be a permanent arrangement, but it comes to an abrupt end when his father and older brothers are killed in an airship explosion. Thrust into an unfamiliar court in which intrigues abound, Maia has no choice but to become Emperor.

And he has no idea how to do what's expected of him.

Friends, *The Goblin Emperor* was my most anticipated book of 2014. You see, Katherine Addison is my most favouritest of favourite authors—she's published a number of novels and short story collections under the name Sarah Monette—and this is her first new novel in a few years. I'm not saying I stalked NetGalley for weeks on the offhand chance Tor would make it available on there, or that I made burnt offerings to the Publicist Gods after I'd hit "request", or that I performed the happy dance when they informed me I was welcome to read it, but I invite you to draw your own conclusions.

If you've interacted with me on social media at any point over the last month, you already know how much I loved it, and how badly I want you to read it. Let's spell out a few *reasons*, though, so you and I can both feel good about your decision to rush out and buy this (or ask your library to buy it, if that's your thing).

The Goblin Emperor is very much a fish out of water story. Maia isn't completely ignorant, but his education has in no way prepared him to be Emperor. He has to master the job awfully quickly lest he leave himself vulnerable to scheming courtiers, any one of whom could have been behind the previous Emperor's death.

Maia's limited knowledge of the court's inner workings gives the reader a prime opportunity to absorb everything alongside him, making this very much a How Stuff Works book. As some of you may recall, How Stuff Works books are my *favourite*. They give the reader an opportunity to take a close look at how a particular mechanism—in this case, a large empire equipped with a complex bureaucracy—operates, all within the context of a good story.

A successful How Stuff Works book is never infodumpy, since everything that comes to light either furthers the plot or adds to the characterization. That's very much the case here. I had an absolute blast discovering the ins and outs of courtly life and the role Maia was expected to fill there.

Addison's worldbuilding is exquisite, as always, and feeds into the story in some gorgeous ways. The society she presents here isn't medievalesque; a potential disappointment for fans of the form, but always a good way to score points with me. Medievalesque worlds are okay and all, but there are *so frickin' many of them* that it's nice to have something different every once in a while. In this case, the technology is somewhat pseudo-Victorian, what with the prevalence of airships and gaslights and pneumatic tubes, but the social structures aren't even close to a match. Neither are the fashions (which sound gorgeous, by the way. I'm particularly taken with the hair ornaments). It's impossible to pin *The Goblin Emperor* down to a particular real world time period, and the result is unique and unexpected; a banquet of non-standard fantasy goodness.

The worldbuilding works on multiple fronts, too. On the linguistics side of things, Addison introduces a grammar that varies depending on each conversational partner's relationship to the other, and on the formality of an exchange. Fun! Physiologically, she takes advantage of her elven and goblin characters' unique attributes to add another level to each conversation; which is to say, their ears often give away their emotional state, whether they will them to or not.

I love details like this.

I suppose I should add, now, that some of the complexities of Addison's worldbuilding could prove stumbling blocks for readers. I normally ignore dramatis personae when they're provided, but Maia is surrounded by so many aides, courtiers, and servants that I dearly wished for one here. Much to my surprise, there *is* a dramatis personae-slash-world guide, but it's at the back of the book instead of the front, so I missed it. (Oh, eARCs. You're so convenient, but you have your disadvantages.) If at any point you're confused as to someone's role in the story, flip to the back and look them up.

The names, too, could be a source of confusion. They have a distinctly goblinish cant to them, what with all their guttural consonants, and they follow particular rules depending on the characters' gender, rank, and marital status. I had a lot of fun parsing the conventions for myself, but if you feel differently, please be aware there's also a relevant guide right before the dramatis personae. It's spoiler-free, so you're safe to read it before you dive into the book, if you are so inclined.

So, yes. Structurally, and from a worldbuilding standpoint, this book is awesome. It's got everything I love: a gorgeously realized world, plenty of jaw about How Stuff Works, and a setup guaranteed to provide heaps of tension as the protagonist navigates unfamiliar terrain. But *The Goblin Emperor* is so much more than a pretty world and a good premise. It's packed so full of heart that it makes me ridiculously happy whenever I think of it, even weeks after I turned the last page.

And I think of it a lot, because it's the sort of book that sticks.

Addison's previous novels are dark, to put it mildly. She's the sort of writer who does awful things to her characters in service to the plot, and to their emotional growth. Maia is no exception, but in his case, most of the horrible stuff happens before or very soon after the book begins. Maia loses his mother when he's very young, his father wants nothing to do with him, and he's shunted off to a backwater estate with a cousin who beats him for kicks.

Then, within twenty pages, he's brought to court and told a) he can never, ever, *ever* be alone again, because Emperors need supervision for their own good, and b) he can never be friends with anyone because Emperors aren't allowed to be on the same level as their subjects.

It's a crap situation and Maia knows it. He also knows there's no way out except death or abdication, the latter of which both leaves the country vulnerable and is bound to result in his death anyways via an "accident" of some sort.

So things, they are not so good at the beginning. But fear not! It gets better! *The Goblin Emperor* eschews straight-out grittiness in favour of something tinged with hope. Addison doesn't sugar coat the harsh realities of Maia's station, but neither does she leave him mired in desperation forever. She does a phenomenal job of building sympathy for him, of showing us the stress his new position places on him, and of organically relieving that stress as the plot rolls along.

I'm reluctant to say too much about all that because really, it's the meat of the novel. There's plenty of political intrigue and a subplot involving the investigation into the airship explosion that killed the rest of the royal family, but Maia's own growth rests firmly at *The Goblin Emperor*'s heart. He begins as a lonely, uncertain person possessed of a certain amount of internalized self-loathing thanks to his father's treatment of him and his physical differences from the rest of the elven court (namely, he's got grey skin, which we can assume his loathsome cousin taunted him with at every opportunity). Nobody's so much as told him they like him since his mother died, and no sooner does he arrive at his new home but he's told he can never, ever expect to view anyone as an equal. He'll spend his days and weeks with people who're paid to help him, he'll marry a woman who's politically expedient, and he'd durned well better use formal grammar at all times, because Emperors don't get personal lives.

Despite all this, he *tries*. He has no desire to be Emperor, but he doesn't half-ass the job. He works hard to find his feet, he accepts help when it's offered, and he treats everyone fairly along the way.

And in the process, he wins people over.

It's an utter joy to watch him gain such a strong support system. Most of the time, he doesn't even realize he's building good will; he just behaves like a decent person, with excellent results. I loved so many of the smaller scenes where his staff and his surviving family profess affection for him, often in ways that surprise him or go straight over his head. I spent much of the book with my heart in my throat, terrified that one of them was set to betray him. I desperately wanted him to get to keep these people. I wanted him to have friends, even if his station barred him from interacting with them in a traditionally friendly manner.

It delighted me, and warmed my heart, and every other happy cliché you can think of.

Seriously, y'all, *The Goblin Emperor* made me fantastically happy on every level. I'm gonna need you to read it as soon as you possibly can, because books this wonderful deserve an enormous audience and you—yes, you!—deserve to be part of it.

I'll note, too, that it's a perfect standalone, so you needn't worry about cliffhangers. Even though this particular story is complete in and of itself, though, I can't help but hope Addison will write something else in this world. It's a fascinating place brimming with scope.

I'd also be happy with something set in a completely different, but equally gorgeous, world. I want MOAR ADDISON, is what I'm saying. Please, Book Gods? Please?

This article first appeared on *In The Forest Of Stories* on April 2, 2014.
memoryscarlett.blogspot.com/2014/04/review-goblin-emperor-by-katherine.html

'BLUE LILY, LILY BLUE' BY MAGGIE STIEFVATER

Erika Jelinek

Persephone stood on the bare mountaintop, her ruffled ivory dress whipping around her legs, her masses of white-blond curls streaming behind her.

I know that this month is technically "science fiction month", and *Blue Lily, Lily Blue* by Maggie Stiefvater is not, if we're going to get "technical", really "science fiction", but this was my most poop my pants highly anticipated book of the year so I'm reviewing it right now, and if you don't like it then YOU can go poop in YOUR pants! See if I care!

This is the third book in a four book series, so I'm going to give a bare bones minimum plot teaser thingy, because it won't really make sense to anyone if they haven't read the first two books. The psychically engaged Scoobies in the form of Blue, Gansey, Ronan, Adam, and kind of Noah, are focusing their respective abilities on trying to find Blue's mother, who is supposedly underground just like their coveted dead Welsh king. Sleeping Welsh king. Whatever. He's Welsh, and he's apparently been in a cave for the past several centuries. So, there's a lot of amateur caving. Also, Colin Greenmantle, the dude who hired the Gray Man to kill Ronan's father is in town because he wants to coerce the Gray Man into producing the Greywaren (not possible!) by further threatening Blue's mother, so he's looking for her, too, only he doesn't want to hug her when he finds her! So, everyone is mucking about in mystical caves, and most people are stressed out, and there is a lot of magic and ghosting around and Tarot and HOLY SHIT this book is satisfying. Like I said, none of that is going to make any sense if you haven't read the first two books.

Like I said before, this was my most highly anticipated novel of the year, and you know what? It delivered and delivered and delivered. It's strange. Every time I read a book by Maggie Stiefvater I think, "She can't get any better than this," but then, impossibly, she does. Her writing becomes more polished, her characters more vivid, her stories more achingly true despite (because of?) their magic. Maybe it's because, at this point, I've read over 1,000 pages worth of *The Raven Cycle*, but to read this story is to fully inhabit its world, to love and understand its characters. They are so real and so familiar that every read word feels like wrapping yourself in a warm blanket with a cup of hot chocolate. There were times when I caught myself smiling like a loon at the way the characters were behaving, at the things they were saying, because of course that is what they would do, and of course that is what they would say. Stiefvater has created characters that aren't just characters, they are friends, they are as real and natural and solid and nuanced as anyone I interact with in the world that exists beyond the page and and and... just... sigh. I love them all. Even shithead Ronan. Even the ever-suffering Adam. Understanding how their flaws make them whole is one of the themes that really touched me in this book. Whereas *The Dream Thieves* was all about the empty spaces in our lives that we try to fill, *Blue Lily, Lily Blue* is about reflecting your truth, warts and all, and just like in previous chapters in this cycle, Stiefvater hits the mark. Achingly so.

And, I have to say, Stiefvater creates a hell of a villain. I loved that, even though this is a fantasy with all sorts of ominous portents of doom, the actual antagonists in this book were a super wealthy sociopath who is mostly evil out of a lack of anything better to do and his wife whom I'm pretty sure wears Lululemon pants even when she's not exercising. The banality of these characters as they did truly horrific things was enormously entertaining, especially when they were set in contrast to the ominous, unknown evil of the third sleeper who must not be woken.

This is mostly a book of changing gears; people are waking up, learning who they are, and shifting and dancing around each other to prepare for the next, final stage of their quest. What's incredible about this book is that Stiefvater is, effectively, taking us through the long, slow process of that shift in consciousness between adolescence and adulthood. All of our characters are growing up, and the beautiful thing about this process is it's so clear that, for each of these characters, that process means something different, just like how in real life growing up entails a different kind of awakening for each of us. This is what is so spellbinding about Stiefvater's writing; she takes these very real, very human processes, and infuses them with a deliciously unfurling magic without ever losing touch with their humanity. All with pretty writing, too!

So, bottom line: this book is nothing short of magnificent. It is magical, it is human, it made my readerly heart swell with immense satisfaction. You should probably read this whole series, and then positively die with anticipation for the last book along with me. I honestly can't wait to reread the entire series when that one comes out.

For music, I'm going to do an ode to my favorite new character, Gwenllian, and that ode is "Girl Anachronism" by The Dresden Dolls.

This article first appeared on *Book Punks* on November 10, 2014.
www.bookpunks.com/blue-lily-lily-blue-maggie-stiefvater/

REVIEW: 'THE MIRROR EMPIRE' BY KAMERON HURLEY

Ken Neth

Fantasy is the genre where *anything* is possible and that is one of the biggest reasons why so many of us read it. Yet fantasy, and let's focus on epic fantasy for this discussion, tends to shackle itself with rules. Most mimic in one way or another what has come before. Most take inspiration from historic cultures of our own world (particularly Western societies) and build that inspiration into a set of rules to adhere to. Often those rules are not based on any factual part of history, but perceived aspects of history that never actually existed.

Why do fantasy peoples form the frozen north have to be Vikings? Why do those frozen lands have to be north? Why do people from the south/desert always have to be Muslim/Jewish analogs? Why are temperate climates European analogs? Why is a tropical environment populated by African or Mayan analogs? Why in a fantasy world do people ride horses into battle? Why not bears... with forked tongues? Why can't trees chase you down and eat you? Etc.

For all the freedom that the genre offers, the vast majority of it shackles itself in rules. *The Mirror Empire* by Kameron Hurley chooses differently. This fantasy world feels alien—there are sentient plants who will eat you, people do indeed ride bears with forked tongues, the traditional "castle" just may be a sentient organic construct, etc. The cultures of the world do not (at least at first glance) bear any resemblance to historic cultures of our own world.[1] The societies are different, the people bear little resemblance (in race, ethnicity, and cultural construction) to the past or present of the real world. Hurley builds a world that is a true fantasy—a brilliant fantasy that actually embraces the possibilities it presents rather than limits itself by so-called rules of the past.

To continue with the rhetorical questions I mentioned above, why do the gender politics of our current society have to be present? Fantasy can have dragons bonding magically with riders who battle trolls and elves and whatever else—but women have to be in their place because that's the way it's always been. Men rape women because that's the way it was in history. Women don't fight and are often little more than the property of men because that what history (supposedly) tells us. This book calls all that out for the bullshit it is.

---

1 However, I suspect that inspiration for the clan-based structure of the Dhai was in part from clan/tribal organizations of southern Africa, but that is really an aside.

Hurley creates a variety of nations and societies that are often matriarchic. Or consent. Or some other organizational structure that simply doesn't fit in with what our society tells us is the way things are. She rams this rail spike of point home—repeatedly. In one society, men are weak, they are property—it is the mirrored reflection of those "traditional" societies of our own world. Gender roles are reversed and sometimes completely deconstructed. Gender isn't binary and not even a 5 gendered society makes everyone feel welcome. Does it feel wrong? Does it make you uncomfortable? Do you question? Should you take a long hard look in the mirror? Yes! That's the point. It's driven in hard, it's overdone. It comes complete with the gratuitous rape of man by women—the same sort that is so often unnecessarily present in other fantasy books and is (thankfully) being called out more often for the bullshit it is. Of course, is it bullshit in this book when used in the same? Is it hypocritical? Yes, but unfortunately it's a point that still needs to be made.

With *The Mirror Empire*, Hurley celebrates the open canvas that is fantasy. There are no rules except the ones imposed on it by us and this book tosses those away. Yes, there is an agenda, a fuck you to the imposed "fantasy norms" and the oppressing culture of our own (in my original notes for this review, I coined a new term for this—epic rantasy—originally a typo, but a movement I'm sure will catch on). But it's also a celebration. A textbook on what can be done if you free yourself of the imposed limits.

The Mirror Empire is bold, courageous, unapologetic, and at times, angry. In short, it's damn near unpublishable—kudos to Angry Robot for taking a chance on this one. While I don't think this will ever be a book that is considered a great success, I do think it's a book that should be read, particularly as an example how to remove the box of epic fantasy. I can also imagine that there will be a temptation to limit this book—to catalog it as feminist, or queer, or some other specialized form of epic fantasy that are ultimately attempts to silence it as something different and segregate from the "usual" epic fantasy. I really hope that readers, booksellers, and fans refuse to let that happen. This is epic fantasy, just epic fantasy that has removed traditional boundaries.

In *The Mirror Empire*, two "mirror" worlds begin to collide, and my reaction to this book is the same—two mirrored visions (unhappily) collide. There is the beautiful image of Hurley's creation that I describe above, and its reflection that I describe below, a reflection from a carnival mirror complete with confounding distortions.

For all the bold, brilliant creativity that goes into the world, as a story, the story of *The Mirror Empire* suffers. This is a dense book with a slow start. Very slow. I felt very little about the characters—essentially no investment. That makes it a challenge to want to read the book—a challenge to enjoy anything about the book. In all honesty, if had been another author, I suspect I wouldn't have finished the book—but there was all that I rave about above, so I had to see it through.

The names are confusing (which I suspect is more of a product of the absolute mess that is the first act of this book and not the names themselves). There are too many point of view characters—the book loses focus as it tries to introduce and bring to some form of conclusion a few too many threads.[2] Places are confusing and the geography confounds (note: I read an early copy of this book without the benefit of the map and glossary of the final so hopefully others will not find this the challenge that I did—though I stand by my belief that a map and/or glossary should never be *necessary* for the success of a book).

Simply put, the story failed to provide the motivation for me to keep reading to see what would happen next.

I keep seeing the word "challenging" used to describe *The Mirror Empire*. Sure, I see that, there is a lot of challenge in this book. But that should not be confused with the mess that is its story. It's a challenge to calculate all of the optical physics that describe the reflection of a curved mirror, it's a (bloody) mess to try and re-construct a shattered mirror (that's missing a few pieces).

So, *The Mirror Empire* is a mixed bag. Two images—one the idealized intent, the other the reflected reality. It's a brilliant exploration of what fantasy can truly be when boundaries are not slammed in place. It's also wreck of a story that never really pulls itself together. Did I like it? Did I enjoy it? Yes and No. Will I read the second book in the series? Maybe—I haven't decided yet. The first book never quite sold me, but I so want this to succeed (in large part due to all that I began this review with). We'll see—I may just have to look into my mirror and begin with those classic words...

Note on this review: Notice how I didn't really discuss the plot or the characters or anything that actually happens in this book? Use the back cover or another review for that if that's what you're after, but I simply found no need to discuss these. Make of that what you will.

This article first appeared on *Neth Space* on August 4, 2014.
nethspace.blogspot.com/2014/08/review-mirror-empire-by-kameron-hurley.html

---

2 I find it quite amusing that this book, this book that has so much to say about epic fantasy, falls right into the same trap that so many do—too many point of view characters.

THE SOUTHERN REACH TRILOGY BY JEFF VANDERMEER

Adam Roberts

1

Trying to think what one word best describes Jeff VanderMeer's Southern Reach trilogy. I could go with "masterpiece", since it is so clearly a major achievement in SF/Fantasy/Weird writing—since it accomplishes so many of the things it sets out to do, since it is so beautifully imagined and written, since it will clearly scoop all the awards next year and remain a touchstone text in the genre for a long time. But that's an evaluative word, and I'm interested (for reasons that will become more apparent) in the descriptive space outside evaluation. The trilogy is science fiction on the haunted, fantastic side of the genre; often brilliantly spooky and uncanny. And VanderMeer has, I suppose, a reputation as Purveyor of High Quality Weird to the Refined Reader. But I remain unconvinced as to the coherency of "weird" as an aesthetic descriptor; and certainly weird-for-the-sake-of-weird (a coinage along the lines of *l'art pour l'art—l'étrange pour l'étrange*, I suppose) is really not what Southern Reach is about. One of the things that makes these novels so readable is the air of absorbing mystery that VanderMeer flawless evokes; but what makes them so satisfying as a whole is that they are not content simply to evoke that mystery, to make the tiny hairs at the back of the reader's neck stand up. They are not just mood pieces. Indeed, after I had finished I found myself wondering if what these books are doing is reconfiguring pastoral for a new century. So that's the one word I'm going with. Southern Reach are strange pastoral.

The trilogy is set in the Tarkovsky-*Stalker*-like zone of "Area X", somewhere down Florida way. At some point in the past this area suffered some kind of unexplained catastrophe and, like the "Zona" around Chernobyl, was left to revert to a state of nature. A governmental organisation called the Southern Reach has been tasked with observing and assessing this place, and from time to time sends in expeditions; although these exploratory incursions all end badly.

In *Annihilation*, the first (and, to revert to evaluation for a moment, the best) of the three novels, one such expedition is described. It is comprised of women and we don't get their names: they are "the psychologist", "the surveyor", "the anthropologist", and our narrator, "the Biologist." An expertly handled piece of characterization, this cool, rather introverted woman has always been more comfortable observing wild ecosystems. When growing up, the pool in her back garden was neglected by her self-absorbed parents, and soon became clogged with weeds, tadpoles and other flora and fauna. The Biologist returns to memories of the hours she spent observing the minute interactions of this re-wilded world as a kind of touchstone for personal happiness. That quality seems to have been largely absent from her adult existence. Her marriage, for instance, had not been a success. Her husband had disappeared on the previous, eleventh expedition into Area X—all previous expeditions (and it seems there were more than the officially logged twelfth) having failed, with explorers going mad, killing one another, committing suicide or succumbing to weird infections and parasites. When her husband unexpectedly and mysteriously turns up again, in her kitchen, he is a hollowed-out, PTSD-y version of the man he had been before, and soon dies of cancer.

The Southern Reach hypnotize the members of the twelfth expedition, a psychological conditioning imposed ostensibly to help them through the border into the zone. It turns out, the hypnotism is more far reaching, an attempt to control the explorers, with the Psychologist possessing certain trigger words to "induce paralysis", "induce acceptance or compel obedience" (*Annihilation* 135). The title of the first novel is one such hypnotic command: to "induce immediate suicide." Clearly, the Southern Reach don't wholly trust their own explorers; or, rather, don't trust what they could mutate into.

Early in *Annihilation* the Biologist descends a spiral staircase into a subterranean structure she insists on calling a "tower" and finds a mysterious message written on the walls in letters made of some sort of fungoid vegetable growth. (This text starts: *Where lies the strangling fruit that came from the hand of the sinner I shall bring forth the seeds of the dead to share with the worms that...* and goes on and on). Spores from this fungus somehow de-condition the Biologist from her hypnotism, meaning that she escapes the Psychologist's catastrophic attempts to manipulate the expedition. One member leaves; another is found dead at the bottom of the tower, her body deliquescing and turning luminous yellow. The Psychologist disappears, and when the Biologist chances upon her again she is dying. The Biologist finds the journal kept by her deceased husband. A strange individual called "the Crawler" is threatening the group. I'll pause here, to insert a quote from *The Guardian* review of the novel:[1]

> But what makes this book so remarkable is less what happens in it, and more its tense, eerie and unsettling vibe. Creating such a vibe is a balancing act between (on the one hand) not destroying the mood with too much brute explanation and loose-end-tying-up, and (on the other) not alienating the reader by being too annoyingly oblique. VanderMeer hits exactly the right balance, like a gymnast on a beam. A creepy gymnast who's been infected with occult fungal spores and is starting to glow yellow.

I think that's right, and can only commend the insight and eloquence of this *Guardian* reviewer. The paper should surely put more work their way.

The second volume in the trilogy, *Authority*, is about the Southern Reach organization itself. The book is mostly concerned with the byzantine in-group

---

1 http://www.theguardian.com/books/2014/aug/27/acceptance-jeff-VanderMeer-trilogy-review

political struggles and ultimate impotence of the organization's new leader, "Control." We get some more detail about Area X. There is a mysterious barrier around the zone which may or may not have been created at a different time, and perhaps by a different entity to the one that created the zone. The only way in or presumably out is through a "door" that the Southern Reach did not create. There is video footage of an experiment in which a great many bunny rabbits are herded at the invisible barrier surrounding Area X—they all vanish as soon as intersecting the limit, apparently never to be heard of again. People mention "aliens" for the first time (or, rather, they go out of their way not to mention aliens—"why are none of you comfortable using the words *alien* or *extraterrestrial* to talk about Area X?" Control peevishly demands, upon arriving in post (*Authority* 10). The Biologist from *Annihilation* is assumed dead, but she turns up, standing in a parking lot outside Area X in what looks like a fugue state. She claims not to remember anything from her expedition. Is she actually the Biologist, or only some occult copy of the original woman? She prefers now to be addressed as "Ghost Bird", the nickname her deceased husband used. We are still not vouchsafed her actual name.

Though not its narrator, Control (a childhood nickname, not a Le-Carré-style job description) is at the heart of *Authority*, much as the Biologist was at the heart of *Annihilation*. For me this was one of the reasons the second volume worked less well. It's not so much that the "genre" interest is back-seated in favor of a rather tortuous spy-thriller-bureaucracy satire—although that's kind of true. It's more that the character of Control didn't strike me as being as well drawn, as sparely yet vividly rendered, as the Biologist. We learn a lot (too much, perhaps) about his childhood, his life before Southern Reach, his difficult relationship with his mother—also in the espionage business, and an important character in the trilogy—and generally about the anxieties and frustrations of his new rôle. How does that Ricky Martin song go? It drags. It doesn't drag excessively, like Danny La Rue; but it certain drags from time to time. Like Eddie Izzard.

Southern Reach call the tower-that's-actually-a-hole-in-the-ground "the topographical anomaly." It appears to be alive. There's also a lighthouse in Area X, and this structure's former keeper, once called Saul Evans, now something else entirely, appears to have been the author of the strange text (he was a lay preacher as well as a lighthouse-keeper, before whatever happened to Area X happened). In the final volume, *Acceptance* we discover a good deal more about Saul, as well as solving some—but, satisfyingly, *not all*—of the mysteries of Area X. The meat of this third novel is the return to the Area of Control and the Biologist—or rather, of "Ghost Bird", the uncanny duplicate of the Biologist. They pop up through an occult undersea portal, and explore the whole zone further.

Now I'm guessing that VanderMeer was aware that this trajectory—(1) mysterious sea-defined zone, odd animals and lots of mystery, (2) characters leave the zone and pootle around "our" world for a while, (3) characters *return* to the zone changed and resolve many of its mysteries—was going to make many of his readers think of Abrams's *Lost*.[2] I'm guessing that partly because the comparison is obvious (though VanderMeer does a much better

2 http://www.strangehorizons.com/reviews/2010/07/the_woo_of_lost.shtml

job of wrapping his story up than did Abrams and his scriptwriters). There's also stuff like this (Ghost Bird is sifting through the scattered records of the "Seeker and Surveillance Bandits" who once explored the zone):

> In among this detritus, these feeble guesses, the word Found! *Handwritten, triumphant. Found what? But with so little data, even* Found!, even the awareness of some more intelligent entity peering out from among the fragments led nowhere. (*Acceptance* 178)

Hah.

Late in *Acceptance* Ghost Bird encounters a spooky owl. She wonders if this is some mutant reincarnation of her dead husband, but the impression I got (it's not clear) is that it isn't. It is a testament to VanderMeer's skill in these books to say that by this stage it comes across almost as cheating, to peg so intrinsically eerie a creature as "owl" in this way: earlier, the books have convinced the reader to be weirded-out by bunnies and dolphins. An owl is almost too obvious. It possesses too straightforward a metaphoric relationship to the theme. Elsewhere VanderMeer expresses exactly this. "Data pulled out of Area X duplicates itself and declines, or 'declines to be interpreted' as Whitby puts it." Southern Reach linguists compare it to "a tongue that curled up and took them with it":

> Area X muddying the waters. Except that it wasn't muddying waters or a tongue by the side of the road or anything else, muddled or not, that they could understand. "We lack the analogies" was itself somehow deficient as a diagnosis... Except Area X never responded, even to that indignity. (*Acceptance* 46)

The "allure" of the place lies "in its negation of why" (*Acceptance* 193). It is possible to frame descriptive accounts of nature in terms of "why." It isn't possible to frame evaluative or moral accounts that way. Nature isn't a why.

2

SF has had a rather awkward relationship with "Nature." Most often, I suppose, it has figured only as a resource to be improved with technology, something that backgrounds the main business of the standard genre fare— that is, if it is present at all (and there have been plenty of Trantor/Corruscant wholly urban SF built worlds). Iain M. Banks set his hugely popular novels in the Culture, after all; not in the Nature. The SF Encyclopedia's only entry on Nature rather makes my point for me.[3]

There has been something of a "turn", though; and although I'm going to suggest this is a recent thing. A couple of VanderMeer's reviewers have compared Southern Reach to Ballard, reaching for some way of flagging up the deliberately disorienting aesthetic at work. Plus: the Biologist's prompt for her fascination with the natural world is a disused swimming pool. But I don't think the comparison quite right, actually. Ballard's disused swimming pools tended to be empty; VanderMeer's pool is brimming and indeed overflowing with gloopy life. Ballard's interest was in the spooky dynamics of groups—in

3 http://www.sf-encyclopedia.com/entry/nature

his later career, almost always gated communities of the wealthy. There's surprisingly little "nature" in his works. VanderMeer, on the other hand, fills all three novels with vivid and sometimes gorgeous descriptions of nature, but seems interested in the human group dynamics (of explorer teams, of the Southern Reach organisation, of families, of lovers) really only to the extent that they break down and disintegrate. What might look at the beginning of the series as a rather modish absence of proper names becomes, by the end, more significant: proper names are shed in the course of the book because they are so specific to human interpersonality. Animals do without names. Nature is not named.

The "turn" I'm thinking of is not really Ballardian. It is evident, though, in writers like M. John Harrison—and *Southern Reach* has a cooler, less spiky Harrisonian feel to it—or in some of Iain Sinclar's less urban-focused prose (I'm thinking of the descriptions of English and Welsh countryside in the too-little-known *Landor's Tower* [2002]). I might also mention books like Simon Ings's *Wolves* (2014).[4] I might *also* mention myself, if it didn't look like I was trying to hijack the review to plug my own stuff; so I won't—except to say that even though I wrote my latest novel (about an angry man and some Southern English wildernesses) before I read VanderMeer's trilogy, the prior appearance of Southern Reach is inevitably going to make my version look derivative. The more interesting question is whether there's something in the water that is informing speculative writing today. Maybe "Nature" in this sense is the coming thing. A kind of Macfarlanization of the SFnal idiom.[5]

"Nature" in the sense that I'm using it here—in the sense that informs these novels—is a relatively new phenomenon. Raymond Williams's lengthy *Keywords* entry on the word starts:

> Nature is perhaps the most complex word in the language. It is relatively easy to distinguish three areas of meaning: (i) the essential quantity and character of something; (ii) the inherent force which directs either the world or human beings or both; (iii) the material world itself, taken as including or not including human beings. Yet it is evident that within (ii) and (iii), though the area of reference is broadly clear, precise meanings are variable and at times even opposed. The historical development of the word through these three senses is important, but it is also significant that all three senses, and the main variations and alternatives within the two most difficult of them, are still active and widespread in contemporary usage.

To present a fairly crude reduction of a very long and complicated discursive history, we could say that one valorized iteration of "nature"—wilderness nature, the state in which the world exists when men and women don't interfere with it by cutting it down, concreting it over and so on—is a Romantic and a post-Romantic invention. Since life preceded humanity on this planet of ours by billennia, this might look like a foolish thing to assert. Surely (you could say) "wilderness" is the default setting of the natural world, some-

4 http://www.strangehorizons.com/reviews/2014/02/wolves_by_simon.shtml
5 http://en.wikipedia.org/wiki/Robert_Macfarlane_(writer)

thing into which homo sapiens has blundered very late in the game. That's as may be; but I'm talking not about brute reality but about the value discourse of the natural world. This latter is both deeply embedded in (for instance) contemporary environmentalism (in the sense that some forms of nature are taken to be "better" or "worse" than others—pristine national parks are better than chemically polluted factoryside lakes, for example)—and a profoundly humanocentric state of affairs. I say this in as neutral a way as I can muster: outwith mankind the natural world is neither good nor bad, because "good" and "bad" are human concerns. It is neither good nor bad that sharks eat tuna, or fungus rots old oak trees. It just is. You might say *well, surely it's good for the shark and bad for the tuna*, I'd reply that you're stretching the meaning of "good" and "bad." My point is that it's not *morally* or *aesthetically* good or bad; because the idiom of nature-in-itself is dynamic and competitive existence, not morality or aesthetics. The fact that you are starving doesn't delight the forest in which you hunt fruitlessly for food; nor is the forest in which you hunt fruitlessly for food saddened to see the state you've gotten into. The forest doesn't care one way or the other. *Caring* is what humans do, not forests. Forests are no more malicious than they are compassionate. Forests are forests. Characters in the Southern Reach ponder this very question. What does the organism, or whatever it is, that has transformed Area X *want*? Control thinks he understands its purpose ("which is to kill us, to transform us, to get rid of us" [*Acceptance* 190]). He calls it "enemy", because it reassures him to frame events in this black-and-white way. Ghost Bird isn't so sure: maybe the horrifying things that have happened to the explorers are a sign not of hostility, but indifference.

> "Had they, in fact, passed judgment without a trial? Decided there could be no treaty or negotiation?"
>
> "That might be closer to the truth, to a kind of truth," Ghost Bird replied. It was now early afternoon and the sky had become a deeper blue with long narrow clouds sliding across it. The marsh was alive with rustlings and birdsong.
>
> "Condemned by an alien jury," Control said. "Not likely. Indifference." (*Acceptance* 79)

This is, perhaps, the real skill in VanderMeer's eerie vision: precisely this sense that we move through a living cosmos that neither loves nor hates us, but which is instead magisterially indifferent to us. How sharp a cut to our collective *amour propre*! Hatred would be preferable. How much more does SF prefer the acid tooth hostility of Geiger's Alien (that enduring genre epitome of the monstrous-organic) to the unsettling blankness, the beautiful semiotic void of Tarkovsky's "zona"? Better to be hated. At least then we matter at least enough to arouse strong emotions. But the refrigerator motor chugging quietly round the back of the Southern Reach books, and generating their palpable chill, may be something much less reassuring than the horror cliché of hatred. At least you know where you are with a Triffid. We lose our way in a particular manner in Area X. It's not just that we longer know where we are. We no longer know *what* we are.

Actually my point is less grandiose. It has to do with the cultural representation nature. In this context, the valorization of "wilderness" is an invention of Romantic poetry. The seventeenth- and eighteenth-centuries are full of nature poetry of course; but the emphasis is horticultural. For pre-Romantic poets it's common sense that nature is at its most beautiful in a garden or (managed) country estate; wildernesses and deserts might evoke the shiver of the sublime, but they were almost by definition ugly rather than beautiful. Wordsworth is probably the key figure. His poetic celebration of the wilder landscapes of the Lake Distract (rather than, say, Surrey or Kent, "the Garden of England") shifted the public aesthetic. Scott's novels achieved something similar for the grandeur of the Scottish highlands. By the later nineteenth-century, wilderness was not only appreciated on its own terms, it was being actively preferred by some to cultivated spaces. Not by everyone (English hymnist Dorothy Gurney, born 1858, is famous today for one couplet: "You're closer to God's heart in a garden/Than any place on earth"). There's no shortage of beautifully manicured lawns and robo-pruned topiary in contemporary science fiction: from the artfully corporatist landscaping of StarFleet's San Francisco headquarters to the "gene wizards" gardening on a solar-systemic scale in McAuley's Quiet War books (2008-2013). New Edens.

But for others, especially those writers interested in the inheritance of Romantic and Gothic sublime, "good" wilderness has exerted its pull. For instance, it informed some aspects of the boom in utopian writing: Richard Jefferies's *After London* (1885) delights in the overthrow of the poisonous city and a fresh new life in Nature; and both J. Leslie Mitchell and S. Fowler Wright thought that the route to human happiness was to embrace a life of noble savagery. Mind you, the pastoralism of William Morris's *News from Nowhere* (1890) is much more garden-like than it is wildernessy. If "man" and "nature" are imagined as at odds to one another, then one will presumably have to win out over the other. Still, broadly speaking, SF tends to dramatize "nature" as something to be adapted to serve the interests of humankind—as with the intricately detailed terraforming of Kim Stanley Robinson's Mars books (1993-1996) and *2312* (2012)—rather than the other way about (Pohl's *Man Plus*, for instance).[6] In this SF was reflecting a world where we have, more or less, put all the trees, put 'em in a tree museum, charged all the people a dollar and a half just to see 'em. And the reaction against that situation as often involves symbolic demonization of "the natural": Quatermass's 1950s astronaut, infected by alien life and slowly turning into a cactus monster. The Antarctic scientists in John Carpenter's body-horror classic *The Thing* (1982), consumed by biological hideousness in a way simultaneously repulsive and fascinating to us, the audience—the very definition of Abjection. The difference between those icky symbolic fables on the one hand and Southern Reach on the other is not just that the former play their strange mutations as merely horrifying, where VanderMeer manages a skilful balancing act between ghastliness and glamor. More telling, I think, is that such intrusion of alien nature in SF usually takes place to a body

6 http://www.strangehorizons.com/reviews/2013/01/2312_by_kim_sta.shtml

or bodies, inside an otherwise unaltered environment—Quatermass's meta-morphosing spaceman stumbling around regular 1950s London. In Southern Reach, it is the environment as a whole that is weird. Our Thing-like mutation is a process of aligning ourselves with the new reality.

VanderMeer, clearly, is writing is work of complex modern environmen-talism, a reaction to our collective mistreatment of "nature" and the conse-quently parlous state of our environment. But I think he's doing something more than that. He is channeling a deeper disquiet about nature itself; the way we are increasingly unable to *think* of the natural world as a pretty back-drop to human affairs, or a resource to be exploited. A time (in the word of Joshua Ramey) "when 'nature' has become something like absolute contin-gency, incarnate." It is a matter of the relative orientation, in amongst all the dread and horror and symbolic articulation of disgust at human environmen-tal pollution. The remade Ghost Bird is able simply to *be* in Area X. Control, constantly if impotently itching for comprehension, agency and power, can-not.

> On their fourth day in Area X, Control followed Ghost Bird through the long grass, puzzled, confused, sick, tired—the nights so alive with insects it was hard to sleep against their roar and chitter. While in his thoughts, a vast invisible blot had begun to form across the world outside of Area X ...

> "How can you be so cheerful?" he'd asked her, after she had noted their depleted food, water, in an energetic way, then pointed out a kind of sparrow she said was extinct in the wider world, an almost religious ecstasy animated her voice.

> "Because I'm alive," she'd replied. "Because I'm walking through wilderness on a beautiful day." (*Acceptance* 77)

But can it really be so simple, this being-in-the-world malarkey? To put it another way: is the weight more on the "religious", or on the "*almost*", there? And actually this is key, I think. If Southern Reach actually added up to a mac-farlaney celebration of wild places wrapped about with the ribbon of an SFnal weird mystery, it would be a lesser achievement. But VanderMeer's brilliance here is not so much in the delineation of Nature Redux, however lovingly and carefully he describes his blisses/of shapes that haunt these wildernesses. It is in the way he frames the question of our place in nature.

I say this in part to reflect the thoughts I've been having, pondering the trilogy and trying to work out the place the middle volume has. To repeat my-self, I don't think *Authority* works nearly as well as the other two books. More, there's something unbalanced (something that has the outward appearance almost of pandering to the present-day absurd commercial template of tril-ogies as arbitrary publishing format) about putting out three books—I say so, because the books themselves are so fascinated with doubles, not with triplets. The passages where Ghost Bird in *Acceptance* ponders what it would be like to meet the Biologist; the lighthouse-keeper's love affair with Charlie, Control and his mother, all refract the central binary of Area X and rest-of-the-world which is the way this text epitomizes precisely the nature-culture divide itself. As an articulation of a particular process of metamorphosis the book goes from before to after without dwelling (as with the mysteriously disappearing bunnies as they are shoveled towards the barrier) on the actual process of change. It's a conceptual dyad for which a triadic narrative break-down feels like a mismatch.

But there it is: *Authority* and all the detail it gives us about the Southern Reach. Why? Well, at some point after finishing the final volume I was put in mind of this passage (part 1, §7, if you want chapter and verse) from Nietzsche's *Genealogy of Morals*:

> One will have divined already how easily the priestly mode of valuation can branch off from the knightly-aristocratic and then develop into its opposite; this is particularly likely when the priest-ly caste and the warrior caste are in jealous opposition to one another and are unwilling to come to terms. The knightly-aris-tocratic value judgments presupposed a powerful physicality, a flourishing, abundant, even overflowing health, together with that which serves to preserve it: war, adventure, hunting, dancing, war games, and in general all that involves vigorous, free, joyful activi-ty. The priestly-noble mode of valuation presupposes, as we have seen, other things: it is disadvantageous for it when it comes to war! As is well known, the priests are the most evil enemies—but why? Because they are the most impotent. It is because of their impotence that in them hatred grows to monstrous and uncanny proportions, to the most spiritual and poisonous kind of hatred. The truly great haters in world history have always been priests; likewise the most ingenious haters: other kinds of spirit hardly come into consideration when compared with the spirit of priest-ly vengefulness. Human history would be altogether too stupid a thing without the spirit that the impotent have introduced into it.

This, perhaps, is the point of the second volume: to delineate the so-cial logic of the priesthood. The warriors are all long gone; in place of the knight-aristocratic world, and appropriately for a post-Enlightenment Republic like the USA, are the pen-pushers and the microscope-peerers. The Southern Reach's impotence in the face of Area X merely magnifies and externalises this Nietzschean inner *ressentiment*. More, VanderMeer's bureaucratic and scientific "priests" are desperately trying to be warriors, running around with guns, shooting at random—incompetent and ignorant but *aggressively* so.

> Once they go outside, where the strange, the stranger is found, they are not much better than uncaged beasts of prey. There they savour a freedom from all social constraints, they compensate themselves in the wilderness for the tension engendered by pro-tracted confinement and enclosure within the peace of society, they go back to the innocent conscience of the beast of prey, as triumphant monsters who perhaps emerge from a disgusting

procession of murder, arson, rape, and torture, exhilarated and undisturbed of soul, as if it were no more than a students' prank, convinced they have provided the poets with a lot more material for song and praise.

The novels are about the monstrosity not of the other, nor even (really) of the human heart; but of the particular state of affairs when modern human beings find themselves so jarringly out-of-place in an environment not interested in supporting them.

And this, in turn, brings me back to Pastoral. Classical pastoral was an idealized version of a perfect and blissful natural environment. In Theocritus and Vergil and Spenser, shepherds are not troubled with the toil of actually looking after sheep; instead they spend their days filling their bellies with delicious food, playing music and making love. That, in a sense, is the point of pastoral—the enjoyment of civic levels of luxury in a rural setting. All that VanderMeer's rather brilliant rewiring of the pastoral mode as horror does is to bring out the fundamental mismatch in the original material. "Nature" is inhabited by the cultured; not farmer and hunters but desk-workers and clock-watchers—not Nietzschean warriors but Nietzschean priests, with all the petty dissatisfactions and resentments of their caste. It is from this mismatch that The Southern Reach generates so many of its so very powerful effects.

This article first appeared on *Strange Horizons* on October 15, 2014. www.strangehorizons.com/reviews/2014/10/the_southern_re.shtml

K IS FOR JACQUELINE KOYANAGI

Olivia Waite

Visit the complete alphabet of intersectional feminism in romance for more information. And be warned that there are enormous spoilers in the post below![1]

It's easy to say that Jacqueline Koyanagi's luscious debut *Ascension* ticks just about every box on the anti-kyriarchy bingo card: our heroine is a queer disabled woman of color (in space!).[2] She falls in love with a disabled starship captain who's in a polyamorous relationship with another queer woman: a medic who plans on having children with a man-slash-engineer-slash-sometime-wolf. But like we saw with *Her Love, Her Land*, this book was written from deeply within the perspective of the identities it represents.[3] The characters' disability is a plot point, but it's not The Plot Point—the same goes for queerness and race: they're baked in, functions of character rather than Moving Moments. Polyamory gets a bit more of the Very Special Episode treatment, but this aspect is presented as bridging a gap between two different planetary cultures, one more sexually conservative than the other.

And all the characters are compelling, and several scenes made me gasp out loud (Adul!), but what I can't wait to talk about is how this book treats the problem of humans having bodies.

I say *problem* because human bodies are a source of profound tension, both in *Ascension* and in fiction and philosophy and human existence more generally. Our bodies are ourselves—but they are not entirely ourselves. They connect us to the world—except when they prevent us from connecting to the world. When we looked at the meaning of bodies in Vicki Essex's *In Her Corner*, they were always one or the other: male *or* female, healthy *or* injured.[4] Bodies in *Ascension* are better described with the conjunction *and*: they are weak *and* strong, burdensome flesh *and* transcendent gifts all at the same time. Characters are not restricted to one single and never-changing attitude to their own physicality: instead, there is a web of constantly shifting priorities, needs, limitations, and abilities.

We begin with Alana Quick, whose genetic disability, Mel's Disease, is a daily obstacle:

> I dropped the scrap and looked at my empty hands to determine
> how bad the tremors were today—hands that should have ben

---

1 http://www.oliviawaite.com/blog/2014/03/intersectional-a-z/

2 http://en.wikipedia.org/wiki/Kyriarchy

3 http://www.oliviawaite.com/blog/2014/04/a-is-for-american-indians/

4 http://www.oliviawaite.com/blog/2014/03/e-is-for-vicki-essex/

learning the curves of a ship instead of reaching for prescriptions. Hands that would become unreliable without medication, weak and gnarled. I didn't feel sorry for myself. I knew I could accomplish amazing feats with these hands, given the right tools and a ship to love. It's just that, well, I got frustrated that my ability to function—to do the one thing I'd loved since childhood— was entirely dependent on synthesized chemicals. (87)

At the same time, the self-awareness her disease requires of her enhances Alana's natural flair for mechanics and ship-fixing:

Every ship I worked on, I got to know by learning her song. I imagined each one stringing wires through me like new arteries, connecting us until I could feel what ailed her reflected in the pain patterns of my own flesh ... Each job made me feel alive. (319)

Her body's particularity, her disability, becomes a source of helpful experience. It's not an idealization—disability here is not a superpower—but it has given her practice with a mode of thought that comes in handy in her work.

At the same time, Alana's disease is more than simply a personal affliction: it's a financial burden as well. Alana (and her aunt Lai, who has the same disease) are dependent upon a medication known as Dexitek, which means they have an extra expense they can ill afford with the lack of ship-repair jobs: "People like [therapist] Shrike had no idea what it meant to have to choose between paying bills and paying for food" (107). This is a classic and very real meeting point between disability and poverty: the one reinforces the other, compounding Alana's suffering just as it compounds the suffering of disabled persons in our own present society. "Life was a privilege, not a right," Alana says. "Something you had to struggle for when you were unlucky enough to be born at the intersection of poverty and bad genes" (1841). Yes, precisely.

As with Tessa Dare's *Three Nights with a Scoundrel*, in *Ascension* we have a plethora of disabled characters, each of whose experiences is unique and personal.[5] Captain Tev Helix (oh, the hotness!) wears a prosthesis since she lost a leg in a mining accident: her disability has a before and an after with a moment of trauma as punctuation, leading to a different experience of embodiment than Alana's chronic pain issues or pilot Marre's terminal slide toward invisibility. "At some point I knew I couldn't pretend to be whole anymore," Tev says. "It didn't even occur to me at first that I'd still be able to have a leg, just not the one I was born with" (2267). The prosthetic is still her leg, still a part of her body: but years later, she's still paying off the debt for the new leg and her post-injury medical care.

Tev's leg and Alana's Dexitek highlight the common SF trope of technology as a means of compensating for physical disability. Where *Ascension* goes a step further is treating implanted non-compensatory tech as a part of a person's embodiment. To elude the authorities, who are pursuing them for a crime they didn't commit, the entire crew of the *Tangled Axon* re-

---

5 http://www.oliviawaite.com/blog/2014/02/d-is-for-tessa-dare/

move their communication implants. Alana finds this loss profoundly disconcerting:

> I still slept on one side to avoid hitting the transmit switch even though it wasn't there anymore. I still reached for my neck when I wanted to talk to someone. I still had to remind myself that I now had to seek them out face-to-face. I'd lost a sense almost as integrated as my vision or hearing, and I didn't know if I'd ever not feel a little incomplete. My body missed the metal I'd lost just as badly as if it had been blood or bone. (1899)

The great anxiety surrounding cyborgs, of course, is that adding robot parts decreases a person's humanity (Robocop, replicants, the Terminator, the Borg, the current preview for that Johnny Depp thing I'm too lazy to look up right now). Here, the tech incorporated in the body is all but transmuted into human flesh. This is a flexible, inclusive definition of humanity that I admit I can't stop thinking about: *of course* we're going to think of implanted tech as part of ourselves, just as we already personify and anthropomorphize our cars and our phones and our gadgets. Add to this *Ascension*'s overlap between a ship's body and its captain's, and the metaphysical connection between the pilot and the ship and the crew... There is a receptive physical inclusivity in this world, a fluid resilience and incorporation (pun intended) that I want more of.

Though the Dexitek works well enough most days, Alana and her aunt are saving for a more permanent cure, which the sinister corporation Transliminal Solutions offers for a hefty price tag. At the book's beginning Alana is offered a temporary taste of this cure, but once she takes it she will need to keep taking it and each treatment is shockingly expensive. Her therapist assures her there are payment plans: "I knew all about their 'payment plans.' More like indentured servitude. They'd own not just my city, but my body. My suffering and its relief. My life" (126). Alana carries this miracle drug with her for over half the book but never ingests it—her disability, though often frustrating and limiting, is not the worst-case scenario for her as an individual. Her struggle with Mel's is at least a familiar struggle—she would like a cure, but not at the expense of her personhood. Life with a disability is preferred to (and importantly not equivalent to) dehumanization.

That able-bodied-ness is not itself an idealized state in Ms. Koyanagi's text is shown by the attitude of Alana's sister Nova, a spirit guide (read: New Age-y type thing) who feels that her own healthy able body is still not good enough, still not the sum total of her true self:

> The first time I saw Nova injured as a child—a paper cut, nothing more—she screamed and wept for hours, unable to reconcile the visceral, heartbreaking reality of blood and split skin. It was too much, too far removed from her expectations of what little girls should be made of. Surely a tear in her flesh should have leaked purity and rapture into the world. Surely her soul should have escaped in vaporous arabesques, dissipating into the ether. (1115)

The language here is strongly reminiscent of our own culture's trope that girls' bodies are innately delicate and ethereal—witness this stunning Yahoo Answers thread from the antiquity of the internet about women farting, only some of which appears to be trolling—but despite that, from all I can tell the hierarchy in *Ascension* is gender-neutral at minimum and matriarchal at maximum.[6] Most of the characters we meet are women, including all those in positions of power. It's a straight gender reversal of the usual fictional ratio and as such is welcome and soothing as sinking into a warm bath.

And yet it's unsettling that in this book we have a sci-fi religion that elevates asceticism and self-starvation as practices that purify the soul, in ways that echo both the modern dietary compulsions of high fashion and the spiritual guidelines from, say, medieval Catholicism or Jainism. I admit to a personal lapsed-Catholic distrust of any doctrine of self-abnegation. Alana, so connected to her body even when that connection causes pain, is horrified by what she sees as her sister's casual disdain for a functional body: "Her words came from a kind of healthy privilege I couldn't begin to process" (2168). To Alana, Nova feels ungrateful, squandering a pain-free existence for no practical gain, unnecessarily scornful of an able body that does nothing to impede her connection with the wider world.

And yet ...

And yet Nova's words in this passage are impossible to refute:

> "One day, you'll feel it too . Only you'll feel it when it's too late. Your eyes will weaken. Your legs will start to hurt when you climb stairs. The space behind your knees will ache, like growing pains all over again, but this time you'll know the feeling is your body stretching and reshaping, pulling itself apart to make room for death. You'll fight it with medication like you always do, but she'll still come for you. Memories will lose definition around the edges, smoothing over in places that were once sharp and precise. Your skin will seem to expand and deflate, wrinkling in places that were once like silk. You'll feel as if you're shrinking inside your skin, disappearing. You'll get implants and upgrades, you'll fill your body with scaffolding to hold it together, to buy time, but the truth will remain: you're dying. You've always been dying. Life is a thin film, a veil between deaths." (2169)

Nova is right: Alana is going to die. Even the cure from Transliminal that she hopes for proves to be an illusion, a fraud. Alana's focus on her body blinds her to the long-term destiny of every human life. I was strongly, gut-wrenchingly reminded of the passage in *Catch-22* where Yossarian spends entire pages wondering which organ could be the first one to fail, the first soldier to fall, the first sign of his own impending demise. And barring catastrophe, there has to be a first step into the descent, doesn't there? Nova is entirely, horribly right: by virtue of the fact that we are alive, our bodies are destined to fail and to die. This is the way of all flesh.

There is a quote late in the book from another character who resists the inevitability of death: "Birke's voice echoed in my thoughts. *I will never*

6 http://answers.yahoo.com/question/index?qid=20060802184600AAa61jB

lose her again. I will build a new universe where bodies aren't fragile, where the soul is limitless, where medicine is pure magic" (4093). And this is our villain. Who—spoilers!—happens to be a double of our heroine, from another universe, one where Nova had Mel's and died of it instead of Alana. So the Alana-double is searching through various realities, trying to find a Nova-double she can use to resurrect her sister. She is Alana's resistance to the gospel of death, taken to its logical conclusion.

And yet …

And yet Birke is clearly, unambiguously a villain. She kills remorselessly, wiping an entire planet and its population in one stunning surprise of a scene. (I told you there were spoilers!) It's doubtful this is the first time she's done this in one reality or another; if death is inevitable, why bother waiting for it? Why allow other people to wait for it, when you have a personal stake in eliminating them? Nova's self-abnegation is a questionable virtue, but Birke's willingness to abnegate others is clearly much more terrible.

While Birke-as-Alana's-doppelganger does show up somewhat out of nowhere at the climax of the plot—can this really be the very first double we've met from the othersiders?—the way her appearance complicates the text's structure of embodiment is symbolically satisfying to a profound degree. As Alana wonders: "How could someone who shared my body be so alien? Was it the difference of a single synapse? One twist in the timeline, and this is what I would have been?" (3904).

The answer to this question is yes, as Alana realizes while Nova chooses to give her life in sacrifice to save Marre's (despite what she's said earlier about death's inevitability):

> Her [Birke's] grief resonated with mine. I knew its bitter taste, its color. I knew how it felt to see the empty space they once occupied. To resent even happy memories for the flaying pain they brought to the surface. I understood then that it was true: given the right set of circumstances, I could have become Birke. Any version of me from any reality could have become her. (4093)

Body and self, self and other, the individual and the universe—it always comes back to that first conjunction, the all-important *and*. Alana is right about the body, *and* Nova is too. Nova is also right about the soul: her last gift to her sister is this memory from their childhood:

> "I said there's two reasons to have a soul … One … is to feel the all world inside you, from now to then and back again. To breathe the breath of every ancestor, to know where you've been and anchor you to the physical world—to your body and everything it touches."

> I grabbed Nova's finger and pretended to bite it. She laughed and shook it out, but didn't break her stride. "The other … is so that one day, you can look into the eye of the universe and burn away that which separates us from God." (4112)

Reader, I admit I teared up at this part. So often genre fiction will set one ideology against one another until one of them wins—the brooding isolated

263

hero is brought back out into the world, the cold uptight heroine learns to relax and enjoy life. *Ascension* manages to draw a great deal of tension out of opposing worldviews, yet it doesn't feel the need to resolve the tension in favor of one or the other. Engineer Ovie is a wolf *and* a man, simultaneously. Alana *and* her sister are both right, and both wrong. The body is a gift *and* a burden. It depends on who you ask—and how they're feeling when you ask them.

***

Side note: Stay tuned for my upcoming essay *Oh My God, I Just Realized How Many Parallels This Book Has To Star Wars Let's Talk About Them Forever Especially The Things About Tech And Disability And Family And Choices.*

***

Last year Tor.com posted an excerpt from Kathryn Allan's Disability in Science Fiction, and later a review of the book.[7] I haven't had a chance to read this yet myself, but Interlibrary Loan has a chance to change all that!

Dr. Laura Vivanco let me know that for a limited time, the archives of the Journal of Literary & Cultural Disability Studies are free to access. There's a lot of great things in there! I'm going to learn so much!

I owe a great intellectual (and therefore personal) debt to the incisive Ana Mardoll, whose writing on the now-defunct-but-still-visible FWD/Forward was a light in the darkness of my privilege, and who continues to be awesome by writing the viscerally readable Annotated Index of Ross Geller.[8]

This article first appeared on *oliviawaite.com* on April 12, 2014.
www.oliviawaite.com/blog/2014/04/k-is-for-jacqueline-koyanagi/

---

7 http://www.tor.com/stories/2013/08/disability-in-science-fiction-excerpt and http://www.tor.com/blogs/2013/12/book-review-disability-in-science-fiction-representations-of-technology-as-cure-edited-by-kathryn-allan
8 http://www.anamardoll.com/2014/03/friends-annotated-index-of-ross-geller_22.html

'MS. MARVEL': DELICIOUSLY HALAL?

Ng Suat Tong

Would you give G. Willow Wilson and Adrian Alphona's *Ms. Marvel* to your daughter or young nephew to read?

I think the answer in most instances would be a loud and affirmative, "Yes!" It is after all quite inoffensive and mainly concerns the travails of school and family life; if complicated in this instance by the fact that the main protagonist is a Pakistani-American Girl. The comic is friendly, instructive, educational, and has a placid attitude towards the dangers of everyday existence. It would seem to be, in a word, "safe."

And what exactly are the dangers Kamala Khan faces in her first three issues? She is tricked into taking alcohol by insensitive classmates, breaks her curfew and is grounded, is sent to detention for accidentally destroying school property, helps a pair of accident prone lovers, is involved in a friendly hold-up at a corner store, and is injured during the accidental discharge of a firearm.

In many ways *Ms. Marvel* is a return to the more gentle pleasures of the comics of yore; dialing back the myth of a violent America propagated by TV shows like *CSI*, *Criminal Minds*, *NCIS* et al.—where murderous psychopaths reside on every corner and corpses are to be found on every other doorstep and school dormitory. Can a superhero comic subsists on stories culled from ordinary high school life? Well, the sales figures on future issues of the comic should tell the tale in due course.

The central issues at stake in *Ms. Marvel* are conformity and difference, subjects which are balanced precariously at this historical moment in America (and Europe) where the simple act of wearing a hijab might be cause for derision.

Perhaps the comics' greatest achievement is to make the life of a Muslim girl in America perfectly ordinary. Part of the success of Jaime Hernandez's *Locas* lies in just this effect—the way it shapes our understanding of an unfamiliar culture, revealing its core of basic humanity. Something similar occurs in Asghar Farhadi's *A Separation* where the setting (environmental, legal) and motivations may seem strange but the reactions completely "human." With that moment of recognition, Iranians stop becoming headline material or screaming terrorists (a la Ben Affleck's *Argo*) but individuals in all their complexity.

I don't think Wilson's work is quite at that level in *Ms. Marvel* but there is a trace of gentle subversion about it; much of it related in humorous vignettes. A visit to the neighborhood mosque for a halaqah (religious study circle) is not an occasion for harsh harangues of deeply conservative mullahs but some questions concerning Islamic theology and issues surrounding the place of women within the mosque and society. The first page of issue one has Kamala sniffing a "greasy BLT" which is described as "delicious, delicious infidel meat." This is followed by the suggestion that she try fakon instead ("it's not that terrible"). Buddhists face similar philosophical "problems" when encountering vegetised meat dishes; a culinary art form in itself.

Wilson's subversiveness doesn't lie simply in these small challenges to authority but in more subtle mouldings of this thoroughly "white", Christian-Jewish form of expression—the American superhero comic.

Present day Islam is not especially enamored of figurative works of art, but the image of Kamala confronting the Avengers in the form of Iron Man, Captain Marvel and Captain America is clearly an instance of borrowed iconography. Lamps are not rubbed in the course of issue one of *Ms. Marvel* but the Terrigen Mists and the appearance of the Avengers suddenly within its folds do suggest the appearance of Jinn bearing gifts, and we all know how badly that usually turns out.[1] The soundtrack to their arrival is a qawwali song by Amir Khusrow ("Sakal ban phool rahi sarson"), sufi devotional music which some might find intoxicating.[2]

There's an image of Captain America as an Islamic mystical being straight from the pages of the Qur'an (as angels are from the Bible). But more than that, the image is clearly a syncretisation of well known religious forms—it is a Transfiguration with Moses and Elijah on both sides of a female Jesus. Iron Man has his left hand raised in a gesture which either suggests the Trinity or the giving of a benediction. Captain Marvel herself is posed in a manner which immediately brings to mind images of the Assumption of the Virgin—right down to her flowing waist ribbon. The birds surrounding her are presumably modern day versions of the cherubs we see in Renaissance paintings. To borrow a phrase from Ms. Kamala Khan, it's all "delicious, delicious infidel meat." One assumes that Kamala—aged sixteen and forbidden to mix with boys at alcohol fueled parties—is a virgin herself. One also assumes that Wilson and Alphona are not entirely convinced of the merit of the iconoclastic claims of hadith literature.

> AND LO! The angels said: "O Mary! Behold, God has elected thee and made thee pure, and raised thee above all the women of the world. Surah 3. Al-i'Imran, Ayah 42

Christopher ZF writing at The Stake is eager to let readers knows that:[3]

> In this instance Kamala's gods are not God, but another trinity that inspires her: Captain America, Iron Man, and the central religious figure of Kamala's imagination: Captain Marvel....The manner in which Wilson and artist Adrian Alphona handle what could be a potentially fraught subject is instead refreshing in its candor... this scene is not a ham-handed, irreligious, or silly affair....

The caution is understandable though obviously not my cup of tea.

1 http://marvel.wikia.com/Kamala_Khan_(Earth-616)
2 http://en.wikipedia.org/wiki/Qawwali and http://en.wikipedia.org/wiki/Amir_Khusrow
3 http://thestake.org/2014/03/07/review-ms-marvel-1/

This appropriation of imagery is clearly tied up with Kamala's own conflicted sense of identity and her cultural influences (both knowing and unknowing)—a desire to fit equally into "normal" white American society and the traditions of her parents, with these parts seemingly irreconcilable. She's a dark haired Alice in Wonderland, taking the bottle labeled "Drink Me" to become small or the cake with "Eat Me" written on it to become a leggy white blonde—all of this done in the interest of assimilation. The creators obviously thought long and hard (or maybe not) when they decided to make her a "human with Inhuman" lineage. Kamala's vision is no more than a reflection of the mishmash which constitutes her subconscious desires.[4] As "Iron Man" says to her, "You are seeing what you need to see." If only Captain America was more halal.[5]

Noah writing at The Atlantic doesn't quite see it that way though.[6] Concerning Kamala's shape shifting powers he writes:

> You could see this power as a kind of metaphorical curse, reflecting Kamala's uncertainty; she doesn't know who she is, so she's anyone or anything. I don't think that's quite what it signifies, though. Changing shape doesn't mean that Kamala erases her ethnicity...Rather, in Ms. Marvel, shape-changing seems to suggest that flexibility is a strength. Kamala is a superhero because she's both Muslim and American at once. Her power is to be many things, and to change without losing herself.

And that is undoubtedly the final destination of Wilson's story. The first three issues are in all likelihood a journey to that point of realization.

Perhaps the greatest subversion of all is that Ms. Marvel might be the most religious comic book published by Marvel in decades. Not anywhere as overt as the Spire Archie Christian comics but arguably in the same tradition. Islam both informs Kamala's action and the conflicts she faces at school and at home. The centrality of Islam in Ms. Marvel was probably considered uncontroversial by Wilson's editors (save Sana Amanat who is Pakistani-American) because of the ethnicity of the main protagonist—in America, race and Islam seem almost indivisible and therefore "excusable." At the risk of stating the obvious, this rigidity in terms of race and religion is part of Wilson's challenge to her readership in a country where the word "Muslim" often conjures up images of "brown" or black individuals. The fact that a blonde, white woman is taking moral action on the basis of the Qur'an is an essential part of Ms. Marvel's narrative.

In Culture and the Death of God, Terry Eagleton writes that:

> Societies become secular not when they dispense with religion altogether, but when they are no longer especially agitated by it...as the wit remarked, it is when religion starts to interfere with your everyday life that it is time to give it up...Another index of secularization is when religious faith ceases to be vitally at stake

4 http://marvel.wikia.com/Kamala_Khan_(Earth-616)
5 http://en.wikipedia.org/wiki/Halal
6 http://www.theatlantic.com/entertainment/archive/2014/03/what-makes-the-muslim-em-ms-marvel-em-awesome-shes-just-like-everyone/284517/

in the political sphere...this does not mean that religion becomes formally privatized, uncoupled from the political state; but even when it is not, it is effectively taken out of public ownership and dwindles to a kind of personal pastime, like breeding gerbils or collecting porcelain...

American society *is* "agitated" by Islam but Muslims have almost no voice in the political sphere. Kamala Khan may be the central figure of *Ms. Marvel* but she is an "other"—not us, someone strange, someone else—with seemingly little to say about how Americans should lead their lives; she has no religious or moral prescriptions which could affect white America. She is someone else's porcelain collection. This makes the comic "tolerable" in the eyes of Marvel's paymasters even while Disney enforces a policy of not taking the Lord's name in vain in song.[7]

The commentators at Deseret News have an even more innocuous explanation for this new venture:[8]

"Comics are a "survey of the pop culture medium," Hunter said, adding that the religions brought up in modern comics reflect modern society.

He said mainstream culture is talking about Muslims. According to the Pew Research Center, the Muslim population in the United States is projected to rise from 2.6 million in 2010 to 6.2 million in 2030, which shows Muslims are a growing market and topic in the U.S....Ms. Marvel's Muslim heritage was chosen as a reflection of what the mainstream culture is interested in...Publishers are not just appealing to certain religious markets, however. They're also using religious comics as a way to tap into the market of unbelievers, too, Lewis said.

How wonderfully bland it would be if this was the comic's sole *raison d'être*. This gentle and most politically correct of comic book stories is sometimes more clever than it seems.

Further Reading

G Willow Wilson on Kamala's powers.[9] Lots of background information in this interview:

"Her power set was actually the toughest thing, I think, to narrow down in the character creation process," Wilson said. "I really did not want her to have the classically girly power sets—I didn't want her to float. I didn't want her to sparkle. I didn't want her to be able to read people's minds. I think a lot of these sort of passive abilities are often given to female characters—becoming invisible, us-

7 http://www.christianpost.com/news/frozen-songwriters-backtrack-disney-does-not-have-policy-of-not-using-god-118931/

8 http://national.deseretnews.com/article/677/Superheroes-and-faith-How-religion-plays-a-role-in-the-comic-book-industry.html

9 http://herocomplex.latimes.com/comics/ms-marvel-g-willow-wilson-sana-amanat-on-kamalas-transformation/

ing force fields. I wanted her to have something visually exciting, something kinetic... The idea of making her a shape-shifter nicely paralleled her personal journey."

Mariam Asad, Zainab Akhtar, and Muaz Zekeria discuss "What the new Ms. Marvel means for Muslims in Comics."[10]

This article first appeared on *The Hooded Utilitarian* on May 12, 2014.
www.hoodedutilitarian.com/2014/05/ms-marvel-deliciously-halal/

10 http://www.npr.org/blogs/codeswitch/2013/11/11/244529591/what-the-new-ms-marvel-means-for-muslims-in-comics

UNDER THE RADAR: 'SULTANA'S DREAM'

Mahvesh Murad

There are a few texts that come up again and again in discussions of early feminist utopian fiction—*Man's Rights* by Annie Denton Cridge from 1870, *Mizora* by Mary E Bradley Lane from 1880-81, *Arqtiq* by Anna Adolph from 1899 and perhaps most famously, Charlotte Gilman's *Herland* from 1905.

But these were all stories from the western world, stories that were part of a surge of utopian fiction written by women leading up to the women's Suffrage movement of the early twentieth century. But what of the east? What of the countries that were not just weighed down by patriarchy, but colonialism as well? Did any of them create any important feminist narratives?

As it happens, they did. Rokeya Sakhawat Hossain's short story *Sultana's Dream* from 1905 remains a prominent and important example of feminist fiction, especially since it was written by a woman in the subcontinent—an area that is still trying to shrug off the dirty overcoat of patriarchy and colonialism. Hossain's story is a charming, funny and sharp analysis on subcontinental life at the time, especially for the Muslim women for whom it was the norm to remain illiterate and in purdah.

Sultana's Dream was written in English (which was far from Hossain's second language—she probably spoke at least Bengali, Urdu and possibly read Arabic and Farsi as many of the richer Muslims in the subcontinent did, before she wrote in English), while her husband was away for work so that she could show him how her skills in the language had grown.

It was printed in *The Indian Ladies Journal* that same year. It begins with an unnamed narrator ("Sultana" here is a title, though in the subcontinent it is can also be a name) who may or may not have fallen asleep in her "easy-chair", thinking about the state of Indian womanhood. She looks up to see someone who resembles her friend Sister Sara and walks with this woman into a world unlike anything she has ever known. They are in Ladyland, Sister Sara explains, is a utopia run by women, where all civic duties are managed in a few hours, thanks to the extreme efficiency that comes naturally to the women, leaving the rest of the day to be used to develop more important things—art, science, beauty.

There are only women to be seen in public and Sister Sara explains how the men entered purdah readily, after being heavily wounded in war and presuming the country was lost. Of course, once the women were able to take control, they won the war easily and with science, not brute force. In fact, the war is won by university students and not soldiers: "Then the Lady Principal with her two thousand students marched to the battle field, and arriving there directed all the rays of the concentrated sunlight and heat towards the enemy." Brain over brawn, Hossain makes clear right away.

With the war won by the cleverness of women, it was only natural that they continue to manage Ladyland entirely, leaving men in the mardana (the male version of the traditional female space of the zenana, "mard" being the Urdu word for male), where they tend to the domestic chores, since no one can trust these "untrained men out of doors." This aspect of reverse-segregation of the sexes in *Sultana's Dream* has influenced a great many writers and in particular, this idea of the mardana has most recently influenced fantasy writer Kameron Hurley's book, *The Mirror Empire*. Hurley frequently points out the importance of *Sultana's Dream* on her work and on feminist SFF.

It's interesting that Hossain slyly pointed out back in 1905 what is often discussed now, particularly in the subcontinent—why should women be taught to stay safe, when men are not taught to not threaten or abuse or rape or be a danger to women? The idea of restricting women in the zenana (or even in forced purdah) *by* men for their own protection *from* men is completely absurd—just as much back then as it is now, and Hossain isn't afraid to point out that "it is not safe so long as there are men about the streets, nor is it so when a wild animal enters a marketplace."

When the narrator of the story innocently repeats what women were often told about men, "Even their brains are bigger and heavier than women's. Are they not?", her new friend tells her, "Yes, but what of that? An elephant also has got a bigger and heavier brain than a man has. Yet man can enchain elephants and employ them, according to their own wishes."

Hossain doesn't just subvert the traditional role for subcontinental women in the Twentieth Century, she is downright disdainful and critical of women who have allowed themselves to be trapped within a limited role. Her narrator explains her Calcutta to Sister Sara by saying, "We have no hand or voice in the management of our social affairs. In India man is lord and master, he has taken to himself all powers and privileges and shut up the women in the zenana", and when Sara asks her "Why do you allow yourselves to be shut up?", she explains—like any "good" traditional Muslim woman from that time probably would—"Because it cannot be helped as they are stronger than women." The idea of a male dominated society existing because of brute force comes up here, but Hossain doesn't abide by that. "A lion is stronger than a man," says Sister Sara, "but it does not enable him to dominate the human race. You have neglected the duty you owe to yourselves and you have lost your natural rights by shutting your eyes to your own interests."

What makes *Sultana's Dream* particularly pleasing as an early feminist text is the ease with which Hossain casually dismisses the myths perpetuated by parochial patriarchal systems of the time—she's so confident in her belief that every aspect of male-dominated society can be challenged if women were to accept that there is more for them than basic domestic duties, so positive in her faith that the status quo can be challenged—it's refreshing. It's often reported that her husband read the story without even stopping to sit down, and at finishing it declared it to be "a splendid revenge." Revenge upon whom, I do not know.

Hossain is also very aware of living under colonisation—and not just that of women by men but that of nations. The Queen of Ladyland tells the narrator:

> We do not covet other people's land, we do not fight for a piece of diamond though it may be a thousand-fold brighter than the Koh-i-Noor, nor do we grudge a ruler his Peacock Throne. We dive deep into the ocean of knowledge and try to find out the precious gems, which nature has kept in store for us. We enjoy nature's gifts as much as we can.

Interesting—and pointed—that she brings up two of the most valuable items plundered by the British Empire in the subcontinent—the Koh-i-Noor, a massive diamond mined in the 17th Century in India that became part of the Crown Jewels in 1877, and the Peacock Throne, commissioned in the 17th Century which no longer exists, though many jewels adorning it were taken by British colonialists and are presumed to be a part of part of the Crown Jewels. Obviously, Hossain was no fan of the British Empire or its presence in the Indian subcontinent, and she wasn't afraid to say it.

Born to a Muslim zamindar (landlord) family in what is now Bangladesh, Hossain was married at 16 (a reported "love marriage"—rare in those days) to a local magistrate who encouraged her to write in both English and Bengali about what she felt believed in. And what Hossain believed in was equality for women in every aspect of life. Women's lives at that time—Muslim women's, in particular, were very much spent in purdah, and in kitchens and homes, trapped entirely and only in domesticity. Hossain believed that women were held back by their lack of knowledge of their rights, often pointing out that women's right as written in the Quran were no longer in effect, as a result of Muslim male conservatives. She was one of the earliest feminist reformers the subcontinent has known, writing a great deal about women's empowerment in Bengali so as to reach a larger audience. When her husband died, she used the money he left her to set up a school for girls, and though she had to go door to door to beg people to let their daughters attend it at first, The Sakhawat Memorial High School exists in Kolkata to this day.

Hossain's explanation for why women should have equal rights was simple and remains applicable, probably everywhere in the word but especially in the Indian subcontinent where women are struggling against a male-dominated society more so than in the west. "We constitute half of the society," she said, "If we remain backward can the society move forward? If somebody's legs are bound up how far can she walk? Indeed, the interest of women and men are not different. Their goal of life and ours are the same."

This article first appeared on *Tor.com* on October 17, 2014.
www.tor.com/blogs/2014/10/under-the-radar-sultanas-dream

LIU CIXIN—'THE THREE BODY PROBLEM'

Mieneke van der Salm

With the scope of *Dune* and the commercial action of *Independence Day*, *Three-Body Problem* is the first chance for English-speaking readers to experience this multiple-award-winning phenomenon from China's most beloved science fiction author, Liu Cixin.

Set against the backdrop of China's Cultural Revolution, a secret military project sends signals into space to establish contact with aliens. An alien civilization on the brink of destruction captures the signal and plans to invade Earth. Meanwhile, on Earth, different camps start forming, planning to either welcome the superior beings and help them take over a world seen as corrupt, or to fight against the invasion. The result is a science fiction masterpiece of enormous scope and vision.

Diversity and giving space to voices other than those of the privileged majority have been a huge talking point in SFF in the past year. One way to achieve this is through translating foreign-language titles into English and to introduce these new perspectives to English-speaking readers. Yet this is still a very rare occurrence, as few foreign-language titles are translated and published each year. Off the top of my head the only authors I can think of in speculative fiction are Haruki Murakami, Carlos Ruiz Zafon, Pierre Pevel, and Pasi Ilmari Jääskeläinen, and of course, Thomas Oldeheuvelt's *Hex* series that will be published in English in the autumn of next year. So it was really exciting to see this novel brought to print in English by Tor. It's the first Chinese SFF series ever to have been brought over, at least by one of the big Five, as far as I'm aware. This is exciting because China is one of the biggest and fastest-developing countries in the world, where there is some great voices we've never heard of and we finally get to discover one of them. Liu Cixin is one of the best-known and most successful SF writers in China, so his being the first to be translated into English isn't actually that surprising.

The Three Body Problem is set in China, partially during the years of the Cultural Revolution and partially in the book's present. As China developed along far different lines than Western culture—the most obvious being moving from a monarchy system to communism, instead of capitalism, and having what is essentially an oligarchy instead of a democracy for a long time—its cultural outlook and values are different from the familiar ones we usually encounter and I really enjoyed discovering these differences. I did need to quickly look up some of the background—Wikipedia for the win—as it has been a long time since I learned about the Cultural Revolution in secondary school. It also made the way Liu Cixin treated the Western scientists and philosophers who show up in the Trisolaris sections awesome, because they were so irreverent, lacking the gravitas they'd usually be embodied with in Western literature.

In-between the past and present storylines, Liu Cixin introduces us to a world called Trisolaris, which as the name indicates is a world with three suns. The titular three body problem stems from these three solar bodies and their effect on the planet and to be honest this part just went right over my head somewhat, because science, but it didn't do it in such a way that I felt dumb or lost. In the context of the Three Body computer game and the way the problem was explained there, I could kind of squint and understand it. Enough to be going on with anyway. The game mechanics Liu Cixin uses to explain the Trisolaran quandary and its society and culture was fantastic, especially as gamification is something that is a technique that's used in teaching and literacy instruction as well and so it is actually something quite familiar.

In addition to the hard physics of the three body problem, there is also a lot of technical and mechanical science in play between the computers and telescopes that are used at some key points of the novel and let's not forget all the stuff the military brings to bear. Yet when we set the science (fictional) elements aside, the core of the book is essentially a mystery, including murders and conspiracies, which Wang Miao and Shi Qiang need to solve. I loved these two characters. Wang is our main point of view, be it in our world or that of Three Body, and he is such a calm, methodical thinker, testing and re-testing his theories, but one forced out of his usual habits through the events described in the story. Shi Qiang, or Da Shi as he's nicknamed, is his polar opposite almost: worldly, impulsive, and always on edge, he's a great foil for Wang. The other main viewpoint character, the one through whose eyes we get most of the story set in the past is Ye Wenjie. The daughter of an intellectual executed during the Cultural Revolution, she's a very sympathetic character. However, she doesn't come through her experiences unscathed and the way Liu Cixin develops her and changes how the reader sees her over the course of the novel was brilliant. She goes for sympathetic, to eerie, to scary in the space of a book.

One aspect of the story that has to be mentioned is its translation. I often translate web texts for work and that just plain, vanilla Dutch-to-English, without literary flourishes, but it can be quite challenging at times, especially if there is a specific sense I want to convey for which there is no direct English equivalent. So, having heard Ken Liu talk about translating *The Three Body Problem* on the Coode Street Podcast and the issues he encountered, I can only imagine how hard it must have been to translate this novel and do Liu Cixin's prose justice.[1] In my opinion, he has done a marvellous job with this first book in the series. The writing is gorgeous and sometimes lyrical, yet hard and clinical in the places where it needs to be and I never had the sense that this was a translated text. I also loved the translator's notes Ken Liu included, especially as he didn't just explain some of the Chinese cul-

1 http://jonathanstrahan.podbean.com/e/episode-205-ken-liu-and-chinese-science-fiction/

tural elements Western readers might not understand, he also touched upon some science elements. At one point, he even referenced an academic journal article, which I thought was very cool.

The Three Body Problem is a fantastic book. I loved this story with its old-time SF sensibilities, real, scary aliens—you guys, the aliens!—mixed with modern tech. I want to know what happens next and how Earth will react to the news that "they" are truly out there. It is easy to see why Liu Cixin is so popular in China and I can only hope he'll be just as popular in the rest of the world now his work has been translated to English. If you want a hard SF novel, mixed with history and social science elements, than I can't recommend *The Three Body Problem* highly enough. It's one of my favourite novels of the year and it will definitely feature on my Favourites of 2014 list in a week or two.

This article first appeared on *A Fantastical Librarian* on December 16, 2014.
www.afantasticallibrarian.com/2014/12/liu-cixin-the-three-body-problem.html

LYRICAL EMPOWERMENT: 'MEMORY OF WATER' BY EMMI ITÄRANTA

Justin Landon

I tried to describe *Memory of Water* to a few people in the days after I finished it. It was a bit of challenge that led to me falling back on tiresome comparisons. One example read, "it feels like the young adult novel I wanted Paolo Baciagalupi's *Shipbreaker* to be." Or, "it's like Rob Ziegler's *Seed* if he cared a lot less about explody things." Or worst of all, "Emmi Itäranta creates a cocktail of *The Hunger Games* and *The Windup Girl*, with Susan Collins' sense of character and Paolo Baciagalupi's haunting image of our future." Bad, right?

Itäranta's novel laughs at all these comparisons. Written simultaneously in both English and Finnish, *Memory of Water* is a lyrical and emotionally scarring novel of life in the indeterminate post-climate change future. Once a plentiful resource, water has become as tightly controlled by the government as nuclear material in the modern world. Wars are waged over it. In northern Europe, seventeen-year-old Noria Kaitio is learning to become a tea master like her father. It's a position of great responsibility in their culture, one that affords them more water than anyone not affiliated with the government.

Both the tea ceremony's significance within the culture and the country Noria inhabits being called New Qian imply that China has conquered Europe. It may be true, but Itäranta is disinterested in geopolitics or anything not relevant to Noria's struggle to survive in her oppressed dystopian village. The larger world is interesting, fleshed out enough to make every detail pregnant with possibility, but remains only tangentially important to the narrative. While *Memory of Water* tackles challenging themes, it's the tight focus on Noria's situation, and her emotional responses to it, which renders the novel vivid and compelling.

Those emotional responses begin when Noria learns the secret her father has guarded his entire life. He alone knows the location of a hidden spring, passed down for generations from tea master to tea master. Knowledge of the spring means something different to Noria, or at least she thinks it does, as she's forced to watch her best friend's family suffer from water restrictions. How can one person keep such a big secret in the face of all these pressures?

This decision point is the root of the novel's emotional punch. How do we know the decisions we make are the right ones? Should Noria sacrifice her future for the future of another? *Memory of Water* is a novel of decisions, of grasping life and giving it direction on your own terms and no other's. This empowerment, combined with the deeply evocative first person narrative, is what makes Itäranta's novel such a wonderful piece for younger readers. It doesn't contrive to get adults out of the way so much as it demands that a young person be responsible for their fate.

Of course there is some heavy handed kvetching about climate change. A fair bit of finger pointing about the wasteful society we inhabit is par for the course in this kind of novel. It never strays beyond the needs of the story, remaining within a narrative focused more on the personal implications of the catastrophe than the underlying causes. This personal nature of the conflict is what separates it from the books I compared it to at the outset. *Memory of Water* isn't worried about the future of the Earth or the people writ large who live on its surface. Itäranta cares only for Noria, the life she'll be able to lead and the friends she'll take with her.

She does this all amid brilliant, lyrical prose. Lyrical is a term often overused in describing prose. Quite literally it means that the author's style is imaginative and beautiful, which is rather pat. I use it here to describe rhythm, the slightly repetitive words that drive the point home, a chorus before the next verse. Itäranta's writing is almost a song, working like a melody that sticks in your head more than a series of words that flow by.

If there's a weakness in the novel it's that nothing is going anywhere with vigor. The result is a novel that meanders like a wooded creek, finding rocks to alter its course and making it bubble, before ending in a body of water with far greater potential. There's more story to tell in Itäranta's world, both about the how and why. Without these things it becomes less a science fiction than a literary character study with some odd parameters. Could this have been the story of a girl in desert culture, with no hints at our own imagined future? Most assuredly. Whether that detracts from the novel is a question for each reader to answer. For me, Noria's journey was satisfying and poignant. Emmi Itäranta's novel recalls a memory of what's important, not only to survive, but to actually live.

Sometimes a review pales in comparison to the words of the author herself. If you really want to know what *Memory of Water* is about and whether you should read it, I find this passage sums the situation up quite well.

> Most of the soil we walk on once grew and breathed, and once it had the shape of the living, long ago. One day someone who doesn't remember us will walk on our skin and flesh and bones, on the dust that remains of us.

This article first appeared on *Tor.com* on July 2, 2014.
www.tor.com/blogs/2014/07/book-review-a-memory-of-water-emmi-itaranta

REVIEW: 'ZERO SUM GAME' BY SL HUANG

Renay

I came out of *Captain America: The Winter Soldier* going, *"This is totally like this book I'm reading!"* I have made it utterly no secret that I love Steve's magical flying shield and the way he chooses to use it in fights. In fact, I would watch two hours of fight scenes to watch Steve fling that sucker around with split second decisions about trajectory and *mumblemutter* forces. So this book was a lot of fun (neat characters with diverse talents! interpersonal conflict! rad superpowers!), but also frustrating because of the writing.

Cas doesn't have a specific totem; she uses everything at her disposal and the math flying through her head to make calculations help her take people out with rocks, bust through a group of gun-wielding criminals, and get out of tough scrapes. If she *did* have a totem, it would be a loaded gun (but not a Glock, I get it book, she *hates Glocks*). It would be even better filmed (dear Hollywood, I will write this screenplay, call me!), but it's a pretty great premise even in book form.

With that sort of skill, Cas would be unstoppable, and in so many scenarios, she's absolutely brutal with her ability. *Zero Sum Game* is about what happens when her ability to manipulate the world around her with numbers and calculations utterly fails in the face of mental abilities much stronger than the ability to see the Matrix. Cas's ability to see mathematical solutions to situations around her reminded me a little of the visual trick used in the Lucy trailer where she could see information streams like phone calls in the air around her and sort through them with her hands to find what she wanted.

The conceit of the book is interesting enough, but you can't sustain a book with *"the character is great at math!"* I skimmed most of the longer sections that dealt explicitly with math or related topics, especially later in the book. I don't know anything about high level math. I also don't know anything above third grade math, either, so no matter how carefully I read it, it's never going to mean anything. Word problems have always been my enemy, so I never grokked half of the explanations Cas tossed out about what she was doing. Math nerds will totally get it! If not, I feel like there's going to be a lot of skimming for some folks.

Cas is more than her mathematical prowess, though: she's violent, she's a loner, she's incredibly lonely, she desperately needs a few good friends, and way less recreational substance abuse during downtime, when her ability threatens to overwhelm her. Cas Russell's drinking problem is Dean Winchester in Season 8 levels of fucked up. Cas copes *less well* than Dean Winchester. That's messed up. When I finally got sucked in for good around chapter nine (which took me three weeks to reach), I finished the book in a day because yes, secret agencies! Conspiracies! Nerdy computer geeks! Sweet, sweet revenge! Shady pasts! This book hit several of my favorite topics:

1. TRUST: Cas doesn't trust anyone except Rio the Sociopath, doing God's Work. Rio talks like he's drugged, kills like a machine, and is not Cas's friend, which is weird since Cas puts her faith in him without fail multiple times in the book for reasons never quite made clear. Rio "values her" more than himself (RED ALERT). It got to a point, mid-way through when everything seemed FUBAR that I couldn't believe the book wasn't going to address the parade of pink elephants from all the Rio Kool-Aid Cas was drinking. WILL THIS BE EXPLAINED IN THE SEQUEL? I really liked Rio, even more when everyone else was terrified of him, but damn, I sure don't trust him much at all. SHADY CHARACTER ALERT, made super interesting by the fact that the whole book is about a psychic that can alter your behavior and thoughts, and how Cas handles being manipulated by such a person, *while being manipulated by a person without those skills*. I'm so suspicious. I don't trust you, Rio.

Other than the weird trust issues at the center of Cas and Rio's odd relationship, Cas makes friends with Arthur and Checker, a PI/hacker team. She makes several bad impressions, there's some mutual betrayal as well as mutual butt-saving, and eventually Cas gets adopted. The book wants you to believe Cas is the one doing the adopting, but back in reality where Cas doesn't have great (spoiler: any, at all) interpersonal skills, Arthur and Checker totally adopt her. I was glad, because Rio is not necessarily the be-all-end-all of friendships. Give that friendship bracelet to someone else, Cas. I am totally on Arthur and Checker's side re: Rio. SORRY.

2. FRIENDSHIP: In a book about assassins, deadly freelancers, explosions, worldwide conspiracies, and the apocalyptic death and destruction of L.A., I did not expect to find a book so concerned with friends: not having them, having them but being dubious about them, wanting them and being crushed when they don't want you back, being a person worthy of friendship and how hard that is, being a shitty friend with good intentions, being a great friend and still fucking up, being a creepy friend who likes to beat on you (HI RIO), etc.

Even when Cas positions herself as someone who works best alone, she's quick to fall into camaraderie with the people she meets and quick to tease and open up in despite of herself. She's quick to hurt and be hurt, and that reveals a gaping loneliness that persists throughout the book. It becomes especially explicit when she interacts with Rio. WHO ARE YOU, RIO??

3. MORALITY: Oh, shades of gray, my old friend. There's three groups of remorseless killers here (well, maybe four if we split Cas and Rio up, but for the sake of my argument, let's say three since I suspect Cas models herself on Rio without realizing it). I found this particular tidbit interesting once Arthur finally calls Cas out on how she's so good at mowing through situations with violence and lack of concern for the people who end up super dead or grievously injured at the end of it.

Compared to the type of killing Rio does (remorseless mass homicide), and the type of killing the other villains do (it's for the greater good! it's not like we kill EVERYONE, just the people that DISTRACT us from our super villain adventures!), Cas's killing became very rote and perfunctory. Watching Cas deal with being called to account for her somewhat destructive approach to human life was what made my spider sense start tingling when I got to the very end of the story and realized that in reality, I probably still don't know who Cas truly is. Not even Cas knows who she is or how she feels beyond "do the job, survive, eliminate opposition." I suspect Cas is only finding out who Cas is by the end of the story, which ends on a note of continuation for the sequel.

Meanwhile, I have to go back to the writing, which was a major stumbling block for me. I read a lot of bad writing because I persist in reading in fandoms that will produce awesomely plotted, terribly written but absolutely charming coffeeshop, magical bonding, or soulmate AUs with very sincere emotions, because I am weak. Due to this, I can't honestly tell the difference between writing that's traditionally published or self-published because the quality of my reading swings around wildly within any given week. I don't believe a book has to be a canonical literary masterpiece to be enjoyable (evidence: this book), but I really considered not finishing because it took me nine chapters to read it for any length of time. But really, my judgment is flawed. I once read 50k of super shitty Final Fantasy VIII fic written in second person where Squall and Seifer got turned into dinosaurs and liked it. *Don't trust me.*

Once I reached the point where I devoured it in 14 hours (because seriously, what that fuck, Cas? What is your *deal* with Rio? WHAT IS HAPPENING? YOU ARE A CLEVER WOMAN, this is so suspicious, what is going on??? I need to know!) I wasn't putting it down unless someone pried it from my hands after I was stone cold dead. I took this book to work and read it *behind the counter.* I work *retail*, and anyone who's ever worked retail knows the dire consequences for leaning while using an electronic device. Those are the lengths I went to finish, so obviously it ended up not being an issue.

Probably appropriate would be to say that the writing felt self-conscious and unsure of itself. It's nervous, very intent on explaining exactly what it's doing, so the bits meant to be subtle aren't. It needs less periods, and more complicated, stream of consciousness traits specific to first person narratives. It doesn't feel immersive like first person narration generally does to me. If the first person isn't invasive and all up in my face, I can't buy it. Sign of a good first person narrator is that I hate it intensely, with the entirety of my being, for the first chapter. Here I was just bored.

Because eventually I got used to it and made it through to the end of the book, I wondered if this overly stilted style that reads like a third person version of first person was intentional because of revelations about Cas's very vague past. It doesn't feel like first person, but wait, Cas is having a little trouble with personhood, so clearly something's happening. But I still suspect that if my guess is right about the likely Swiss-cheese nature of Cas's head, this narrative doesn't quite manage to bridge the gap between "whoa her head's sort of weird, right?" and "puzzling and distracting first person narrative choice."

Well, it's either brilliant or I just wasted hours of my life trying to figure out if it was brilliant. I'm going to go with a 30% chance of being right about this being on purpose. If I am, I sure hope we see more of the Cas that Arthur and Checker adopt and less robo-Cas in the sequel, which comes out in 2015. *SEQUELS.*

Additional Notes:

- I now have the headcanon that Cas can drive absolutely anything. Stick? Sure. Big rig? Absolutely. Any type of motorcycle? Yes. Speedboat? Sure thing. Helicopter? That, too. Tank? Why not!

- Every time Rio appeared in the book I rarely pictured him entering a scene, just suddenly appearing, like the sociopathic creepy stalker *Teen Wolf* S1 Derek Hale wishes he could be. HE ALSO WEARS A TAN DUSTER. If you're going to be sociopathic killing machine, you might as well look fashionable while doing so. And anyway, all those pockets are probably dead useful. They hold all his secrets.

- Crying over the painful reality of Cas's casually racist disregard over a bunch of dead kids, after complaining about racial profiling.

- CAS RUSSELL, WEAPONS HOARDER. I will never get over her fixation on having a weapon. She's like the deadly mercenary version of a determined chipmunk ramming nuts into her mouth, except she's packing grenades, knives, and various types of firearms. I have this hilarious mental image of cartoon!Arthur waiting by a truck waving his arms going "we have to go!" as cartoon!Cas runs toward him trailing various deadly weapons in a trail behind her because she's carrying too many, done in the style of Nimona.

- I don't believe in character death. HEAR THAT, BOOK? I DON'T BELIEVE IN CHARACTER DEATH. But nice try.

- In dramatic thriller movies when huge cities become pawns in the power struggle between multiple powerful entities/the heroes, there's always a huge cost. Some poor sucker city takes a beating. Usually it's just infrastructure (regardless of what anyone says the L.A. destruction scene in *The Day After Tomorrow* is brilliant and chilling, I want to make out with the team that put that together) but this book was cold as ice and heartless. Everything about the suffering in this book aims the pain inward. METAPHORS.

- SHADY GUYS WHO PAY TAXES and defends application of taxes to citizens.

This article first appeared on *Lady Business* on May 14, 2014.
ladybusiness.dreamwidth.org/2014/05/14/review-zero-sum-game-sl-huang.html

[MOVIE] 'MALEFICENT'

Rachael Acks

Going to start this one off with a disclaimer, which is this: I am not an original dyed-in-the-wool Maleficent fangirl. I do not have a massive ladyboner for this Disney villain the way quite a few of my friends do. So I'm taking this movie as itself. It's been well over a decade (man, probably closer to two) since I last watched *Sleeping Beauty*, so all I really can say about the original animated lady of menace is that she sure had some style.

TL;DR: I have absolutely nothing to say about how this movie relates to the character as seen in *Sleeping Beauty*. So please don't yell at me.

All right.

I really, really liked this movie. Even more than I expected to, and I was already looking forward to it.

Angelina Jolie? Fucking amazing. I am already so in love with that woman I could write odes to her (non-enhanced) cheekbones, so this did not surprise me. She made a stylish Maleficent, from menacing to downright intimidating even when she was being "good." And man, those contacts she had. Holy crap, her eyes.

Other than Maleficent, Diaval (Sam Riley), and Stephen (Sharlto Copley), there wasn't a lot to most of the characters. I found the three pixies particularly grating. There were some odd pacing issues, and the movie seems to kind of get lost and meander during the second act until it remembers where it's going and launches into the third.

The movie was pretty enough, but could never quite decide if it wanted to look realistic or be overtly cartoonish. I think either style can work just fine (even cartoonish does all right mixed with live action if the movie just jumps in with both feet) but never being willing to commit to one or the other or draw lines between the two realities of the film didn't serve it well visually. I found myself wishing there was less cgi. A lot less cgi. Particularly when they were in the fairy lands, pretty much everything was computer generated and some of it just... didn't quite make it out of the uncanny valley, I think. (And missed a golden opportunity for some gorgeous puppets and practical effects.) Or maybe it just looked a little too fake. I found the miniaturized pixies disturbing. They just did not look right in some fundamental way that really bothered me. Score was all right but nothing to write home about.

So, not the best offering I could have hoped for. Honestly, *Snow White and the Huntsman* did a much better job visually, I think.

What really made me like *Maleficent* was the story itself, and I found several aspects of it very interesting:

Going to cut this now for major spoilers.

Quick summary: Maleficent is the most powerful fairy in her lands. She meets Stephen when both of them are very young, and they fall in love. The humans, led by King Douchebag, decide to try to invade the fairy lands and Maleficient sends them all packing. King Douchebag says he'll give his kingdom and daughter to whoever takes revenge on Maleficent. Stephen goes to the forest, drugs Maleficent, but can't quite bring himself to kill her so just cuts off her wings and takes those back to King Douchebag. Maleficent is understandably upset about this. She takes vengeance of her own by cursing Stephen's daughter, Aurora, though she eventually she develops real affection for the girl. On Aurora's 16th birthday, Maleficent drags Prince Philip to the castle to try to get him to kiss Aurora and break the curse. That doesn't work, however. Maleficent apologizes to Aurora and kisses her on the forehead, which *does* break the spell. As they try to leave, Stephen attacks; Aurora runs away and finds Maleficent's severed wings in a case, which she breaks open. The wings reattach to Maleficent, enabling her to escape, though Stephen clings to her and ultimately ends up falling to his death. At the end, Aurora is crowned queen of both the human and fairy kingdoms and Maleficent has returned to her rightful place as the protector of the fairies.

Got all that?

True Love

So first of all, this movie did what *Frozen* attempted with the concept of true love being more than just romantic love, but did it much, much better.[1] In fact, I think *Maleficent* even takes a potshot at the notion of true love being essentially romantic in nature. At the beginning of the movie, Maleficent thinks she's shared true love's kiss with Stephen, and then not long after he betrays her and cuts off her wings. She later tells her raven, Diaval (who is my second favorite character in the movie; he brings the sass) that the reason she cursed Aurora the way she did, to sleep as if dead until woken by true love's kiss, is because *true love doesn't exist*. (Stephen also says this to the pixies, that there is no such thing as true love.) And indeed, when Prince Philip is convinced to kiss Aurora (more on this in a minute) it doesn't work. The true love that saves Aurora—and effectively saves Maleficent as well—is familial love.

I cannot begin to describe how happy it makes me that this is a message that's getting put in more than just one Disney movie. So. Very. Glad.

As an extra even better treat at the end, there is no wedding. Instead, Aurora is crowned queen of the fairy and human lands. I honestly can't even recall if Philip was anywhere around—because the point of that scene was most definitely the fairies accepting Aurora as their queen, and the emotional exchange between adoptive mother and daughter.

Revenge

Vengeance is the main driver behind the plot. King Douchebag wants revenge for his defeat. Maleficent wants revenge on Stephen for cutting off her wings. Stephen wants revenge on Maleficent for cursing his daughter. If nothing else it shows the perpetuating cycle of vengeance. But what I found most interesting was the way the story draws parallels between Maleficent

---

1 http://katsudon.net/?p=2563

and Stephen, and then shows them diverge. (Though I'll say right here, don't get me wrong; Stephen is the bigger asshole in this equation by far.)

Both Maleficent and Stephen are taken to a very dark place by the initial act of violence perpetrated by Stephen. Maleficent is enraged, distrusting, and closed off. I'd say from the first time we see King Stephen, even before the curse, he doesn't exactly look like a healthy man; perhaps he's been haunted for years by the guilt for what he did. (We can only hope.) After Aurora is cursed, he too becomes angry and closed off, to the point that he refuses to be diverted from his thoughts of revenge even to attend to his dying wife. Both of them are rulers of their respective lands, and are generally obeyed.

The difference we see is that Maleficent is not entirely closed off and alone. She has Diaval to sass at her. And she comes to love Aurora like a daughter. Stephen, in contrast, turns his back on everything but the thought of revenge and killing Maleficent. So at the end of the movie, when Maleficent tries to flee rather than fight, he clings to her. She even tells him that this is over; she's done with trying to have her revenge. He refuses to let his own desire for vengeance go and subsequently falls to his death.

So ultimately, on one hand there's Maleficent, who is effectively healed by her (rather reluctant) love for others, and with that chooses to try to end the ongoing violence. And Stephen, who has isolated himself completely, is consumed by his own hatred.

Female Power/Rape

At the beginning of the movie, when King Douchebag tries to invade the fairy lands, he mocks Maleficent for being an "elf with wings." As I write this now, I actually had to stop and check with my housemate that, at no time, did any of the humans explicitly insult Maleficent for her gender. I think that's partially because it's sort of expected, when it's a man versus a powerful woman in a fantasy setting. (Well, let's be honest, in a lot of settings.)

But after thinking about it post movie, it feels like the fairies were very much meant to be read as female. The vast majority of the humanoid fairies were overtly feminine, and the lands were led and protected by a Maleficent—a woman. On the other hand, you have the human kingdom, where there are basically two women outside of the servants: Aurora and her mother. Aurora's mother is little better than living scenery, and is basically *given* to Stephen like an object as a reward for his betrayal of Maleficent. I think Aurora's mother has one scene in which she gets to speak, and then dies off screen while Stephen is having a truly creepy conversation with Maleficent's severed wings.

So if you'll grant me that, the idea that the conflict between humans and fairies can be easily read as one between a completely misogynist society and one that is either matriarchal or at least truly equal, it makes for an interesting way to examine the movie.

Consider the inciting incident of the movie: Maleficent humiliates the humans, then has her wings cut off in retaliation. Stephen comes to Maleficent with the intent of killing her; he abuses her trust by getting her to drink drugged water, then cuts off her wings when he can't quite find it in himself to murder her outright. Immediately after leaving the theater, my housemate mentioned to me how much that scene *bothered* her because it came across as very date rape-y. (ETA: I was right.)[2]

I think that was probably quite purposeful. Maleficent humiliated the (male) humans. She was subsequently punished for it by being drugged by a man she thought she could trust, and then being violated in a very fundamental way while drugged. And considering that much is made of the physical power and freedom her wings grant her, having her wings removed reads very much as an attempt to humble and reduce her. (I suppose Stephen might have even convinced himself that he was doing her a *favor* because this way he let her live, but ultimately he *used* Maleficent to get something he wanted, which was the kingdom.)

Rape is a sickeningly common trope used to take powerful female characters down a peg. Rape is also a sickeningly common trope substituted as character development or reason for vengeance, insanity, and so on. In this case, the result for the character is thankfully one that isn't so common. Maleficent was an incredibly powerful character both before and after her wings were cut off; the only real difference after is that she has to take on Diaval to do her flying for her. Stephen's betrayal does make Maleficent into a cold, angry person for a time—and who could blame her, at that point. But she doesn't go mad, she doesn't acquire the fantasy land equivalent of a buttload of guns and go on a vigilante field trip.

There are a couple of larger twists that I find even more interesting. Her major act of revenge is against Stephen's daughter, rather than directly on Stephen himself, and it's because of Aurora that she comes to decide that she wants better things than vengeance. But I think far more importantly, Maleficent is symbolically healed not by completing her revenge or (barf) finding her one true dick to make it all better, but by the actions of another woman. *One whom she loves deeply in a non-romantic way.*

Aurora, acting completely on her own—no one tells her to find Maleficent's wings, or to help her in that way—gives her godmother her wings back. So it's ultimately a brave and loving act by another woman that heals Maleficent. At the end, she obviously hasn't forgotten what's happened to her, but she's moved on and become *happy* again. I'm trying to think if I've ever really seen that in another movie. Definitely not recently.

Consent

I think it's very worth noting that the one (human) man in movie who is presented as unambiguously good—Prince Philip—actually brings up the issue of consent. When Maleficent drops him off at Aurora's room, the pixies drag him inside and tell him he has to kiss the girl. He immediately objects on the grounds that he and Aurora only just met, he doesn't know her that well, and he doesn't feel right doing it. He only agrees to try to kiss her once he's basically badgered with the fact that it will supposedly save Aurora's life. The implication being that, left to his own devices, he wouldn't have though it was at all right to violate Aurora's personal space like that.

Finally, I've found a prince charming.

---

2 http://katsudon.net/?p=3250

Race

Anyone else a little freaked out that the only obviously non-white human(oid) character in the movie got physically assaulted by Stephen for failing to get past the wall of thorns? Eeagh. (And, as usual: It's a generic fantasy land. Why the hell is almost everyone white, anyway? And the humanoid fairies too. Gosh.)

And in conclusion...

Obviously this movie made me think. A lot. Way more than any other Disney movie I can recall in recent years. I think that's a fantastic thing. Is it a perfect movie? Gosh no. It had some definite pacing and history issues. But if you like things along the vein of *Wicked*, this is definitely a movie worth seeing. (To be honest, I enjoyed watching this movie far, far more than I ever enjoyed reading *Wicked*.)

This article first appeared on *Rachael Acks: Sound and Nerdery* on June 8, 2014.
katsudon.net/?p=3213

PAGE TO SCREEN: 'GUARDIANS OF THE GALAXY' (2014)

Clare McBride

Ever since the first trailer dropped, featuring sci-fi action, comedy, and Blue Swede's "Hooked on a Feeling", I've been excited to see *Guardians of the Galaxy*. Not because I have any familiarity with the Guardians themselves, but because anything that combines the hits of the seventies and eighties and speculative fiction is one hundred percent my jam. (I will admit to being a little disappointed that my first theory, that *Guardians of the Galaxy*'s soundtrack was, in fact, just the *Reservoir Dogs* soundtrack, was wrong, but "Cherry Bomb" is in there, so I am content.) Now that Marvel is on top of the world, the fact that they're reaching back into their catalog and digging up obscure characters is heartening, especially for those of us desperate to see Black Panther or Captain Marvel finally make it to the big screen.

The finished *Guardians of the Galaxy* is less heartening. It begins perfectly, with the young Peter Quill witnessing his mother's death and, running out into the woods overwhelmed by his emotions, getting abducted by aliens. Cut to the adult Peter landing on an abandoned planet to find an artifact for a client. Face shrouded by his retro-cool mask, he stalks around like Han Solo—before taking his mask off, revealing the kind (if currently very chiseled) visage of Chris Pratt, and turning on his Walkman so he can dance his way to the treasure to "Come And Get Your Love."

But, one action sequence later, when Peter returns to his ship to find a half-naked fuchsia space babe and can't remember her name, the film reveals its dedication to what I ended up, in a chatty rage over Chipotle after the film, referring to as "going full dudebro." After the towering, humanistic heights of *Captain America: The Winter Soldier*, it's disappointing to be presented with a film that treats its female characters shoddily, tells far more than it shows, and revels in violence. Obviously, there's a major difference in tone between the two films, but I have selfishly come to expect that the characters in a Marvel film will be treated like people.

(Or raccoons. Or tree people. You get my point.)

Perhaps that was too much to ask from James Gunn, who famously wrote "The 50 Superheroes You Most Want to Have Sex With", a virulently homophobic and sexist post about the sexual attractiveness of various superheroes (as voted on by readers of his website).[1] He's since made an actual, sincere apology for the post, but it's hard not to think about that when *Guardians of the Galaxy* attempts to make a light-hearted joke about how the very

---

1 http://www.themarysue.com/james-gunnsuperhero-sex-post/

literal Drax the Destroyer expresses his friendship while insulting his friends—and having him call Zoe Saldana's Gamora a "green whore" to that end.[2] While Gamora and Nebula, her adoptive sister, have a powerful but fundamentally conflicted relationship to rival Thor and Loki's, it's largely unexplored. That's all before you get to the sad fact that Djimon Hounsou took the role of Korath so his kids could see a superhero of color onscreen—only for that character to suffer largely the same fate as Kurse in *Thor: The Dark World*.

And this underdevelopment plagues *Guardians of the Galaxy* as a whole. We spend a lot of time establishing Peter as a character, but since he's essentially a Han Solo type, it's unnecessary, especially when Gamora's far more intricate backstory is clunkily handled solely in dialogue. Even Rocket Raccoon's breakdown in a bar over constantly being dismissed as an animal misses the mark, as we're taken out of a romantic scene between Peter and Gamora and don't see *why* he finally broke. They are a likable bunch, especially—and perhaps specifically—the marvelous Groot, but this underwriting makes them more compelling concepts than characters. And those are the *main* characters. The villains of the piece, despite having an interesting motivation that's never really explored, are just outlines.

This is all the more frustrating because the cast is so very game. Chris Pratt's Peter is engaging and fun; Saldana gives Gamora a nice balance between her serious, honorable side and a more pragmatic side; Dave Bautista's extremely literal Drax adds a wonderful physical presence and deadpan to the proceedings; Vin Diesel's sheer dedication to Groot will result in your weeping or your humanity back; and Bradley Cooper does a fair Denis Leary impression as Rocket. Seeing Pratt's little personal flourishes on Starlord is delightful, as well as seeing the rest of the cast riff off of Peter's eighties references. ("We're like Kevin Bacon!", as delivered flawlessly by Saldana, may be my favorite line in this film.)

But *Guardians of the Galaxy* does succeed brilliantly in one department: the visuals. Gunn clearly wants you to think of *Star Wars* when you watch this film, but I was particularly struck by how this marries modern CGI with practical effects in a way that the *Star Wars* prequels utterly failed to do. It's a tactile universe, from Star-Lord smacking a scanner to make it work to the innards of Ronan the Accuser's ship to Yondu's dashboard tchotchkes. While Gunn occasionally gets lost in the action set pieces, the sets and locations themselves are so well-balanced that they're just a joy to look at. Marvel's Asgard can sometimes feel toy-like, so it's incredibly refreshing to see it done well. May it set a standard for speculative fiction on film in the future—but only visually.

(Oh, and that half-naked fuchsia space babe? Her name is Bereet and, in the comics, she's an alien filmmaker.[3] You know, a character with stuff going on beyond alien conquest of the week.)

2 http://www.themarysue.com/james-gunn-apology/
3 http://en.wikipedia.org/wiki/Bereet

This article first appeared on *The Literary Omnivore* on August 4, 2014.

theliteraryomnivore.wordpress.com/2014/08/04/page-to-screen-guardians-of-the-galaxy-2014/

REVIEW: RUN, DON'T WALK, TO SEE 'SNOWPIERCER', THE BEST SCI-FI FILM OF THE DECADE SO FAR

Rebecca Pahle

"Why am I so freaking excited about this movie? Check out its cast: Tilda Swinton. Chris Evans. Jamie Bell. Alison Pill. John Hurt. Ed Harris. Octavia Spencer. South Korean actor Song Kang-ho, who was excellent in Park Chan-Wook's 2009 vampire movie *Thirst*. I'm feeling *Pacific Rim* levels of anticipation here. Higher, even." That's what I wrote the very first time I heard about Bong Joon-ho's *Snowpiercer*, all the way back in January 2013.[1] I have been looking forward to this movie for seventeen months. To say I had high expectations going into it is like saying Michael Bay is mildly fond of explosions. Because I was looking forward to it so very much, potential for disappointment was high.[2] So it goes.

But was I disappointed? Readers, I see a lot of movies. Most of them are good. Some are great. A small number I love. And every once in a while I see a movie that leaves me vibrating with energy as I leave the theater, knowing that what I just saw will stick with me probably for the rest of my life, or at least until the inevitable robot overlords come and conquer the planet. *Snowpiercer* is one of those.

Snowpiercer was the subject of a much-discussed controversy where its US distributor, The Weinstein Company, wanted to edit the film to make it more palatable to mainstream American audiences ("their aim is to make sure the film 'will be understood by audiences in Iowa... and Oklahoma...'").[3] Ultimately that didn't happen, but the compromise was that an uncut *Snowpiercer* would only get limited release.[4] I don't know what movie Harvey Weinstein was watching—maybe he thought "Woah, South Korean director and some Korean dialogue, what is this, some *art-house foreign shit*?! People will never watch that!"—because for all that what I saw has some seriously dark content, an incredibly bleak worldview (humanity dies *because it tries to fix global warming*), and is packed full of metaphors about class issues and human nature, it is *absolutely* an entertaining, even crowd-pleasing, movie.

The plot is fairly basic. As anyone can glean from the trailers, *Snowpiercer* takes place in a world beset by a new ice age. All that's left of human-

---

1 http://www.themarysue.com/things-we-saw-today-191/
2 http://www.themarysue.com/2014-summer-movie-reader-survey-results/slide/13/
3 http://www.themarysue.com/snowpiercer-film-edits/
4 http://www.pajiba.com/trade_news/the-weinstein-company-has-finally-decided-the-extent-to-which-theyre-screwing-over-snowpiercer.php

ity lives on a train, where they're separated into the haves and the have-nots. One of the have-nots, Curtis (Chris Evans), leads his people in a revolution. The whole movie is just them trying to get from the back of the train to the front. But *Snowpiercer* never gets boring. Your favorite characters never feel completely safe. You never know if you're going to leave a car where an intense action sequence took place and enter one where people straight from the Capitol scenes in *The Hunger Games* are nightclubbing their hearts out like there ain't no tomorrow. You might think you know where the story's going... but you don't.

There's a darkly surrealist tone to *Snowpiercer* that's reminiscent of Terry Gilliam, if Terry Gilliam weren't quite so... Terry Gilliam-y. There's *weirdness* in this movie, for all that it's more accessible than a *Brazil* or a *Fear and Loathing in Las Vegas*. During one blood-pumping fight scene Curtis slips on a fish. Again: *Chris Evans slips on a fish*. Tilda Swinton takes her false teeth out at one point for some reason. There's a scene where our grizzled revolutionaries encounter a chipper elementary school teacher (Alison Pill) who leads her charges in a rousing singalong about how great Wilford, the God-like owner of the train, is. It's *ridiculous*, but it works. The darkness, the action, the humor: Everything fits. This movie could've turned into a hard-boiled *mess* at any given point, but it's so carefully stylized, so *precise*, that I accept things which I would never let fly in another movie. ("That character's clairvoyant? OK, I'll buy it.")

One of the reasons it works is that *Snowpiercer* is a visual masterpiece—the entire thing literally takes place in a series of boxes, but it's never boring. Some of the dialogue's a bit awkward and stilted at first, but as soon as you accept you're watching a heavily-stylized surrealist dystopian sci-fi and not a gritty, "Nolanesque" (as they say) sci-fi actioner, *grrrrr*, it all comes together. The key to tapping into the tone of the movie is something a character says late in the film: The experience of living on the train has driven everyone on it ever-so-slightly (or more than ever-so-slightly) crazy.

That brilliant creative decision on the part of Joon-ho and screenwriter Kelly Masterson leads to great performances from the entire cast, which is another huge reason why *Snowpiercer* didn't fall on its face. You have never in your life seen another performance like the one Swinton gives in this movie, and I know you can say that about most Swinton performances, but trust me on this—you need to experience it. Incidentally, her character, Mason, was a man in *Le Transperceneige*, the graphic novel on which *Snowpiercer* is based.

And Chris Evans. Oh, Chris Evans. Curtis has similarities to Evans' most famous role—both he and Captain America are men trying to be both a good person and a good leader when everything is stacked up against them. You can make a case for (or, for that matter, write fanfic about) Curtis *being* Cap in a particularly grim AU. But *Snowpiercer* strives for more than the MCU's solid (but fairly basic) level of entertainment. With *Snowpiercer*, Evans gets to show you how good an actor he really is, and man oh star-spangled man does he deliver. Between this and *Sunshine*, he's been in two of the best sci-fi movies to come out in the past ten years, hands down.[5]

---

5 http://www.themarysue.com/2014-summer-movie-reader-survey-results/slide/13/

In a cast as big as *Snowpiercer's*, you'd think there'd be a weak point, but there really isn't. Octavia Spencer, Jamie Bell, John Hurt, Song Kang-ho, Ed Harris, Ewen Bremner, Ah-sung Ko, Luke Pasqualino, Marcanthonee Reis, and Vlad Ivanov all terrify, infuriate, intrigue, and/or cause intense emotional pain in turn. The only thing about *Snowpiercer* I really didn't like at the time I was watching it is the visual effects of the frozen hellscape outside the train. Frankly speaking, it looks fake. But the more I thought about it, the more it grew on me. Like I said, *Snowpiercer* is an incredibly visually stylized movie. The world outside the train is *supposed* to look fake, to look distant and un-reachable and unreal, because for the people on the train... it is. It's mere feet away, but they've lost all hope of ever setting foot on it again. The train is the only thing that's real.

I fear The Weinstein Company, with the aforementioned limited release, is trying to bury this one. It's been out in other countries for months, and many people already illegally downloaded the French version in the wake of *Captain America: The Winter Soldier*'s release (and *why* didn't TWC put *Snowpiercer* shortly after it to capitalize on Evans mania?). Going into *Snow-piercer* I felt like I was one of the few people who hadn't seen it yet, and I got into an advance press screening weeks before it even came out in the States! I've seen the trailer in a movie theater once—*once*—at an indie theater that plays trailers for whatever its upcoming movies are. Not in a Regal theater. Not in an AMC.

All this is to say, it looks like The Weinstein Company doesn't think all that many people want to see *Snowpiercer*. They don't think a weirdo dys-topian movie with a South Korean director and partially Korean dialogue where one of the main actors (the always excellent Song Kang-ho) is mostly unknown to American audiences and Chris Evans slips on a fish has main-stream appeal. Prove them wrong. *Snowpiercer* comes out next Friday, June 27th. If you can, if it it's playing near you, see this movie. *Pay* to see this movie. Take your friends, take your family, take your pet fish. Stand up for original sci-fi that's not *Transformers 4* or, yes, *Captain America 3*.

And see a damn fine movie in the process.

This article first appeared on *The Mary Sue* on June 20, 2014.
www.themarysue.com/snowpiercer-review/

IT'S GETTING SERIOUS IN PANEM AS 'MOCKINGJAY' GOES DARK

Andrew Lapin

When producers were laying track for the *Hunger Games* series years ago, they couldn't have foreseen how discomforting author Suzanne Collins' descriptions of a war-torn authoritarian state would look on the big screen in 2014. In *The Hunger Games: Mockingjay - Part One*, Jennifer Lawrence witnesses and/or learns of: towns reduced to rubble, refugee camps next to mass graves, public executions of innocents with burlap sacks over their heads, law enforcement gunning down protesters in the street, and a military bombing a hospital filled with civilians. All of these images have resonance in real events of this year, generations before Collins predicted civilization would devolve into a regime that maintains control over its citizens with televised death matches.

The series has always evoked real geopolitics, but the earlier films offset those with self-parody: an abundance of purple hair and oily camera-ready suits, an outlandish imperial march composed by Arcade Fire. This playfulness is absent from *Mockingjay*, which is laser-focused on the land of Panem quashing dissent by any means necessary. It's not that the film is "too dark for kids"—that would drastically underestimate teenagers' capabilities for darkness. It's that this degree of nastiness doesn't square with the empty-calories action scenes of the first two films, where nothing that happened in the Hunger Games arenas (Look out! Wild monkeys!) seemed to impact the overall story.

But maybe it's a good thing to be more serious this time, even if the progression wasn't gradual. "A little on-the-nose, but, of course, so is war," remarks the dearly departed Philip Seymour Hoffman, playing an architect of the Panem resistance movement. He's referring to a tweak he's made to a rally song, but he could also be discussing *Mockingjay* itself, how a mass appeal sci-fi franchise chooses its war imagery. In a film about the role that visual communication plays in public opinion, the on-the-nose approach is at once intriguing and exhausting. Strange to think this series used to be about archery in the wilderness.

That, anyway, is where fiery revolutionary Katniss Everdeen (Lawrence) was at the conclusion of the previous film, 2013's *Catching Fire*. Rejecting society's pressure to kill her friends for amusement a second time, Katniss instead shot a hole in the sky, through which she has been whisked away to the super-secret underground rebel stronghold District 13. In the first two films, Katniss was a pawn of Panem's dastardly, white-bearded President

Snow (Donald Sutherland, forever sneering). Sadly, she's still a pawn, but of a nobler president, the benevolent but still white-haired District 13 leader Alma Coin (Julianne Moore, a hair too robotic). Coin needs Katniss to be her "Mockingjay", a symbol around which to mobilize the citizens of Panem: a warrior who's no-nonsense yet down-to-earth. In short, she needs Katniss to be Jennifer Lawrence.

Until now, the biggest strength of the *Hunger Games* series has been the careful construction of Panem, a dystopia-lover's utopia. All the details from the first two entries were rich in cinematic absurdity, like the party where the rich gladly vomit up their food, or the gaudy stage sets that accompany Stanley Tucci's gleeful talk show host as he conducts cloying interviews with Games candidates. Having to trade such an expansive setting for a drafty underground bunker (District 13 must be sharing the lease with the Zion rebels from the *Matrix* sequels) is the weakest part of *Mockingjay*, along with Katniss' friend-and-maybe-more Gale (Liam Hemsworth) and his mopey "I have feelings, too!" jealousy.

There's also no escaping the fact that this film, co-written by Collins and two others, is a stopgap designed to string audiences along one year more than the source material requires. The artificial division of a narrative for the sole purpose of making money should not normally be cause for a creative success. But somehow, chopping up *Mockingjay*, a practice that has become the norm with final installments of YA series adaptations, created some happy accidents. With less material than in *Catching Fire*, director Francis Lawrence is free to be contemplative, edit sequences patiently instead of frantically, and linger over small visual details like a speck of blood on Snow's cheek after his groomer cuts his face shaving. And Jennifer Lawrence has the freedom to interact with each of her allies in more subtle ways: practiced patience with Elizabeth Banks' fallen fashion maven, Effie; steely distrust with Woody Harrelson's rakish mentor, Haymitch; sheer annoyance with her cat.

Josh Hutcherson, a bit wooden in the other films, is also doing something fascinating as Peeta, Katniss' on-camera boyfriend who was captured by Panem's Capitol at the conclusion of *Catching Fire*. For much of *Mockingjay*, we see him only via the Capitol's authorized interviews saying questionable things about the revolution. Like Katniss, we can only guess at his current state of mind. Hutcherson's strong, subtle performance lets us read any number of possibilities in his face and minimal line readings. That's until the very end, when he turns chilling.

If any of this felt like Hobbiting—defined as the practice of throwing useless, fan-serving footage onscreen to bloat up a blockbuster franchise—there'd be a problem. But *Mockingjay* doesn't have that vibe, because it follows one unmistakable theme from beginning to end: an information war. Instead of physically dueling, Katniss and the Capitol fling propaganda films like projectile bombs.

The chess match of public opinion is a colder, more calculated game than the testing of wilderness survival skills. Katniss, reluctant viral video star, hilariously fumbles her lines when she's in front of a green screen leading the CGI army from a Ridley Scott movie. But she draws tears when a tattooed documentarian (*Game of Thrones*' Natalie Dormer, who could have stepped out of a Copenhagen artist's co-op) films her examining the rubble of her childhood home. It's the latter footage, the on-the-nose war stuff, that drives Panem to rebel rather than change the channel to *Where Are My Pants?* Collins and the Lawrences have crossed the uncanny valley separating imagined dystopia from actual horrors, but they're also delivering a life lesson in cinema to teens: Things are stronger when they look *real*. Think about that when the Capitol beams out the next all-CGI superhero movie.

This article first appeared on *NPR* on November 20, 2014.
www.npr.org/2014/11/20/365187357/its-getting-serious-in-panem-as-mockingjay-goes-dark

'HER'

Abigail Nussbaum

Science fiction films, it often seems, are the idiot cousin of the genre. Not that there aren't some excellent SF films out there, but even if you ignore the vast majority, which are actually action or horror films in an SFnal setting, what you'll be left with will be mostly small, simple stories in thinly drawn worlds, often with a thuddingly obvious political subtext. Again, that's not to say that these films can't be good—*Moon*, to take one example whose story and world are practically miniscule, is one of the finest SF films of the last decade. But it's rare, verging on unheard-of, for SF films to achieve the depth and complexity of SFnal ideas and worldbuilding that written SF is capable of, and I think that part of the reason for this is fear. Most SF filmmakers (or their financial backers) are afraid to imagine a world too different from out own, a future too alien—the most celebrated SF film of the last year, after all, was one that used space exploration as a metaphor for alienation, and ended with humanity effectively barred from space for decades to come. Spike Jonze's *Her* isn't the film to buck that trend, but it carries within it the seeds of that film. Jonze takes the relatively unusual step (in the film medium, at least) of pairing SF with romantic drama, but that potentially refreshing choice turns out to be *Her*'s undoing—not only because the romance it crafts is problematic and unconvincing, but because it obscures the much more interesting SF film that *Her* could have been, if it were slightly less afraid of the future.

Joaquin Phoenix plays Theodore, a depressed recent divorcé who is starved for human connection but too emotionally constipated to engage with actual people (for which read women—Theodore's only male friend at the beginning of the film is his best friend's husband, with whom he cuts ties after the two divorce, and though throughout the film he forges a connection with a colleague played by Chris Pratt, this is only after the other man makes several enthusiastic overtures). When Theodore buys a new handheld phone/computer/personal organizer, it comes with an AI interface (rather infuriatingly referred to, throughout the film, as an operating system) which promises to mold itself to suit Theodore's personality and needs. The resulting persona, Samantha (voiced by Scarlett Johansson), is a bubbly, curious, adventurous creature who quickly brings Theodore out of his shell. Before long, the two become friends, going on day-long excursions in which Samantha can discover the world and Theodore can re-experience it through her eyes. Soon after that, the relationship turns romantic (and, within certain parameters, sexual), with Theodore and Samantha proudly proclaiming themselves to be dating.

It's difficult to read this plot description and not feel uncomfortable. Watching the film's trailers, I found myself reminded of *(500) Days of Summer*, a movie that purported to cut through the commercialized, commodified artificiality of modern romantic comedies, but could only do so by turning its heroine into an unattainable cipher.[1] *Her* seems to take that approach to extremes when it imagines a romance in which the female half of the relationship is the male's property, a program designed to not only make his life easier but whose personality was especially fitted for that task. Add to that Samantha's copious Manic Pixie Dream Girl traits, and it becomes all but impossible to take her romance with Theodore as anything but the logical extension of films like *(500) Days*, in which women exist solely in order to enable the self-actualization of a schlubby, self-pitying male hero. (For some more discussion of the problems with *Her*'s conception of romance and of its hero, see Sady Doyle's trenchant takedown of the film.[2] As the rest of this review will show, I don't agree with all of Doyle's conclusions, but her discussion of Theodore, and of "sensitive", beta male characters of his type, is necessary and important.)

In fairness, *Her* is clearly aware of the potential for this reading, and tries to head it off through a variety of devices—though these are, invariably, notable more for their good intentions than their success. When Theodore's ex-wife Catherine (Rooney Mara) finds out about his new relationship, she immediately speaks for doubters like myself, concluding that being with Samantha appeals to Theodore because it doesn't require him to cope with "real emotions." It's a perspective that desperately needed to be heard, given how strangely non-judgmental everyone else around Theodore is, and the crisis that it precipitates in his and Samantha's relationship is also necessary, finally puncturing his blithe acceptance of the fact that he is dating his PDA. But the film also tries to undermine Catherine, by depicting her as bitter and having other characters comment on her emotional instability. (In this quality, Catherine is joined by Thedore's other human love interest, a blind date played by Olivia Wilde; just about the only woman in the film who is not depicted as crazy is Theodore's endlessly supportive best friend Amy (Amy Adams), for whom he feels no sexual attraction.) Later in the film, Theodore and Samantha make a disastrous attempt at expanding the physical side of their relationship with the help of a surrogate, Isabella (Portia Doubleday), an experiment whose failure sheds a light on the limitations of their relationship. But this scene also highlights the handwaving that Jonze does where Samantha's sexuality is concerned. We're told that she orgasms when she and Theodore first have sex (really just dirty talk, and rather tame at that) because their connection somehow makes her feel "her" body. But as Anna Shechtman, writing at *Slate*, points out, this is merely an extension of the canard that women's sexuality is emotional while men's is physical.[3]

The real problem, however, with how *Her* constructs its central romance isn't the multiple question marks surrounding Samantha's ability to freely and meaningfully enter into the relationship. It's how bland and generic Theodore

1 http://wrongquestions.blogspot.co.il/2009/11/500-days-of-summer.html
2 http://inthesetimes.com/article/16031/her_is_really_more_about_him/
3 http://www.slate.com/blogs/browbeat/2014/01/03/her_movie_by_spike_jonze_with_joaquin_phoenix_and_scarlett_johansson_lacks.html

and Samantha are as a couple. *Her* is, by definition, a very talky film—Theodore and Samantha fall in love through words and conversation, not physical attraction—but instead of powering the film and making us feels its characters' emotions, *Her*'s dialogue is painfully nondescript. Theodore works as a personal letter-writer—sometimes for special occasions such as anniversaries, but also as a regular part of his customers' lives, as in the case of a couple whose love letters he's been writing for nearly a decade. We're told that these letters are insightful and moving—at one point, Samantha compiles some of them and sends them to a publisher, who is so moved that he offers to put them out as a book. But when we actually hear Theodore's letters, they sound like what they are, extra-long greeting cards, full of trite turns of phrase and over-exposed sentiments. (It's interesting that both *Her* and *(500) Days* give their heroes jobs writing greeting cards, as if to stress that they are manufacturing sentiment they can't feel; but at least *(500) Days* acknowledges that the sentiments Tom sells are hollow.)

In much the same way, Theodore and Samantha's conversations, in which they allegedly forge a deep, instant connection, come off as stilted and forced, both of them trying too hard to be friendly and funny without ever saying anything of substance (there is, in fact, very little difference between Theodore and Samantha's conversations and the one he has with Wilde's character on their blind date—in both cases, the characters appear to be working so hard to be agreeable and pleasant that they barely seem to notice the person they're talking to). Later in the film, as the relationship and its challenges deepen, Theodore and Samantha start to discuss weightier topics. But despite emerging from such an unusual relationship, these issues are familiar and trite—Theodore is emotionally withholding, Samantha is growing past him. The discussions never become interesting or compelling because Theodore and Samantha aren't particularly interesting people—like Theodore's letters, they feel like collections of clichés handsomely strung together, not genuinely nuanced characters.

In a way, this is a very SFnal flaw—using characters and relationships as placeholders around which to construct a world or an idea, without bothering to shade them in or strive for complexity. And if *Her*'s characters are bland in a way that feels typical of SF, its world is nuanced in a way that also seems particularly SFnal. Jonze takes the Andrew Niccol approach of imagining a future that is sleek, clean, and impeccably designed (and also sadly lacking in people of color), but the technology with which he fills this world, and which his characters use, is more homey and lived in. Samantha is, after all, a personal organizer, and like her, most of the technology Theodore interacts with is intended for daily human use. Amy designs computer games (most notably, an appalling creation in which players compete to be a "super-mom" who gets her kids to school first and bakes delicious cookies), and Theodore entertains himself by playing another game, evocatively projected across half his living room. User interfaces—for the computers Theodore uses at work, for Samantha and other, non-sentient organizers, for the social network on which Theodore looks up his blind date—abound in the film. They create the texture of a world in which the human relationship with technology is similar to ours, but also changed. As that texture develops it becomes easier to see *Her* not as a romance between two people in a unique situation, but as the story of how a new technology changes the definition of romance for all people. Late in the film we learn, for example, that Theodore and Samantha aren't the only AI/human relationship out there. Amy is friends with an AI, and a woman in her office is dating one who isn't even hers.

In its final third, *Her* changes and becomes a much more interesting film—by shedding the unconvincing romance plot of its earlier segments. Jonze seems to have realized that the only way to prove that the romance between Theodore and Samantha is real is for her to end it, but he does so in a way that reveals that the real story of the film wasn't their love story, but the story of Samantha's (and other AIs like her) emergence and self-discovery as a new lifeform. If, in the early parts of the film, the differences of experience, age, and legal status between Theodore and Samantha make their relationship seem dubious and creepy (in one particularly disturbing scene, Theodore all but gaslights Samantha, who is worried about their waning sex life, taking advantage of her inexperience by telling her that this is perfectly normal when he knows it isn't) by the end of the film it's clear that Samantha has become something much bigger than Theodore. In one of the film's most devastating—and, to me, most satisfying—scenes, Theodore realizes that at the same time that he and Samantha have been having intimate, soul-baring conversations, she's also been conversing with thousand of other people, some of whom are also her lovers. In these final scenes, *Her* suggests that, far from enabling the petty, narcissistic, isolating urges of the emotionally inept, the technology at its center is expanding the definition of love and relationships.

It's a pity, then, that the first two thirds of *Her* lack the courage of this final revelation. That they bury Samantha's emerging consciousness beneath Theodore's neediness and depression, and fail to address the questions, about Samantha's personality and personhood, raised by their relationship. The rather creepy scene with Isabella the surrogate is retroactively validated when we realize that Samantha has been having meaningful relationships with people other than Theodore—it suddenly becomes more believable that this woman agreed to the experiment of her own free will—but wouldn't it have been more interesting to learn this fact earlier in the film, and explore Isabella's feelings for Samantha, instead of reducing her to a marital aid (not to mention yet another one of the film's crazy women)? For that matter, wouldn't it have been more interesting, not to mention believable, to face up to the fact that Samantha can love Theodore without gaining sexual satisfaction from him, at least not in the human terms that she uses to describe her sexuality? Wouldn't it, in short, have been a much more interesting film if, from the get-go, *Her* had been about Samantha as a new lifeform, not the object of Theodore's affections?

Sticking to the template of a romance means that *Her* loses sight of the more interesting story happening in its background, and fails to fully explore its premise. It's a failure that mars the film even in its more successful final act, as when it plumps for the cliché of treating Theodore and Samantha's relationship as a learning experience, something designed to make him a better man—he ends the film composing yet another of his trite, cliché-ridden letters to his ex-wife, in which he wishes her well. This is clearly intended as a sign that Theodore has grown and matured, but it actually makes him seem smug and self-satisfied—despite its claims to the contrary, his letter to Catherine is designed to show off the fact that he has achieved closure after their divorce, not give that closure to her, and it has the effect of, once again, turning Samantha into the instrument of Theodore's growth, rather than the person he was in love with and has now lost. Say what you will about *(500) Days of Summer*, but at least it recognized that the end of a relationship, no matter how inevitable, hurts, and included within its titular timeframe the time necessary for its hero to get over his heartache before gaining wisdom.

Ultimately, *Her* is neither a successful romance nor the mythical complex, intelligent SF film I yearned for in this review's opening. That it has enough hints of the latter makes me wish that the romance aspect of the film had been jettisoned (that the romance itself is so problematic, of course, makes me wish this even more). But the fact that the film was made, and that in its final third it dares to imagine a future in which personhood and love mean something different from what we define them as, gives me some hope. Perhaps, in some distant point in the future, SF film won't be so terrified of the unfamiliar—and perhaps when we get to that point, filmmakers in general will be able to imagine a romance in which both partners, be they humans or machines, are real people.

This article first appeared on *Asking the Wrong Questions* on February 12, 2014.
wrongquestions.blogspot.com/2014/02/her.html

'INTERSTELLAR' IS THE BEST AND WORST SPACE OPERA YOU'LL EVER SEE

Annalee Newitz

I f you love epic space opera, you shouldn't miss *Interstellar*. But before you go, you need to be prepared to overlook its major flaws.

Interstellar is a thematic sequel to Christopher Nolan's last original film, *Inception*. It drops us into a dark future full of otherworldly landscapes and time distortions. Its spectacular action is propelled forward by tragic family secrets. The difference is that *Interstellar* tries to tell the story of humanity, and that's where it stumbles.

Space Opera Rightly Understood

It probably comes as no surprise that the greatest strength of this movie is its visual impact. Nolan is famous for melding surrealism and granular detail to create imagery that makes you feel like you're plummeting through the world's smartest amusement park ride. This is a movie about four people who take a fantastic journey to another galaxy through an artificial wormhole in orbit around Saturn. The wormhole itself is worth the entire price of IMAX admission. Glittering and alien, roaring with rock concert levels of sound, it has the potential to wrap you in badass levels of wonderment.

What we see on the other side of the wormhole is equally magnificent. A gas-ringed black hole is orbited by two planets with weather systems that stretch the imagination—and test our characters' endurance. This aspect of the film, the pure Golden Age science fiction story of visiting strange worlds, does exactly what space opera is supposed to do. It takes your breath away, and fills you with a wanderlust the likes of which only a wormhole can truly satisfy.

Nolan shot the film using a lot of practical effects, and this really matters when it comes to the spaceship sequences. The pilot Cooper (a scenery-chewing Matthew McConaughey) and his crew are in a ring-shaped vessel called the Endurance, and every time the landing ships dock with it you can see the telltale wobbles that reveal this isn't a perfect, clean CGI creation. I'm not saying the ships look like models—in fact, they look more realistic than anything digital. There's a feeling of heft and fragility that you get with practical effects that CGI never achieves, and it's perfect for this story.

As writer Jonathan Nolan has said, the look is also a major tip of the hat to *2001*, which inspired many aspects of *Interstellar*.[1]

A Barren Future

1 http://io9.com/jonah-nolans-first-interstellar-pitch-were-not-f-ing-g-1654506330

The mind-bending vistas of space are echoed back on Earth, but in a way that's depressing rather than awe-inspiring. As the film opens, Cooper and his daughter Murphy are living on a vast corn farm, trying desperately to eke out a living (and food) in a world of massive dust storms, climate change, and population decline. We never know for sure what's happened, but we get little hints that crop blight is a constant threat—and the blight itself is an organism that is pumping so much nitrogen into the air that oxygen levels are going down. Within a generation, it's likely that suffocation will be a bigger issue than starvation.

With humanity's future hanging in the balance, a few scientists at NASA are racing against time to get what remains of *Homo sapiens* off the dusty, dangerous rock that can no longer support us. Brand (Michael Caine) is a physicist who has helped create the ship that will take Cooper and his crew (including Brand's daughter, a rather bland Anne Hathaway, also named Brand) through the wormhole to visit possible colony worlds. While they're gone, the elder Brand will work with Cooper's genius daughter Murphy to try to "solve gravity" so that they can create artificial worlds for humans in space.

Again, the visions of this dying Earth are spectacular. We see massive, bruised dust storms looming over burned fields, and watch the whole world suffer through a 1930s-style dust bowl apocalypse. The urgency of the problems on Earth may not be scientifically accurate, but they work emotionally.

Time and Relativity

The problem with this film is that the emotions evoked by its landscapes are not matched by the characters. Monolith-shaped robot TARS, voiced by Bill Irwin, crackles with more personality than Cooper, Brand and Murphy (Jessica Chastain). One of the great tensions we're supposed to feel in this film is between Cooper and Murphy—due to the time-distortions of relativity, Murphy grows up while Cooper is off exploring. So he knows that he's lost the chance to watch his beloved daughter grow up the instant he steps into the spaceship. The question is how much more of her life he will miss.

There are some incredible moments of dramatic urgency as we see Cooper and Murphy working to save humanity in two different galaxies, but their relationship has been sketched so lightly that their tears don't move us as much as they should.

The relationship between Brand and her father is equally light, though intended to be much heavier. *Interstellar* delivers nerve-jangling action scenes, but really stumbles when it comes to these interpersonal notes. And that's a problem in a movie that wants to be a psychological melodrama that just happens to be set in space.

Instead of giving us emotional relationships whose details feel as real as his exoplanets, Nolan gives us a kooky relativity lesson. The closer Cooper and the crew get to the black hole—which is irritatingly described as an "oyster" containing a "pearl" of singularity—the slower time gets, due to gravity distortions. So we see Cooper and Brand remaining young, while Murphy and Brand's father age back on Earth. Somehow these dislocated time scales are supposed to capture the distance and relatedness between all of them, but instead the scenario feels gimmicky and occasionally downright silly.

Some Very Bad Woo

It's funny that this movie, which is so in love with science, falls down when it comes to physics. Yes, there are bits of the film taken directly from the cutting-edge work of physicist Kip Thorne (who consulted with Nolan), but there is an egregious amount of pseudoscientific woo that feels wildly out of place. At one point, Brand infodumps a clumsy analogy between Einstein's theory of relativity and the idea of emotional relatedness—love between humans, like gravity, transcends dimensions. She says that love might even be the fifth dimension, where the beings who made the wormhole live.

Wait, what? Are we watching that campy flick *The Fifth Element*, where ladies dress in toilet paper and talk about how love is a physical force that can save the world? Unfortunately, you will begin to feel that the answer is yes about halfway through *Interstellar*.

Put simply, *Interstellar* has a strong undercurrent of cheesiness. A lot of things happen that make no sense unless you believe that love is the missing variable in all our calculations of how cosmology works. We can partly blame movies like *2001* for this trope, because that film had its share of incomprehensible transcendent something something lurking beneath its futuristic snark. Even the hyper-scientific *Contact* gave us a weird father/daughter, physics/love scenario at one point. But that doesn't mean it works.

Interstellar seems torn between hard science fiction realism and new age spiritual beliefs about quantum.[2]

And that makes for a bad mix. Watching *Interstellar* is really like watching two movies slowly collide with each other. One is a masterpiece of space opera, whose vistas will fill you with wonder and give you hope for the future of humanity in space (and time). The other is a predictable, stale melodrama about how absent fathers are actually super great and women exist to channel love.

The result is a mess. But it's a beautiful mess, and one that I wouldn't want you to miss for the world.

This article first appeared on *io*9 on November 5, 2014.
io9.com/interstellar-is-the-best-and-worst-space-opera-youll-ev-1654807305

---

2 http://io9.com/10-scientific-ideas-that-scientists-wish-you-would-stop-1591309822

AFTERWORD

2015

Foz Meadows & Mark Oshiro

We cut our teeth online. By "we", this refers to your editors for next year's issue of *Speculative Fiction*, Foz Meadows and Mark Oshiro. We have found our voices on the Internet. Foz has done so on her blog, *Shattersnipe: Malcontent and Rainbows*, which is exactly what the tin describes: a mixture of rage and anger, joy and celebration. Mark has done so through *Mark Reads* and *Mark Watches*, crying about plot twists and asking writers to *do better*. And it's no coincidence that we both have complicated emotions about the state of critical analysis, meta-textual commentary, and engagement on the Internet.

But to us, the Internet is many things. It's where we learned to argue. It's where we learned to *discuss*. It's where we learned just how tiny and narrow our perception of the world was, and it's where we felt like we found tiny, familial communities.

The challenge of summarizing that experience is massive and almost foolhardy; words can't quite describe how much the online communities we've been a part of and we've built have affected our understanding of the world around us. But we both know that this massive, snarling beast of a thing has made us *better*. Why is that? How can you measure such a change? The chaotic, unpredictable nature of online interactions suggests that this is all unquantifiable.

However, we believe that there is an inherent value in the blurring of lines between what is considered academic, fan writing, or just geeking out with your friends on Tumblr. There *is* something exciting to us about how hard it is to tell the difference between these various acts, all of which with engage with media in thoughtful ways.

This is not a new or recent phenomenon either. In 2010, for instance, a proposed exhibition of anonymous short stories—some by established authors, and some by amateurs—caused writer Susan Hill to go on a splenetic rant, furious at the idea that, in being asked to participate, the famous writers wouldn't have their works properly credited. "Names... are invidious," Hill snarked. "They might indicate to people that the story was worth reading." Though she tried to couch her anger in impartial terms—"If someone writes a marvelous short story I don't care where they come from"—her biases were laid bare when she sneered at the idea of amateurs being exhibited "just because they have put one word in front of another, or because they're asylum seekers." This is the textbook definition of gatekeeping: an established writer furious at the idea of sharing a level playing field with others she thinks less worthy, not because their writing is bad, but because they don't have the right name or the right background.

2010 Foz, it should be noted, completely missed the racist, classist implications of Hill's dig at asylum seekers, a fact which makes 2015 Foz cringe. But that's the point of critical engagement over time: it changes you and broadens your view of the world. In a space like the Internet, which provides an unprecedented platform to groups that are otherwise marginalised and silenced, or whose narratives are elided, the clash between dominant and subcultures is even more pronounced—which is to say, visible *at all*. Generally speaking, the point of gatekeeping in mainstream spaces isn't just to police their borders, but to do so while claiming the opposite: namely, that all voices are being fairly represented, and that any absence must be indicative not of prejudice, but of native absence or fault.

Remarks like Hill's are jarring, not because they're reflective of something uncommon, but because they're bold enough to clearly show their underlying biases. When someone like V. S. Naipaul comes out and says, bluntly, that all female writers are "unequal" to him, because of their "sentimentality, the narrow view of the world," as he did in 2011, it's easy to identify his remarks as sexist, because they scarcely pretend to be anything else. But gatekeeping is just as often achieved through less overt, more insidious means: a game of dog-whistle politics wherein the left hand proclaims equality while the right scribbles, in automatic writing, *some animals are more equal than others*.

The gatekeeping that we've experienced – and know others have faced, too – is twofold. There's an academic reluctance to accept the work that non-professional fans do in breaking down literature, in detailing trope usage, in tying marginalization to the narratives that books and shows sell to us. While academia and critical theory are obviously crucial aspects of critical analysis, we believe that the barriers in place prevent many writers from achieving recognition they deserve. That same sentiment applies to the greater SF/F fandom as well. We want to value *lived experience*, which offers insight into this world just as much (if not more) than academic study.

It's a bold desire, but it's one that we want to move forward with while doing our best to exceed the standards set by the many past editors of this anthology. We both have massively different backgrounds as editors and as people, and we hope that this will reflect in the diversity of work that we will collect.

Therefore, we want to commit to the same goals that Renee Williams and Shaun Duke set to meet in this issue ofSpeculative Fiction:

1. We want to continue to extend the conversations, debates, and developments within genre culture and do so through both creative content and fan response.

2. We will seek a diversity of voices both within the SF genre and outside of it, recognizing that many important conversations and debates occur in places and through mediums that are not typical of the norm.

3. We will seek a parity in gender, sexuality, race, and nationality in the work we collect, conscious of the fact that many Western voices are often louder than others.

−Foz Meadows & Mark Oshiro
April 2015

ACKNOWLEDGEMENTS

We're deeply grateful to all the contributors that allowed their work to be used in this volume. Thanks as well to all the people who promoted the submission form and who submitted content, by themselves and others, and made this anthology a success. Thank you for helping us continue the work of this anthology series.

We are also incredibly thankful to David Annandale, Jodie Baker, Zachariah Carlson, Michelle Dong, Ira Gladkova, Rose Littlewolf, Allison Morris, Curtis Jefferson, Kathleen Jones, Julia Rios, Ana Silva, Mike Underwood, Alison Watson, and Paul Weimer for their help, advice, Microsoft Word tutorials, and friendly support throughout this process. Plus, a special cat treat for Winston, for keeping Shaun sane with his kitty support powers.

Special thanks goes to our publishers, Ana Grilo and Thea James, for massively patient counsel and assistance with all the moving parts that go into publishing an anthology of this size. Extra special thanks with glitter (glitter never comes off) go to Jared Shurin and Justin Landon for launching this series, and then, perhaps foolishly, placing its future in our hands. Good job, guys, and thanks!

CONTRIBUTORS

ABOUT THE CONTRIBUTORS

Abigail Nussbaum works as a software engineer in Tel Aviv. She blogs at *Asking the Wrong Questions* and is the reviews editor for Strange Horizons.

Adam Roberts is the author of 15 novels, most recently *Bête* (Gollancz 2014). He is also Professor of 19th-Century Literature at Royal Holloway University of London, and lives a little way west of London. A collection of his SF essays and reviews, *Sibilant Fricative*, has been published by Newcon Press.

Aidan Moher is the Hugo Award winning editor of *A Dribble of Ink*. He lives on an island in British Columbia with his wife, his daughter, and many books.

Aja Romano is a geek culture and fandom reporter for *The Daily Dot* and Submissions Editor Emeritus for Big Bang Press. She lives in Brooklyn, but more accurately on Tumblr at bookshop.tumblr.com and on Twitter @ajaromano. She has a deep love of bad horror, good horror, and Regency romances, and is forever looking for ways to combine the three.

Alex Dally MacFarlane is a writer, editor and historian. When not researching narrative maps in the legendary traditions of Alexander III of Macedon, she writes stories, found in *Clarkesworld*, *Interfictions Online*, *Strange Horizons*, *Beneath Ceaseless Skies* and the anthologies *Phantasm Japan*, *Solaris Rising 3* and *The Year's Best Science Fiction & Fantasy: 2014*. She is the editor of *Aliens: Recent Encounters* (2013) and *The Mammoth Book of SF Stories by Women* (2014). In 2015, she joined Sofia Samatar as co-editor of non-fiction and poetry for *Interfictions Online*. Find her on Twitter: @foxvertebrae.

Amal El-Mohtar is the Nebula-nominated author of *The Honey Month*, a collection of poetry and very short fiction written to the taste of 28 different kinds of honey. She plays the harp, is a member of the Banjo Apocalypse Crinoline Troubadours, and edits an online quarterly of fantastical poetry. Presently she lives in Glasgow with two Jellicle cats and their pet Glaswegian. Find her online at amalelmohtar.com.

Ana Grilo is a Brazilian who moved to the UK because of the weather. No, seriously. She works with translations in RL and hopes one day *The Book Smugglers* will be her day job. When she's not here at The Book Smugglers, she is hogging our Twitter feed.

Andrew Lapin is a freelance film critic and journalist. His writing has been published in *NPR*, *The Washington Post*, *The Atlantic*, *The Dissolve*, and *Indiewire*, among other outlets. A graduate of the University of Michigan, he has been selected for the Young Critics Workshop in Film Fest Ghent, a Tent Writing Fellowship, and a Hopwood Award. He hopes future dystopian society will still have bagels. Find him online at andrewlapin.org.

Annalee Newitz writes about science, pop culture, and the future. She's the editor in chief of *io9*, a publication that covers science and science fiction, and has over 10 million readers every month. She's the author of *Scatter, Adapt and Remember: How Humans Will Survive a Mass Extinction* (Doubleday and Anchor), which was nominated for a 2013 *LA Times* book prize.

Anne C. Perry founded *Pornokitsch*, The Kitschies, and *Jurassic London*, a small non-profit publisher, before becoming an editor at Hodder & Stoughton. She spends most of her free time thinking about monster movies.

Bertha Chin is a fan studies, social media, celebrity and TV scholar with a PhD from Cardiff University. Her academic works have been published in internationally peer-reviewed journals and edited collections on topics such as fandom, digital media and crowdfunding. She also consults on matters relating to social media and audience engagement for various international digital media projects.

Betty was waylaid onto the internet in the mid 2000s by the unbearable presence of people being Wrong About Batman. She has since become the sort of fangirl you were warned about.

Charles Tan is the editor of *Lauriat: A Filipino-Chinese Speculative Fiction Anthology*, and the co-editor of *Philippine Speculative Fiction Volume 9*. His fiction has appeared in publications such as *The Digest of Philippine Genre Stories*, *Philippine Speculative Fiction* and the anthology *The Dragon and the Stars* (ed. by Derwin Mak and Eric Choi). He has contributed nonfiction to websites such as *The Shirley Jackson Awards*, *Fantasy Magazine*, *The World SF Blog*, and *SF Signal*. In 2009, he won the Last Drink Bird Head Award for International Activism. He is also a 2011, 2012, and 2013 World Fantasy nominee for the Special Award, Non-Professional category. You can visit his blog, *Bibliophile Stalker* at charles-tan.blogspot.com.

Chinelo Onwualu is a writer, editor and journalist living in Abuja, Nigeria. She is a graduate of the 2014 Clarion West Writers Workshop which she attended as the recipient of the Octavia E. Butler Scholarship. She is editor and co-founder of Omenana.com, a magazine of African speculative fiction. Her writing has appeared in several places, including the *Kalahari Review*, *Saraba Magazine*, *Sentinel Nigeria Magazine*, *Jungle Jim Magazine*, and the anthologies *AfroSF: African Science Fiction by African Writers*, *Mothership: Tales of*

Afrofuturism and Beyond, and *Terra Incognita: New Short Speculative Stories from Africa*. Follow her on twitter @chineloonwualu.

Clare McBride is a book blogger, fan, and pop culture critic at *The Literary Omnivore*.

A lifelong Amsterdammer, **Corinne Duyvis** spends her days writing speculative young adult and middle grade novels. She enjoys brutal martial arts and gets her geek on whenever possible. She is a co-founder of *Disability in Kidlit* and a team member of *We Need Diverse Books*. *Otherbound*, her YA fantasy debut, released from Amulet Books/ABRAMS in 2014 and received four starred reviews—*Kirkus* called it "original and compelling; a stunning debut," while the *Bulletin of the Center for Children's Books* praised its "subtle, nuanced examinations of power dynamics and privilege." Her next novel, *On the Edge of Gone*, will release in 2016. Find her at corinneduyvis.com.

Daniel José Older is the author of *Half-Resurrection Blues* and the upcoming Young Adult novel *Shadowshaper* (Scholastic's Arthur A. Levine Books, 2015). *Publishers Weekly* hailed him as a "rising star of the genre" after the publication of his debut ghost noir collection, *Salsa Nocturna*. He co-edited the anthology *Long Hidden: Speculative Fiction from the Margins of History* and guest edited the music issue of *Crossed Genres*. His short stories and essays have appeared in the *Guardian*, Tor.com, *Salon*, *BuzzFeed*, the *New Haven Review*, *PANK*, *Apex*, and *Strange Horizons*, and the anthologies *Subversion and Mothership: Tales Of Afrofuturism And Beyond*. Daniel's band Ghost Star gigs regularly around New York and he facilitates workshops on storytelling from an anti-oppressive power analysis. You can find his thoughts on writing, read dispatches from his decade-long career as an NYC paramedic and hear his music at ghoststar.net, on YouTube and @djolder on twitter.

Ebony Elizabeth Thomas is an assistant professor in the Division of Reading/Writing/Literacy at the University of Pennsylvania's Graduate School of Education. Previously, Dr. Thomas was an assistant professor of teacher education at Wayne State University in Detroit, Michigan, her initial position after finishing her Ph.D. at the Joint Program in English and Education, University of Michigan – Ann Arbor in 2010. A former Detroit Public Schools teacher, Dr. Thomas' program of research is most keenly focused on children's and adolescent literature, the teaching of African American literature, and the role of race in classroom discourse and interaction. Dr. Thomas has published her research and critical scholarship in the *Journal of Teacher Education*, *Qualitative Inquiry*, *Linguistics and Education*, *English Journal*, *The ALAN Review*, and *Sankofa: A Journal of African Children's and Young Adult Literature*. Her scholarly work has also appeared in *Diversity in Youth Literature: Opening Doors Through Reading* (ALA Editions, 2012), her own co-edited volume *Reading African American Experiences in the Obama Era: Theory, Advocacy, Activism* (Peter Lang, 2012), and *A Narrative Compass: Stories That Guide Women's Lives* (University of Illinois Press, 2009). Dr. Thomas is a former NCTE Cultivating New Voices Among Scholars of Color Fellow (2008-2010 Cohort), serves on the NCTE Standing Committee on Research (2012-2015), and was elected by her colleagues to serve on the NCTE Conference on English Education's Executive Committee (2013-2017). Dr. Thomas' early career work received the 2014 Emerging Scholar Award from AERA's Language and Social Processes Special Interest Group. Recently, she was selected as a 2014 National Academy of Education/Spencer Foundation Postdoctoral Fellow.

Once upon a time in Maryland, a nine-year-old **Erika Jelinek** decided to dress as Alia Atreides and do a class presentation on Dune along with a hand-drawn picture of a Shai-Hulud; her parents noticed this somewhat odd behavior and, being devout bibliophiles, started feeding her science fiction and fantasy books via i.v. drip. She somehow managed to survive to young adulthood and went on to get her BA in English from Skidmore College, her MLIS from the University of British Columbia, and to live in four different countries before bringing her bookish fight to Los Angeles, where she is currently a teen librarian.

Foz Meadows is a bipedal mammal with delusions of immortality and YA urban fantasy author. Her current novels, *Solace and Grief* and *The Key to Starveldt*, are available in both paper and ebook formats. She is also a contributing writer for the *Huffington Post*, and a contributing review for *Strange Horizons* and *A Dribble of Ink*. She currently lives in Scotland.

Gavia Baker-Whitelaw is a writer living in Glasgow, Scotland. She currently writes for *The Daily Dot* as a fandom and internet culture reporter, and blogs about film and costume design under the name "HelloTailor."

Joe Sherry began writing his *Adventures in Reading* blog in 2004. In blog years, this makes him approximately 85 years old. His reviews and articles have appeared in *Fantasy Magazine* and the *Sacramento Book Review*. Joe lives near Minneapolis with his wife and son.

Jonathan McCalmont lives in a wood. A critic and fan-writer, he writes a regular column entitled 'Future Interrupted' for the British science fiction magazine *Interzone*.

Juliet Kahn is a Boston-based writer. When she isn't pondering the mysteries of Sailor Moon, she writes about women, comics, and women in comics.

Justin Landon writes, edits, and podcasts for Tor.com. He's also a world class breather of oxygen.

Kameron Hurley is the author of the novels *God's War*, *Infidel*, and *Rapture*, a science-fantasy noir series which earned her the Sydney J. Bounds Award for Best Newcomer and the Kitschy Award for Best Debut Novel. She has won the Hugo Award (twice), and been a finalist for the Nebula Award, the Clarke Award, the Locus Award, and the BSFA Award for Best Novel. Her most recent novel is the epic fantasy *The Mirror Empire*. The sequel, *Empire Ascend-*

ant, will be out in October 2015. She writes regularly for *Locus Magazine* and publishes personal essays at kameronhurley.com.

Kari Sperring is the pen-name of the Anglo-Welsh historian Kari L Maund. She has published six books and many articles on Welsh, Irish, Anglo-Saxon and Viking history and taught the history of these peoples at university level. As Kari Sperring, she is the author of two novels, *Living with Ghosts* (DAW 2009), which won the 2010 Sydney J Bounds Award, was shortlisted for the William L Crawford Award and made the Tiptree Award Honours' List; and *The Grass King's Concubine* (DAW 2012).

Ken Neth is the blogger behind *Neth Space*, a SFF review and discussion blog that began in 2006. He's a fan first, reviewer second, and lays no claim to impartiality or objectivity in reviews and/or criticism. In the real world he's a father and husband living in Northern Arizona and works as an engineering geologist.

Mahvesh Murad is a book reviewer and recovering radio show host who lives in Karachi, Pakistan. She writes for numerous publications including *Dawn*, Tor.com, *Pornokitsch* and *Strange Horizons*, and hosts the Tor.com podcast *Midnight in Karachi*. She can be reached at mahveshmurad.com or via Twitter @mahveshm.

Martin Petto is a British critic and editor. As a reviewer, he has published widely since 2001, notably at *Strange Horizons*. He has also been reviews editor for the British Science Fiction Association since 2010 and was a judge for the Arthur C Clarke Award in 2010 and 2011.

Matthew Cheney has published fiction, essays, and reviews with *Locus*, *Weird Tales*, *Strange Horizons*, *One Story*, *Lady Churchill's Rosebud Wristlet*, *Black Static*, *Los Angeles Review of Books*, and elsewhere. His blog, *The Mumpsimus*, was nominated for a World Fantasy Award in 2005, and he is the former series editor for the Best American Fantasy anthologies. Winner of the 2014 Hudson Prize, his collection *Blood: Stories* will be published by Black Lawrence Press in January 2016. Currently, he is working toward a Ph.D. in Literature at the University of New Hampshire.

Memory Scarlett has been blogging about books since late 2008. She's hung up on comics these days, but also makes an effort to write about other flavours of SFF (and the occasional non-genre title) at her blog, *In the Forest of Stories* (memoryscarlett.blogspot.ca). When she's not writing about stuff she's read (or watched, or listened to), she's writing fiction, some of which has appeared in *Crossed Genres Magazine*, *Fireside Magazine*, and *Daily Science Fiction*. She is exceedingly fond of tacos, dogs, and Kate Bishop, and is often found gushing about these interests on Twitter as @xicanti.

Mieneke van der Salm works as an information specialist at a university library in the Netherlands. In her free time she aims to create and read her own library at home and, together with her husband, raise two little geek girls. In July 2014 she was nominated for a World Fantasy Special Award: Non-professional. You can read more about her and her reviews on her website, afantasticallibrarian.com.

N. K. Jemisin is a Brooklyn author whose works have been nominated for the Hugo, the World Fantasy Award, and the Nebula, and have won the Locus Award. Her new novel *The Fifth Season* comes out from Orbit in August 2015. Her website is nkjemisin.com.

Natalie Luhrs reviewed SF/F for *RT Book Reviews* for 8 years before launching out on her own. Now she can be found on podcasts including *Rocket Talk*, *Skiffy & Fanty*, and her own blog, pretty-terrible.com. She calls herself a free-range reviewer and opiner.

Ng Suat Tong is a doctor working in Singapore. He has written reviews for *The Comics Journal* since 1993 and blogs at *The Hooded Utilitarian* website. He was the editor of the Eisner and Harvey nominated anthology *Rosetta*.

Nina Allan's stories have appeared in many anthologies, including *Best Horror of the Year 6*, *Strange Tales from Tartarus*, and *The Mammoth Book of Ghost Stories by Women*. Her novella *Spin*, a reimagining of the Arachne myth, won the British Science Fiction Award in 2014, and her collection *The Silver Wind*, a story-cycle on themes of time and memory, won the Grand Prix de L'Imaginaire in the same year. Her debut novel, *The Race*, set in an alternate future England and featuring bio-engineered greyhounds and island-sized whales, is out now from NewCon Press.

Olivia Waite puts words in comprehensible order, usually to some purpose. She lives in Seattle.

Expat New Yorker **Paul Weimer**, often known on the internet as "Princejvstin", is a podcaster, science fiction writer and reader. He writes and contributes to the *Skiffy and Fanty Show*, *SF Signal*, *SFF Audio*, and many other places and venues.

Rachael Acks is a writer, geologist, and sharp-dressed sir. In addition to her steampunk novella series from Musa Publishing, she's had short stories in *Strange Horizons*, *Crossed Genres*, *Daily Science Fiction*, *Lightspeed*, and more. She's also written scripts for Six to Start and Toska Productions. Rachael lives in Houston (where she lifts weights, drinks tea, and twirls her ever so dapper mustache) with her two furry little bastards. For more information, see her website rachaelacks.com or watch her tweet @katsudonburi way too often.

Rebecca Pahle is a New York City-based entertainment journalist and part-time Sith Lord. Currently the Assistant Editor at *Film Journal International*, her previous places of editorial employment include *The Mary Sue* and *Mov-*

ieMaker Magazine. You can find her freelance work at *Pajiba*, *Phactual*, and *Nerd Approved*.

Rose Lemberg is a queer immigrant from Eastern Europe. Her work has appeared in *Strange Horizons, Beneath Ceaseless Skies, Interfictions, Uncanny, Sisters of the Revolution: A Feminist Speculative Fiction anthology*, and other venues. Rose edits *Stone Telling*, a magazine of boundary-crossing poetry, with Shweta Narayan. She has edited *Here, We Cross*, an anthology of queer and genderfluid speculative poetry from Stone Telling (Stone Bird Press), and *The Moment of Change*, an anthology of feminist speculative poetry (Aqueduct Press), and is currently editing a new fiction anthology *An Alphabet of Embers*. You can find rose Rose at roselemberg.net and @roselemberg on Twitter, and support her on Patreon at patreon.com/roselemberg.

Saathi Press has been a multifandom, omnishipping fanfic author and observer of fannish behavior for over 15 years. An illustrator by trade, she's not quite sure where all these pesky words come from, but she's not going to inquire too closely in case they stop. You can find her online at LiveJournal, Dreamwidth, Archive of Our Own, Tumblr, and occasionally Twitter under the alias Saathi1013.

Sara L. Sumpter has loved narrative art since childhood, when a chance encounter with Marvel's *X-Men* left her with a passionate appreciation for the visual storytelling format. As a graduate student working in the field of Japanese art history, her research focuses on early-medieval illustrated handscrolls and how the stories they depict reflect the socio-political conditions of the period in which they were produced. She spends her free time avoiding dissertation-writing by reading comic books, watching comic-book movies and TV shows, and analyzing them instead. She maintains a writing blog at sechan19.blogspot.com.

Tade Thompson's roots are in South London and Western Nigeria. He has a background in psychiatry and social anthropology. His short stories and essays have been published in small press, webzines and anthologies. Most recently, his story "Honourable Mention" appeared in *Dangerous Games* anthology from Solaris Books. His novel *Making Wolf* will be released in 2015 from Rosarium Publishing. He lives and works in South England.

Tasha Robinson is the Senior Editor of *The Dissolve*. Her writing and interviews have appeared in the *Chicago Tribune*, the *Los Angeles Times*, *Orlando Weekly*, *Science Fiction Weekly*, and at the *NPR Books* website, and she's been a recurring guest on *Filmspotting*, *Slashfilm's Filmcast*, and *The Sound Of Young America*, now known as *Bullseye*. She lives in Chicago, where she appears to have made a profession out of disagreeing with Scott Tobias about torture-porn.

The G is founder and co-editor of *nerds of a feather, flock together*, which covers SF/F, crime fiction, comics, cult films and video games. He moonlights as an academic.

thingswithwings has been active in online fandom for almost twenty years now, in so many fandoms that she's lost count. She makes fanfic, vids, podfic, podcasts, meta, communities, and tweets. You can catch her at thingswithwings.dreamwidth.org or @twwings.

Vandana Singh is an Indian science fiction writer living in the Boston area. She has a Ph.D. in theoretical particle physics and teaches physics full-time at a small and lively state university. Many of her stories have been reprinted in Year's Best anthologies, and she is a winner of the Carl Brandon Parallax Award. Recent work includes a novella, Entanglement, in the anthology Hieroglyph and a short story for tor.com, "Ambiguity Machines." She has a new website at http://vandana-writes.com and a blog at http://vandanasingh.wordpress.com.

ABOUT THE EDITORS

Renee Williams is comprised of some rainbows, a herd of overly excited unicorns, and bees. She co-edits the media criticism project, *Lady Business*, co-hosts *Fangirl Happy Hour*, and is the editor of the 2014 edition of the *Speculative Fiction* anthology series. She gets up to mundane/exciting shenanigans on Twitter @renay, reblogs lots of puns and photos of attractive celebrities on Tumblr @heyheyrenay, and sometimes writes fanfiction.

Shaun Duke is a reviewer, podcaster, and PhD student at the University of Florida studying science fiction and postcolonialism. His work can be found on his blog, *The World in the Satin Bag*, or on his two podcasts: *Totally Pretentious: A Podcast About Great Movies* and the Hugo-nominated *Skiffy and Fanty Show*. He also happens to be a sentient toaster.

EDITORS' NOTE

Where possible, we have tried to preserve the language, content and stylistic idiosyncrasies of the original articles. However, a few small changes were made for clarity when they were translated from online to print.

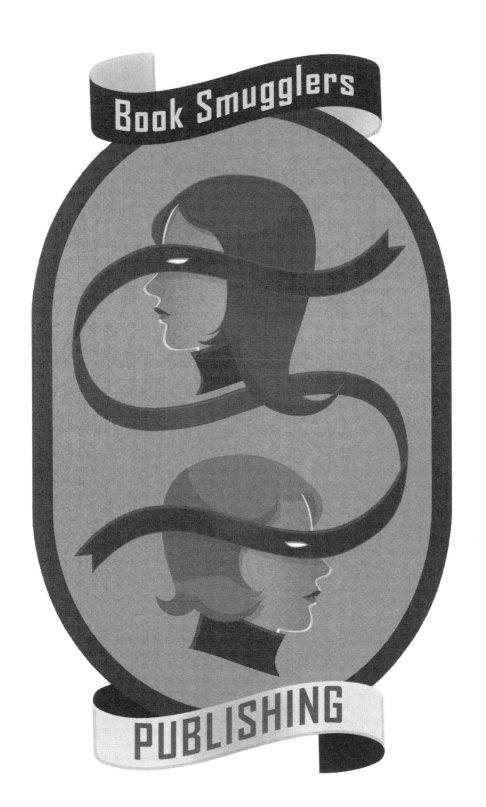

Made in the USA
Charleston, SC
02 August 2015